CAC

D0462490

REVENGE of the LAND

REVENGE of the LAND

A Century of Greed, Tragedy,
and Murder on a Saskatchewan Farm

by

MAGGIE SIGGINS

M&S

Copyright © 1991 Maggie Siggins

First trade paperback edition 1992

All rights reserved. The use of any part of this publication reproduced, trans-
mitted in any form or by any means, electronic, mechanical, photocopying,
recording, or otherwise, or stored in a retrieval system, without the prior written
consent of the publisher – or, in the case of photocopying or other reprographic
copying, a licence from Canadian Reprography Collective – is an infringement of
the copyright law.

Canadian Cataloguing in Publication Data

Siggins, Maggie, date.
Revenge of the land

Includes bibliographical references and index.
ISBN 0-7710-8155-3 bound   ISBN 0-7710-8156-1 pbk

1. Pasqua Region (Sask.) – History.   2. Murder – Saskatchewan – Pasqua
Region.   3. Saskatchewan – History.   I. Title.

FC3549.P37S5   1991   971.24'4   C91-095082-2
F1074.5.P37S5   1991

Designed by K.T. Njo

Printed and bound in Canada on acid-free paper.

McClelland & Stewart Inc.
The Canadian Publishers
481 University Avenue
Toronto, Ontario
M5G 2E9

For my husband, Gerry,
and my daughter, Carrie-May

Contents

Preface

Something explodes in a young man's mind and murder ensues. In these violent times, this is not such an uncommon occurrence, even if the victims are the killer's grandparents. But this particular crime is one with unusual underpinnings. The slaughter took place in an ordinary kitchen of a prairie farmhouse and in the flax field of a farm that is as rich and fertile as any on the Canadian plain. The wealth of the land, it seems, has everything to do with the tragedy.

This is the history of one particular farm, 640 acres of black-brown clay, located seven miles south of Moose Jaw, Saskatchewan. It was chosen because a ghastly murder occurred there, but a commitment was undertaken: no matter how uneventful or commonplace, the story of every person who owned even a part of that land from 1883 to the present would be faithfully chronicled. The subsequent research revealed that of the eight men – always men because the wives, like most women, are lost in written history – whose names appeared on the title, not one lived a mundane life, not one escaped a fate full of astonishing surprises. How could they, when from the moment the first sod was turned, revenge was heaped on each who dared to violate the land?

This history explodes all the myths about the homesteader, proud and determined, who, with great satisfaction, after years of perseverance and hard work, passes the family farm on to his sons and his grandchildren. The one true pioneer in this saga, the man who came West and planted the first seeds, was utterly defeated – not so much by the environment, although that took its toll, but by an unfeeling and arrogant government bureaucracy. The second owner, a Mountie, who came to know Indian culture as much as any white man could, was done in by his insensitive and stupid superiors in the force, his own naïvety, and, most destructively, by the cut-throat moneylenders who milked the pioneers of everything they had.

Greed emerges as the dominant theme in this book. For the men who owned this land were often not dedicated "toilers of the soil"; most hated getting their hands dirty. They were businessmen who hired other people to do the hard work. They were land-speculators who got rich by exploiting anybody who showed signs of weakness. The defeated, down-and-out half-breed was their favourite prey.

The families of these "land-flippers" formed the upper crust of the new towns like Moose Jaw. The men were stewards of the grandiose churches they helped build; their wives held "At Homes" every Thursday afternoon, when tea was served on Coalport china by Chinese servants. Their children grew up with unrealistic delusions of grandeur.

Even those owners who were dedicated farmers were infatuated with the wealth that they were sure could be squeezed from the "Last Best West." They became obsessed with owning more and more land and exploiting that land for every cent of profit, and worked themselves into early graves. Or, with a roll of the dice, they threw away their life's work on worthless stock certificates. Or they hoarded their wealth like squirrels in fall, until others were made violent with envy and impatience.

The terrible crime is only the climax of this drama. For over a hundred years, malevolence, unrequited ambition, and greed stalked the land. This book is about how the West was really won, and by whom.

Acknowledgements

I am greatly indebted to my researcher, Tracy Stevens, whose sleuthing ability was often amazing. Without her perseverance, skill, and hard work, this book would not have been possible. I would like to thank Xuelin Bai for her assistance in tackling the *Moose Jaw Times*, Gail Bowen for reading the manuscript with a writer's eye, and John Aitken for scrutinizing it from a farmer's perspective.

I would also like to express appreciation to the staffs of the Saskatchewan Archives Board, Regina; the Moose Jaw Public Library Archives; the Moose Jaw Land Titles Office; the office of the Court of Queen's Bench, Moose Jaw; the office of the Court of Queen's Bench, Regina; the Gabriel Dumont Institute; and the Prairie History Room of the Regina Public Library. They were unstinting with their time and effort.

Finally I would like to thank the Canada Council for its assistance.

14-16-25 W2

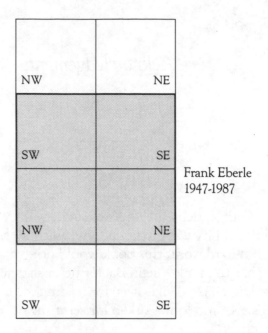

Frank Eberle
1947-1987

11-16-25 W2

The retribution was horrible. An elderly couple, made rich by the land, fell victim to an anguished young man, himself maimed on the land. On a cold fall day, everybody gathered on the farm to say goodbye to their neighbours of forty years – and to gawk with morbid curiosity.

The Auction

November 4, 1987

When Val Lewis arrived at the Eberle farm at eight o'clock in the morning, she was astonished to find seventy people already milling about. The auction wasn't scheduled to start for another two hours. She went into the Quonset hut where the luncheon booth had been set up, and quickly organized the coffee urns. The brewing would take a good hour. By that time, she thought, people would be freezing and in need of a cup of hot, strong coffee.

It was a raw, blustery morning, the sky a leaden grey. "Certainly suitable for the occasion," Clara Turner shivered to herself. She was there only to please her father. Years before, at the tail end of the Dirty Thirties, Albert Slywka had worked as a farmhand for the Eberle brothers, and he could hardly contain his curiosity. "I hear he'd done real good," he told Clara when they first heard the news.

"Why didn't you go and visit him before it was too late?" she asked.

"Not the friendly type. He and the wife kept to themselves," was his reply, no more laconic than usual.

That morning, in his eagerness, he had dressed and eaten breakfast before Clara had even opened her eyes. When the disc jockey on the radio had chirped that the first sting of winter was in the air, she had insisted that her father put on an extra sweater.

By the time they had driven the thirty-seven miles from Regina to the little town of Pasqua, it was nine a.m. Since the auction was still an hour away, Clara was astounded at the heavy traffic on Highway 39 headed towards the Eberle farm. A good two hundred vehicles were already parked, more half-tons than cars, so she had to find a spot in a field some distance from the yard. Albert was surprised to find so many out-of-province licence plates. Alberta, Manitoba, North Dakota, South Dakota, Montana were all represented. "Beats me how they found out about it," he said. His daughter explained that details of the auction had been broadcast on radio and television newscasts all across Canada and the United States.

By the time Clara and Albert got to the Quonset hut, the coffee was ready –"The usual Saskatchewan dishwater," Clara said to herself as she stirred the pale brown liquid – and Val Lewis had been joined by a dozen helpers. One of their number had laughed when he spotted the 300-gallon tank. "Think you got enough water there," he called out sarcastically. By the end of the day hardly a drop would be left.

Cecil Champion began frying hamburgers on the grill. He would not stop for the next eight hours. Gertie Aitkin's hot dogs were so popular that she never had a chance to poke her nose outside to see what was going on. The slices of lemon-meringue pie must have been delicious, because they sold by the hundreds. All eighteen people who manned the luncheon booth that day were volunteers, people who lived in the neighbourhood. They were there raising money for the Pasqua Community Hall.

Pasqua squats on the flattest prairie found anywhere, about a mile north of the Eberle farm. The highway sign announcing the hamlet reads, Pasqua. No Services. It's a sad commentary on what once was a bustling little place, and, since it was the junction between two major rail lines, the Soo and the CPR, was rather prominent. Time had whittled away at its importance, and in the last few years it had become downright derelict.

A dozen years before, Don McKnight had arrived in town and almost overnight had created a vast graveyard of junk. A shabby old train station had been transported by truck from Hearne, Saskatchewan, and with it an ancient caboose in which McKnight lived for a while. In the fields surrounding these antiques were parked row upon row of ancient, stout-nosed Hudsons. Gold, silver, blue, red – they sat dolefully, crumbling slowly but surely into prairie dust. They were of little value, since McKnight wouldn't dream of selling them. "You couldn't buy the dirt off them," says Walter Champion.

Actually McKnight and his debris finally did the community of Pasqua a favour. The townsfolk and the neighbouring farm-ers became so determined to get rid of him and his wrecks that they planned a general clean-up, tearing down the rickety build-ings, filling in abandoned wells, convincing a certain recluse to paint and repair his property. But it was the brand-new community hall, where fowl suppers, bingo games, and fiftieth wedding anniversaries would take place, that was meant to rekindle the spirit of the Pasqua district. Already the concrete foundation had been poured, the rafters erected, the insulation and wiring installed.

Val Lewis and a few others had been working on the building during the Thanksgiving weekend after the missing-persons reports had been filed, when police were searching the Eberle property. People kept driving up and asking questions. Says Val, "Everybody just shut up. The whole community said, 'Okay, we're not gonna say a word.'"

The money raised by manning the luncheon booth would provide the finishing touches for the hall. But that wasn't the only reason Pasqua people worked so tirelessly that day. Frank and Kay Eberle had lived in the district for forty years and in their own reclusive way had supported the community, had even volunteered a substantial donation towards the hall. Their neighbours were merely showing their respect by serving coffee and pie to the crowd. After all, even the curiosity-seekers who didn't intend to spend one cent were, in a strange sort of way, guests of the Eberles.

Meanwhile, outside the Quonset hut, Jim Low was getting ready to start the auction. His father had bought the business in 1972, and ever since taking an auctioneering course in Mason City, Iowa, Jim had worked for Low's Furniture and Auction in Moose Jaw, the nearest big centre to Pasqua. Low's specialized in estate auctions, and had presided over hundreds of them, but the Eberle case was a little different. For one thing, Jim Low and his workers had a terrible time cleaning the place up.

The Eberle farm, once a model of order and efficiency, had been trashed. In the house, garbage and clothing and dirt were strewn everywhere. The smell of the backed-up toilet was nauseating, but the stench from the fish was worse. It had fallen behind the freezer, and had been left there to rot. The cupboards, the pantry, and the chests of drawers all had to be cleaned out. Anything not considered of value was taken to the dump. Including Kay and Frank's wedding pictures.

The usually immaculate farmyard had looked like a war zone;

grain strewn everywhere, beer bottles thrown about, Kentucky Fried Chicken containers and pizza boxes littering Kay Eberle's garden like mutant weeds. It had taken Jim Low weeks to get the place cleaned up and items for sale catalogued and put on display, but on this cold November morning, everything was ready.

Unlike most of his customers, Jim Low did not sport the usual baseball hat with Canadian Herefords or Cargill written on the front; his merely said Low's Auction. In a shirt and tie and overcoat, he was dressed more formally than most of the crowd. But then, his was important business.

Just past ten he jumped up on a half-ton truck and began his spiel into the microphone. "Dollar, who'll give me two. Two, who'll give me three. Three, who'll give me five," and on and on, a whine that cut through the bitter, cold wind all day long.

The first bidding was for small farming items – chains, shovels, pieces of sheet metal, a large assortment of tools. Harvey Brentnell, who had first met Frank Eberle years before when Frank farmed a section near Belle Plaine, wasn't too interested in the small stuff. He thought he recognized some of it from other dispersal sales. Frank had loved auctions and would buy any old thing. "He'd take the stuff home and wouldn't know what to do with it and so put it in the shed just like the rest of us do," Harvey said. What interested him was in the huge barn with the FRANK P. EBERLE sign prominently displayed. This was where Frank had created his unique grain-storage system, supposedly just as efficient as the elevators in town. For years Harvey had heard people talking about it, and just last April, when he had run into Eberle at John Deere's spring open-house, he asked if he could come around and take a look. Frank seemed genuinely pleased at the idea. "I'd really like that," he said. But Harvey had got busy and the visit never materialized. Now, as he inspected the huge granaries, his admiration for the old man increased. He suddenly felt a sharp twinge of regret: he would never be able to tell him how impressed he was.

Frank's farm implements held little appeal for Harvey's sister Edith Benson; she was more interested in the household things. Just the other day she had come across a picture of Kay Eberle taken about 1948. Edith's husband had operated a wholesale gas-distribution outlet, and the Eberles were regular customers, so that Edith and Kay saw each other often in those days. Kay was thirty-three at the time, and attractive, with her soft hair curly around her face and her small, rather sharp features. In the picture she is kneeling in her garden tending a tomato plant, but she's looking straight at the camera and smiling. That's the way Edith Benson wanted to remember her.

Edith wandered into the outbuilding where all of the Eberles' personal effects were laid out on tables. She watched, feeling more and more upset, as people rifled through boxes of sheets and towels and bedspreads and dishes. These things looked new, never used, and she surmised they might have been anniversary or Christmas presents, not opened before. Then she spotted the mirror. It was a heavy Hobbs mirror, unframed, the kind you hang above the chesterfield instead of a painting. They had been popular in the early 1950s; Edith had bought an exact replica when she was first married. Reflected there she could see Kay's personal effects being fingered and gawked at by God knows who. It was as though all her secrets, the very enigma that had been Kay Eberle, were on display for the whole world to ridicule. Edith could hardly hold back her tears.

Judy Dixon felt the same way. Her aunt and uncle had been the most private of people and yet here were complete strangers picking through their belongings, driving over their property. The security guards had been kept busy all day shooing away the curious who insisted on peeking into every window, every door. A couple of teenage boys had even broken into the house, only to find that it had been stripped of everything. "Kay and Frank must be rolling over in their graves," one of the visitors said.

Judy Dixon was furious about the dispersal. "If that had been my parents' place I would not have allowed that to go on," she told a friend. She was even more angry because the relatives had been given so little to remember Kay and Frank by. They'd been invited to the Eberle house and told they could chose a personal memento, but "they [Guaranty Trust] were very particular. If you pointed out a dish or a little piece of furniture, they'd say, 'Well no, that's not available. It's going to auction.'" Judy took

Kay's Christmas cactus, a lily, and some geraniums. Other relatives were allowed a few pictures and some old clothing. Just as she was leaving the Eberle house, one of the cousins spotted the family Bible. Kay and Frank's only child, Carol Anne Ostrander, had not even wanted that.

By three o'clock in the afternoon, Low's auction had distributed 1,098 "paddle" cards. That didn't represent the number of people bidding, however. Most husbands and wives shared one card, as did groups of two or three. Nor did it indicate the number of visitors that descended on the Eberle farm. In fact, people willing to spend money were probably in the minority. All day curiosity-seekers had come and gone in swarms. They often seemed disappointed, and Val Lewis wondered what they thought they were going to find.

The Pasqua Community Club had run out of food on several occasions. Val's husband, John, had been dispatched to Moose Jaw to buy more hamburgers and hot dogs. The main roads were clogged, but since John had been a school-bus driver for years, he knew the back routes well and made good time travelling the thirteen miles back and forth to town. He reported that the only parking now available was over a mile away. The wind was coming up; the weather had turned even more cold and miserable.

Val Lewis was making coffee when a woman with a deep southern accent accosted her. "You take me out and show me where Kay and Frank were both buried," she demanded.

"I'm not going anywhere, lady," Val replied.

"I'll go over your head then. Get me your boss."

"I'm the boss here," Val hissed, thinking to herself, How ignorant can people be?

Clara Turner had lost track of her father. Albert had been so interested in Frank's tools and implements, had met so many people he knew, that he was wandering about in seventh heaven. For a seventy-eight-year-old he had remarkable energy. Clara realized she was in for the long haul and had picked up a bidding card. She fancied herself a connoisseur of Eastern European immigrant furniture and artifacts, and she thought she might spot something interesting. But when the bidding began on Frank and Kay's household goods – their rather nice bedroom-suite, a corner china cabinet, knickknacks, pots and pans, crocks – she realized most items would be beyond her means. She did spot two picture frames she liked; they weren't antiques, certainly, but they were old and interesting. Clara assessed their worth to be about $25, but bid to $50. "In at $275," the auctioneer had barked in conclusion.

Clara didn't mind the genuine antique-collectors paying a hefty amount – the man who bought Frank's old Studebaker truck obviously loved it – but she couldn't abide the ghouls who paid outlandishly high prices for things like a cracked butter dish simply because of the gruesome circumstances.

As the hard grey light darkened, the top items, the big draws, finally came on the auction block. These were the tractors and the combine, the field equipment, which were the heart of Frank's farming operation. Much to the surprise of the crowd, the bidding did not go as high as expected. The top bids for the year-old Hesston 80-90 tractor and the International Harvester 784 tractor, only slightly older, weren't bad. The forty-two-foot Doepker rodweeder and the John Deere twenty-one-foot drill (for seeding) did all right. But the bidding on the six-year-old combine, Frank's pride and joy, was slow. The machine had been found plugged and battered, and although it had been serviced back to the pristine condition in which Frank Eberle always kept it, the farmers in the crowd remained leery. Rumours circulated that agents for Guaranty Trust had stepped in and made the final bid, later selling the combine for a higher price through a dealer.

By five o'clock every single item had been sold. Although Jim Low was cold and exhausted, he felt pretty good. The auction had brought in $150,513, certainly a respectable effort.

The Pasqua Community Club was satisfied too. A $500 profit had been cleared on the pies and hamburgers. The irony of this was not lost on Val Lewis. That was exactly the amount that Frank Eberle had promised to donate towards the hall but had not been able to deliver.

There were many things on the Eberle farm that weren't sold, or even picked up by the curious, because people didn't realize the significance of them. Kay's flowerpot holders, for instance, told everything about her. They were everywhere: on the porch steps, attached to window ledges, hanging from nails in trees. Made from the frames of discarded lamps, they had been decorated with the green and red plastic snaps, each with a date stamped on them, that were used to close the cellophane wrapping on loaves of bread. Whether Kay thought these utilitarian things were really beautiful didn't matter; it was a way of getting rid of nuisance items without having to throw them out. For bred in Kay's bones was a hard, sometimes even cruel, pioneer spirit, a frugality that was almost psychotic, a deep-seated aversion to wasting anything, even ten dollars to get one's hair done at a beauty parlour. After the divers had scooped her corpse out of the septic tank and taken it to the morgue, Judy Dixon's husband, Bob, had gone to identify the body. What had horrified him was not her partly decomposed face, or even the bullet hole in her forehead, but how utterly ordinary she looked, as though she was about to start the day's chores. She was dressed in brown culottes, a T-shirt, an apron, socks, old shoes; the outfit she always wore to pick weeds in her vegetable garden, a garden not of beauty but of utility. For it hurt Kay Eberle to have to spend one cent on a can of tomatoes or green beans.

Albert Slywka insisted that, before returning to Regina, his daughter drive him to the northern part of the Eberle farm. He wanted to look at the fields where Frank grew his money-making flax. "A wonderful farmer was Frank. A very well-to-do farmer. Wanted to pass his know-how down to the next generation, was all. Would have done anything to keep the farm in the family. He loved that land more than his life, I guess."

Clara Turner did not tell the old man what she had heard that day. As the police were searching that same field, they had spotted something that stopped them in their tracks. In *rigor mortis*, Frank's hand, as white as a prairie primrose, had popped out of his shallow grave and seemed to be waving at them, pleading for help.

PIONEERS
and
BUCCANEERS

Carmichael

14-16-25 W2

Dougald Carmichael homestead 1883-1897		Colin Carmichael homestead 1884-1906
NW	NE	
Dougald Carmichael pre-emption		Colin Carmichael pre-emption
SW	SE	
NW	NE	
SW	SE	

11-16-25 W2

He had had such high expectations. After all he had long experience as a farmer, he was known for his patience and endurance, and he had saved the grubstake he knew was necessary to start up a farm properly in the West. Never did he think he would be so utterly defeated, and by forces so beyond his comprehension. After a few years he began to think that the land craved revenge.

~ I ~

Gristle tough as an old buffalo's was what Dougald Carmichael thought of when his new Verity plough bit into the virgin prairie; after the gravel, a three-inch knot of knee-high grasses, bright yellow silverweed, purple prairie clover, dwarf roses. Through the four-inch rip churned the black-brown soil, so rich, so heavy, so fecund, that Carmichael could already see the lush golden wheat growing before his eyes – easily twenty-five to forty bushels an acre, at least a dollar a bushel, just as the propaganda pamphlets had described. The promised Garden of Eden.

Although it was early May, in two hours he was sweating profusely. His oxen – Ring and Coon his little boy Ed called them – thick ropes of saliva hanging from their muzzles, plodded on like good soldiers. But as they passed the north end, their big, doleful eyes had fastened on the glitter from the slough, and Carmichael realized that next time around, whether he wanted them to or not, they'd head that way. So when he got there he rested for a few moments while they slushed up the brown water.

As he sat contemplating the vastness around him, he noted the bones of buffalo and other beasts bleached white, like winter rabbits frozen stiff, strewn everywhere about the flat prairie. A chill went up his spine. Sometimes he thought his wife, Rebecca, might be right. As she saw it, this was a place of the macabre, the brutal, the repulsive. It had been the stench that accosted them that early spring which had set her in that conviction.

The previous winter the railroad workers, hundreds of them, had allowed their horses to graze along the creek and on the open prairie, and in the severe winter, the animals had frozen to death. The local population of coyotes and buzzards was not large enough to strip the carcasses clean. When warmer weather arrived, the remains thawed and the spring breezes carried a stench that was putrid, revolting. "I've smelled it before," Rebecca grumbled, "so I know what it is. Gangrene!" She was beginning to loathe the West.

But for Dougald Carmichael this was a minor matter, not casting even a shadow on the dream for which he had struggled long and hard.

He'd grown up in New Brunswick, English Settlement, King's County, a peaceful place of rolling hills and subsistence farms. "I spent my boyhood picking rocks," Dougald would often say. "Damn things popped right up from hell."

His father, also named Dougald, had fled a similar kind of farm in Dumfries County, Scotland, and so, while he was grateful that the governor of New Brunswick had presented him with a land grant of 200 acres of virgin scrub, he often wondered if he was any better off in his new homeland. In 1834 he married Agnes Haney, eleven years his junior, also a recent immigrant. The couple had six children, Dougald junior being the middle son.

The Carmichaels hewed a poky farm out of the virgin timber and bush, and eventually grew the types of vegetables and grains that the heavy clay soil would support. The farm was convenient to the river, so that the produce could be hauled to Saint John by boat, but even so it provided only a meagre, worrisome living. In the Carmichael family, the talk about the vast fields out West, "the new granary of the British Empire," never ceased. "Our entire farm would be considered nothing more than a mere field in the North-West," the father often said.

To Dougald, Junior, Queen's County was not only a place of pocket-sized farms but also of limited and confining ambition. He grew up with a sharp hunger for land, and a yearning to head West. For years he worked at odd jobs, as a ninety-cent-a-day labourer on the railroad, a bartender in his uncle's hotel, a carpenter, a farmhand. Coin by coin he saved his money, until, painfully and slowly, $1,000 had been accumulated. "A damn fine outlay to forge this wilderness into the best wheat-growing farm in the West," he bragged to Rebecca. At age thirty-three, he was strong, wiry, and fit for the hard work he knew lay ahead.

Dougald wouldn't even wait until the railroad had been completed. He would have the *best* free land available. "It'll all be gone if we wait for the end of steel," he insisted. And he was right. In one year, every decent homestead in a radius of twenty miles around the town of Moose Jaw would be reserved.

During 1882, Dougald worked as a carpenter in Toronto, saving every cent he could. At the end of that summer, leaving Rebecca, his son, and his baby daughter there, Dougald travelled to what at that time was the end of the track, the old buffalo hunting-ground formerly called Pile of Bones. He spent a few days outfitting himself in the cluster of shacks and tents that made up that rag-tag city, which, because it had recently been designated the capital, had been given the grandiose name of Regina in honour of Queen Victoria herself. "No city with the possible exception of Sodom and Gomorrah has ever been founded in less congenial circumstances," wrote a wag at the time. Dougald Carmichael was so single-minded in his pursuit of his farm that he probably didn't notice.

Dougald debated long and hard – he was a frugal man who had slaved for every cent in his pocket – and finally bought a team of yoke cattle. They could live off the land, while horses would require grain with their fodder. "In warm weather you just let them loose on the prairie at night and in the morning their bellies will be full," the dealer had told him. Oxen would not depreciate in value – "They'll provide many a meal when they finally drop," Dougald later told his wife. She snapped back, "And I bet you need teeth like a squaw to bite into them."

Most important, however, was the invaluable help these tireless beasts of burden would provide in taming the virgin prairie. "If the plough strikes a boulder hidden in the soil, they'll stop dead, and not damage their harness, while a horse'd get finicky and try and break loose," the dealer had said. But Carmichael was experienced enough at farming to know how infuriatingly slow the big, plodding animals could be.

"Once the first crop is off the ground, I'll get a good team of Clydesdales," he told himself.

When the mountain of supplies was piled into the wagon – everything carefully chosen, from the five pounds of Red Rose tea to the six tins of Prince Albert tobacco, to the hundred-pound sack of flour, to the flax-burning stove, to the pitchforks, the plough, the harrows, the seed grain, and the seed potatoes – he headed fifty miles straight west towards the infant town of Moose Jaw.

The spring had been wet and the summer had come early, so on that lovely September day the prairies were still a lush green. As sunset approached, the flat land shimmered in rich, glorious gold. By the time Dougald Carmichael had reached his destination, he had fallen in love with the magnificent prairie. He did not know, of course, that the spring rains of 1882 would be the last to fall for five years.

Moose Jaw was even more primitive than Regina. The grey tanks used to store water for the CPR engines were just being put up, and they represented the town's most impressive architecture. As one old-timer later described that period, "All Moose Jaw was was five ragged tents already turned brown by the elements situated between the train depot and the coal sheds."

That a community, even one so dishevelled, existed at all demonstrated the almighty power of the Canadian Pacific Railway. A year before, only a cluster of Sioux Indian lodges and two log cabins built in the 1860s by the Métis brothers Paul and Xavier Denomie gave even a hint of the boom town that was about to blossom with the coming of the rail.

Actually, though, this had always been a favourite place. Twelve miles upstream from where the Moose Jaw Creek meets the Qu'Appelle River, at exactly the spot the Assiniboines and the Blackfoot Confederacy announced their boundary, it was an oasis of clear water and aspens, and basket and pussy willows. For centuries nomadic hunters had used this protected place, which was called The Turn, to rejuvenate, and also to perform religious rites thanking the Great Spirit for a bountiful life. In the early 1800s the Métis also discovered the peace and comfort of the place and liked to rest there after the great buffalo hunt. Not only did it provide shelter but it was a business hub; as part of the old Hudson Bay trail from Fort Garry, it was the only point on the Moose Jaw Creek where squeaking Red River carts, loaded with pemmican and furs, could cross the Qu'Appelle Valley with ease. Then the buffalo suddenly, tragically, disappeared, and the Great Plain waited to be transformed.

In January 1882, the Canadian Pacific Railway, then in the process of building a railway across the country, made a startling announcement that put Moose Jaw on the map.

From the time a trans-Canada railway had been conceived in the early 1870s, the designated route was the one first followed by the earliest explorers and *coureurs de bois* – west, and then north from Winnipeg through the "fertile belt" of the North Saskatchewan River, via Battleford and Fort Edmonton, then through the Rocky Mountains at Yellowhead Pass.

In the spring of 1881, a handful of CPR brass, godlike, decided that the railroad would be moved south, running close to the U.S. border. Suddenly, all early surveys were swept aside. The new route headed due west from Winnipeg, through the dry-lands of southern Saskatchewan and Alberta, through the high Kicking Horse Pass in the Rockies, through the Selkirk Mountains, to Kamloops and Port Moody on the Pacific.

It was a gamble. In the obstreperous eastern press, the southern regions of the Prairies had long been designated a desert. "The lack of firewood and good water will render this portion of the North West a hell on earth," was a typical journalistic non-opinion. Could settlers be persuaded to come here? It might mean an expensive propaganda campaign, but at least the CPR would not have to deal with scheming land-speculators, who were already entrenched along the northern route. The railroad would have absolute control over the fate of hundreds of little communities scattered along the line. There was one other reason for the change in plans: railway bosses felt the new route could compete for freight and passengers with the Northern Pacific, the trans-national railway just being completed south of the border.

It wasn't hard to figure out the significance of The Turn on Moose Jaw Creek. It was exactly the right distance – 330 miles – from Brandon, the CPR's most westerly division point, to be designated an important railway centre. As well, there was plenty of available water for steam engines – over 700,000 gallons a day would be needed – and well-travelled trails by which the railroad could bring in supplies during construction. What an economic underpinning for a new town! There would be jobs in repair shops, jobs building houses for railway employees, jobs in the shops, and businesses that would surely sprout up with a growing population. And in that spring of 1882, Henry

Battell from Cobourg, Ontario, one of the few who actually planned to settle permanently in the area, had hitched his oxen to the plough and broken ten acres. By late summer, settlers were streaming in by ox and horse teams. By winter, speculators were already vying for choice lots in Moose Jaw, which was shaping into a real town.

When Dougald Carmichael arrived that September, the first person he talked to was the good-natured Felix Plante, who had just opened his dry-goods store. Plante was a dapper French-man, a raconteur who loved his whisky. He explained that the community was in an uproar; just a few days before, a band of whisky traders from Missouri had stolen nine horses and six mules from the American trading company, Leighton Jordan. "Such goings-on will give the place a bad name," the Frenchman complained. "It's getting so we have to bed down with our horses every night so they won't get stolen from under our noses."

Dougald Carmichael moved into Moose Jaw's only hotel, a large tent with a dirt floor and a cook-stove in the middle, layered on all sides by wooden bunk-beds. Another settler of the time described it thus: "Billy Dixon kept a boarding place, and apparently it kept him, for he was fat, jovial, and Irish, with a dislike to the Police, who, the Summer before, had inconsider-ately taken his team, waggon and outfit away from him because he had some kegs containing a fluid much in demand." Dougald Carmichael might have joined the all-night poker games if he hadn't been such a cautious man, and so tight with his money.

He was determined to find "the best damn homestead" possi-ble. No more rock-picking for him; on the prairies nature had already managed the exhausting job of clearing. The kind of land Dougald would have liked, with sweet water, sheltering hills, and lots of timber, was found in the beautiful Fort Qu'Ap-pelle area. But his brother told him not to bother searching there. "Land's all squatted on already," he said.

Duncan Carmichael, Dougald's junior by ten years, had arrived a few months earlier. He had not saved the nest egg his brother had, and so he had to watch every cent. He had actually walked from Regina to Moose Jaw. Mac Annable, an early settler, met up with him at Cottonwood Creek in the Qu'Appelle Valley. "The stream was a swollen torrent that day. I saw a man in mid-stream making a crossing of the ford on foot. He was dressed in nothing but what nature had given him, a bundle of clothing balanced atop his head." Duncan was a clever young man and quickly learned the knack of reading the tin markers on the survey posts. He had already helped dozens of new settlers find land, so naturally he took his elder brother under his wing. Duncan had already entered for his own homestead in an area southeast of Moose Jaw, and he had paid $10 to have it ploughed up so he could build a sod hut. He recommended that Dougald stake out land just a few miles away, the northwest one-quarter of section 14, township 16, range 25, west of the Second Meridian.

Dougald quickly rode out to inspect the plot. Digging through the tangle of high grasses, he grabbed a handful of that rich earth, pressed it to his nose, and took a long exhilarating sniff. Whether he knew it or not, he had stumbled across some of the best wheat-growing land in the world.

When he arrived there the Dominion Lands Office in Regina was crowded with nervous, sweating men. Like Dougald Carmichael, they were all new arrivals to the West, about to register the one-quarter section of prairie land they had chosen. The regulations were not complicated. The homesteader must construct a dwelling-place on his farm, reside there for at least six months in each of three consecutive years, and attempt to break ten acres of virgin land a year. After that, he could apply for a patent, and ultimately be presented with clear title. But an ambitious settler could immediately double the size of his farm. For another ten-dollar fee, the government allowed him to take up an interim claim on a quarter-section adjacent to his homestead and later purchase it at the price prevailing at the time of his entry. Carmichael took advantage of both these opportunities: the northwest portion of 14-16-25 W2, was to be his homestead, the southwest one-quarter, his pre-emption.

After he had completed the necessary forms, the clerk advised him, "Be very careful to keep a complete record of the time you stay on your land. They mean to be strict about

enforcing the rules." Carmichael would later kick himself for
not paying more heed to this man's advice.

Dougald took the opportunity in Regina to buy the good
quality lumber he wanted. It wasn't easy riding it back to Moose
Jaw on running-gear, several boards tied on to two sets of
wheels. On top of this contraption sat a keg of nails, rolls of
tarpaper, and bundles of roof shingles. It was an uncomfortable
journey, but Dougald was determined to build the best house he
was able – not just to protect his family from the erratic weather,
although that was certainly important, but to etch a dramatic
stroke on the forbidding landscape. This would be the beginning of his struggle to make fruitful what he considered to be the
wild, frightening, defiant prairie.

Although the huts made of mud and sod, popular with many
early settlers, were cheap, warm, fireproof, and didn't crack,
Dougald Carmichael rejected the idea outright. "I'm not a
bohunk peasant," he told his neighbour Tom McWilliams. "I'm
not accustomed to the fleas and bedbugs that dirt floors and
mud walls attract." He'd build a proper house of lumber, with
three windows, a door on hinges, a floor of poplar boards, and a
roof of two thicknesses of elm board with tarpaper in between,
covered with shingles. It would be only fourteen feet by twelve,
but he considered it a good beginning.

For eight days in October, Carmichael camped on his land, a
tent sheltering him in the chilly nights. Because he was a skilled
carpenter, in that time he built the house and a stable for the
oxen, horses, and two pigs. Two neighbours, who were to
become fast friends, and his brother helped him out.

In February 1883, Rebecca and the two children, four-year-old
Edward and two-year-old Stella, arrived with Colin Carmichael,
another brother six years younger than Dougald. Fortunately,
they had been able to travel all the way by rail, since the CPR now
regularly ran passenger trains to Moose Jaw; however, the line
had not yet been ballasted, so the ride was a slow one. Colin
Carmichael chose a homestead and pre-emption directly adjacent to Dougald's, the east half of 14-16-25 W2.

While a few other settlers had already built on their land, they
were mostly young bachelors; the Carmichaels were the first

family in the area south of Moose Jaw to actually live out on the prairie. Though Rebecca didn't complain too bitterly, Dougald could tell she was profoundly shocked. Even positioning the marble-inlaid sideboard, the one piece of furniture she had shipped, hanging the curtains, and laying the rugs didn't help much. "One day soon you'll have a house with lathed and plastered walls and with an upstairs," he promised her. But she only looked angrily at him and huddled closer to the stove.

During their first winter the weather was so ferocious that settlers talked about it for years after. Temperatures sank to thirty-five to forty degrees below zero and stayed that way for weeks on end. "I woke up yesterday morning and my eyelids were frozen solid together. I had to rub them to get them thawed out," Rebecca wrote in her first letter home to her father. She was terrified of the savagery howling outside her door. When blizzards rattled the little shack as though it had been caught in the maw of a tiger, she wouldn't allow the children to go out. Big feed buckets served as temporary chamber pots, and only when the stink was unbearable did Rebecca do the uncivilized thing and throw the offensive waste outside. Stella and Ed laughed when the bright yellow urine etched exotic patterns in the startling white snow.

There was so much snow, so many blizzards and white-outs that year, that Carmichael had trouble finding his way to the stable and his hungry livestock until he discovered the expediency of throwing forkfuls of manure as signposts along his path.

Relations between the adult Carmichaels became strained. Rebecca felt cruelly deceived. When they had first talked about coming West, Dougald had hunted up a pamphlet printed by the Dominion government. She could see herself in the enchanting picture it painted, busy churning butter, pruning the fruit bushes, weeding the garden. In her spare time she'd likely be inspired, the propaganda insisted, to paint the exquisite prairie landscape, or at least embroider a pillow with the scene. But it was nothing like that, nothing at all. Even Dougald's promise that they would plant trees and gardens full of purple violets and tomatoes and cucumbers was received now with scepticism.

When spring arrived, Rebecca didn't cheer up much, especially after being assaulted by the carrion stench of dead horses and livestock lying about the prairie. But Dougald managed to keep his spirits high; he'd soon be working the land, and that always brought him comfort. His most pressing chore, however, was to find water and dig a well.

He thought he was right when he selected the spot – buffalo willows and badger holes pointed to water. He had to dig down with his pick and shovel through the glacial clay and then the sand, his brothers hauling the filled baskets and pails up with long ropes. He'd never say it out loud, but he was scared down there. He knew that damp gas, suddenly seeping from the bowels of the earth, had poisoned unsuspecting well-diggers before. And then there was the recent death of homesteader John McFarlane. While McFarlane was easing the cribbing of his well into place, it had come crashing down on him. Just as his wife and children managed to get him out of the hole, he babbled his last words, something about the highlands of his native Scotland.

Dougald Carmichael was relieved when, at forty feet, the earth suddenly grew moist. Once the water started trickling in, he anxiously drank a little – and spat. A mouth full of rusted nails would not have tasted worse. The water was a red-brown colour, so hard and full of minerals it couldn't even be used for the garden or the cattle. With a heavy heart, Carmichael realized he'd have to haul water from a creek a couple of miles away.

That spring Dougald broke fifteen acres of land. He had expected to accomplish more, but he hadn't realized how back-breaking the job of ploughing virgin prairie could be. The quality, water-retaining gumbo that made his acreage such superb land, also made it difficult to work. In addition, Moose Jaw was exploding, money was to be made, and Dougald Carmichael fully intended to be part of the action.

~ II ~

"Moose Jaw was very lively that May and June. It was the end of passenger traffic west, there was a floating population of between two or three thousand and the sound of hammers was heard from daylight till dark," Henry Dorrell, another early settler, later recalled. The CPR still hadn't announced where the divisional terminus would be, and speculators, who had rushed to buy up the town lots, held their breath. Finally a train of flat cars, carrying the timbers of the roundhouse that was once located in Regina, arrived. John Rowe, a sign painter and the Carmichaels' friend, became even busier. "Working twelve and fourteen hours a day, I still can't keep up with the business," he said, quickly adding, "but I ain't complaining." Annie Hoburg, an entrepreneur of great ingenuity, opened the Rail Road Restaurant on Main Street, which immediately became the hub of a thriving bootleg business. Many new arrivals, mostly men "baching it," were still living in tents on the outskirts of the city, and her establishment offered welcome relief from loneliness and a constant diet of mashed beans.

At the beginning of March 1883, the village of Moose Jaw consisted of four stores and thirty houses. By the end of that month it boasted six stores, five saloons, one drugstore, two blacksmith shops, three hotels, and forty houses. By May 1, over a hundred buildings had been, or were in the process of being, constructed. Businesses included twenty general merchants, five lumberyards, three livery and feed stables, two bakers, one drugstore, two furniture-dealers, two blacksmiths, two tinsmiths, two harness-makers, two barber shops, two churches, a dozen hotels and restaurants, and seven lawyers. "Moose Jaw! The Future Great Central City of the North-West. The Prettiest Townsite on the Canadian Pacific Railway," was the banner headline on the first edition of the *Moose Jaw News.* The only businesses lacking, the paper reported, were a tailor and a laundry. "The first to come here will surely make their fortunes!"

Dougald Carmichael was itching to jump into the action, and fortunately he had a few dollars in his pocket to do just that. As well, he had found a partner with similar resources and ambition.

Robert Allison, his wife, and their seven children had arrived that spring from Ontario. They had settled on the quarter-section lot not far from Carmichael's, only to discover that it was situated in the Mile Belt, the stretch of land twenty-four miles either side of the railway from which the CPR was to choose odd-numbered sections of the best land. The federal government and the railway were battling over this selection process, and early settlers like Allison still did not know whether they'd be allowed a free homestead or whether they'd have to hand over five dollars an acre to the Canadian Pacific. Whatever the case, the burly settler was eager to make money.

Both Carmichael and Allison were master carpenters, easily capable of erecting the crude board structures that predominated in western towns at the time. Together they formed a partnership: with Carmichael supplying most of the cash and Allison the labour, they would build and operate the Enterprise House, a hotel to accommodate the influx of newcomers.

It opened in June of 1883 on High Street, just east of Main, and advertisements were immediately placed in the *Moose Jaw News*: "ENTERPRISE – First-Class Accommodation For Permanent and Transient Boarders – Charges Moderate – Every Attention to the Comfort of Guests – Carmichael & Allison, Proprietors." To attract customers, Rebecca insisted they paint its plain wooden face bright red. T. E. McWilliams, his wife, and six children ate their first Moose Jaw meal there that summer. "Better than most of the other grub available," was McWilliams's assessment.

The food was good because Rebecca Carmichael was the cook. It was a struggle, since supplies were frightfully expensive: bread cost fifty cents for three loaves and beefsteak "tough as hide" soared to forty cents a pound. "I paid ten cents each for frozen apples," Rebecca complained to her husband, who blamed it on freight charges. "It's that damn CPR squeezing every cent they can from us homesteaders," he scowled.

Nevertheless, Rebecca had been happy to leave the farm, if only for a while: Edward could go to school, even though, as the inspector noted, it was "dark, unsanitary and unsafe, wedged at the back of a printing office above a pool hall." The fee per child was fifty cents a week, and Rebecca had had a terrible time wheedling it out of her husband. "Once we get more on our feet, then Edward can go," he said.

"We might be dead by then," was her reply.

Yet for Rebecca there was more to do in town than simply talk at Dougald. There were friends to gossip with, church services to attend, and country picnics to bake pies for. She even sang in a concert at Moose Jaw's first Victoria Day celebration. Still, as she wrote to her relatives, the village scribbled along Moose Jaw Creek wasn't exactly Paris on the Seine. The grass was so high in the middle of the streets that Edward caught garter snakes there on his way to school. Dogs ran wild – "We should get rid of the large number of worthless curs which are no good to man or beast," the *News* suggested – and cattle and horses roamed about making no distinction between the town and the wide-open plain. The animals that had frozen to death in the winter were still lying in the streets that spring. As the newspaper said, "It is thought by many of our citizens that some steps should be taken to remove and bury the carcasses of animals lying in a putrid condition around the city. . . . They are likely to provide a fruitful source of disease."

"The heaps of manure all over don't exactly make Moose Jaw a jewel of a city either," Rebecca complained to her husband. That she regularly had to chase "immoral, loose" women, on the lookout for paying customers, away from the Enterprise door-step didn't do much to enhance her impression of the town.

The summer of 1883 was a difficult one for Dougald Carmichael. Not only was he running the Enterprise – Bob Allison was a fine carpenter but not much of a manager – but he travelled the seven miles to his land every day except Sundays, even though he kept a hired hand. The state of his crop was uppermost in his mind. There had been little rain in the spring until June, when it poured heavily for a few days. This made the Red Fife wheat shoot up rapidly, but there seemed to be something wrong. The crop wasn't ripening equally; some of it was shrivelled, and that took away from the healthiness of the whole. He later realized that many of the seeds had not been planted deep enough to benefit from the moisture trapped in the subsoil clay base. And, as worrisome as the prospect of a puny crop was the news from the East.

The good times that had begun in Canada in 1879 had suddenly vanished. Worried about the effects of an economic recession on central Canada's manufacturers, Sir John A. Macdonald's government had raised duties on farm machinery from 25 to 33 per cent. Carmichael's dream of purchasing a new Monitor grain-seeder vanished. Even more ominous, grain prices were falling drastically. In 1881 a bushel of wheat brought $1.33; by that summer the going rate was eighty to eighty-five cents a bushel.

On September 7 there was an early frost in the Moose Jaw area. Although it hadn't been that severe, the millers and grain-dealers claimed that all the wheat had been frozen, and they refused to pay top price.

"They say it's hardly good enough for chicken feed, which isn't the truth at all," Dougald complained.

"I'd say not one-tenth of the crop was frozen," added Allison. "The buggers are just trying to cheat us as usual."

Farmers got only fifty cents a bushel, which hardly replenished the Carmichaels' dwindling savings. The propaganda pamphlets had insisted that this chocolate loam, together with the clay subsoil, was "so famous for holding moisture that crop failure was virtually impossible. Your first crop might pay for the entire farm." Dougald Carmichael laughed when he thought of this "silly boast." Still his resolve to make a go of it did not weaken.

The Carmichaels were well aware that the homestead regulations required that they spend six months a year on their farm, so that November they moved back to the land. Dougald added an eight-by-ten-foot addition to the shack, which Rebecca used as a cooking-house. The Enterprise had been left in the hands of a hired manager, but by December business was suffering under his stewardship and the Carmichaels decided that they had better be in attendance for the festive season.

They returned to Moose Jaw just in time to experience the town's first violent labour strike, and since so many of the boarders who daily sat around their dining-room table were involved, the Carmichaels watched events with nervous interest.

Out of the blue, the financially strapped CPR had announced that the wages of its locomotive engineers and firemen were to be cut. Naturally, the railroad workers' union was outraged, and from Winnipeg to the Rockies, workers walked off the job. Violent incidents were reported along the line – engines were tampered with, soap was dumped into the water tanks, brawls broke out between union members and scabs. When the union threatened trouble at Moose Jaw, the divisional superintendent wired the North-West Mounted Police headquarters in Regina for help. "I selected the biggest men we had to make the best impression," Sgt. Frank Fitzpatrick later recalled. Thirty-five of his most intimidating, their loaded revolvers and Winchesters on display, arrived and immediately cleared the CPR yard of the "great number of irresponsible and unnecessary employees hanging about." The police were not there simply to keep order; they were used as strike-breakers. With the help of management and scabs, they managed to maintain intermittent mail-and-passenger service over the line. In fifteen days the walkout was over; the engineers and firemen took a cut in pay and went back to work. "Never pays to go against the bosses," Carmichael remarked. "Especially when there's only one employer in town."

But the strike was not the event that made that Christmas so memorable in Moose Jaw. It was the dirty, mean, election campaign that got under way by the end of December.

Since the population was now large enough, it was decided that Moose Jaw should be incorporated as a town. This historic event would take place on January 19, 1884, and the first municipal election followed a month later.

A bemused reader of the *News* noted of the mayoralty contest, "It was a fight from the drop of a hat." John E. Ross, pioneer and Liberal real-estate agent, against R. L. Alexander, land-speculator – the Ross Clique versus the River Street Gang – and the character assassination, name-calling, and dirty tricks were astonishing. Alexander's daughter fell on icy Moose Jaw Creek one evening, and a skater ran over her hand, badly cutting it. Surely the assailant must have been a Ross supporter. The

Alexander group claimed yes. When the proprietor of the Occidental Hotel, a Ross loyalist, opened his door one night, a fist landed in his mouth. The assailant fled before anyone could get a good look at him but, as the pub owner said, "The thug's an Alexander supporter, sure as damn."

Moose Jaw citizens didn't pay much attention to party affiliation: what mattered was who you knew well enough to do you the most favours.

On a bright February morning with the temperature stuck at minus thirty degrees, the burghers of Moose Jaw, the lucky ones whose ownership of property gave them a vote, lined up outside the schoolroom in the Foley Block. They were waiting to inform the clerk of their choice (there was no secret ballot). Since he was the proprietor of the Enterprise House, Dougald Carmichael was among this landed gentry. There's no record of which candidate he favoured, but certainly his ballot counted. Ross won by only one vote, 109 to Alexander's 108. The new mayor's elated supporters celebrated by congregating at Allen & McKenzie's brewery and toasting Ross's victory. He, of course, provided the drinks free. Actually it wouldn't have made much difference to Moose Jaw if the other candidate had won; Alexander and Ross were of the same class, same philosophy. In fact, 75 per cent of the new council were businessmen, boosters, and free-enterprisers, and this would set the tone of Moose Jaw's government for years to come.

Carmichael and others felt the election was something of a joke; the politicians weren't calling the shots, anyway. The townsite trustees, acting on behalf of the CPR, refused to pay their taxes, so there was little money to do what a town council was supposed to do: construct sidewalks, set up schools, hire police.

Yet the election was important. It symbolized the gelling of a community and the beginning of a support network that would mean life and death to the farmer out on the merciless prairie.

Dougald Carmichael knew well this sense of being overwhelmed by his environment, and went out of his way to help newcomers, showing them the best land available, putting up and feeding their families for no fee, lending them his team to get wood, using his carpentry skills to erect stables and houses. He was the first to admit that he had an ulterior motive: the sooner homesteaders settled, the quicker a school would be established that his children could attend. But Dougald's willingness to help newcomers also involved something far deeper; although he never would admit it to Rebecca, the vast landscape frightened him, made him feel utterly vulnerable. How to protect his family from the ominous forces he could feel in the dead of winter? His farm was anything but an ally.

This was one reason he let Robert Allison talk him (and three others) into founding the Valley Lodge No. 1 of the Independent Order of Odd Fellows. Allison was named Noble Grand Master, and Carmichael, because of his acknowledged sense of responsibility and respect for authority, was made the warden.

In the Odd Fellows' odd world, the warden symbolized venerability and wisdom, so Carmichael was made to don a white wig and beard (cotton stuffing from pillows), dress in a black robe (Rebecca's one good dress), and turban (Rebecca's hat), and carry a cane. "Listen to the voice of wisdom, speaking from age and experience and let it sink deep into your heart," he would sing out during the Lodge's initiation ceremonies. "In the practice of friendship, love and truth will be found the best safeguard against the ills of life. Forget it not! Forget it not!"

"You're just like little boys playing around the schoolyard," Rebecca scolded. But belonging to a fraternal society made Dougald feel better. In not too many years he would have to rely on its charity.

The Carmichaels were back on the farm by January 1, 1884. Since Dougald had to travel back and forth to Moose Jaw to oversee the Enterprise House, Rebecca found herself alone with the children for much of that bitterly cold winter. She could hardly muster her courage, especially after she learned of the tragedies that occurred that January. A three-year-old girl, the only child of Rev. G. B. Davis, the well-liked pastor of Moose Jaw's Baptist church, and his wife, Flossie, died of smallpox complicated by pneumonia. Two weeks before, the couple had buried their infant son. And on a nearby farm, a three-month-old baby, lying in bed alongside its mother, froze to death. The father had gone looking for food.

By the spring of 1884, Moose Jaw's boom times had started to dwindle. The railway construction gangs had moved out, and although there were still plenty of paying guests, mostly settlers *en route* to somewhere else, half a dozen hotels – the Ottawa, the Enterprise, the Brunswick, the Moose, the Occidental, the Queens – were competing for their few dollars. Dougald Carmichael and Robert Allison decided to call it quits. An ad was placed in the *Moose Jaw Times*: "To rent: The proprietors having to go on their land, the Enterprise House is now to rent on easy terms, apply at the house on High Street East, Carmichael and Allison." When no one showed any interest, the partners decided to close the hotel, at least for the time being. Allison was desperate for money to feed his seven children and had found a job carting along the CPR line. Carmichael was determined to produce a decent crop.

Spring came late that year, and was very dry. Dougald Carmichael had traded in his oxen for three horses, so the thought of ploughing that virgin gumbo didn't appeal to him much. More important, government experts were advising farmers to plant smaller, rather than larger, areas, so the entire crop could be harvested before the frost. Carmichael broke only one more acre, but planted the fifteen prepared the previous year.

Fortunately, rain fell in July, and the wheat sprang up lush and green. With his brothers on hand to help with the harvesting, Carmichael decided he could afford to invest some time in refurbishing the Enterprise. The Carmichaels returned to Moose Jaw on July 29, and the hotel re-opened on August 3. The *Moose Jaw Times* announced it was "to be managed solely by Dougald Carmichael. We wish him all the best." Rebecca Carmichael responded to their kind regards by sending the editors a big bunch of radishes from her garden.

All through August and into early September the sun drenched the prairies. The heat was so intense it looked like liquid gas playing about the heads of the shrivelling plants. The government agent at Qu'Appelle reported, "The crops have not been so abundant as was expected from the rapid growth and appearance through the early summer." Carmichael put it another way. "The crops aren't worth taking off the ground." Two years in the North-West and his golden dream was rapidly turning into a black nightmare.

Thank God there was another way of earning a few dollars. Early that spring, the Carmichaels had carefully set small grass fires. On the dark burnt grass the spectre-white bones of buffalo stood out and were easily spotted by Edward and his mother. They worked hard because they knew Felix Plante paid five dollars a ton at his Buffalo Store. Almost every homesteader took advantage of the bonanza. Along the tracks west of the Moose Jaw railway station the piles of bones were so gigantic that they looked like Arctic snowdrifts, weirdly incongruent in the hot August sun. It was terrible, Dougald thought, that a crop of ghosts brought in more money than a crop of wheat.

The Carmichaels' growing suspicion that their future was doomed in the West was further reinforced the following winter. Rebecca and Dougald always claimed that it started in the ovens of George Robinson's bakery next door. Robinson insisted that the boarders at the Enterprise were careless with their pipes or, perhaps having indulged in a drink or two too many, had tipped over a lantern. Whatever the case, on a cold March night in 1885, flames engulfed the two buildings. Only minutes after the last boarder had staggered out, the Enterprise House collapsed in a pile of ashes. The Carmichaels' entire investment went up in smoke.

"Maybe it's not such a tragedy," Dougald said to a distraught Rebecca. "After all, we came out here to be homesteaders not hotel-keepers." By March 24, they were back on the farm.

~ III ~

Spring came early that year, 1885, bringing some rain and plenty of sunshine, but ironically it didn't much help the Carmichaels' farming operation. The North-West Rebellion had flared, and Dougald felt obliged to offer his services.

The previous summer the Carmichaels had read newspaper

reports about the return of Louis David Riel to the North-West. They had a vague impression of him as a hot-headed, anti-British traitor, a religious fanatic bent on goading his people into rebellion. That the Métis might have good reason to be discontented, or that their grievances pertaining to land claims might be fully justified, never occurred to Rebecca or Dougald. Nor did they have any idea that Riel and his followers were being used as scapegoats by businessmen and land-speculators in Prince Albert and Battleford, whose dreams of enormous wealth had vanished when the CPR changed its route southward. These people were determined to provoke a war between the Dominion government and the half-breeds, because they believed a military campaign would result in a heavy injection of cash – just what the Prince Albert clique needed.

The Carmichael family also had no idea that a small war in the North-West was just what the government of Sir John A. Macdonald was hoping for. By 1884, with the cost of constructing the difficult southern route soaring, the Canadian Pacific was on the verge of bankruptcy, despite the incredible subsidies already granted by the Conservative government. Macdonald knew Canadians would balk at yet more tax dollars being funnelled into the CPR trough. A conjurer's act of persuasion was needed, and it materialized miraculously in the form of a rebellion of French-speaking, Catholic Métis. Macdonald knew the Loyal Order of the Orange, especially in Ontario, would react with fervent patriotism. They had never forgotten that, fifteen years before, during another rebellion, Riel had executed one of their own, the obnoxious Thomas Scott.

In the fall of 1884, rumours had circulated that the Métis scattered in the communities of Fort Qu'Appelle, Willow Bunch, and Battleford, and along the South Saskatchewan River – at St. Laurent and St. Louis, Duck Lake, and St. Antoine-de-Padoue (Batoche) – were becoming dangerously militant and that the North-West Mounted Police might take Riel by force.

Neither Carmichael nor the other settlers with whom he often chatted were very sympathetic toward the half-breeds – "wild, gypsy-like people with black streaming hair and colourful, filthy clothes" was how Rebecca described them in letters home. But they didn't consider them a real menace, either. However, if Riel's rhetoric sparked the Indians to revolution, that was something the population around Moose Jaw was deathly frightened of. For good reason.

After the Battle of Little Big Horn and the massacre of Custer's troops in 1876, about five thousand Sioux Indians, led by Sitting Bull, had fled to Canada. For years they roamed, aimless and hungry, around the southern Wood Mountain area. In 1881, Sitting Bull had finally been persuaded to accept the amnesty offered and had returned to the Dakotas. Most of his tribe had gone with him, but one group remained determined to stay in Canada, and they took up residence in the valley of the Moose Jaw Creek, just outside the town.

Once the Carmichael farmyard was invaded by a family of Sioux. Three large men, dressed in their customary blankets and floppy hats, walked into the house unannounced, leaving the women and children outside. Rebecca was terrified, especially when they began to make menacing gestures. But Dougald, who was a more sensitive person, realized that all they wanted was something to eat. Once they had had their fill of bread fried in goose grease and topped with berry jam, and had drunk some tea, they sauntered away.

"They live in teepees, so they're not accustomed to knocking," Dougald explained to his wife.

"One day when they arrive naked as the day they were born, smeared with that war paint and whooping it up, you won't be so nonchalant," she responded.

Although a feeling of unease and fear permeated the North-West that winter of 1885, the citizens of Moose Jaw were still shocked when, on April 2, news arrived that one week before the North-West Mounted Police had been defeated by the half-breeds in the first battle of the rebellion.

On St. Joseph's Day, March 19, a provisional government with Louis Riel as God's prophet, had been established by the Métis. Upset at this development, Supt. L. N. F. Crozier sent a hundred armed men to Duck Lake to secure the food and arms of the village store. As word of their approach reached the warriors, they gathered near the town, and scattered for cover when the police drew near. There was an attempt at mediation, but it ended in violence. Twelve of Crozier's men were killed and eleven wounded in a battle lasting thirty minutes. Only at Riel's intervention were the survivors allowed to flee to Prince Albert.

A week later, the Cree of Frog Lake rose up and killed priests and Indian agents whom they believed were withholding food supplies.

Panic swept Moose Jaw. "We're defenceless; there's hardly a rifle in the town," cried Rebecca's friend, Mrs. Bellamy. "And yesterday one old squaw came into our cottage and told me we were all going to be killed and she had picked out our place for her own." A home guard with Henry Battell as captain was formed, and plans for the evacuation of women and children were drawn up; the CPR agreed to keep an engine ready for quick evacuation should the town be attacked. The Carmichaels had their trunk packed in case they had to flee their farm.

But in only a few days the panic eased. The Winnipeg Light Infantry arrived in Moose Jaw on their way west to Calgary. They stumbled off the trains, clutching their brown bags – there had been a shortage of issue knapsacks – and the New Testaments and temperance leaflets that had been thrust into their hands at various points along the route. One lad flashed a poster that read "Shall French Rebels Rule Over Our Dominion?" "They were just green kids – store clerks and school teachers. Some were in tears they were so exhausted from the trip west," one observer later wrote in his journal. Still, the people of Moose Jaw treated them as heroes. They were marched into the various hotels and fed "a damn fine meal" – the last they might have for days.

On the morning of April 9, a scout arrived in the area to recruit teams and freighters to haul supplies for the troops. Would Dougald Carmichael join? He hesitated – but only for a minute. It would mean putting off spring seeding a dangerously long time, but on the other hand the pay was ten dollars a day, which at that moment seemed a fortune. But even more important, Dougald Carmichael, son of lowland Scottish immigrants, had been raised to cherish the British empire. While he was growing up in New Brunswick, his friends had all been children of United Empire Loyalists. It was natural, then, for him to join those Odd Fellows who sent a telegram to the 90th Winnipeg Rifles stationed at Qu'Appelle, "Stick together boys, do your duties. God Save the Queen!"

Twenty-five of the fifty teams travelling with Lieutenant-Colonel W. D. Otter's second division were from the Moose Jaw area, including one driven by Dougald and Colin Carmichael. The loading point was Moose Jaw. The supplies – everything from oats and hay to corned beef and ammunition – the horses, and the teamsters themselves were shipped by train, two hundred and forty-five kilometres west to Swift Current, at that time nothing more than a brick station, a roundhouse for two engines, and six other assorted rickety buildings. From there the soldiers and freighters would head north.

Camp was set up on the hill north of town, the wagons forming a corral, with horses and teamsters in the middle. As Jud Battell, who was in the same wagon train as Carmichael, wrote in his memoirs that the men woke up in the morning to find themselves covered with six inches of snow.

Otter and his division travelled thirty miles north to the Saskatchewan River, where the ménage was loaded onto flat-bottomed boats. It took two days to get the soldiers, the freighters, their wagons, horses, and supplies across the river. The group then proceeded to Battleford.

Rumours circulated that teamsters had already been abducted by Indians, so scouts were regularly sent out to ensure that the road was free of ambush. Battell was amazed to see several wagons piled high with goods simply abandoned on the side of the road. They had been left there by freighters who regularly hauled on that route. "When the scouts told them the Indians were rising in rebellion these truckers just drove off the trail into low places or coulees and left their wagons there, got on a horse's back and rode for home."

The wagon train travelled quickly, averaging a remarkable forty-five miles a day. It was feared the people of Battleford were starving to death.

Since Battleford had been the capital of the North-West Territories (from 1876 to 1882) before Regina had snatched away the
honour, the town boasted several imposing government buildings and stately homes. Hungry Cree, once encouraged by the
Métis' Duck Lake victory to declare war on the whites, would
naturally head there. The townspeople had just enough time to
flee their houses and take refuge in the fort on the southern
bank of the river, which was protected by a cannon and pretty
well invincible. From there, day after long day, they watched the
sack of Battleford.

Joseph Kinsey Howard, in *Strange Empire*, his biography of
Louis Riel, vividly describes the scene. "Weeping, the gently
reared Canadian and English women watched . . . as the Indians, hysterical with delight, danced into the neat little houses
and out again, ripping off their own blankets and donning the
precious silk gowns and party bonnets."

Once Battleford had been demolished, the Indians spread
into the surrounding vicinity, looting and then setting fire to
"anything that would ignite." A settler and an instructor who
had been sent to teach Indians how to farm were assassinated.

After the frenzy was over, the Cree returned to Battleford
determined to wait until hunger pried the white man from the
safety of his fort. The Indians apparently did not know that a
two-month food supply had been laid in. The Canadians didn't
starve, but since there were five hundred penned in an enclosure
two hundred yards square, they were uncomfortably crowded,
cold, and often ill.

As Otter's militia and the freighters approached on a snowy
April 24, the Indians fled and Battleford was liberated. Jud
Battell recalled, "In the fort we found several hundred souls, all
crowded in together and with provisions enough to last only
two days. They were hysterical with joy when they realized that
the militia had come."

Dougald and his brother Colin became instant heroes the
moment the people of Battleford saw what they were hauling – a
mound of corned beef.

Eventually thirty teams volunteered to join Colonel Otter's
pursuit of Chief Poundmaker, another Cree Indian who had

infuriated the whites, but the Carmichaels were not among them. They hadn't yet seeded, and if they were to have any crop at all that year, they would have to do so immediately. The rebellion was pretty well over anyway. The final dust-up between General Fred Middleton and Louis Riel had occurred at Batoche on May 9, and the Métis had been defeated.

By May 20, Dougald Carmichael was back on his farm. After the seeding was completed, and at the urging of Rebecca, he spent much of his teamster's earnings improving the homestead. The house was moved onto a cellar, which the three Carmichael brothers had labouriously dug out, and three of the walls in the house were reinforced with concrete. The stable was torn down and a larger and more sturdy one built. Dougald at last felt his roots growing deeper into the prairie soil.

Most of the good land near his and Colin's farms had been settled, so there now existed a community of sorts, built along the railway. The CPR had called the little hamlet through which its line passed Pasqua, after a famous Cree chief. There were only a few buildings, strung out in a row like Indian beads, across from the train station. There was the station-master's home, as well as a post office, a boarding-house, and a general store. It was here that the farmers gathered to grumble about the weather, the CPR, and the Tory government. That July, the conversation was more heated than usual. One of their number, Joseph Young, had sent a letter to Ottawa that caused some anxiety in Pasqua. It read:

> To the Right Hon. Sir. J. McDonald (*sic*) G.C.B
> Sir,
> Being a friend and supporter of your administration I take the liberty to inform you of a fact that is injurious to your interests here and depreciated by your friends and gives your enemies a chance to denounce.

Young's disturbing information had to do with the CPR's station agent at Pasqua, an American immigrant, L. S. Carruth. He had entered for a valuable homestead half a mile from the station, but had not, according to Joseph Young, lived on it one day. Young considered that Carruth was "a Yankee and an

Anglo phobist" and claimed that Carruth hadn't applied to get the deed to his homestead because he didn't want to take the obligatory oath to the Queen. "He finally decided to swallow that although he does not intend to hold his allegiance long. Only until he can turn his speculation to account and get back to Yankeedom with its proceeds," Young wrote to the prime minister.

Young was also concerned because Carruth had been given a job as a telegrapher. If the Americans invaded, Carruth would be in a prime position to sabotage the Canadian defence. "Such places should only be held by loyal Canadians or Britons," Young wrote, and suggested that his friend John Brookfield, Pasqua's postmaster and a loyal British subject like himself, should replace the Yankee traitor.

Sir John personally ordered A. M. Burgess, Deputy Minister of the Interior, to look into the case. Burgess wrote Young, thanking him for the information, promising him that his name would not be revealed by the inspector who was investigating the matter, and requesting him to inform on any settler he felt might be breaking the homestead regulations.

Young promptly did so – he got the postmaster John Brook-field to write the letter – naming anyone he didn't like or he felt had slighted him. David Dustin, the brothers Thomas and William Bennie, James Trodden, and T. E. McWilliams did not live on their land and were therefore breaking the rules, he insisted. There followed that summer an investigation that generated bitter feelings in Pasqua for years afterwards. Who were the speculators keen on bagging a homestead, prov-ing it up, and selling it out? Who was willing to suffer the hardships of the pioneer life, to put down roots, help build the community? The village of Pasqua heaved with accusation and innuendo.

The report of homestead-inspector Thomas Swan exonerated everybody named by Young and Brookfield. David Dustin's wife ran the boarding-house in Pasqua, a quarter mile from his homestead, so the family slept there. But Dustin was on his land, slaving away every day. "He is a good settler and no doubt a bona fide one." Both the Bennie brothers were "industrious settlers trying hard to get along." It was true that Trodden was away working for the railway and his wife was living in Moose Jaw so the children could go to school (there was then no school in Pasqua), but, when times got better, the inspector concluded, "I think he will be a good settler." McWilliams had to take odd jobs off his land to feed his large brood, "but he is very industrious and hard working, deserving some favourable consideration."

But what of that "damn Yankee speculator," "the deep-dyed Fenian" – Carruth, the CPR agent? The inspector found that, although he slept at Pasqua station, he "devotes all his time to labour on the land" situated three-eighths of a mile away. "His wife attends to the duties of the station through the day which are very light, the trains arrive during the night." Carruth might not be getting much sleep, but he was certainly working hard to fulfill the homestead regulations. "I'm sure he'll make a good settler and be reconciled to the country."

During his investigation, Swan discovered why Joe Young had been so vindictive. He had asked for permission from the Regina land office to be absent from his claim "and being informed that he would have to comply with the law, he resolved that he would make others do the same."

"Complaints arose from a motive of jealousy, if not of vindictiveness," Swan concluded. "I anticipate no further trouble in the matter." Swan was wrong. Two months later Young squealed on another settler, Malcolm Gillies, eventually driving him and his son off the land.

It took the community a long time to get over the ill will generated by nasty games played by Young and Brookfield. "You should go and give those two a piece of your mind," Rebecca Carmichael told her husband.

"Better we stay out of it altogether," Dougald replied. Later he would regret that he hadn't paid more heed to the drama played out that summer: how easy it was for one homesteader to betray another.

While Dougald was away doing his bit in the North-West Rebellion, he had been amazed when the soldiers from the east had complained that the prairies were monotonous. "Grass, buffalo tracks, and bones and little slews of water, that's all there is to look at," one young recruit had grumbled. When the wheat was growing tall and strong, as it was this summer, it made Dougald think of the sea, a yellowish green ocean, gently swelling in the wind, and for once he didn't long for his native New Brunswick. This was his land, and it was beautiful.

August brought perfect weather – until the morning the Carmichaels woke up to discover that, over the water left out for the pigs, there glimmered a thin layer of ice. Dougald rushed to his fields and found the worst: his wheat that had been standing so sturdy and green had been transformed into black spectres, wasted soldiers ravaged by some cruel enemy. As the agent at Fort Qu'Appelle reported, "There was an abnormal frost on August 23rd which devastated the crop." It also devastated the Carmichael family. For the third year in a row, Dougald would not make a cent from his wheat. His savings were depleted, his family close to destitution.

A terrible winter followed. The Carmichaels lived on cracked wheat and milk. "Wheat cracked same as horse feed," was how Dougald put it, and in later years he would repeat it over and over as though it were a family scandal. Little Stella was scalded with boiling water that toppled from the stove, and Rebecca developed a severe cough that went to her chest. There was no money for doctors or medicine for either one.

On a particularly vicious day, when the granules of snow were seeping through the walls of their house, Rebecca pleaded with her husband, "Dougald, this place isn't fit for man nor beast. God's given us enough warnings. We must leave at once." But Carmichael wouldn't hear of it. He was determined to prove up his homestead claim; in this, his third year, the family would have to live on the farm for six months no matter what happened.

In what seemed like a day, the harsh winter turned into summer, spring somehow overlooked. The hot wind from the southwest began blowing in May. Farmers, feeling the fine dirt on their skin, whispered of drought worse than in any other year. By the time Carmichael was ready to seed his fifteen acres, the earth was so hard he had trouble keeping the walking plough in the ground. Even the Saskatoon berries dried on the bushes.

It did rain. As the Moose Jaw correspondent for the *Regina Leader* put it, "It fell in torrents. It was something alarming – something frightful. . . . In half an hour the streets were flooded. . . . the water in High St. covered the steps leading to the post office. The prairie was a sheet of water and hail – no land to be seen save the hills."

And yet in a six-mile radius around the town not a drop fell. "It was so dry and the cracks in the ground so large that a person could throw in a rock," one pioneer later wrote. There was a downpour in early July, but it proved too little too late to save the crops. It was the last straw for Dougald Carmichael. He would later write, "The potatoes had ripened in June and then shrivelled up. After the July rain they started to sprout and grow again. To me this was a signal to get out." What finally defeated him was the realization that the odds were stacked against an ordinary man like him ever taming his land; luck was laughing at him, knowing he had no chance. The only way of gaining control of his life, Dougald finally realized, was to leave this ill-fated place.

Carmichael tried to sell his livestock – five horses, two cows, two calves, and eleven pigs – and his equipment – two ploughs, a harrow, a wagon, and a buckboard. But "everybody was in the same position – everybody trying to sell and nobody buying." He got rid of some of his stuff, for which he received only two hundred dollars, an amount that barely covered his debts.

On July 16, a neighbour told Carmichael that the CPR was looking for men to work on the rail line in the Rocky Mountains. As well as a wage, he would receive his train fare to Vancouver. Dougald immediately hitched his wagon and rode into Regina. The CPR agent said there was still room for him, but "The next day's crew will be the last we'll ship out."

Carmichael panicked. What was he to do about getting title to his land? Did he have to pay for his pre-emption before he left? After settling his debts, he had hardly one cent left from selling those possessions he could get rid of. As he often did when he was in difficulty, he sought out the most important Tory in town.

Nicholas Flood Davin was Dougald Carmichael's hero. A flamboyant Irishman, a poet and raconteur, he had first made his name in Toronto as an orator, journalist, and lawyer before he sought even greater opportunities in the North-West. Immediately on his arrival in Regina, he had founded a daily newspaper, the *Regina Leader*. Carmichael used to read it often, both because the paper's conservative outlook reflected his own and because the editor wrote with passion. Davin was a man who believed that anyone who stuck by his guns, even someone as insignificant as Dougald Carmichael, could get rich in the North-West. Soon to be a Member of Parliament, Davin had grown accustomed to being asked for advice by desperate home-steaders. He tried to calm Carmichael, but, disappointingly, did nothing but point him in the direction of the land office.

Carmichael had a long and careful conversation with A. J. Fraser, the local agent of the Dominion Lands Office. Fraser told him three important things: one, that Carmichael had put in the required time to make good his claim both on his home-stead and his pre-emption; two, the pre-emption did not have to be paid for immediately; and three, that his witnesses – those neighbours who would vouch that he had complied with the regulations – need not swear their affidavits in Regina, but could do so at some later date in Moose Jaw. Feeling relieved, Carmi-chael signed up with the railway.

Rebecca and the two children were to stay with Colin Carmi-chael until Dougald could scrounge up their train fare. (Dun-can, the youngest Carmichael brother, had already left; he ended up a miner in Fairview, British Columbia.) As he was locking up the house, the furniture and tools he hadn't been able to sell stacked inside, Dougald said to his wife, "Don't worry. We'll have enough money saved by next spring to return." Rebecca's response is not known.

~ IV ~

Working on the railway was one of the "roughest experiences" Carmichael ever had. As part of the gang stabilizing bridges throughout the Rockies, he laboured an average of ten hours a day, seven days a week, and when bad weather intervened, he made up for lost time by working in the moonlight. The food was awful – "loads of pork fat and beans with bread and molasses for dessert" – but he earned $2.75 a day, which he considered a royal wage.

He reached Vancouver in February of 1887. The year before the city had been devastated by a fire. Twenty people lost their lives and every building except for a hotel and the mill had burnt down. Rebuilding was going on fast and furious, and Carmichael found his skills as a carpenter in demand. He was able to send his family train fare even earlier than he had anticipated, and Rebecca and the two children joined him in May.

But Dougald was still determined to get back on his prairie land as soon as he could. More than anything else in life, he longed to be his own man, and farming, he realized, was his only ticket. He was shocked, then, when he received a letter that spring from his old friend and business partner Robert Allison, reporting that Carmichael's application for patent to his homestead was running into trouble.

Allison was one of the two men – Duncan Stalker McVannell, a neighbour, was the other – who had agreed to vouch that Carmichael had complied with the homestead requirements. When Dougald was contemplating leaving the North-West, A. J. Fraser had told him that his witnesses could swear their affidavits in Moose Jaw, but when Allison approached the agent there, he refused to accept it. "Wouldn't listen to a word we said," Allison wrote. "Claims everybody's cheating about how long they stayed on their farms. Says farmers been swapping testimonials like they were berry pies. Insisted he wouldn't take our statements unless you were standing beside us."

Not only did Carmichael not have the cash to return to the

prairies, he also wasn't feeling well enough to make the long journey back. He was in a quandary until he heard that Thomas White, the Minister of the Interior, was in Vancouver on business.

The Carmichael family had long supported the Conservatives in New Brunswick and had worked hard for them, so Dougald had no hesitation in approaching White. After describing his hard time – "I can't think of losing between $800 and $1,000 in money besides my time. It's too much for a poor man to lose," he told him – White agreed that Carmichael's witnesses could swear their affidavits without him being present, but they would have to do so in Regina. By this time McVannell, a thirty-three-year-old bachelor, had left his homestead and was working somewhere in British Columbia. Dougald wrote to his brother Colin, requesting that he step in for McVannell. On September 16, both Colin Carmichael and Robert Allison swore their affidavits in Regina. Immediately afterwards, a certificate of recommendation for a homestead patent was issued, but it was never signed, not by the local agent nor by the land commissioner. Dougald Carmichael was about to engage in a bureaucratic battle that would make his struggles in the North-West seem like a tea party.

In the fall of 1886, someone had lied about Dougald Carmichael, telling the land-inspector that Carmichael could not possibly have fulfilled the residency requirements because, for much of the previous three years, he had been away working as a fireman on the Regina and Long Lake Railway. It was a total fabrication, but it wormed its way into Dougald's record, causing terrible damage and proving almost impossible to eradicate. Carmichael never found out who told the lies, but he had a pretty good idea that it was either David Dustin or T. E. McWilliams.

Dustin was so poor that he had arrived in the Pasqua district in July of 1884 without even a tool to work with. Carmichael tried to help the man, but when Dustin developed the habit of stealing shanties of absent homesteaders to use the lumber for building his own house and stables, Carmichael expressed his disapproval. The two had a bitter argument and never spoke again.

Tom McWilliams was a gregarious man, well liked by everybody except Dougald Carmichael, who said, "He was another man who served me mean."

At first, they had been good friends. One day in 1885 they were out riding together, looking for some interesting land that McWilliams might take up as a homestead. They arrived in the Dirt Hills, some twenty-five miles south of Moose Jaw, where they spotted some strange white patches on the face of several cliffs. Eventually Carmichael went to Regina to see if the land was available for homesteading. When he discovered it was, McWilliams filed a patent, with the agreement, according to Dougald, that "if it were to amount to anything, we were to have equal shares."

After the Carmichaels fled the North-West, McWilliams sent a sample of the soil to Ottawa to be analysed; mineralogists there said it was very rare, a high-quality clay suitable for use in lining furnaces or in cookware. Thirteen years later, McWilliams would lease the mineral rights to a conglomerate of Moose Jaw businessmen about to establish the Dominion Fire Brick and Clay Company. Three years after that he would sell the 320 acres to British Columbia entrepreneurs for $11,000. Never once did he acknowledge Carmichael's part in the discovery of the property.

In his earlier inspection of Dougald Carmichael's property, Thomas Swan had noted two other facts that were erroneous: he estimated the Carmichaels' house to be worth only $25 – later the value would be set at $200 – and he insisted that only eight acres of land had been broken, when in reality double that amount had been cropped. These were significant errors, since those who were not bona fide homesteaders but merely landspeculators did not pour money into their houses or barns, because these added little or no value to their property, nor did they bother to cultivate the land. Another black mark was fixed in Carmichael's file.

On September 26, 1887, the Dominion Lands Office in Winnipeg sent a note to Regina regarding Carmichael's claim. "Tell the inspector to take evidence under oath in this matter and to ascertain the true facts and survey the railway authorities with reference to the time applicant [Carmichael] has been in their employ."

A letter that was supposed to be sent to Dougald was also written, informing him that his application for the patent to his homestead and pre-emption had been turned down, "owing to the fact that the statements made by your witnesses were very unsatisfactory." The land commission office claimed they didn't know Carmichael's address, and the letter was never sent.

In May of 1888, Carmichael wrote asking for more information. A pathetic note crept into his letters, which would become a recurring melody, "I had to leave the Farm for a time in order to make something to live on, got starved out on the Farm, not getting my crops out of the four I put in on account of the dry seasons."

The following month he received a letter telling him that, "owing to some conflicting statements," a further investigation had been ordered, but as yet this report had not been received.

When he had still heard nothing by July of 1888, Carmichael sent another letter to Winnipeg.

> I was surprised to hear that any statement had been made to debar me from getting my farm. I was the first to go to that neighbourhood to live with my family and every honest man there knows that I put in my full time and over through dry seasons which made very hard times. . . . I done the best I could under the circumstances which every honest settler there knows. I can't imagine what the statements are or who made them. . . . I think I done what is required of me and intend to do more when I find the crops grow. . . . Please inform me who made the report and what the statements were.

The land commissioner had no intention of revealing such information, but he did order his Regina office to "shake the inspector up in this matter."

The inspector, John Rogers, finally made it to the Pasqua area in late August. His report was straightforward. Everybody who knew Dougald Carmichael claimed he had fulfilled all the conditions of the Homestead Act. Even his old enemy, Tom McWilliams, spoke highly of him. "I believe that he was a bona fide settler and that he will return and make of his place a home."

The land-inspector concluded, "This Dougald Carmichael has never been in the employ of the Canadian Pacific Railway in this locality. When absent from his homestead, he was living in Moose Jaw, keeping a hotel."

None of this made any difference. That September, Carmichael was shocked when he received a letter informing him that his entry for his land and his pre-emption was "long ago liable to cancellation." The land office insisted that he had put in the required six months' annual residency in only two years and "even this is not clearly established by the evidence of your witnesses."

By this time, Carmichael was seriously ill. While working on the railway, he had injured his back, and recently he had developed a chest cough that doctors thought might be the first stages of tuberculosis. Rebecca blamed his poor health on his experience in the North-West – all the hard labour, worry, and financial setbacks he had suffered had taken their toll. He was "flat on his back," as he put it, and broke. His only hope for the future was to again pull political strings. After all, he had been a long and devoted Tory supporter.

As soon as he heard Edgar Dewdney was in town, he made his way, pale and shaken, to the Hotel Vancouver. Dewdney had been the former lieutenant-governor of the North-West Territories, and was presently the powerful Minister of the Interior. A brusque, discourteous, and insensitive man, he listened to Carmichael, but his great mutton-chop whiskers twitched with impatience. He promised to look into the matter but did nothing concrete. "The difficulty appears to be that you have failed to put in the full amount of residence on your homestead required by law," he later wrote.

Dewdney's office may have stirred things up a little, though, because the Dominion Lands Office in Winnipeg admitted that a mistake had been made. Originally the bureaucrats had claimed that Carmichael had carried out his duties in the second and third years, 1884 and 1885, but not in the first, 1883. Now they changed their collective mind. Carmichael had remained on the land the necessary time in 1883 and 1885, they decided. It was in 1884 that his time in residence was short, but by how much they wouldn't reveal. They did make one concession: his homestead entry would be protected until May 1, if he promised the commissioner that he would be back on the land by that time "to complete the necessary duties on your homestead." Carmichael wrote back immediately, informing the commissioner that he was ill and without funds. "I could bring fifty witnesses to prove I put in all the time required by law" he insisted.

The Fosters, an influential Tory family, hailed from Carleton County, New Brunswick. Although this was some distance from King's County, the Carmichaels had known them for years. It was appropriate then, Dougald thought, to seek help from the most illustrious member of the clan: George Foster, Canada's Minister of Finance.

The building boom in Vancouver now over, Carmichael was desperate for work, and he wrote Foster asking him to provide a reference for a job in the Customs department. Although the minister pulled a few strings, that position never materialized. Carmichael thanked him for his effort, but added, "I suppose I may as well give up trying to get what is called a good position that I can make a living at." And perhaps hoping Foster might be tickled by guilt, Carmichael asked him to sort out the problem with his prairie farm, pointing out that he had been sick three months out of twenty-four, that he had no money to buy a team, provisions, and tools, never mind pay for a pre-emption – "160 acres is not enough land to farm successful in the N.W.T. in order to have pasture and land to plough ahead one year of cropping."

That same day Carmichael wrote the Dominion Lands Office, saying he still wanted his pre-emption. In the reply of April 21, 1890, he was informed that his application for this quarter-section would not be disturbed if he returned to his homestead in May and completed his settlement duties. But Dougald had hardly enough money to buy food that week. And Rebecca's cough had grown worse. "If you go back there, you go alone," she informed her husband.

A deadline of May 15, 1890, had been set for Carmichael to return to his homestead. When, on May 16, there was no sign of him in the Pasqua area, his old business partner in the Enterprise House, Robert Allison, made an application for inspection of Carmichael's land. This forced the issue; if the local agent for the Dominion Lands Office decided that Carmichael's claim was void, Allison could apply for the land himself. "So that's what you have old friends for," Rebecca remarked drily.

In despair Dougald turned to George Foster, and again the Minister of Finance intervened. As a result, a homestead-inspector was once again dispatched to the Carmichael farm. His report was rather depressing: two windows had been removed from the house; the post and poles that formed the stable had been taken away; all the furniture and tools inside had either been stolen or vandalized.

Once again Carmichael and his two witnesses were asked to swear before a notary public that their information was correct. Dougald did so in New Westminster. He had located his old friend, Duncan McVannell, and he was able to give a sworn statement in Vancouver. Allison could not be asked again – he now had his eye firmly set on Carmichael's land – so another neighbour, John Buchanan, stepped in. Their affidavits spelled out exactly how long Carmichael had lived on his land: in 1883 from mid-February to the end of May, and November and December, a total of six and a half months; in 1884 from January to July, seven months; in 1885 from March until June of the following year, sixteen months.

It seemed clear-cut, but the Dominion Lands Office didn't find it so. The inspector had talked to farmers in the neighbourhood, including Robert Allison, who had applied for his old friend's land, and David Dustin, the man who had borne a grudge against Dougald since 1884. Someone was still claiming that Carmichael had worked on the railway for most of the three years.

On August 15, 1890, the land commissioner informed Carmichael that, upon examining the inspector's reports and the statements of his two witnesses, he had concluded that Dougald had "completed but two years residence on the homestead."

How the bureaucrat arrived at this was not stated. "As you have not kept the promise [of returning to his land by May 15] your entries are liable to cancellation by default." The only way he could save his homestead was to return immediately to the West.

By this time Carmichael was just getting back on his feet – he had landed a job as a motorman on the just-completed Vancouver Street Railway – but he was still in no shape to return to the gruelling work on his farm. In desperation, he wrote again to Edgar Dewdney, Minister of the Interior.

Carmichael was informed that he had until April 15 of the following year to get back on the land or "your entry will be cancelled without further notice and the applicant [Robert Allison] for cancellation will be allowed to acquire the land."

Once again Carmichael prevailed upon influential Tory friends, but nothing came of it. When the April 15 deadline for Carmichael's return to Pasqua passed, Allison's two sons immediately filed for entry. But they resisted paying the $150 the government demanded for improvements made by Carmichael. "The house is old and decayed and the storms of last season have left it almost worthless. The roof is of no use and the house is only worth what old lumber is in it," one of the Allison sons wrote. The inspector agreed and reassessed the value at $40.

In June 1891, Dougald Carmichael was told that he no longer had any claim to his farm in the North-West. Other men might have thrown up their hands in despair; Carmichael, in his meek and mild manner, called on yet another Tory politician.

Gordon Corbould was a young and successful lawyer who had left the high society of Toronto to make his fortune in the pioneer town of New Westminster. In the 1890 federal election, he ran as a Conservative and was elected as the Member of Parliament for that constituency. When confronted with Carmichael's plight, he actually seemed to have some sympathy for the man and said he would do his best. He convinced John A. Hall, the acting deputy Minister of the Interior, to order yet another inspection, which resulted in a report like all the others. "The neighbouring settlers seem to think that he [Carmichael] put in his full time." By this inspector's calculations Carmichael was short a mere twelve days from having resided six full months in 1884-1885.

After receiving this report, Hall immediately sent a telegram to the Dominion Lands Office in Winnipeg. "West half 14, 16, 25 W2 Dougald Carmichael. Take no action on cancellation till further advised."

Dougald Carmichael gave a shout of joy when he heard the good news, but it took only a week for his jubilation to evaporate. The bureaucrats were were still not willing to give him his due; he could have his homestead and exemption, but only if he paid for it. The asking price, $2.50 an acre, wasn't bad, Carmichael admitted, but he simply didn't have $800 to purchase the two quarter-sections.

On February 29, 1892, Carmichael wrote Gordon Corbould, who secured a three-month extension for him. Dougald desperately tried to borrow from friends and relatives, but these were hard times in Canada – the depression was having an impact, and he could not even raise a third of the amount. In July of 1893, once the Allisons had given up, a farmer named Robert Craig entered for the northwest quarter of 14-16-25 W2. The unthinkable had happened; Carmichael had finally lost his homestead.

The same year, because of his recurring illness, he also lost his position as a streetcar motorman and began eking out a living with odd carpentry jobs. In 1894, the Carmichaels moved to Aldergrove near New Westminster, to work on a farm owned by Dougald's uncle, Alexander Carmichael. It was pleasant enough, but the small farm was nothing like the vast spreads of prairie wheat that he was used to, and Dougald often quarrelled with his uncle. Dougald's son, Ed, now in his early twenties, kept urging his father to return to the North-West. Finally, in 1901, the Carmichaels – Dougald, Rebecca, Ed, and Stella – boarded a train bound for Alberta.

The Carmichaels had reached Medicine Hat when news came that Nicholas Flood Davin, the former proprietor of the *Regina Leader*, had committed suicide in a Winnipeg hotel. Depressed by his defeat in the election of 1900 and at the same time grieving over a lost love, he shot himself in the head. For

Dougald, it was not only the death of his hero but the squelching of all those dreams of a glorious future in the Great West, which Davin had come to personify in Carmichael's mind.

For the next few years the Carmichaels roamed about Alberta, Ed working on farms and ranches, Dougald serving as a bookkeeper in small-town businesses, doing odd jobs, never settling, never prospering. Dougald was haunted by his lost Saskatchewan farm, and couldn't cease talking about it. Everywhere he went he carried a large leather bag, like doctors use, stuffed with correspondence relating to his prairie homestead. His reading each evening was one letter or another from a bureaucrat. "I'm sure it was Dustin that did me in, but then again maybe it was McWilliams or that fish Joe Young," he'd rattle away at Rebecca, who grew increasingly impatient with the conversation. She was sick to death of both his long-lost farm and his battles. Wanting to embrace his old dream, yet frightened of it, Dougald had imposed this peripatetic, fretful life on her, and she resented it.

Rebecca finally became ill, and in 1904 they returned to Vancouver. At age fifty-four, Dougald was again trying to make a living doing odd carpentry jobs. He felt particularly bitter about this, because the news from the West was glowing: crops were excellent, and farmers were not only making a decent living but expanding their operations. All of this made Dougald Carmichael mourn for his lost land all the more.

One day, near Christmas of 1904, he was passing the office of Robert G. MacPherson, the Member of Parliament for Vancouver-Burrard. Carmichael had never approached MacPherson before because he was a dreaded Liberal, but on the spur of the moment he stepped inside. Much to his surprise, Carmichael found in this Grit someone sincerely interested in helping him.

When the Liberals had defeated the Conservatives in 1896, the dynamic Clifford Sifton had been installed as the Minister of the Interior. He was under no illusions and called his ministry, "a department of delay, a department of circumlocution." He set out to change that. The land office in Winnipeg that had caused Carmichael so much heartache was abolished because of its frustrating, even cruel, treatment of homesteaders. Someone who had tried as hard as Dougald Carmichael to become a good farmer was no longer to be treated with contempt.

In February 1905, at the urging of Robert MacPherson, a memorandum was compiled that put Carmichael's situation simply and definitively: "According to the present practice of the Department, the duties performed by Mr. Carmichael entitle him to patent for land." Still, his case was caught in the maw of bureaucracy and floated around the Dominion Lands Office for another two years. Finally after repeated urging by MacPherson, Frank Oliver, the then Minister of the Interior, turned his attention to Carmichael's plight. In January 1907, he sent a brief letter to J. W. Greenway, Commissioner of Dominion Lands. "It appears that a man named Carmichael, who formerly had a homestead near Pasqua, but who had to go West on account of hard times, had completed the duties entitling him to patent but that the Department later on cancelled his entry. Under these circumstances you should allow Mr. Carmichael to purchase at $1, without conditions, any available even-numbered quarter sections."

Since good farmland was selling at between $65 and $150 an acre at the time, this was a victory for Dougald Carmichael. After twenty-one years of bureaucratic flim-flam, a powerful politician could take up his pen and in three minutes finally effect justice.

~ V ~

The Carmichaels now had to find a good quarter-section of farmland; no easy task, since most of the ideal homesteads, including the ones around Pasqua, had long ago been entered for. Ed had worked as a farmhand around the Medicine Hat area, and had some idea about where the best land was located. But on inquiry he discovered that all of his choices were already spoken for. Finally Dougald Carmichael decided to travel to Ottawa to confer with officials in the Department of the Interior.

Robert MacPherson was outraged at the treatment Dougald

had received over the years and wrote a note asking department officials for their help. "He is well worth any little courtesy you can show him." Dougald was shown maps of land still available.

After his meetings with the civil servants, Dougald Carmichael continued on to visit relatives in Saint John, New Brunswick, but was immediately summoned back to Vancouver.

Three years before, the Carmichaels had returned to the warmer climate of the West Coast because Rebecca's health was deteriorating. Ever since her first experience on the farm, she had been susceptible to chest colds, and in the bitter cold of Alberta's winters she had become seriously ill with bronchitis. In Vancouver, she did not improve as much as doctors had hoped, and on February 16, 1908, at age fifty-four, she died. Carmichael thought bitterly how his triumph had so quickly been diminished. It was his old nemesis, his land in the North-West, taking revenge on him, he was sure. He became more determined than ever to find a good farm, something of value he could leave to his son. In June he returned to Moose Jaw.

He couldn't believe it was the same town he had left twenty-two years before. Moose Jaw was in the middle of a fantastic boom. A new post office had just been built on Main Street, a virtual fortress of stone, bigger than most city halls. The towers and domes of magnificent churches – Methodist, Presbyterian, Anglican, Catholic, Baptist – soared above the city. Electric light, sidewalks, and telephones had been installed, and there was even talk of an electric street-railway. Moose Jaw was now a most sophisticated place, where world-famous violinists played at the Opera Hall, and where Japan's Prince Tashimi had stopped over on his cross-Canada tour. Dougald's old friends who had waited out the bad times were all doing very well indeed. He didn't bother to look them up; his was hardly a success story, and he hated those expressions of sympathy. He settled in a boarding-house and rented a horse and wagon.

He made one trip back to his old land. He felt a pang of jealousy to see the fields on his homestead and pre-emption lush with young green wheat. He noticed, however, that his brother's land had reverted back to prairie and was overrun with grasses – the only sign of Colin Carmichael's effort was the vague outline of what had been the cellar of his cabin. Colin, after some struggle with the land office in Winnipeg, had finally got the patent on his homestead. But the same black fate that had tormented Dougald afflicted his brother. Colin disappeared, and nobody could find a trace of him. Finally, in 1906, a relative living in British Columbia had sold the land for $1,920, or $12 an acre, an incredibly low amount at that time.

For several weeks, Dougald Carmichael surveyed the prairie around Moose Jaw, searching for good available land. One hundred and five miles southwest, he found exactly what he was looking for.

After the turn of the century, the Gravel family – Father Louis Pierre Gravel was the most prominent member – had settled in the North-West at a place that naturally became known as Gravelbourg. Settlers from Quebec and the eastern United States followed them, so that by the time Carmichael arrived in the area, the language spoken by most homesteaders was French. French-speakers were not exactly his cup of tea, but the quality of the soil was more important. And he could see great possibilities. The land was almost as fine as that on his farm at Pasqua. Although it was a long haul to the nearest elevator, Carmichael knew it wouldn't be too long before a branch line of the railway arrived. And then Gravelbourg was sure to boom. He filed for the northwest one-quarter of 16-11-4, west 3rd, and was informed it was still open.

The Carmichaels, père et fils – Stella had married and was living her own life – immediately began to plan their return to the prairies. A large enough nest egg would be needed to provide the most up-to-date farm implements, so that life on the prairie would not be so cruel this time. And Dougald had long ago realized that a quarter-section was not enough land to ensure a decent living; he would have to convince the government that he was entitled to a pre-emption or, failing that, buy more land. Fortunately, for the first time in years, the Carmichaels were in a position to save some money. Ed had returned to Vancouver and was working as a mail clerk for the CPR and as a carpenter in his spare time. Through political connections, Dougald had finally landed the secure, good job he had always longed for, as a clerk for the Inland Revenue Office. "It'll take us about two years to raise the necessary cash, then we'll be sailing high," he told his son. But the misfortune that had sat on Dougald Carmichael's shoulder like an ugly black crow ever since he tackled the North-West struck once again.

On March 23, 1911, Edward Carmichael was working in a building being constructed at Third and Bayswater streets in Vancouver. He had just finished cutting some two-by-fours on the second floor when someone yelled that black thunderclouds were fast approaching. Ed got halfway down the stairs before a mighty gust of wind shook the structure, causing it to collapse inward. Ed was hit in the neck by a wall plate and died instantly. He was thirty-four years old.

The tragedy took away any zest for life Dougald Carmichael possessed. He decided he was too old and too worn-out to farm. On August 15, 1915, two years after the railroad arrived at Gravelbourg, in the midst of the biggest bumper crop the West had ever experienced, Carmichael sold his Saskatchewan land to a West Coast accountant for a reasonable price. Thereafter he remained in Vancouver, living a sad, peripheral existence, moving from one boarding-house to another. His daughter, Stella, had years before married a tug-boat captain, Andrew Halcrow, an immigrant from the Shetland Islands. The couple had no children and, for reasons unknown, daughter and father had become irreparably estranged.

Dougald kept his position in the tax office until he was well into his seventies. "He was always talking about the hard times he had suffered in the prairies and how he had served his country fighting against the Indians in the Riel Rebellion and how his reward was to be poorly treated by the government he and his family had worked hard for," a member of the Odd Fellows recalled.

Dougald Carmichael died of tuberculosis on May 6, 1935 – a lonely, embittered man.

The only relative who cared about him was his niece, Annie Folkins, and according to the death-notice forms, she didn't even know his correct age – she was wrong by four years – nor did she have any idea of the names of his mother and his wife, or what country his father had emigrated from.

As if their lives were of no significance, no markers are found on any of the Carmichael graves, not Rebecca's, nor Ed's, nor Stella's, nor Dougald's. If there had been a tombstone on which to write an epitaph, it could have read "Martyrs of Canada's Great North-West; Victims of Canada's Insensitive Bureaucracy."

Aspdin

14-16-25 W2

NW	NE
SW	SE
NW	NE
SW	SE

Thomas Aspdin
(1902-1904)

11-16-25 W2

From the moment he arrived, he was fascinated by the prairies, the pastel colours of a summer sunrise, the violent white-grey of a winter blizzard. He loved the Indian way of life, their culture. Indeed, he fit in perfectly with his environment. Of all the early settlers in the West, he should have succeeded. But he too was thwarted, not only by the land, but by the money-sharks who had already infected the West.

When the call came in the spring of 1873 for young men to join the newly formed North-West Mounted Police, Thomas William Aspdin hesitated only as long as it took him to put down his pen. It wasn't just that his job as a clerk in a dry-goods establishment was tedious, or even that he thought he could make his fortune – the basic pay of seventy-five cents a day was puny even then. No, his inspiration was something far more high-minded than that.

In his boyhood, he'd gobbled up books like *The Last of the Mohicans* by James Fenimore Cooper and *The Great Lone Land* by William Butler, memorizing whole sections from them. Thirty years later he could still recite Butler to his children: "In winter, a dazzling surface of purest snow; in early summer, a vast expanse of grass and pale pink roses; in autumn too often a wild sea of raging fire. No ocean of water in the world can vie with its gorgeous sunsets; no solitude can equal the loneliness of a night-shadowed prairie." On the walls of his childhood bedroom he had hung the colour pictures he found in rotogravures – his two favourites were reproductions of *The Buffalo Hunt* by Carl Weimer and *Big Snake, A Blackfoot Chief* by Paul Kane. It was these outrageously idealistic pictures that seared into his imagination an image of the Canadian West as a wonderfully romantic place where free spirits dwell, far from corrupt civilization. His relatives and friends had not been at all surprised when, in 1872 at age eighteen, he had set out from the cramped family farm in Yorkshire for Canada.

A cousin, James Aspdin, had already set up a blacksmith shop in Muskoka, Ontario, but he had written that it was difficult to make a living in the beautiful but untamed place. "It would be to your advantage to put aside a little nest egg before trying your luck in this country." So at first Thomas Aspdin had reluctantly stayed in Ottawa, where he found a job as a clerk.

However, he still yearned for wilderness and his first encounter with a "Noble Savage." When news of the Cypress Hills massacre reached the capital, he was outraged. "Wholesale

Slaughter of the Indians," "Another Outrage on Canadian Soil." As the story unfolded in the *Daily Citizen*, he read every word.

The Cypress Hills region, in the south at the Alberta–Saskatchewan border, is the highest point in mainland Canada between Labrador and the Rocky Mountains. Lodgepole pine, white spruce, balsam poplar, and aspen made it a sanctuary for a wide variety of birds, animals, and plants. But it was also a dangerous no-man's land, a rendezvous for white whisky traders. In May of 1873, a band of "wolfers," Canadian and American whites who made their living trapping wolves, slaughtered thirty-six Assiniboine, believing that the Indians had stolen their horses.

As news of the massacre spread east, more and more unsavoury details were added. That the Indians were not quite as innocent, nor the merchants quite as cold-blooded as depicted in the press, mattered not at all. Public outrage and anti-American sentiment hastened a bill through Parliament which gave birth to a police force, civilian in structure but military in discipline and bearing. Its purpose was to uphold British law and order along Canada's uncivilized border, which meant protecting Indians from unsavoury American bootleggers. Thomas Aspdin thought he was doing his duty to Big Snake when he volunteered.

The North-West Mounted Police was to be an élite force, consisting of the most superior young men to be found in Canada and Britain. But Tom Aspdin felt confident about his chances. He was in splendid health; the recruitment doctor who examined him reported that he was blond, blue-eyed, five-foot-eight, 160 pounds, with good nerves, and of "splendid muscular development." He felt comfortable around horses (never mind that he had little experience actually sitting in the saddle; many of the other recruits were in the same position). He was relatively well-educated and certainly literate; he had often been praised for his fine penmanship and essay style. And as for his character, in Yorkshire he had been brought up in the Church of England to be a hard-working, morally proper young man.

The authorities agreed with this assessment, and soon after

he submitted his application, Thomas Aspdin became the four-
teenth man to swear an oath of allegiance to what would soon
be called the most glamorous police force in history.

At the end of a lovely September, Aspdin and his fellow
recruits assembled at Collingwood on the shore of Lake Huron.
From there they made preparations for a journey of 1,000 miles
to Lower Fort Garry near Winnipeg, where they would spend
the winter in training.

Aspdin was among the first contingent of forty men to leave
aboard the lake steamer *Cumberland* on October 4, 1873. Fortunately, the 500-mile trip through Lakes Huron and Superior to
Port Arthur went smoothly, the Indian summer smiling
benignly.

The next stage, 450 miles along the Dawson Route, which ran
from Thunder Bay in the east to the Red River district of
southern Manitoba in the west, was more strenuous, but the
weather held and the group reached the Red River safe and
sound on October 22. The second contingent, which arrived
four days later, had a similar experience. The third group, however, was not so lucky. Their lake crossing was so rough that
everyone but one tough Scottish sergeant suffered terribly from
sea-sickness. Blizzards and bitter cold accosted them on their
march from Port Arthur. "It was so cold our boots were frozen
solid so we had to wrap our feet in our underclothes. We
marched bootless for the last ninety miles," a young recruit
breathlessly told the others. If his fellow constables did not
express as much sympathy for their luckless colleagues as they
might have, they soon felt sorry for themselves. Because of the
early freeze-up, their winter uniforms would not arrive until
spring. For the next five months they flopped around in clothes
too large for comfort and far too flimsy for the severe climate.
More infuriating, their revolvers were not to arrive until the
following July. "How can you feel like a policeman without a
gun," Tom Aspdin's chum Jimmy McKernan complained.

Lower Fort Garry, also known as the Stone Fort, had been
built in 1831 as a Hudson Bay trading post. It was sufficiently
grim to provide a suitable environment for pounding raw
recruits into disciplined constables. As Tom Aspdin would later

admit, the nine-month sojourn there was sheer torture. Each morning when they woke, they prayed that the temperature had fallen below minus thirty-six degrees Fahrenheit, for only then would the dawn-to-dusk drill, supervised by the shrill and badgering Sergeant Sam Steele, be postponed. To be flung onto the ground by a crazed horse and then humiliated further by Steele's belly laugh was common, and something Aspdin and the others remembered with pain long after.

The living conditions at Lower Fort Garry were terrible. One young man wrote to his parents, "Mornings we get bread and water and a kind of tea, the rest of the day the same."

"I'd as soon be in a penitentiary as in this place. We have been treated more like brutes than men," another complained.

Thomas Aspdin cheerfully endured such hardship, considering the toughening process essential to forming stiff-backed, fearless mounted policemen. When, on one occasion, the complaints grew shrill around him, he yelled, "Oh, shut your face! What did you all come out here for anyway?" Then, to work off his anger, he went skating on the frozen Red River, not noticing that the temperature was minus forty below.

To make himself "of more worth to the force," Aspdin joined a class to learn the technique of horseshoeing, given by the farrier major. For this, a fee of $1.00 was extracted from his weekly pay of $5.15. He would come to loathe the work and soon wished he hadn't been so diligent.

In early June, the 150 men prepared to leave Lower Fort Garry and head south for Dufferin, the headquarters of the Canadian section of the Boundary Commission. Dressed in their shiny black leather boots, tight red tunics, and black breeches, with little pillbox hats tilted on their heads like cherries on a cake, their pistols and cartridges in their belts, they at last looked like a real police force. But there was much disaffection in the ranks. As the three divisions of new recruits who just two months before had been mobilized in the east arrived, the Fort Garry veterans could be heard to yell, "Suckers!"

By the time the force was ready to head west in July, thirty-one men were absent without leave. Nevertheless, once the force was assembled, the parade was an astonishing sight, consisting of 73 freight wagons, 114 Red River carts, 2 nine-pounder field guns, 2 brass mortars, field kitchens, mowing machines to make hay *en route*, and 93 cattle destined to be eaten along the way. It stretched for two miles. But after just two days on the road, another dozen constables took advantage of the proximity of the American border and bolted. The desertions continued, exacerbated by the nightmarish march west – a trek of 1,000 miles, which has been seared into the collective memory of the North-West Mounted Police.

Tom Aspdin's good friend, Constable James Finlayson, wrote during the ordeal: "Camped on the open plain near a swamp. No water. No wood. No supper." Two days later his diary noted that he had one flapjack for breakfast. "Lucky to get that. Supper the same as I had for dinner. Nothing!"

Despite bitter cold and terrible sunburn, thick mud that sucked off boots, flies and mosquitoes that drove men and horses mad, Tom Aspdin uttered not a word of complaint. "What a desolate, ugly place," remarked his friend, Lawrence Nobbs, as they scanned an area where prairie fires had completely denuded the vegetation.

"Fascinating, with a beauty of its own, I'd say," was Aspdin's response.

In early October – after several groups, mostly the sick and faint-hearted, were spun off in different directions – the main body, including B Division to which Aspdin belonged, finally reached the junction of the St. Mary's and Belly rivers. There, audacious in the bright sunlight, stood Fort Whoop-Up. It was the most notorious of the whisky outlets built by Americans on Canadian soil to circumvent the U.S. laws prohibiting the selling of alcohol to natives. The memory of the American flag cheerfully fluttering above its stumpy turret stayed with Tom Aspdin forever.

The Indians liked their liquor to pack a wallop, and the white traders were pleased to cater to their whims, concocting a brew of raw alcohol, heavily watered and spiced with tabasco, red peppers, and Jamaica ginger, and coloured with tobacco juice or ink. This rot-gut was potentially as dangerous to the physical and psychological health of the natives as that great annihilator, smallpox, had been. The Canadian government wanted the bootlegging stopped at once.

The first and most important task of the young police force was to demolish Whoop-Up. The field guns and mortars that had been dragged across the prairies were trained on the fort, the men properly positioned. Then, when all was ready, they watched in astonishment as Colonel James Macleod, with his sidekick, Jerry Potts, a bow-legged half-breed and invaluable scout, sauntered up and hammered on the front gate. It was opened by an American named David Akers. "I'm sorry my partners are away on business," he said. "But won't you and your men join me for dinner?" So, instead of their first shootout, the Mounties sat down to a meal that included fresh garden vegetables, the first they'd had for months.

A thorough search was made of the place, and when not a drop of liquor turned up, Macleod deduced that, as soon as the bootleggers had heard his Mounties were approaching, they had quite wisely fled.

He was so impressed with the solid construction of Fort Whoop-up that he inquired about buying it as a winter headquarters for his detachment. Unfortunately, the price Akers quoted was far too high for the niggardly force. Macleod ordered his tired Mounties to get ready for another three days of travel westward.

When they finally reached their destination, Oldman River, they were immediately broken up into construction crews. By December, most of the log buildings for the new Fort Macleod were completed, and the drafty tents at last vacated.

~ II ~

"Crude" was how Aspdin would later describe the life at Fort Macleod. Since their lovely red uniforms were now in tatters, the Mounties appeared on parade dressed in old blankets, buffalo coats, hats they'd made themselves from felt, and trousers cut from buffalo hide and tied around their boots to hold them together. The food was terrible, and boozing endemic. "You'd be shocked to know how much whisky the boys here can get their hands on," one officer wrote his mother. "I don't touch the stuff myself, but I can't say as I blame them." Perhaps as a reaction to this, Aspdin became something of a teetotaller, and as a result the subject of much teasing.

When the warm chinooks arrived, the temperature would zoom up by as much as sixty degrees in a few hours. The roofs of the barracks leaked oozing mud. Once, after hours of patrol duty, Aspdin and his friend James Finlayson fell into their bunks, dead to the world. They didn't hear the roof caving in, but once the cold muddy liquid hit them in the face, they sprang from their beds "like jackrabbits." Thereafter, they slept with sheets of oil-cloth pinned above them. Indeed, sleeping arrangements came to symbolize the rough life of the Mounties for Tom Aspdin. For the thirteen years that he was in the force he slept on what was the standard issue, planks of wood laid across trestles. "The most uninviting couch on which it has ever been my misfortune to seek repose," is the way one police officer put it.

Yet despite all the hardships, Thomas Aspdin, the intellectual, the romantic, thrived. On patrol duty he would stare for long periods at the strange prairies, bewitched by the changing light, the fusion of otherworldly colour. Every kind of wildlife interested him, from the pronghorn antelope to the red-necked grebe. As his contact with members of the Blackfoot Confederacy grew, his fascination and respect for the Indian culture blossomed. In this he was unusual among his fellow police officers.

Although it wasn't considered correct to mouth the American sentiment "The only good Indian is a dead Indian," the North-West Mounted Police, British-stock almost to a man, seldom questioned the predominant wisdom that they were a civilizing force taming an inferior and unproductive race. Constable Thomas La Nauze, writing to his mother in Ireland, gives an example of this soft racism. "I don't see much of the noble savage about them; the squaws put me in mind of the west of Ireland people, going about with various coloured blankets, and the general appearance much resembles the pictures one sees of the distressed Irish."

While Aspdin certainly felt paternalistic towards the Indians – he came to believe that life on a reserve was preferable to starvation – he developed a genuine appreciation of Indian culture. He noticed the intricate bead-work on a papoose sling, understood the symbolic importance of the Sun Dance, admired the Indian hunting ability. Within a few years he could speak five Indian languages, and his knowledge of Indian folk-lore was admired by natives and whites alike.

The Mounted Police spent the winter of 1873-74 dumping illicit booze into the snow, throwing the bootleggers into improvised jails, and confiscating their furs, wagons, and horses. Within three months the whisky trade, which had flourished for a decade under the noses of the American authorities, was wiped out. As well, Macleod had met with the chiefs of the Bloods, Peigans, and Blackfoot and had convinced them that the Mounted Police were there for their own good. This laid the foundation for the treaties that would eventually sequester them on reserves. With the booze peddlers gone and the Indians placated, the Mounties could spread their authority further throughout the Canadian West. In May 1875, Major James Walsh and B Division set out for the Cypress Hills, some 156 miles east of Fort Macleod.

While many of his fellow constables grumbled, Aspdin was excited at the prospect of travelling into even more remote parts of Indian country. After all, this was the site of the Cypress Hills massacre, the event that had goaded him into joining the force two years before.

Situated in the valley of Battle Creek, surrounded by wooded hills, the location for the new fort was pleasant enough, but had one serious drawback: it was almost indefensible against marauding Indians. Within days the place was surrounded, but all the Indians did was sit and enjoy the amusing spectacle of thirty Mounties sweating as they built their log fort.

Almost immediately a village sprang up around the stockade: trading stores supplied by Bakers and Powers, the Fort Benton merchant kings, a log billiard hall, a crude hotel, a restaurant, and a barber shop. The Indians joined in the commotion, and hundreds of lodges were set up nearby, a situation that would have flabbergasted the Americans. Everyone was on hand for the ceremony at which the place was officially named Fort Walsh after the popular superintendent, or, as he called himself, Major James Morrow Walsh.

Life soon settled into a routine. As well as carrying out the usual duties involved in patrolling the prairies, Aspdin worked as the fort's farrier. In the winter of 1875 a huge black gelding fell on top of him, badly injuring his back. He spent a month in the infirmary and was never again fully free of pain. The job of blacksmith was loathsome to him thereafter.

The following fall Thomas Aspdin requested a discharge from the Mounted Police. Whether it was his injury or the poor pay and living conditions, whether he was tired of blacksmithing, or whether he was merely doing what everybody else had done – by 1876 more than half the original recruits had left – is not known.

Certainly Muskoka was on his mind. "A gorgeous primitive country with lots of wildlife, deer and bear roaming about," he told a fellow constable.

"And black flies and mosquitoes," was the other fellow's reply. Tom decided to go and see for himself.

His cousin James, a dynamic, gregarious young man, had not only been appointed postmaster but had managed to get the Muskoka hamlet where he lived named after himself. The village of Aspdin was situated in the south end of Stisted County, and at the time of Thomas's visit it consisted of a small hotel, a general store, and a blacksmith shop. Tom Aspdin applied for and obtained a grant in concession five, lot 13, very near the property of James and another cousin William, who had also arrived from England. But it was still difficult to make a living. The job of clearing such rocky, wild land was daunting, and there was little farming possible. The lumber industry hadn't developed in a major way, and the tourism that would later bring prosperity was still only a pipe-dream. After poking about the area for several months, Thomas Aspdin finally decided his future was in the West.

His family claims that, because of his fluency in Indian languages and his knowledge of the terrain, the United States

Cavalry offered him a position as a scout. The first band of Sioux who had been involved in the Battle of Little Big Horn in Montana was beginning to drift north, and the Americans wanted someone like Aspdin to funnel information about this movement. But, according to his grandson Maurice Williams, as soon as he understood how unjustly the U.S. military treated the Indians, he quit. The North-West Mounted Police was a far more humane organization, he felt, and so he decided to re-enlist. He arrived back at Fort Walsh in the spring of 1877, just in time to encounter the influx of Sioux that was seeking refuge from the American army.

Years later, when he loved to spend evenings talking about the early days in the West with his friend, the Assiniboine chief, Dan Kennedy, he described that June day:

> We reined up our horses and from a vantage point watched a long column of rising dust. At first we thought it was a buffalo stampede. However, when they approached closer it turned out to be not a herd, but a whole tribe of Sitting Bull's Hunkpapas.
>
> They were all mounted, even the women with the papooses strapped to their backs and the children clinging to the horse manes, with their feet tucked in under the sureingles. Their rich trappings and beautiful regalia were wonderful to behold. I never saw so much bead work and porcupine quill embroidery. We feasted our eyes on the magnificent spectacle.

Perhaps because of his experience with the U.S. Cavalry, Thomas Aspdin always maintained that the Americans were deceitful and cruel in their treatment of the Sioux. The U.S. government had, after all, signed an agreement specifying that white men were not to enter the Black Hills of the Dakotas unless the Indians gave them permission. With the first scent of gold, prospectors began pouring onto the reserve; by 1874 the American public was clamouring for a geological survey of the Black Hills. To oversee this exercise, the arrogant and reckless Lieutenant-Colonel George Armstrong Custer was sent in, with 1,200 soldiers, four Gatling guns, sixty scouts, and a great wagon train of provisions. The Sioux remained patient, despite this outright violation of its 1868 treaty, until Custer yelled to the world, "There's gold in the grass roots. Come and get it!"

Inevitably there had to be a showdown between the furious Sioux and Custer's troops. But what surprised the world and outraged the Americans was that, at the valley of the Little Big Horn, the U.S. Army suffered the most humiliating defeat of its history. The Indians baited the Blue Coats, and then waited in ambush. After the bloody clash, not only had the lieutenant-colonel himself been slaughtered, but so had 264 men of the Seventh U.S. Cavalry.

Even as his warriors were mounting their victims' superb army horses, the great Sioux chief, Sitting Bull, could smell defeat. He knew the terrible wrath of the entire U.S. Army would soon descend on his people, and to prevent wholesale slaughter, he ordered a march northward.

Sitting Bull would have been astonished if he knew that, during his stay in Canada, he would become an intimate friend and admirer of a Red Coat commander.

If ever a true-life Sergeant Preston existed, it was the indomitable Major James Morrow Walsh. He was Thomas Aspdin's greatest hero. In his early thirties, heartbreakingly handsome, with posture that never relaxed and a spirit of iron to match, Walsh was considered courageous in a police force where being brave was taken as a given. His legend was cemented the day he met Sitting Bull.

Walsh, in his eccentric dress – a cheeky black slouch hat, a lived-in buckskin jacket (which he wore whenever he wasn't sporting his patrol tunic laden with gold braid), and knee-high U.S. calvary boots – rode defiantly with twelve policemen and two scouts into the camp of three thousand angry, surly Sioux, to meet face-to-face with a man the Americans considered a ruthless killer and the most dangerous Indian on the continent. The great chief, his smallpox-pitted face as hard and worn as old grainy wood, flashed the medals his grandfather had been awarded by George IV for fighting on the British side in the War of 1812. "I'm a child of the Great White Mother," he insisted. "I have buried my weapons."

"You are safe as long as you obey the Queen's laws," said Walsh, as his men stared at the American scalps still hanging out to dry, the guns grabbed from the hands of dying American soldiers, now carried by proud warriors, the horses marked with the brand of the U.S. Army, tied outside the Indian lodges.

This policy of appeasement was bitterly resented by the Americans. In their view, the murderous savages sat close enough to the border to threaten U.S. military posts, but far enough to be safe from counterattack by the Blue Coats. The Americans wanted the Sioux forced back onto U.S. soil, so they could control them. And while the Canadian government disapproved of American Indian policy, it was concerned about the tension developing between the two countries. Somehow Sitting Bull had to be persuaded to return to the States. Would he at least meet with high-ranking American military and officials on Canadian soil? Sitting Bull at first flatly refused – "How can we go and talk to White Men with blood on their hands?" he asked. But the ever-patient Major Walsh kept after him, and finally, because a friendship based on mutual admiration had developed between the two men, Sitting Bull agreed.

Thomas Aspdin was on guard duty in the mess hall at Fort Walsh when the meeting got under way on October 17, 1877. He later told his children that he could hardly keep from bursting into laughter when Sitting Bull swept in. He was wearing an outlandish wolfskin hat, an old ragged shawl, and what Aspdin particularly admired, a pair of beautifully beaded moccasins. Ignoring the Americans completely, he shuffled up to Colonel Macleod and amiably shook his hand. Then he squatted on a buffalo robe spread on the floor, resolutely turning his back on the American visitors.

Nothing was accomplished, of course. Sitting Bull said, "Once I was rich, plenty of money but the Americans stole it all in the Black Hills. What should I return for? To have my horse and my arms taken away? I have come to remain with the White Mother's children." American General Alfred H. Terry promised him peace and freedom, but Sitting Bull would not believe a word. The next morning the Americans left, and the chief went back to his camp at Wood Mountain.

Thomas Aspdin would later tell Chief Dan Kennedy that he thought the following year was the most explosively dangerous in the short history of the Canadian West. There were two possible situations that the Mounted Police wanted to avoid at all costs. The first was conflict among the Indians themselves. The Blackfoot, Assiniboine, and Cree had not exactly welcomed the American Sioux with open arms; the Sioux had been traditional enemies, and the Blackfoot Confederacy didn't want them hunting on their buffalo range. There was a real possiblity that a ferocious war would flare along the entire western border and suck in both the American army and the Canadian police force.

But the other scenario was even more disturbing. What if a confederation of Indian tribes could be forged by someone as brilliant and determined as Sitting Bull? The Mounties knew such an alliance would have the numbers and fighting strength to drive whites from the frontier. Somehow the Indians had to be kept pacified.

Because of his fluency in Indian dialects and his genuine interest in their culture, the natives liked and trusted Tom Aspdin. He spent long days on patrol duty in their prairie camps, discussing, appeasing, promising. And the information he brought back to his superiors was invaluable. The force must have thought he was doing a good job, for in July of 1878 he was promoted to the rank of corporal.

In August he was sent to survey Sitting Bull's summer camp, located at Wood Mountain, eighty-five miles southwest of Moose Jaw. Aspdin was shocked to discover that many Sioux were hungry. The previous winter had been mild – "week followed week with the same genial sunshine and there was little snow," one Mountie reported home. The prairie was very dry, and in spring grass-fires erupted along the border, preventing the already depleted buffalo herds from making their usual trek northward from the United States into Canada. But as bad as the situation was that summer, it was merely a portent of the disaster that was to follow the next year.

The American Sioux had been told that, while Canada would provide a safe refuge for them, they were not under treaty, and the "Great White Mother" owed them nothing; enough ammunition to kill a few buffalo would be provided, but no food rations, and certainly no reserve. Canada was still looking for a way to ease strained relations with the United States, and starving the Sioux back to the Dakotas seemed a reasonable solution.

As much as Major Walsh admired Sitting Bull – "In my opinion he is the shrewdest and most intelligent living Indian, has the ambition of Napoleon and is brave to a fault," he once wrote – he was opposed to giving the refugees their own reserve. Unhappy Indians who were living on American reserves would pour over the border, he insisted, "and would, I fear, prove injurious to our settlers and Indians."

There's no record of what Corporal Aspdin thought about the dilemma, but he probably agreed with Walsh. He admired the handsome major unreservedly, even idolized him, and although he recognized the value of Indian culture, he was not one to buck the establishment.

Though life at Fort Walsh remained primitive, some refurbishing and an addition of storage buildings rendered it slightly more homey than when Aspdin had first arrived. In a letter, Aspdin's old friend Tom La Nauze described it thus: "I scribble to you now in the long room, containing fifty beds, the fellows on each side of me playing cards and further on a fellow at the flute, others singing and talking so it is not easy to write proper."

Definitely lacking, though, was romance. Another friend of Aspdin's, Frank Fitzpatrick, wrote "no white woman was in the country. . . . I never saw one for three years." Dances were held, to which neighbouring Métis and Indian young ladies were invited. Tom Aspdin, who had been too young to leave a girlfriend back east, admitted that he was attracted to many of them. "They were beautifully dressed," he later said. "And some were very, very good-looking." At that point the encounters were casual, but Aspdin's young appetite had been awakened.

That spring of 1879, another series of grass-fires sprang up along the boundary line from Wood Mountain to the Rockies, turning the prairie into an ugly black wasteland. Once again those buffalo wintering in the United States were deterred by lack of grazing from migrating north, and those that had remained in the north of Canada stayed there. Because the fires had started almost simultaneously at several points along the boundary, it became obvious that arson was involved. Rumours spread that the culprits were the Blackfoot, who, it was said, would do anything to pressure the Sioux into returning to the Dakotas and moving off their hunting range. Thomas Aspdin never believed this, for the simple reason that the Blackfoot Indians suffered almost as much as the Sioux. Years later he would tell his friend Dan Kennedy that he believed, even at the time, that it was the Play-ku-tay, "white vandals," who had lit the fires; that they had been hired by the American government to prevent the buffalo migration to Canada and thereby force the Sioux back to the States.

Whoever set the blaze achieved his purpose: the buffalo were trapped in the United States, and General Nelson Miles's troops patrolling the border prevented Canadian hunting parties from travelling south. By summer, not only had the buffalo disappeared completely from the Canadian plains but so had all small animals and game birds. "It was a terrible situation. There wasn't a deer, a rabbit, even a gopher to be seen," Aspdin later recalled.

Fort Walsh was besieged by five thousand hungry Blackfoot, Cree, Blood, Sioux. Aspdin's friend Frank Fitzpatrick wrote of meeting thirty ravaged Indians just outside Fort Walsh. "They looked like a delegation from some graveyard. There were men, women, and children with their eyes sunk back in their heads and all with the look of despair about them."

Inspector Cecil Denny of the NWMP wrote about the desperate Blackfoot. "I have seen them, after I had an animal killed, rush on the carcass before the life was out of it and cut and tear off the meat, eating it raw."

The Canadian government realized that, unless provisions were sent quickly, mass starvation and an accompanying international scandal would result. For one thing, the Treaty Indians were entitled to food in times of emergency. Five hundred head of cattle, 91,000 pounds of bacon, 100,000 pounds of beef, 20,000 pounds of pemmican, and 800 sacks of beef and flour were doled out. And since Indian horses were too weak even to carry the small bags of food to the nearby camps, police wagons had to be stocked and sent out to assist the starving who could not make it to the fort. Keeping track of all this quickly developed into a nightmare – until Thomas Aspdin took over the distribution of supplies.

Since his re-engagement, he had been assigned more and more administrative work – his education and previous work experience were assets in this – and during that chaotic summer he worked around the clock literally saving lives. Throughout, as his superiors noted, he remained calm and patient in his encounters with the desperate.

When a Cree named Swift Runner was charged with having eaten his mother, brother, wife, and six children, most of Aspdin's fellow police officers raved about the "bloody savage." Aspdin's reaction was more sympathetic: "Starving, destitute men are dangerous, desperate men," he said.

Starvation among the native population wasn't the only calamity that fell on Fort Walsh that summer. During the previous three years, outbreaks of Mountain Fever, a typho-malarial infection, had killed a number of people in the surrounding settlement. In the early summer of 1879, 10 per cent of the garrison was down with the infection. Thomas Aspdin felt sick much of the time – his back still bothered him and he suffered from chronic indigestion. But as he later wrote, "In trying to get the supplies to those poor Indians, who could worry about his stomach?"

As autumn approached, the situation was becoming even more desperate, and Tom Aspdin wasn't surprised when disaster finally struck the Mounted Police.

On November 17, 1879, two new recruits, Marmaduke Graburn and George Johnston, decided to pick some greens for the evening meal from a vegetable garden that had been planted just outside Fort Walsh. This completed, they were returning to the Fort when Graburn realized he had forgotten his axe and lariat, and rode back to fetch them.

He did not return that night, although his horse showed up, and the next morning a search party combed the snow-covered hills. In a deep, bushy coulee, Graburn's body was found, a gaping bullet hole in the back of his head. He was the first Mountie to die at the hands of the natives, murdered by a Blood Indian rather inappropriately named Star Child.

Star Child, an irascible, rat-faced young man, was considered a terrible nuisance, because he was particularly insistent in begging for food. The impatient Graburn had lost his temper with Star Child, calling him "a miserable dog." While Tom Aspdin was saddened by the death, he later told Chief Dan Kennedy that, if Graburn had acted as a proper Mountie should, he'd still be alive.

With his second three-year term almost up, Aspdin spent sleepless nights deciding whether he should re-engage in the Mounted Police. He still held his land grant in Aspdin, Muskoka, where his indomitable cousin, James, was making a name for himself as an entrepreneur. There might be a future for him there. On the other hand, Tom was by now enthralled with the vast open spaces of the prairies. The Mounted Police had started a beef herd near Fort Walsh, and he found himself attracted to cattle-ranching. No question in his mind that rounding up calves in the invigorating spring was far more exciting than plodding behind some portly Clydesdale and a plough. But he had by now seen enough of the lives of struggling homesteaders to realize he'd need to save a sizeable grubstake, whether he decided to farm or ranch. And he was doing well as a Mountie; he was now acting quartermaster at Fort Walsh, and there had been promises of promotion and a pay raise.

On June 5, 1880, Aspdin signed up for another three-year stint. The president of the Board of Officers that assembled at Fort Walsh to formalize the re-engagement was a nervous, morose little Englishman who was hard of hearing, named Francis Dickens. Aspdin had once politely asked him, "As I admired your father beyond reason, I wonder if you would autograph my copy of *David Copperfield*." While the officer had obliged, he had signed the book with such ferocity that the pen ripped the page.

That August, Aspdin was sent to investigate conditions in

Sitting Bull's camp. The Sioux were summering at what they called *Wichisto*, or "A Creek in the Shape of Arms," which the white man would soon rename Moose Jaw. Aspdin was shocked at the state they were in. Since they weren't eligible for food rations, they, of all the Indians, suffered the most from hunger. They were so weak and ill that when a small herd of buffalo was sighted seventy miles away, they did not have the strength to go after them. Sitting Bull, still hoping for a reserve in Canada, resolutely refused to consider returning to the States, but Aspdin noted that more and more of his followers were crossing over the border.

There was another incident that fall that shocked and disheartened Thomas Aspdin. Major James Walsh was transferred to an unimportant post in Qu'Appelle Valley. The powerful in Ottawa had decided that Walsh's relationship with Sitting Bull had delayed the Sioux's return to the United States, and he had fallen out of favour. Two years later the major retired from the force altogether. Aspdin always felt that his admiration for Walsh, which he never tried to hide, was one reason his career in the Mounties did not reach the lofty heights that, in 1880, he thought it might.

But he was so busy that he didn't have time to think about the future. An epidemic of Mountain Fever had broken out again at Fort Walsh, and the police surgeon, John Kittson, tracked down the source of the infection to a swampy area littered with carcasses of dead buffalo and horses. In rainy weather the swamp water overflowed, polluting Battle Creek, the fort's source of drinking water.

Dr. Kittson insisted the entire garrison take up camp near a clear spring of water while the fort was fumigated, whitewashed, and the floor was replaced. The men would live under canvas for two months, and since Aspdin was now in charge of the quartermaster stores, it was his duty to see they were fitted out as comfortably as possible. It was a difficult chore. It rained or snowed almost every day, and the tents provided were old and "sieve-like." Many fell sick with colds, rheumatism, and throat infections, and when they finally returned to the fort, the fever immediately broke out again.

In October, Superintendent Edmund Dalrymple Clark succumbed to the infection, the first officer to die in the service of the Mounted Police. He had joined the force the same time as Aspdin, and the two men had become fast friends despite the differences in rank. Clark's death exacerbated the depressing atmosphere and low morale at Fort Walsh, and Aspdin was not unhappy when he was informed that he was being transferred.

On May 1, 1881, he was promoted to staff sergeant and made acting quartermaster at Wood Mountain Post, southwest of Moose Jaw near the American border.

~ III ~

For years the valleys of Wood Mountain had been a favourite spot for Métis and Indian hunters. (It was considered Assiniboine country, but Cree and Saulteaux also frequented the area, often after bloody battles for possession.) The deep coulees offered shelter, wood was abundant for burning and building, and, most important, there were plenty of buffalo.

The North-West Mounted Police had set up a post at Wood Mountain years before, considering its close position to the American border strategically important in their ongoing pursuit of American whisky-runners. Although the Mounties had abandoned the post once the bootlegging had been contained, Wood Mountain became significant again when Sitting Bull and his Sioux chose it as their favourite camping ground.

The post was merely a cluster of log shacks that had once belonged to the Canadian Boundary Commission surveyors. "It offered neither accommodation, comfort, or defence," was how one constable put it. The Mounties would look out the windows of the barracks, down into the deep wooded coulees, and would either imagine or sometimes actually see the shadows of Indian warriors. Even when Aspdin arrived, Wood Mountain Post was crude. His bed, the measuring stick he habitually used to judge how primitive conditions were, was a buffalo-hide hammock, stretched between a wall and a stake driven into the floor.

Aspdin's job as quartermaster involved looking after all the constables' kits, weaponry, ammunition, and food supplies. "He'd have to have had a sharp idea about what's going on," speculates RCMP historian and museum curator, Bill Mackay. "If the uniforms were getting a little worn, he was looking at thousands of miles and many months before he could replenish them from the Ottawa suppliers." Only fifteen constables and five officers were stationed at Wood Mountain, so his job would not have been too onerous, had it not been for the fact that upon his arrival, the farrier left, and he had to perform these duties temporarily as well as his own. Ever since the horse had fallen on him he had loathed the work, but he couldn't resist the pressure put on him by his superiors, or the fifty cents a day extra pay he was offered. He would later write, "I kept fifteen horses shod beside doing waggon work and other jobs. . . . I had often to be in the shop before Reveille in order to do the work in time to attend to my many other duties."

He was rather resentful of this imposition, and began thinking that his Muskoka property might have been a better alternative. But that summer he received bad news from Aspdin, Ontario.

The lumber industry had begun to boom in Muskoka and Thomas's cousin James, always the ingenious entrepreneur, decided a dam was required on nearby Black Creek to supply water power to a sawmill. It was something of a disaster. A description remains of what happened that memorable summer: "Thomas Lakeman built the flume and penstock. A turbine was installed in the penstock. Then bang! Part of the mill machinery landed on the premises, the rest of it was scattered for two miles back on the road." James left the area soon after.

It's doubtful whether Thomas would have settled in Muskoka anyway, for that glorious autumn he met and immediately fell in love with a Sioux princess who was just as beautiful as any depiction he had ever seen in a Kane or Weimer painting.

We-ah-hoska – her English name was Mary – was the daughter of Black Moon, the hereditary chief of the Teton Sioux. Also called Loves War Number One, Black Moon was renowned as a witty and clever master of ceremonies and a wise judge in civil and criminal affairs. His great-grandson John O'kute-sica (LeCaine in English) once wrote, "When Loves War could not persuade or trick the truth from a person or party in a serious or important case tried by him, he always called upon Supernatural Powers to aid in judgment and with never failing results."

Black Moon had three wives – all full sisters – and their nephew was none other than Sitting Bull. In fact, Sitting Bull, who was not a hereditary chief, may have derived his political power from his connection with Black Moon. Fortunately, Black Moon was an admirer of the younger man's military genius and had agreed with the tactics Sitting Bull had used in his bloody encounter with Custer.

Black Moon was conservative, "an old-fashioned warrior," who so disdained white man's ways that he refused to use a gun against the Blue Coats – although, according to his daughter, his bow and arrow did almost as much damage. The Black Moon family was in the vicinity when Custer and the Seventh U.S. Cavalry attacked, and Mary, who was sixteen at the time, always remembered that day. In the confusion, she had not been able to find her beautiful sorrel pony, a gift from her father. She had taken another horse, but her brother had come across her pony and had ridden it into the battle. After the fighting was over, Mary found it lying on the ground in great pain. It had been shot in the back, and had to be put out of its misery. "It was a sad day for me when my pony died," Mary Blackmoon later recalled.

Black Moon and his tribe of three thousand reached Canada months before Sitting Bull arrived. They settled near Wood Mountain, and it wasn't long after he was posted there that Thomas Aspdin spotted Mary Blackmoon.

Even in old age, there was something regal about her. "She had a serenity and grace that amazed us," remembers her grandson Maurice Williams. "Everything she said we considered gospel truth," recalls Eleanor Thompson, a granddaughter. "Whatever she did we considered must be the right thing to do."

In her younger years, she had been stunning. She was exceptionally tall, taller than Thomas Aspdin, and always elegantly slender, with smooth, fair skin (she had never had smallpox), luxurious black hair, a perfectly formed nose, and black almond-shaped eyes. In her youth she dressed in Indian style; when Tom Aspdin met her at a ceremonial dance, she was wearing an outfit her mother had painstakingly sewn – a beaded and fringed dress of white antelope skin, as soft to the touch as bear grease.

Aspdin was immediately smitten by the twenty-year-old Indian princess, but she was leery. Just a few months before his arrival, Mary Blackmoon's cousin had endured a romance with a Red Coat which had been so intense and, in the end, so disastrous, that it quickly became a legend among the Sioux.

Iteskawin, "White-faced Woman," was also a beauty. "Not only her looks, her whole being was magic," recalled her grandson, John O'kute-sica. Certainly Major William Dummer Jarvis, commander of the Wood Mountain Post, found her so; especially after he accidentally ran into her one day at a nearby stream where she was washing her hair, completely naked.

Jarvis was so taken with Iteskawin that, although he couldn't speak a word of Sioux nor she a word of English, he was determined to marry her. At first she was appalled at the idea. As John O'kute-sica said, she deeply feared the white man. "He was considered a spirit man not of this world, out to destroy her race and take away all the Indians loved and lived for."

Her decision to marry the Mountie was a terrible sacrifice for the eighteen-year-old. But she watched as her father returned home from hunting empty-handed and her two brothers and little sister grew even more hungry. Finally she decided that, if the chief of the Red Coats would give food to her family twice a day, she would do what he wished and marry him.

The affair ended badly. Jarvis was a domineering, jealous man, who could hardly wait to take his wife back east and "civilize" her. Not appreciating Indian culture, he misinterpreted a kiss planted on a young warrior's cheek during a dance as infidelity, and, in a flash of rage, he humiliated Iteskawin by dragging her away and twice pushing her to the ground.

Early the following morning she fled southward to the Standing Rock Reservation in South Dakota, where she eventually married Calling Elk, a constable of the U.S. Indian Police Service. Jarvis retired from the force in 1881, "under a cloud," as his record states, and returned to England an unhappy man.

How Mary Blackmoon overcame her antipathy for a white man after this disaster is not known. "My mother, who was Mary's daughter, told me Black Moon simply said to her, 'This white man has done everything in the proper Indian way – he has brought the horses, and said the right words. It would be disgraceful to turn him down.' So, although Mary didn't want to go, she had to," says Eleanor Thompson.

"We believe that Black Moon allowed, or even encouraged, the match as a kind of gift, a symbol of his appreciation for the protection Canada had given him and his people," Maurice Williams says. It might also have had something to do with Aspdin's job as quartermaster; he could easily slip food to Mary and her hungry people.

But there's also a good chance that his romantic success had to do with Aspdin himself. A photo taken at the time shows him to be pleasant-looking in a round-faced, English sort of way, his dusty blond hair parted smartly in the middle, his pale blue eyes serious, his moustache bushy and prominent. But it was probably more his personality that appealed to Mary. He was quite a different man than Jarvis. He could speak her language fluently, and he had an understanding of and respect for her culture that was amazing to her people. "It was always thought in our family that Thomas Aspdin, unlike most whites, had an understanding of Black Moon's place in Indian Society, so that he could appreciate what a remarkable young woman Mary was. And she knew this," Maurice Williams says.

Mary Blackmoon and Thomas Aspdin were formally wed, but only by Indian ritual. He wanted desperately to legitimize his marriage in the Church of England, but he didn't dare, for a very good reason: if his superiors in the North-West Mounted Police had found out about his relationship with the Sioux princess, he would have been drummed out of the force immediately. Not only would the marriage not be permitted, but the mere request would have meant a black mark on his record.

There were several Mounties who got involved with native or Métis women – John O'kute-sica could remember, beside Jarvis and Aspdin, at least four other marriages – and they were not penalized as long as they didn't openly acknowledge the relationship. When the constables were reassigned to another location or were discharged, they were expected to discard these wives, and any children that might have resulted, without a thought. And most did. But Tom Aspdin was madly in love with beautiful Mary Blackmoon and would remain faithful to her for his entire life. He did, however, have a problem. How to make his adored Sioux princess happy in a white man's world?

Aspdin was wise enough to realize that Mary would only be content if she remained close to her family and Indian friends; to be isolated on a farm with only Anglo-Saxons as neighbours would breed disaster. So, when an old acquaintance, Jim Dugan, presented a surprise solution, Tom Aspdin couldn't resist his offer.

In July 1881, Sitting Bull, dejected and destitute, had returned with the last remnants of his tribe to the United States, where, after giving up their horses and weapons, they settled on the Pine Ridge Reservation in South Dakota. Black Moon did not follow him. If anything, his hatred of the American military was even greater than Sitting Bull's, and he was determined to remain under the protection of the Canadians. The banks of the Moose Jaw Creek, just south of the town, became his tribe's favourite camping ground. Mary's sister, brothers, and mother lived there. Jim Dugan also lived there.

He had been one of the earliest pioneers in the Moose Jaw district, settling on a half-section of land – E1/2 of 2-16-26 W2, just west of where Dougald Carmichael had tried to homestead. At Christmas of 1882, Jim Dugan visited Tom Aspdin at Wood Mountain Post and made his interesting proposal.

Although Dugan had built a log house and a cabin, and had broken and ploughed five acres of land, he now wanted to sell his farm. His explanation seemed reasonable to Thomas Aspdin. "He informed me that his wife, who was a French half-breed, was very dissatisfied, as there were none of her folks around that part and that he wished to get to a place where some of his wife's people had settled." Aspdin knew the area well, and considered it one of the most beautiful places in all the

North-West. The land was prairie flat until it suddenly rolled southward. Ash, diamond willows, and chokecherries over-hung the Moose Jaw Creek, which curled like a blue sash through the half-section. This part would provide both water and shelter for his cattle. Even in the fiercest blizzards, livestock were able to survive in these woods; the remaining portion would make superb grain-growing land, he was sure. He decided to take up Dugan's offer.

Dugan was asking $500, which was about the amount Aspdin had been able to save from his $1.25-a-day salary and the sale of his property in Muskoka. He had some money left over, which he had sent to his brother in England to buy passage to Canada. "You'll be needed to help me on the farm," he wrote. He also hired a young man, Jim Philips, to live on the property until he could get there, because "People were cutting down the little wood that remained and selling it in Moose Jaw."

Aspdin's tour of duty in the Mounted Police was up on June 5, 1883, but he had accumulated a month-long furlough, so he was on his land by early May. When he arrived he was surprised to find a piece of paper tacked to the door of the cabin. It was a Dominion Lands Office notice, stating that the area had been recently surveyed and that the nine-by-six-mile area where Asp-din's half-section was located had been reserved for the federal government and the CPR.

At first Aspdin wasn't concerned. He told his brother, recently arrived from England, "Dugan was here before the area was even surveyed. I've bought his squatter's rights, so surely I've nothing to worry about." Thomas continued ploughing and fixing up the shack, since he planned to move Mary in by mid-June. She had already given birth to their first child, a girl they named Alice, born in August 1882.

In the last week of May, the Dominion Lands inspector was in the neighbourhood, and Aspdin decided to clear up the matter once and for all. However, what Inspector Pierce told him came as a profound shock. The government had not yet determined whether or not squatters had any rights at all to reserved land. "The CPR and the Canada North-West Land Co. [the federal government] mean to make a bundle selling this land; they're not going to let the little men like you get in the way." Moreover, since Aspdin was not even a squatter but had bought the land off Dugan, his claim was in even greater jeopardy.

"I advise you not to make any more improvements until the matter's settled," the inspector said. "And that might take several years." With no money and no immediate way to make a living, Aspdin signed on for another three years with the North-West Mounted police. Mary remained with her family at Moose Jaw.

After Sitting Bull returned to the United States, Fort Walsh had been closed down and the headquarters transferred to the new capital of the North-West Territories, Regina. On June 5, 1883, Aspdin was sent there as senior quartermaster.

Both the Queen City and the NWMP headquarters were extremely primitive – in the winter the portable barracks, merely makeshift log huts shipped from eastern Canada, were so drafty that the water froze in the washbasins overnight. As quartermaster, Aspdin had a problem keeping his records straight, because his ink was more often than not a solid block. The one advantage was that Regina was not far from Moose Jaw Creek. The North-West Mounted Police still had no official knowledge of Aspdin's Indian family; in all his considerable correspondence at the time with the force and with the Dominion Lands Office, nowhere was there a mention of Mary or Alice. He was forced to live a double life, and it made him miserable.

Aspdin's stint in Regina didn't last long. In January of 1884, the quartermaster and supply stores were amalgamated. By March, Staff-Sergeant Aspdin was passing through Moose Jaw to say his sorrowful goodbyes to Mary and the baby, on his way 470 miles due west to Fort Macleod, the first post he had been assigned as a young constable.

By this time, the poorly ventilated log cabins of the old fort had been torn down and replaced with well-lit and spacious buildings. The sergeants' quarters were particularly comfortable; there was even a recreation room, where *Punch*, the *Canadian Illustrated News*, and *Saturday Night* magazine could be found. Yet Aspdin found the sixty-odd constables stationed there totally demoralized. The month before, eleven men had run away from the fort, and desertion had become such a problem that the Police Act was amended, doubling the prison term for the offence from six months to a year. Aspdin was told that for seven months they had existed on nothing but bread. "The beef is so rotten that we have to eat out [at the several canteens that had sprung up around the fort] at our own expense so as not to starve to death." Uniforms were in such short supply that the men also had to buy their own clothing – a real hardship, given their low wages. As well, a severe shortage of personnel meant there was too much work. "It has been the custom of this post, when strangers arrive, for men to be detailed off to act as grooms and bootblacks for them, which is not the duty of constables," one police officer complained.

What disgusted Thomas Aspdin the most, however, was the rampant drunkenness. Most of the Fort Macleod men did little else but plot to get their hands on some booze. When two smugglers were caught and their fifty-gallon haul dumped into the ground near the fort, the police quickly gathered up the snow, thawed it in huge buckets, and made punch of it. "Before night fell there was hardly a sober man in the fort," one young recruit wrote in his diary. All-night poker games often led to all-week brawls.

Much of the demoralization stemmed from the federal government's penny-pinching attitude towards the force. As quartermaster, Aspdin found himself in the difficult position of having to deal with legitimate complaints without having the wherewithal to do anything about them. The atmosphere at Fort Macleod was so depressing that he was determined to leave the force as soon as he could.

In April 1884, he wrote a long letter to the land commissioner in Winnipeg, detailing his troubles over the purchase of the Moose Jaw Creek land.

If the government will allow me to make an entry for the land I think I can get out of the force in time to fulfil the [homestead] conditions.

It has been a great set back to me and you may feel assured Sir I would not have gone into the business had I not had

confidence that the Government would do justice and
which confidence I have not lost yet.

He received no reply, probably because the question of squatters' rights had not yet been resolved.

Aspdin desperately missed his wife, who was still living with
her family. William Lethbridge, who is now ninety-five, and
whose mother was a full-blooded Sioux, spent much of his
childhood in the Sioux encampments. On several occasions he
met the daughters of Thomas Aspdin and Mary Blackmoon.
He says the Indians moved continuously, hunting and picking
berries, from Regina to Batoche, Fort Qu'Appelle, and Wood
Mountain, but the long winters were spent on the banks of the
Moose Jaw Creek, about two miles east of town. For protection
against blizzards and cold the camp was set up in heavy bush,
mostly willows, with the lodges surrounded by horses and wagons in corral formation. In the winter, the bell tents were made
of double canvas (buffalo hides having almost disappeared), and
Lethbridge remembers them being quite snug inside. The men
hunted – small game such as ducks were sold to Moose Jaw
butchers – and took odd jobs, such as carting, to make money.
The women worked in town, as domestics and wet nurses for
the Moose Jaw upper crust. Everybody was adept at some craft,
and train passengers disembarking at the Moose Jaw station
were usually met by Indian men in long braids and multi-
coloured blankets selling buffalo horns, polished until they
shone jet black, beaded moccasins, and carved pipes. Mary
Blackmoon was skilled at intricate bead and porcupine-quill
embroidery; her grandchildren still possess wonderful examples
of her work.

There was some sympathy, albeit patronizing, for the Sioux
among the citizens of Moose Jaw. The *News* commented that, of
course, it wasn't pleasant to glimpse a dusky face flattened
against one's windowpane, or to stumble over an Indian on
one's doorstep. "But then, possibly it is not always pleasant to
the red man to have the pale faces haunting his ancient
hunting-grounds, and their screeching engines scaring away his
big and little game."

But most of the bourgeoisie considered Black Moon's people so primitive, so inferior, as to be hardly human.

As a public-relations gesture, a grand pow-wow was staged by the Sioux in downtown Moose Jaw in the summer of 1884. It was an attempt to give the whites a taste of Indian culture, and much work and preparation went into it. Dougald Carmichael and his family were among the spectators. The day after the gala event, the *News* printed the following comment: "It would be hard to conceive of anything more silly, sickening and pitiable."

Aspdin had thought about moving Mary and Alice away from this unpleasant bigotry to somewhere near Fort Macleod – on the sly of course, since his superiors in the Mounted Police must not find out – but he feared for their safety. The North-West Rebellion was about to break out.

During 1883-84 Sir John A. Macdonald had made, in Thomas Aspdin's opinion, a most "stupid, asinine" decision. As part of his government's economy measures, food supplies to already starving Indians were slashed, and cattle-stealing became rampant. The white ranching community began insisting that the North-West Mounted Police enforce the law more vigorously. It was not an easy task. In the neighbourhood of Fort Macleod were camped Blood, Blackfoot, and Peigans, who were considered by the Mounties as the best-armed, best-mounted, and most warlike of all the Plains Indians. "Don't they [the cattle ranchers] realize that in a few days the Blackfoot Confederacy could muster over a thousand warriors?" the Mounties grumbled among themselves. "And what are sixty constables supposed to do against such a force?" That Louis Riel had arrived in Batoche that June and was firing up discontent was an ominous turn of events as well.

Thomas Aspdin was always amazed at how quickly news ricocheted from one Indian tribe to another. The Métis' defeat of Superintendent Leif Crozier (a man whom Aspdin had always disliked for his inflexible attitude towards the Indians) at Duck Lake in March of 1885 reached the Blackfoot long before the Mounted Police courier arrived. While the sound of war drums rumbled in the air, the Mounties dug out rifle pits around the fort, and the two nine-pounder guns were readied.

The Macleod contingent was now below forty men, and had no telegraphic equipment; the only communication to the outside world was a once-weekly postal service – if the courier could get through.

Fortunately Crowfoot, the chief of the Blackfoot Confederacy, still felt as he did in 1877 when he had signed Treaty Number Seven. He said then, "The Mounted Police have protected the Indian as the feathers of the bird protect it from the frosts of winter." By 1885, his confidence in the Mounties had diminished, but not completely. The patience of his young warriors was stretched to the breaking point, however. They were just beginning to realize what a catastrophe the reserve system was.

His obituary, written years later, stated that Thomas Aspdin had seen active service during the North-West Rebellion, "being one of those wounded in the fight of Duck Lake." In a letter written in 1932, Mary Aspdin would maintain that he was wounded in the rebellion, and that she had a medal to prove it. In reality, his service was much more mundane. He remained at Fort Macleod as quartermaster, carefully laying in as many supplies as he could get his hands on, knowing that, in the event that the Blackfoot and their allies declared war, the surrounding white population would assemble in the fort for protection. Aspdin had always had a healthy respect for the Blackfoot fighting ability, and he realized such a siege could last a long time.

Yet he still found time to continue his own personal battle with the Dominion Lands Office.

He had heard that the question of squatters' rights had been settled, mostly in their favour, and he was determined to promote his own case. On January 10, 1885, he again wrote to the land commissioner. "I can only say say that if I lose this place it will take nearly everything I have and I shall have to start afresh. I am ready to go along and fulfil all conditions of the Department as I intend to leave the Police force as soon as I hear I can make an entry."

When by June nothing had been resolved, Aspdin wrote to the Minister of the Interior. "I am informed that other parties who had removed in consequence of such lands being declared reserved under similar circumstances to my own case have been notified that their lands were open to entry." His letter was passed on to Commissioner of Dominion Lands, H. H. Smith, in Winnipeg, who in August of 1885, finally did something about Aspdin's case.

In a letter written to the land agent in Regina, the secretary of the the Winnipeg land office was his usual arrogant, insensitive self. "The Commissioner does not regard Aspdin's claim as a strong one at all; in fact he is of the opinion that it might very well be ignored but in view of the alleged expense incurred by Aspdin in the matter he is willing to allow him the privilege of entry." There was one important stipulation, however. He would have to be on the land by the first day of October, 1886.

Aspdin didn't receive the letter informing him of this decision until mid-August, and he knew he could never disentangle himself from the force in time. He wrote back, offering to buy the land at $2.50 an acre; he believed he could manage the $110 down, the remaining amount payable over three years. This was turned down flatly. "The minister believes he does not possess the authority to sell the land to you – the homestead duties necessary to entitle you purchase not yet having been performed." But he was given an extension until April 15 of the following year.

Aspdin pleaded with the force to allow him an early discharge – it was a matter of only three months, since his term was up on June 5, 1886. But although he had put in twelve years of service, which had been considered outstanding by everyone, his superiors would not "even entertain the idea."

"It was a very strict philosophy then," says RCMP historian and museum curator Bill Mackay, "You signed on the dotted line, now you live up to the contract." Why he didn't buy his way out of the force, which he could have done for $50, remains a mystery. For some reason the choice seems not to have been presented to Tom Aspdin.

He couldn't help but feel bitter. He would later confide to Chief Dan Kennedy that he believed it was his long association with Indians, and his sympathy for them, which put him out of joint with the force. He never escaped from Major Walsh's shadow.

~ IV ~

On April 15, 1886, Staff-Sergeant Thomas Aspdin, sitting far away in his barracks at Fort Macleod, wrote his brother Alfred in Vancouver, "All I had managed to save is gone and there's not a thing I can do about it." Reluctantly, he decided to re-engage in the force, but only for one year.

Aspdin finally found a home for Mary and Alice near Fort Macleod, but shortly after they arrived, he was transferred again, this time further north to Battleford. The only complaint he ever voiced about the NWMP involved the "the terrible expense and difficulty of moving from one post to another in ante railroad days."

He pushed for further promotion, asking a prominent Toronto Conservative, James Beaty, to write a recommendation for him. "He is highly spoken of by his superiors. He is a meritorious officer and so far as I have been able to learn deserves consideration." But Aspdin knew that a promotion to sergeant-major might be a long time in coming; he would have to wait until someone retired. Sick to death of leading a double life – Mary was pregnant again; a second daughter, Anne, would be born in November 1887 – he finally decided, when his term was up, to end his career in the North-West Mounted Police.

There was no pension, no severance pay, for a man who, during his fourteen years of "loyal and efficient duty," did not have one offence listed on his defaulter sheet; not once did he miss the curfew, neglect to clean his saddle properly, give lip to his superiors. "I've never seen a service record that's been devoid of all defaulters before," comments Bill Mackay. "Normally everybody got nicked for something. He must have been what the force likes to describe as 'a man men are made of.'" And yet the only cash that Aspdin was able to walk away with after all those years of hard service was $55.50 in lieu of holiday pay.

He felt he was owed much more. He told the Discharge Board

that over the years he had been promised pay raises by his superiors, but these had never materialized, and now he wanted these commitments made good. According to his calculations he was owed $456.50 in back pay, enough to purchase a decent quarter-section of land. He argued that while he had been the senior quartermaster, he was being paid only $1 a day, while others junior to himself were getting the maximum rate of $1.50. Aspdin pointed out that while he had worked at Wood Mountain in 1883, Regina in 1884, and Fort Macleod in 1886, he had handled thousands of dollars of public money, without a "single discrepancy." "I have invariably been highly praised for the efficient performance of all duties entrusted to me . . . [so that] I cannot see why such a discriminatory and one-sided usage should have been meted out to me," he wrote.

His superiors, once again, would "not entertain" his claim. Two years and many letters later he was offered $68.75, which, out of frustration, he accepted.

Lindstrom Tern, who worked in the headquarter's store in Regina, would write at the time of Aspdin's death, "Tommy's goodness of heart and self-sacrifices were really appreciated by the boys. I can't tell you how many stories I heard about his good deeds around the camp fires of various Northwest Mounted police posts. I only wish the Force had dealt with him more equitably." Not only did he not receive his back pay, but the quarter-section of good farmland he'd been promised upon first enlisting was not forthcoming. This had been a perk offered to recruits before 1879; many had settled in the West through these land warrants. But by the time Aspdin finally left the force, this advantage was no longer available.

His brother, Alfred, had settled in British Columbia and was the chief steward on the Canadian Pacific Steamship Company's Empress line between Vancouver and Hong Kong. (This was not the brother whom Thomas had sent for to work on his farm; Charles E. Aspdin later joined the North-West Mounted Police, and achieved the rank of sergeant.) Alfred suggested that Thomas might think of moving to Victoria, with its "Fine weather and flowers instead of blizzards and grass."

By December 1887, Aspdin was on his way west. Mary and

the two girls were not with him, but it is not known if it was a trial separation or whether he was simply investigating the situation before he sent for them. Perhaps he realized Mary wouldn't be happy away from her family, or perhaps he discovered that his love for the wide-open prairies was stronger than he thought, for six months later he had returned to Moose Jaw.

Over the next few years Aspdin worked at a variety of jobs: he was a bookkeeper for the general store of Felix Plante, the first person Dougald Carmichael had talked to when he arrived in Moose Jaw in 1882 determined to find the "the best damn homestead" available; he ran a transport service for the post office between various rural outposts; he looked after cattle for several big ranchers. As well, he began to build a herd of his own, grazing them on leased pasture, and by 1892 he owned between fifty and sixty head. His cattle were thought to be of such fine quality that he was eventually elected president of the newly founded Moose Jaw Livestock Association.

As early as 1890 he became an agent for the Indian Affairs branch of the federal government, overseeing the Moose Jaw Sioux. They were his wife's people and he remained very protective and sympathetic towards them. He would try and impose government edicts, like the banning of the Sun Dance, as gently as he could. His attitude was resented by some Moose Jaw citizens, the boosters and speculators, who were determined to see the town grow into "the St. Paul of the Canadian West." Scabby, rag-tag Indians didn't fit into this vision.

In January of 1891, a rather startling story appeared in the Winnipeg *Free Press*. Thomas Aspdin, it said, charged that certain individuals had attempted to alarm the white population of Moose Jaw by running around town "howling and screeching as Indians." According to Aspdin, the purpose of these scare tactics was to goad the government into financing the installation of some twenty-five or thirty Mounted Police in Moose Jaw, which would prove an economic boom to the city. These same people had also frightened the Sioux by telling them that the police were about to disarm and murder them, as the Americans had done.

Several weeks later the *Moose Jaw Times* republished the article, but added a mocking footnote: "This appeared in the Winnipeg *Free Press* on the 24th. It is bosh. There has never been an Indian scare. The whole article is rubbish."

Aspdin was furious about this denial and marched into the *Times*'s office armed with a stack of documents. A few days later, the editors admitted they were mistaken.

Aspdin may have won this small battle, but it hardly endeared him to Moose Jaw society. In a few years, his defence of the Sioux was to earn him some powerful enemies.

His attitude towards the Indians was reflected in the way he treated his wife. Remembers his granddaughter Eleanor Thompson: "Thomas Aspdin was never above his wife. When he took her to meet somebody, he always introduced her, 'This is my wife, Mary.' He never tried to hide the fact that she was Indian. In fact, he was proud of it."

In 1891, Mary Blackmoon was thirty years old, and still a beauty. "She dressed in mixed Indian and white fashion," recalls her granddaughter. She wore full skirts with plenty of crinolines underneath, gathered into a set-in belt, which showed off her figure, mutton-sleeved blouses, and high collars. But over the top of this very western apparel she sported colourful shawls and scarves and beautifully crafted bead bags and jewellery. "From what I've heard, my grandfather was the worldly sophisticated one; my grandmother was very feminine, very motherly."

Hers was definitely an Indian household; she liked to do bead- and quill-work, she tanned hides, she dried berries and meat, but she tried to accommodate her husband. She learned to can vegetables that she grew in the garden, and once, when Tom's brother Alfred came to visit, he showed her how to make dumplings to go with her venison stew. Tom Aspdin must have enjoyed her cooking, because he put on a lot of weight as soon as he left the force.

During this period the Aspdin family lived in a large white house, probably rented, on Moose Jaw Creek. In 1890, the Aspdins' third child, another girl, Kate, was born. The happiness surrounding her birth was diminished when only a few weeks later, news reached them that Sitting Bull had been gunned down in a shoot-out with police at his home at Stand-ing Rock Reserve, South Dakota. Aspdin was terribly sorry to hear of the old chief's death, but Mary was devastated. Her father, Black Moon, had also died by this time; while out hunt-ing he had accidentally shot himself with a gun. This was particularly ironic, because he had so disdained the white man's instrument of evil. Mary felt that her links with the past were being severed one by one. "I know she was grateful that her husband was such a good man. That helped her a lot," says her grandson Maurice Williams. "But she also remained tied to her culture."

Aspdin, meanwhile, was determined to get his hands on some land. He wanted a ranch of his own, and he wanted security for his family in case anything happened to him. In July of 1892, he purchased the northeast 1/4 of 19-16-26 W2 for $850. Situated just on the outskirts of Moose Jaw, it was as stunningly beautiful as the land he had bought in 1886. There was a flat upper portion to grow wheat and hay, and then the land suddenly gave way to steep slopes that ran down to the Moose Jaw Creek meandering below. The water was essential for his cattle and his eighty horses. He had always loved horses, and he now planned to become a dealer, buying and selling thoroughbreds. Immedi-ately, he began making extensive improvements to the run-down buildings, and by winter he had fenced almost the entire farm. It seemed a perfect set-up, but there was a shadow lurking which grew darker each year. Aspdin had taken out a hefty mortgage at a high interest rate from the Moose Jaw bank of Hitchcock & McCulloch. Making the payments would become a desperate struggle.

That March, Mary gave birth to another girl. She was a sickly baby, requiring much attention. One day in April, Mary was standing by the window, rocking the fretting infant, when she saw a young Indian lad drive by in a cart and pony. He was heading towards the ford, the shallow spot in the creek that was often used for crossings. The river was particularly high, and Mary became distressed when she didn't see him climb up the opposite embankment. Since she couldn't speak English well enough to make herself understood by the neighbours, and since she didn't dare leave the young children, she could do nothing but wait for her husband's arrival two hours later.

Thomas Aspdin immediately rode to town to get help. A search party was organized, armed with poles and grips to pry loose the ice jams. While the rescuers were hard at it, the pony and cart suddenly popped up out of a hole in the ice. For a brief moment, these ghostly apparitions were frozen in space, but just as suddenly they disappeared forever beneath the surface. The young man's body wasn't found until a week later, and during the whole time, almost the entire Sioux population of Moose Jaw kept walking up and down the river bank, wailing in distress. It was a terrible sound, which disturbed the Aspdin household. Mary told her husband that this was a sign of evil times to come.

Shortly after this tragedy, against his wife's wishes, Aspdin announced he was sending their two oldest daughters away to the Regina Industrial School, a boarding establishment for Indian children on the outskirts of the capital city, which had opened two years before under the auspices of the Presbyterian Church. There were several reasons for his decision: he was a strong believer in a good education, even for girls – at this school, half a day was spent on academics, half a day on the art of housekeeping – and he was impressed with what the institution had accomplished in just two years. Most important, however, he was determined that his children learn English. The language of the home was Sioux, primarily because Mary insisted on it. According to her grandson Maurice Williams, "She was very cagey and in her Indian way she knew a lot but didn't say much. She had the attitude, 'If you want to speak to me, you speak my language.'" Aspdin accepted this, but he was determined the girls would become totally fluent in English.

They had been brought up Indian-style, protected and loved, and they suffered terribly at the school. "My mother was quite bitter about it," says Eleanor Thompson. "When they first went there, they were lonesome, so they sat together and talked Indian. The teachers found them and punished them with the strap." Alice, the oldest girl, had a particularly hard time. With her auburn hair and fair skin, she didn't look like an Indian, and her classmates were unrelenting in their teasing. Slowly the Aspdin girls were "civilized," turned into "proper Christian ladies." A photo taken at the time of Alice's graduation shows her in a long skirt and a jacket made of heavy Irish tweed; she could have arrived from London that day. Yet despite their unhappy experience at school, the Aspdin girls remained devoted to their father.

"They would have done anything he wanted them to," Maurice Williams says. "He was very revered, very appreciated. My mother [Kate] spoke of him until she died; it was Father this and Father that. She never spoke of her mother too much."

It was Aspdin who saw that they were safely ensconced in their dormitories that June of 1893 when they first began school. He then left on a long trip with an old friend, James Bell, herding cattle "to points along the CPR in Manitoba," as the *Moose Jaw Times* reported. While he was away, the new baby grew seriously ill, and she died that August. She was only five months old. The people of Moose Jaw must have rallied to Mary's side, because when Aspdin returned in September, he published a note of thanks in the paper to those "who administered so kindly to my family in time of affliction when it was impossible for me to reach them." Mary Blackmoon never stopped grieving for that baby. Many years later, when she was living in South Dakota, she sent money she had carefully saved to Moose Jaw so that a tombstone could be placed on the child's grave.

But the baby girl's death wasn't the only disaster confronting the family that year. It had become all too clear that Aspdin had made a terrible error in buying the Moose Jaw Creek land. Ironically, it was a situation not unlike the one he had endured ten years before.

When the prairie was originally opened to homesteading, sections 11 and 26 in each township were set aside as school lands. It didn't mean that schools would be built there, but rather that, when the land became valuable, these sections would be sold as an endowment for education. Aspdin's property, NE1/4 of 29-16-26 W2, was originally designated as school land, but since an early pioneer, E. E. K. Davies, had squatted on the land before it had been surveyed, he had been allowed title to it.

Aspdin bought it from Davies for $850. Since he could both farm and raise cattle there, he had considered the place ideal. He quickly realized it was anything but. When his plough cut into virgin soil, he was shocked to discover not rich black earth but sandy gravel. Although these were not drought years, his grain crop "has been burnt out and came to nothing," as he wrote in a letter to H. H. Smith, the land commissioner.

Aspdin had a solution, however. If he could get his hands on the quarter-section directly adjoining his land on the west, he would have about a hundred acres of arable land, enough, he thought, to make his labour worth while. He applied for a homestead entry on NW1/4 of 29-16-26 W2.

But the Aspdin land follies continued. Davies had once entered for this piece of land as a pre-emption, but had not been able to come up with enough money to pay for it. After this, it was claimed by a Church of England minister, who, ironically, was planning to build an Indian industrial school. The project collapsed – "the only Indians living in the vicinity consist of a few straggling Sioux who are not under Treaty with the Government and whom we are endeavoring to induce to return to the United States, which is their country," a government official wrote – and the quarter-section reverted back to school lands. Ever the optimist, Aspdin set out to convince the land commissioner to again reverse his decision and allow him entry for a homestead. He was turned down flat.

Just as Dougald Carmichael had seven years before, Aspdin turned to those friends influential in politics: Carmichael's hero, Nicholas Floyd Davin, the publisher of the *Regina Leader*; James H. Ross, one of the earliest settlers in Moose Jaw, who in 1883 had been elected to the North-West Assembly and was, in 1892, speaker of that body; and D. W. Davis, Member of Parliament for Macleod. All were appealed to for help. "It is simply a matter of getting this land or having to move as I cannot make a living off what arable land there is on my 1/4 section," Aspdin pleaded. It's a measure of how well thought of he was that all of them applied as much political pressure as they could muster.

Davis wrote the Minister of the Interior, "Dear [Thomas Mayne] Daly: I must say that his [Aspdin's] demands seem very reasonable and hope you will try and stretch a point to give it to him as he is a first class man."

In April Aspdin was finally informed that, although he would not be allowed to homestead the land, he would be allowed to purchase it for $3 an acre. He was given sixty days to pay. Aspdin not only didn't have the $480 but he couldn't even manage the first instalment of $120 (the remainder to be paid over three years). He wasn't the only one in dire straits; the entire North-West had been hit by a severe depression. The department did grant Aspdin first a six-month extension and then another full year, but he never could raise the money. The interest on the mortgage that he had taken out with the Hitchcock & McCulloch bank was a whopping 18 per cent, and it was all he could do to manage the payments.

Because of these financial pressures, he worried all the time about his family. How would they exist if something were to happen to him? In 1894, many of Black Moon's people decided to take advantage of land allotments that were being handed out to the Sioux on the Cheyenne River Reservation in the United States. At Aspdin's suggestion, Mary, their three daughters, her mother, brother, and nephew all travelled to South Dakota that spring. Most of the family settled permanently at Cherry Creek Village, although Mary and the children went back to Moose Jaw as soon as their land claims were secure.

By the time they returned, Tom Aspdin had good news. He had been handed a political plum that would bring into the household much-needed dollars.

Booze had always been a problem in the West. The North-West Territories Act of 1875 had established a permit system to control liquor importation; any decision about who among the white population could obtain booze was left entirely to the discretion of the lieutenant-governor. The system didn't work very well. As the prohibitionists pointed out, liquor was run into the country under the most imaginative disguises: in barrels of sugar and salt, in bottles that usually contained fruit preserves, jams, and pickles, and in reconstructed eggs. When

Edgar Dewdney, a man who admittedly liked a strong drink now and then, was named lieutenant-governor in 1881, he loosened up the system. An application for a gallon of whisky for "medicinal use" almost always got approval. His successor, Joseph Royal, issued more permits and allowed 4-per-cent beer to be sold in bars. The Mounties were supposed to police this system full of loopholes, and they found it a nightmare.

Finally, in 1892, against the wishes of the prohibitionists, drunkenness in the North-West Territories was placed on the same footing as in the rest of Canada; permits were replaced by liquor licences for hotels and wholesale outlets. Civilians were appointed by a board of commissioners to supervise these licences. At a time when money was tight, it was considered a fat political appointment.

Aspdin, perhaps because of his former service in the Mounted Police, perhaps because he had powerful political allies, was appointed liquor inspector for the Moose Jaw area. He made about $240 a year, not a magnificent sum, but it was only a part-time job, and this was certainly more cash than most other farmers could muster at the time.

Aspdin quickly realized that the system was failing miserably, especially for those it was designed to protect – the Indians. Although the selling of alcohol to natives was still prohibited, Métis could legally buy booze, and, with the help of white bootleggers, they supplied their Indian friends with as much as they wanted.

The effects were immediately seen in the Moose Jaw Sioux community. Aspdin reported, "Whilst fairly well behaved, the life around town is beginning to show, and some of them have cultivated a taste for liquor. I had one man convicted and fined for supplying liquor and have taken steps to check it as much as possible." When three harvesters from Ontario sold Old Bogue, a notorious drunk who lived in the Sioux encampment, a couple of bottles of whisky, they were arrested and put in jail. One of them pleaded guilty and was knicked $50, a lot of money in those days; Old Bogue was also fined, $25 and costs, which he paid.

But among the drunkards of Moose Jaw, the natives were a

small minority; the real rowdies were found in the white community. "It is quite a common occurrence to see men battered, bruised, and bleeding in our streets, while the noise of their drunken revel is heard until long past the hour of midnight," complained the *Moose Jaw Times* before Aspdin was appointed inspector. "I doubt you can find a town or village in the whole of Assiniboia where the Liquor Licence Ordnance is being so frequently and grossly violated. There seems to be no limit to the number of offences these licenced rum-sellers can commit and not have a single effort made to have the law enforced."

Aspdin tried as best he could to clean the town up, but in his diligence he soon raised the hackles of some leading citizens. On April 2, 1897, Councillor William Hannah, chairman of the Board of Works, moved that Aspdin be fired from his job. "I consider him [Aspdin] incompetent and I'm sure a more suitable man could be employed."

Hannah's displeasure stemmed from an incident that had occurred a month and half before. Aspdin had walked unannounced, as was his wont, into the Brunswick Hotel in the middle of a drunken celebration. "Drinks on the house!" one inebriated gentleman yelled at him. Aspdin ignored their debauch until he spotted Nelson Brown with a glass in his hand. Aspdin knew Brown was under eighteen, and he promptly charged the hotel proprietor, J. H. Kern, with selling alcohol to a minor.

Kern was one of Moose Jaw's leading citizens, and he was able to convince the police magistrate that what the youngster had being drinking was "port wine, a non-intoxicating liquor." The charge was dropped, but Kern was furious at this public humiliation. He and Councillor Hannah were in the same lodge of the Loyal Order of the Orange; Hannah demanded Aspdin's resignation.

Although City Council did not act on Hannah's motion, Aspdin began looking about for other work. He felt the confrontation with Kern was a minor thing, but he was only too aware that some of Moose Jaw's citizens disapproved of him, not because of his zealousness as a liquor inspector but because they considered him a "Squaw Man," an "Indian-lover." For one thing, they had never forgotten what came to be known as the Vigar Incident.

Two years before, a group of Sioux had come galloping into Aspdin's farmyard, yelling that a white man was trying to kill them. Aspdin rounded up two friends, and the trio rode out to a hog farm managed by Charlie Vigar. When Vigar starting screaming insults at them, they tied him up and went for the North-West Mounted Police. Vigar was charged with shooting with the intent to kill. He managed to raise the $800 bail, but he was so furious he counter-charged Aspdin and his two friends with assault.

In court, the hog farmer claimed that the Indians were prowling about, and he simply wanted to scare them off his property. The Sioux countered that he had screamed at them, "The only good Indian is a dead Indian," and then had fired directly at their heads.

After three days of complicated testimony, a deal was finally worked out: Vigar would be acquitted of the attempt to murder, but would plead guilty to the lesser charge of common assault. He was fined $15. Charges against Aspdin were dropped.

Many Moose Jaw citizens sided with Charlie Vigar. They considered the Sioux Indians unsightly nuisances. "We are sick to death of having Indians walk into our houses uninvited, of having them beg for food, of having our children run wild with them," wrote J. D. Morris to the *Moose Jaw Times*. Tom Aspdin had tried to mediate between the two races. At the Moose Jaw Agricultural Fair, for example, he offered a special prize of $2 for the best dog- or wolf-skin mat, home-dressed. This, he thought, would encourage the Indians to participate in the fair, and the whites might also appreciate their culture. What he got for his pains was to be repeatedly snubbed on Main Street.

But there were other reasons that Aspdin finally concluded that his family would be better off elsewhere. Despite his liquor-inspector's wage, he was in serious financial trouble. There was a light crop in 1895, and cattle prices fell through the floor. Aspdin could not make his mortgage payments, and the Hitchcock & McCulloch bank foreclosed, confiscating all of Aspdin's livestock, his cattle and horses, as well as his land.

While Mary Blackmoon was making sure the household goods were firmly secured in the wagon, she didn't shed a tear. She merely looked at Arthur Hitchcock, the banker who was overseeing the foreclosure, straight in the eye and then spat at his feet.

Fortunately for Thomas Aspdin, he still had many important Liberal friends. In July 1897, the Department of Indian Affairs offered him a job as farm instructor on the Assiniboine Carry-the-Kettle Reserve at a salary of $720 a year with a house and garden. He jumped at the opportunity.

At the height of their power, the Assiniboine nation dominated a huge territory in the West, including much of what is now south Saskatchewan, through northern Montana and North Dakota, from the Saskatchewan and Assiniboine river valleys, southward to the area north of the Milk and Missouri rivers. Theirs was typical of the Plains culture centring around the mighty buffalo, "a larder and clothier on the hoof" as historian J. R. Miller puts it.

The Assiniboine were particularly hospitable to the white man, and when the Hudson's Bay Company set up shop, they worked as middlemen between the traders and remote Plains Indians. They hauled furs and pemmican (they were noted for a particularly delicious variety, which mixed Saskatoon berries with the buffalo meat) to Hudson Bay depots, and they distributed everything from tea to muskets to Indians. This contact with the whites cost them dearly, of course. Two smallpox epidemics in 1780-81 and 1837-38 devastated the nation. By 1896 their once-thriving community of 18,000 had been reduced to less than 2,500.

Carry-the-Kettle was one of the Assiniboine chiefs who had signed Treaty Number Four with the Canadian government in 1874. But his band of some two hundred and twenty-five did not settle on a reserve right away, preferring instead to hunt buffalo until they had completely disappeared. During the famine of 1879, they were among the Indians who were forced to beg for their rations at Fort Walsh. Corporal Thomas Aspdin had been in charge of distributing these supplies during this period, and thought the Assiniboine an amiable, non-threatening bunch. He also remembered an unusual custom: their use of dogs as beasts of burden.

Finally in 1883, realizing that their way of life was doomed, they settled on a reserve at Sintaluta, 73.2 square miles, between Indian Head on the west and the CPR's Wolseley Station on the east. Thereafter, they were subjected to paternalistic, rigid reserve management, which set out first to denigrate their culture and then to transform them into a species of Lesser Prairie Farmer. The Indian agent, and a few ranks down, the farm instructor, were the main instruments used in this alchemy.

For much of the time before Aspdin arrived in 1897, the reserve had been dominated by W. S. Grant, a short and beefy man with a thick white beard. As the Indian agent, he had dictatorial power over the lives of "his charges"; they were not even allowed to leave the reserve without a pass signed by him. Since there were no fish or game on the reserve, Grant's job was to teach the Assiniboine to be self-sufficient as farmers. This was not an easy task; it was not flat prairie but wooded, rocky land, which had to be cleared to farm. There were also cultural problems: farming was considered woman's work; a hunter did not concern himself with such domestic chores. Even after the government had spent twenty years trying to interest the Indians in farming, only 425 of the 46,320 acres on the reserve had been ploughed.

Rather than the back-breaking toil of clearing a farm that often didn't produce much, the Indians preferred to eke out a living selling wood and hay, tanning hides, freighting, and working for other farmers. They lived in tents in summer and log buildings, rundown and ramshackle, the rest of the time. Tuberculosis was rampant. Grant reported there were thirty children on the reserve, but most were too sickly to go to school. In 1896, the 214 natives earned $1,140, while the Indian agent alone made $1,200.

When Thomas Aspdin arrived, he found the Assiniboine in an ugly frame of mind, "very much disinclined to do any work at all." Aspdin blamed their sullenness on "outside influences." It's not difficult, however, to read between the lines: the Assiniboine were rebelling against the patronizing, insensitive attitude of Grant and his immediate successor, Sam Swinford. In Grant's yearly reports, the Indians were continually "making rapid progress toward civilization." This included having Christianity rammed down their throats; being forced to send their children to a school they disapproved of; and renouncing important symbols of their own culture. "I advised them to give up their annual Sun Dance as it always comes at a time when new land should be broken," Grant reported.

Aspdin realized at once that he had a problem. As he described in a report to the agency, he found the Indians suspicious, domineering, and perverse: for example, they had pulled down all the fences and sold them for firewood. "I naturally found the situation awkward and the duties onerous," he wrote.

Conditions improved under Aspdin. As Alex McGibbon, the Inspector of Indian Agencies and Reserves, reported, "Mr. Aspdin, after a good deal of patience and perseverance, got things once more into working order and prospects were bright for better showing in the future."

Mary Blackmoon had difficulty adjusting to life on Carry-the-Kettle Reserve. The Sioux and Assiniboine were traditional enemies, and she was looked upon with suspicion. Shortly after the Aspdins arrived, she became seriously ill with congestion of the lungs, which the doctors were afraid would develop into tuberculosis.

Still, there were advantages to living there. The Aspdins were provided with a splendid, three-storey house, with huge windows and a wide veranda. There was a garden, which the three girls tended when they were home on holidays, as well as chickens and cows. All the Aspdins were expert horsepeople, and the youngest, Katie, was particularly daring.

But the hard work was getting to Thomas Aspdin, and he didn't feel secure. In February 1900, he wrote Frederick White, comptroller for the North-West Mounted Police, inquiring if there was a possibility of rejoining the force as a staff-sergeant.

I have been in charge of this agency for 2 1/2 years and am
now getting $60 per month and some rations with a pros-
pect of a little increase *but no supernumeration or pension. . . .*
I may say I am well treated by the Indian Department but
there being no pension and the Reserve not being a nice
place for children to grow up in is my reason for thinking of
a change if I could perceive enough inducement.

Nothing came of the request, and in a few months Aspdin
was promoted from farm instructor to full-fledged Indian agent,
with a corresponding $146 a year increase in pay. Still, the lack
of security for his family preyed on his mind, and it was probably this that made him commit the one truly immoral act of his
life.

Aspdin had always assumed that, because he hadn't been able
to raise the money to buy the quarter-section of land on the
Moose Jaw Creek, he had forfeited all claim to it. He was
surprised then, when in the fall of 1900, a letter arrived from the
Dominion Lands Office informing him that NW1/4 of 29-16-26
W2 was no longer part of the school endowment lands and that
he could buy it for $3 an acre.

Aspdin had no intention of farming this nightmare of
embankment and creek. But Moose Jaw's land boom was just
beginning, and he could see the potential for making some
quick money. He thought of raising a mortgage to buy the
property, until John Hawke Grayson, a Moose Jaw land-
speculator, presented him with a much more lucrative scheme.

The Graysons were early pioneers in Moose Jaw and, as the
upper crust hardened in the frontier town, they emerged as the
élite. Two brothers worked in tandem: William was the establishment lawyer and figurehead, who was charged with aggran-
dizing the Grayson name; John Hawke was a real-estate broker,
whose task was to make the family fortune. Both were prominent Liberals and had known Aspdin for years through this
connection. Although the Aspdin family was living on Carry-
the-Kettle Reserve near Sintaluta, Thomas was still the Indian
agent responsible for the remaining Sioux, living near Moose

Jaw, so he visited that town regularly, and often ran into the Graysons.

In July 1901, John Hawke Grayson told Thomas Aspdin that he would be foolish to pay the government the full $480 for the Moose Jaw Creek quarter-section. "It's hardly worth much more than that," he said. He would arrange a deal. Métis land scrip could be obtained at a cheap price; Aspdin would use this scrip certificate to obtain the land from the government and then he would immediately sell it to Grayson at a profit.

Since Métis were acknowledged as part-Indian by the Canadian government, they were entitled to free Crown land. In order to extinguish half-breed land claims, the Dominion Government had issued what was known as land scrip. The half-breed would take the scrip certificate, which looked like an enormous dollar bill, to the nearest land office and choose the specified amount of available Crown land. On paper, the scheme sounded like a workable idea; in reality it resulted in widespread swindling by unscrupulous, white land-speculators, like John Hawke Grayson.

The Métis whom Grayson chose to fleece in this case was a fifty-year-old trapper by the name of Abraham Beauchamp, from Willow Bunch in southern Saskatchewan. Since Willow Bunch was about thirty-one miles from Wood Mountain, Aspdin probably met the Beauchamp family when he had been posted there with the North-West Mounted Police. Certainly he would know that Beauchamp was poverty-stricken, with a large brood to feed – a man who, in his desperation and defeat, could easily be cheated.

That year Beauchamp had been allotted 240 acres of land scrip from the Department of the Interior. Grayson arranged for Aspdin to buy the scrip from Beauchamp for $250. He then plotted with the Department of the Interior to allow Aspdin to use the scrip to obtain the Moose Jaw Creek land. This was a quarter-section, 160 acres, which left Aspdin 80 acres of land scrip left over. Grayson quickly found him some prime land – none other than Colin Carmichael's pre-emption, one half of the SE1/4 of 14-26-25, which had finally been released for home-steading.

In the late summer of 1901, Thomas Aspdin visited his newly acquired land south of Moose Jaw near the the village of Pasqua. He had some difficulty finding it, until some neighbourhood farmers pointed him in the right direction. It was early evening by the time he dismounted. Immediately he dug out from under the matted growth a handful of dark brown earth. Rubbing it between his hands, he realized at once how fecund, how rich, it was. He sat down in the tangled grass and stared at the shimmering pink-purple sky, stretched above him like the fine Chinese silk his brother had brought back for him from the Orient, and he knew this was the prairie farm he had been looking for for years. He also knew he had to make good on his deal with Grayson.

To buy the Moose Jaw Creek land from the government would have cost him $480. What he had obtained for $250 of Beauchamp's land scrip therefore was worth, at the very least, $750. But as pre-arranged, immediately upon obtaining clear title, Aspdin sold both pieces of land to John Hawke Grayson for $360, making a small profit of $110; in three years' time, Grayson would sell it for five times that amount.

Shortly after the complicated deal was completed, Thomas Aspdin became ill. Alice, his eldest daughter, who had been training as a nurse in a Regina hospital, rushed to Sintaluta to help care for him. One night he told her, "After I'm gone you make sure your mother goes back to the States to be with her own people." Not long afterwards he was diagnosed as having cirrhosis of the liver, a rather cruel blow for a man who didn't drink and had been a liquor inspector.

In the fall of 1905, his brother Alfred arranged for him to travel to Victoria. "The doctors here are better qualified and the treatment more sophisticated," he wrote. On February 9, 1906, shortly after a bungled operation at the Provincial Royal Jubilee Hospital, Thomas Aspdin died. He was fifty-one years old.

As the casket was carried along in the bitter cold, the road from the Carry-the-Kettle Reserve to the Sintaluta graveyard, a distance of three miles, was packed with mourners. Every Indian on the reserve and the entire population of Sintaluta and its surrounds were there to pay their respects to a man they had so admired. The lieutenant-governor of the North-West Territories, Amédée Forget, was in attendance, as was ex-premier Frederick Haultain and Senator James H. Ross. There were many lofty eulogies from many important people. But it was the Assiniboine Chief Dan Kennedy who made Mary Blackmoon weep: "Thomas Aspdin was an honest, kind man who treated the Indian as an equal of the white."

Mary Blackmoon lived for another thirty-nine years, and never once took her precious gold wedding band from her finger.*

---

*Mary Blackmoon lived near Sintaluta until her daughters had completed their education. In 1913, the family moved to the Cheyenne Indian Reservation in South Dakota, where they had been allotted land. Pooling their resources, they built a house and went into the cattle business. Alice and Katie married and had children; Annie, the most beautiful of the daughters, lost her fiancé, a full-blooded Sioux, in War World I. She never married, preferring instead to take care of her mother.

Grayson

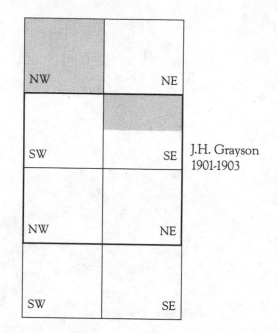

14-16-25 W2

J.H. Grayson
1901-1903

NW

NE

SW

SE

J.H. Grayson
1901-1903

NW

NE

SW

SE

11-16-25 W2

The family had immigrated from Britain to eastern Canada, where they lived comfortably, but they were certainly not wealthy or influential. The father knew that if he sent his well-educated and ambitious sons to the newly opened West, they would likely prosper. They did become rich and powerful, but only through years of exploiting the poor and the humiliated.

~ I ~

John Hawke Grayson glimpsed no romance in the vast prairie landscape. A thoroughly practical man is how he viewed himself. He was a rancher who knew where to find his cattle during the most furious blizzards, but he was also a skilled entrepreneur who made a fortune from real estate, flipping parcels of land like flapjacks. He was a pillar of the Zion Methodist Church, and in that he took much pride. "Grayson is an honoured name in the life of Moose Jaw, and has been for half a century. It has been synonymous with public service, personal attainment and integrity," said the Regina *Leader-Post* when John Hawke died in 1934. What neither the newspaper editor nor the public perceived was that he was the quintessential speculator, a land-shark, who preyed on the weak and the poor. It was through "scrip farming," that he got his hands on Dougald Carmichael's homestead, Colin Carmichael's pre-emption, and Tom Aspdin's eighty acres.

For many years John Hawke – most people called him J. H. or Jack – and his elder brother, William, dominated Moose Jaw; indeed the name Grayson became synonymous with the town's great expectations. They were flipsides of the same coin. Both had round faces, sandy hair, straight, Anglo-Saxon noses, and bushy moustaches. They looked a little like Thomas Aspdin, but then they were Yorkshire men, just like him.

As he grew older, the elder brother would ooze authority – nobody crossed William Grayson, K.C., with impunity – but he was a more refined and compassionate man than John Hawke. "My grandfather was a lovely man, a kindly, generous, thoughtful man," remembers Joan Bidwell. "He kept those great brown tins of Riley Taffy in the hallway closet. You always had candy when you went to see Grandpa."

"I remember him as being rather austere and not too approachable," remembered his grandson, William D. Grayson. "He was always dressed as though he was going to a wedding or a funeral, which he probably was."

John Hawke did not have as much formal education as his

brother, nor was he as cultured. He was rougher and tougher; there was something of the cowboy about him, and he fascinated the various Grayson offspring. For one thing, he kept a bundle of "shin plasters," twenty-five-cent bills, in his pocket, and passed them out whenever he ran into one of the children. He'd take the boys out to the farm and dare them to shoot crows with his rifle – which was a lot more fun than the long lectures on Canada's place in the Empire, or some other dreary subject that William Grayson delivered whenever he ran into one of them.

John Hawke and William married two sisters, the Babb girls of Sidney, Manitoba. Both men were family-oriented, dedicated Methodists, and therefore teetotallers. Neither of them could, or would, dance. But they both knew how to make money. Together they connived to create the family fortune. "Grayson Brothers of Moose Jaw! Farm Lands for sale! 100,000 acres, $3.00 to $10.00 an acre!" proclaimed a handbill, and the accompanying photo showed the two men ever so slightly smiling.

Although in later years there was talk about humble origins, William and John Hawke's father, Michael Grayson, was a prosperous lumber merchant, who in 1868 had immigrated with his wife, Ann, and four children to London, Ontario. By the 1870s he had money enough to send his eldest son to Osgoode Hall in Toronto. William Grayson was called to the bar in 1878 at age twenty-two, and then returned to London, where he articled at an established law firm. Like so many young men at the time, he dreamed of a glorious future in Canada's vast North-West, but his vision had little to do with cultivating the earth. The virgin prairie, he realized, would be a land-speculator's windfall.

In 1881 he moved to Winnipeg and got a job with the law firm Ross, Killam, and Haggart, but a year later he decided that the city was too developed. Hearing that Moose Jaw was booming – lots were selling at a fantastic $575 each – he decided to head further west.

Grayson arrived in the winter of 1882-83 and promptly came down with scarlet fever. James H. Ross, who had come to conquer the West the year before, took the young lawyer to his cabin on Spring Creek and nursed him back to health. Their friendship was cemented the moment they discovered they were both dyed-in-the-wool Liberals.

Grayson had little money in his pocket and was eager to hang out his shingle in the ramshackle tent town of Moose Jaw as soon as possible. He teamed up with another lawyer-adventurer, James P. Mitchell, and that spring the two established their practice in one of the wooden shacks that had popped up like crocuses along the mud river called Main Street. Days later, the Dougald Carmichaels, having just suffered through their first prairie winter, would open the doors of the Enterprise House just around the corner from Mitchell & Grayson. But it soon became obvious to the young lawyers that you didn't get rich quick from legal fees earned by servicing poor farmers. In 1884, Mitchell left Moose Jaw, sniffing out his fortune even further west.

Whether it was his lack of money or his scepticism about whether Moose Jaw would make it as a town, Grayson didn't at first take advantage of the land boom erupting under his nose. In 1885, however, he bought a prime lot on Main Street across from the Canada North-West Land Company. And thus he began his spectacular career as a speculator.

In 1882, the government and the CPR decided to pool their land interests in Moose Jaw and three other prairie towns and divide the profits from the sale of their property equally. But by this time, the railroad was starving for cash, and decided to sell some five million acres of its original grant. The Canada North-West Land Company, a British-Canadian syndicate, was set up to acquire this land. As part of the deal, the company agreed to manage the sale of the jointly-owned CPR-government townsites, and in return it received one-quarter of the profits (the CPR received another quarter and the government one-half.)

In 1886, William Grayson was named the Moose Jaw agent for Canada North-West Land & Townsite Company, replacing the notoriously incompetent White-Fraser, who had no notion of formal bookkeeping but who had kept all the transactions in a jumble in his head. This position yielded Grayson invaluable inside information about the town's real-estate transactions, and by 1890 he had made a lot of money from the 3 per cent commission he charged the company, from the 2 per cent on collections, and from his lawyer's fees on the sales – "Town lots selling fast," he reported in 1891. "Six sold in one week alone." In addition, he himself bought twenty-six prime parcels in downtown Moose Jaw, all purchased from the Canada North-West Land Company, for which he was agent. For years he refused to pay taxes on this land, insisting that, since Canada North-West considered itself exempt from local taxation, so did he. (In 1891, after much protest from the citizens of Moose Jaw, the land company finally agreed to hand over a cash payment of $5,000 for back taxes owed from 1884; at that point Grayson also paid up. But the year before, Grayson had conveniently been named city solicitor, a job which paid only $200 a year but offered many bonuses. He was, for example, able to arrange tax concessions for both the Canada North-West Land Company and for himself until the company was dissolved in 1902.)

In 1890, a go-getter ex-newspaperman, who was to boost the Grayson family fortunes even further, arrived in town. Arthur Hitchcock's parents had immigrated from Leicester, England, to Stratford, Ontario. But small-town Ontario seemed a confining place for so ambitious a young man, and when he was barely twenty, he went to New York, becoming a reporter for the *World*. Hitchcock had a taste for money; he saw himself as a "true English gentleman," who dressed for dinner and enjoyed fresh-cut flowers on his table every day. His idea of paradise was accompanying two obscure members of the royal family duck-hunting. The problem was that his journalist's salary hardly allowed for Tudor-style homes and English butlers. Banking was where a man could make his fortune, so he quit the newspaper business and became an apprentice in one of the principle financial houses. Not surprisingly, after a time, he found this a restricting experience, too. The "opportunities abounding in the Canadian North-West," seemed the only answer, and in 1890, at age twenty-eight, he headed for Moose Jaw – with a queer name like that it had to be an interesting place. From the moment he stepped down from the train, he began his never-ending quest to cultivate important people, and one of the first persons with whom he shook hands was William Grayson.

Grayson was impressed by the former reporter's knowledge of

the New York business community; Hitchcock was impressed with Grayson's growing wealth. The two men formed a bond at once.

A banking firm, Lafferty and Moore, had been renting space in one of Grayson's downtown office buildings. In 1892, that outfit disappeared, to be replaced by another bank, Hitchcock Bros. & McCulloch. (Arthur Hitchcock's brother Alfred, who had returned to England, maintained an interest in the bank, but after a short time the bank was known simply as Hitchcock & McCulloch. H. H. McCulloch was the son of a well-known Moose Jaw physician. There may have been a falling out between the two partners, because in 1898 McCulloch moved his family to Calgary. Some years later, the McCullochs divorced, and Mrs. McCulloch married Arthur Hitchcock. Neither Alfred Hitchcock nor McCulloch took an active interest in the bank's daily activities.)

For the first eight years of its existence, Hitchcock & McCulloch was the only bank between Regina and Calgary, so it did a roaring business. (In 1925 it was sold to the Royal Bank of Canada.)

Hitchcock's bank and Grayson's law office shared the ground floor in an office building owned by Grayson and renovated to facilitate close relations between the two firms; a wicket in an adjoining wall allowed for quick passage of cash and documents back and forth. This was convenient, because Hitchcock would give money to almost any farmer who walked in – "private funds to loan at low rate of interest" ran the advertisement; Grayson operated the legal machinery for the foreclosures that very often followed, especially during the depressed 1890s. As pioneer George Tuxford wrote in 1889, "the regular rate of interest charged on loans was 25 per cent compounded every three months. What farmer has a chance?"

Many of Dougald Carmichael's old friends who had stuck out the drought of the 1880s ended up losing their homesteads a few years later after being caught in the Grayson-Hitchcock maw. The jovial, well-liked Mac Annable, for one, came close to financial ruin.

Annable was one of the first in the Moose Jaw district to go into the horse-breeding business; farmers were grateful to him because he sold stock relatively cheaply, which meant they could switch more quickly from oxen to Clydesdales. He was a kind man, with a big booming laugh. In 1892, in order to expand his business, he borrowed $5,000 at 18 per cent interest from Hitchcock & McCulloch. Hard times hit, and three years later, Annable fell behind in his payments.

Hitchcock arrived one morning at the farmer's stables and demanded, "I want you to turn over your wheat to me, for what you owe me." Annable refused, explaining he would be ruined, because wheat was selling at the all-time low price of thirty-five cents a bushel.

"I owe my men and I owe Tom Baker, the storekeeper. However, I will turn over a thousand bushels on account," Annable promised. Hitchcock wouldn't accept it.

Annable's problems were severe because he had been so lenient with other farmers; he had sold them horses and stock and, knowing their difficulties, had not pressed payment. Hitchcock wanted him to repossess the horses owned by indebted farmers, but Mac thought that this was unwise since times were so tough, and he knew he wouldn't be able to resell them. Hitchcock then proposed that Mac assign the notes to the bank, so that Hitchcock could carry out the dirty job of repossession. "I refused to do this because it would be like treachery to the men who had trusted me," Annable later wrote. He suggested several compromises to Hitchcock, but the banker brushed them aside. Hitchcock wanted cash and was now claiming that the debt had risen to $8,000.

At that point, William Grayson stepped in, trying to bully Annable into handing over his assets by threatening legal action. Finally, Grayson attempted to get an injunction to stop the farmer from shipping his wheat and selling it elsewhere. The judge had habitually used the services of Annable's Livery, Feed & Sales Stable in Moose Jaw, and he knew Mac well. He said, "I have heard a lot of Mr. Annable and I believe there is no one in the Moose Jaw district who had helped the farmers during these years of hard times more than Mac Annable has done. He is not the man to skip out dishonourably and I refuse to grant an injunction." The usually silent bank partner, McCulloch, finally joined in, insisting that Annable be given time to come up with the money.

Mac Annable paid off everybody else before he got around to Arthur Hitchcock, he hated him that much. And in 1901 he was to get a revenge of sorts. When J. H. Ross resigned his seat in the legislature, Annable ran against Hitchcock and whipped him.

It was Arthur Hitchcock who, in 1896, had foreclosed on Tom Aspdin, confiscating his Moose Jaw Creek farm. The banker had claimed the property was worth only $700, and had taken all eighty of Aspdin's horses to make up the difference he owed on the mortgage. Three years later, Hitchcock sold the land for three times the amount at which he had valued it.

In a few years Hitchcock had acquired some seventy-six farms around Moose Jaw; William Grayson eventually grew so rich that he could indulge his passions for collecting valuable art and travelling around the world, and he was also able to send his children to universities in Toronto and New York.

The creation of such wealth required the proper environment, and "the commercial élite" realized how important it was to control the machinery that governed their town. Hitchcock served as alderman for Moose Jaw and tried, unsuccessfully, for a seat on the North-West Territory legislature. The refined, quiet William Grayson wielded power in a different way.

He was a rather inhibited man, certainly not flamboyant, although he loved to give speeches. He always had to be in control, and this may have been the reason he didn't like running for political office. (He also shunned public life for other reasons. When, years later, he was offered the position of lieutenant-governor of Saskatchewan, he turned it down. He realized protocol would dictate that liquor be served at Government House, and, as a dedicated teetotaller, he was loath to do so.) He would serve as mayor of Moose Jaw, but only for one term, preferring to control his fiefdom from behind the scenes.

In 1882, the year he had arrived in the ragged, frontier town, he had organized a campaign to get his friend and fellow-Liberal, James H. Ross, elected to the North-West Council. The day the election writ was dropped, Grayson not only had twenty-eight of the sixty-two eligible voters already in his pocket, but he had had himself named returning officer. He then appointed his law partner, James Mitchell, enumerator, and Ross's partner, H. H. Smith, as election clerk. "Ross's subsequent election with a healthy majority is a foregone conclusion," Grayson told a newspaper reporter – and he was right.

James H. Ross's father, John E. Ross, then decided he wanted to be the first mayor of Moose Jaw. In January 1884, Grayson, from his law office, conducted what would go down as one of the most vicious campaigns in Moose Jaw's history. "I blush for the fair name of our town," is how one *Moose Jaw Times* correspondent put it. Dougald Carmichael had been among those who lined up in weather that sunk to thirty degrees below to cast his vote, and he was one of those who joined the celebrations when John E. Ross won by one vote.

Education was William Grayson's great interest, and in 1884 he ran for trustee of the Moose Jaw School Board. When he lost that election to hotel-owner Harry Bates by four votes, he simply called on his friends, the mayor he had put in office, John E. Ross, and the school-board chairman, Richard Bogue, both of whom were justices of the peace. They ruled that there had been irregularities, so that the election was declared void. It was the kind of manipulation and intrigue that would grease the political machinery in Moose Jaw for years to come.

With the oldest son prospering so remarkably, others of the Grayson clan came West. Albert Kirk Grayson, four years younger than William, arrived a few months after his brother. Certainly the most congenial and kindly of the brothers, he seems to have been the one truly dedicated farmer of the family. He took up a homestead to the northeast of Moose Jaw and built up a successful ranch. In the spring of 1910, Albert was returning home from business in Moose Jaw when one of his horses reared up, possibly frightened by a jackrabbit bounding across the road. While trying to bring the team under control, Albert fell off his rig, catching his foot in the wheel. The horses bolted, and he was dragged to his death. His wife, Willa, was expecting their eighth child. "She wouldn't take any help from the Graysons," recalls Joan Bidwell, "because she resented the family's wealth. She felt like a poor relation."

~ II ~

The third Grayson son, John Hawke, born July 13, 1867, could hardly wait for the day he graduated from the Collegiate Institute of London, Ontario, so that he could head West. By that time he was eighteen and already determined to make his fortune. "J. Hawke was a hungry, grave, ambitious young man," was how homesteader John O'Leery remembered him. He was a different version of William, leaner, more energetic, less given to pomposity and long-windedness, and more willing to compromise the Grayson name.

He arrived in Moose Jaw just in time for the North-West Rebellion, and right away learned a thing or two from his elder brother. When the militia started flooding into the town, many of them young men from influential eastern-Canadian families, William Grayson used the occasion to establish contacts. As Lieutenant H. Bapty's diary pointed out, "April 24, 1885: Passed Regina, Had breakfast at Moose Jaw, Saw Indians painted, Met Grayson, lawyer, there."

"Never know when in the future one of these lads might lead the way to an interesting business proposition," was Grayson's philosophy.

John Hawke's job during the rebellion was to keep account of the freighters who were hauling supplies to embattled areas. He probably recorded how much corned beef Dougald and Colin Carmichael would cart to Battleford.

In May of 1885, about two hundred French half-breeds suddenly appeared on the outskirts of Moose Jaw. They had trekked from Wood Mountain and Willow Bunch, half-starved because of the collapse of the buffalo-hide trade. They said they were looking for work, but all Moose Jaw sat terrified, convinced that they were about to attack "and kill every last white person, man, woman and child." Telegrams were sent to Lieutenant-Governor Edgar Dewdney in Regina, pleading for police or militia reinforcements. Dewdney didn't consider the situation in Moose Jaw to be dangerous, but he did agree to a plan concocted by William Grayson and Mayor Ross. The trader Jean-Louis Légaré was to be signed on as a special constable at a pay of $2.50 a day. In return he would convince the Métis to leave Moose Jaw. You must travel south to the U.S border, Légaré told them. There you'll find Americans sympathetic to Riel. They're plotting rebellion. If you scout them out, you'll be paid, and handsomely.

Forty men, representing all the Métis families, were enlisted, given a few dollars, and sent on a long trek southwards. For nothing. There were no American sympathizers and no jobs as scouts; it had all been a deception. The trip greatly increased the misery of these already-desperate people, but they were effectively dispersed, and the town fathers were hailed as heroes. It would not be the last time the Grayson brothers would use trickery to deceive down-and-out mixed bloods.

A year after his arrival in Moose Jaw, John Hawke entered for a quarter-section, NW 14-17-26 W2, not far from the town, and adjacent to his brother Albert's farm. Although Albert had all the latest farm machinery, as well as seven teams of horses that he was willing to loan, John Hawke did not seem interested in the actual work of farming. During his first four years in Moose Jaw, he didn't build a cabin on the land and cultivated only twenty-nine acres, so he was not eligible for a homestead patent. The Dominion Lands Office, however, had no qualms about selling him the 320 acres (homestead and pre-emption) for $1.25 an acre, which he immediately passed on to his brother William. John Hawke much preferred herding cattle to sitting all day behind two fat workhorses and a plough. During the 1880s, he was hired by several large cattle outfits to manage their stock during the winter.

In 1896, after Hitchcock had foreclosed on Tom Aspdin, he found himself with eighty horses on his hands. Hitchcock approached Mac Annable and asked him to dispose of the horses. Despite the antagonism the two men felt for each other, "business was business." Mac said, "I can probably trade them for cattle but not for cash. I'll take them down the line, and you send a man along to check up on my sales." The "man" chosen was John Hawke Grayson. "On the first of June we started out, equipped with a big tent and camped out every four or five miles as we went. The big tent drew attention to our coming and our purpose and we traded along the road for two months, going as far as Indian Head and from there north. J.H. selected the cattle for Hitchcock who later said he was completely satisfied."

Annable added: "J.H. always boiled his sausages before he fried them. Looked like hell but they were tasty as anything."

The trip was so successful that Mac asked Grayson to go with him the following spring, to sell another 500 head of horses. Each made $1,600, a fair bundle in those days. "The trip put J.H. on his feet a bit. It was practically the first money he had been able to lay up."

John Hawke prided himself on being lean and fit and able to rope a calf with the fastest of cow-punchers. And yet what he was really good at, the skill that would make his fortune far more than branding cows or dealing horses, was a much more mundane occupation – bookkeeping.

He began by clerking in J. J. A. McLean's Staple and Fancy Grocers and then moved over to the larger T. W. Robinson, dry-goods establishment, both in Moose Jaw. In 1890, at age twenty-three, he went to work in his brother's law office as a clerk and general do-everything. It was there he learned the nuts and bolts of land-dealing. Manipulating the government's regulations had developed into a fine art in the Grayson law firm. The fleecing of Andrew Hardie was a case in point.

In June 1884, Hardie made an entry on a homestead that was situated adjacent to the farms belonging to Albert and John Hawke (and later to William). The Grayson brothers thought it would be a convenient spot for their elderly father, who was moving West from London, Ontario. So they devised a means to get their hands on it.

Hardie was working diligently to complete his homestead obligations when he received word in the fall of 1888 that his father was deathly ill. Much would have to be done on his return to the family farm near Longueuil, Quebec, so, unaware of the Graysons' intentions, Hardie asked William to look after his concerns during the time he was gone. Only days after he left, William Grayson asked the land commissioner in Winnipeg for an inspection of the homestead, claiming Hardie had not put in the necessary time on the land.

In June 1889, Hardie, now in Longueuil, received a letter from the commissioner, informing him that his entry would soon be cancelled. In reply he wrote,

> You inform me that William Grayson, advocate, and his brother Albert are arguing the cancellation of my place with the intention of entering for it. Now Mr. William Grayson has been acting as my agent since I left Moose Jaw, and I sent him my application with all particulars to place before you. I have some reason to think that all is not right. Can you keep my case open until I hear more fully from Moose Jaw?

The land-office officials paid no attention to Hardie's request. Two weeks later his homestead was cancelled and Michael Grayson's right of entry granted.

With such an apprenticeship, John Hawke Grayson did well in the real-estate business. He had a sharp eye, a good memory, and a bookkeeper's fastidiousness. Unlike his brother, William, he spent a lot of time out on the prairies, until "he damn well knew every sod hut and willow tree for miles around Moose Jaw," as pioneer John O'Leery put it. His *modus operandi* was both systematic and complicated. As an agent for the Dominion Lands Office, he would assist newcomers to locate on available homestead land – for a fee, of course. (In 1906, the land commissioner called this practice "flim-flamming unwary settlers." Homesteaders were not supposed to need "land-sharks" to help them find good land.)

Grayson would watch as the farms failed and the pioneers' enthusiasm dwindled, as happened very often during the 1890s. When the homesteader was ready to give up, John Hawke was always standing by, ready to hand over enough cash to enable the farmer to leave the area, but nowhere near what the land was worth. If he couldn't talk the farmer into vacating his land, John Hawke would wait until he fell behind in his taxes. The town would then confiscate the property, and Grayson would again be waiting in the wings to buy it at a very low price.

But like his brother, John Hawke understood that it was town property which would eventually bring home the real gold. He bought his first Moose Jaw lot in 1892, and by the time he died, forty-two years later, he owned thirty-eight substantial pieces of property in the city (some of these were entire blocks, incorporating as many as forty lots), as well as a huge chunk of the downtown business section, which he had jointly developed with his brother William.

But this all came later, after Moose Jaw had enjoyed a fantastic boom. In the early 1890s, the town was not exactly thriving. Poor crops, the country-wide recession, and more specifically the failure of the CPR to build the promised branch lines through the countryside all contributed to its anemic health. Pessimism and apathy floated so thick in the air that nobody could even be bothered to run for municipal office. Something had to be done to bolster the family's fortune, and in 1893 William Grayson agreed to run for mayor. As the *News* put it: "His policy will be one of progress and his election will infuse new life and energy into municipal administration, and promote the prestige, progress and credit of our town." But the job took much more of his time than he had anticipated, and he hadn't been able to accomplish what he wanted – massive public works to beautify and develop Moose Jaw. "I regret the council had been unable to float the debentures necessary for civic improvements owing to the tightness of money market," he reported, and stepped down after one term. John Hawke was designated the family politician thereafter.

Meanwhile, J.H. had been busy sticking his thumbs in many different pies. In 1893 he was appointed secretary of the newly established Moose Jaw Co-operative Creamery, the following year he inaugurated the J. H. Grayson Real Estate and General Insurance – "money to loan" – Company, becoming an official land agent for the Department of the Interior, and in 1895 he was appointed by the lieutenant-governor as a "commissioner for taking affidavits," which sent all kinds of diverse business his way. Finally, in 1896, at age twenty-nine, he was elected to the town council, a position he held for six years. While he was never much of a speaker or a debater, he was an influential, energetic power in Moose Jaw, and as chairman of the finance committee, he molded much of the town's development. Ironically, given where his future wealth was to lie, he several times chastized speculators as "those who did nothing to improve the value of land," and then upped their taxes.

Although the population had hardly soared – it had stuck at about twelve hundred people and little industry had developed – the Moose Jaw of 1896 was quite a different place than the ramshackle, matchstick town that had greeted the Carmichaels and Graysons on their arrival over ten years before.

In 1891, a fire had swept along Main Street "like an inferno," killing three people and demolishing seventeen businesses, including the old Foley Block where the first school and town hall had been situated. Tom and Mary Aspdin had spotted the smoke and flames from the veranda of their rented home on Moose Jaw Creek and had rushed in by buggy to aid the injured. William Grayson's large house was damaged but, as he said, "This tragedy is not entirely a bad thing." The town's rickety eyesores had also gone up in smoke.

If Moose Jaw looked like a great city, surely it would become one, reasoned the town fathers, and so they declared that only buildings of fieldstone or brick could be constructed along the main street. The bumper crop of 1892 provided the money and optimism for this construction, which included a new town hall and fire station, St. John's Anglican Church, Moose Jaw Baptist Church, some lovely Victorian homes, and several dozen office and retail buildings (many built by William Grayson). W. W. Bole's new drugstore had oak shelving, two large plate-glass windows adorned with handsome shades, solid oak counters, a new section for books and notions, and a modern dispensary. Moose Jaw was transformed – "As elegant a town as any in the West," boasted the Moose Jaw Times.

There were plank sidewalks and fresh-water delivery, and for a while Moose Jaw citizens enjoyed electric lights.* "The difference in the appearance of the streets since the electric lamps were placed in position has been frequently commented upon," crowed the *Moose Jaw Times*.

As much as their grandiose new buildings, Moose Jaw citizens were proud of their "sophisticated" cultural life. The luscious Katie Putnam wowed a full house with a great performance in *Love Finds a Way*; the Literary Society fiercely debated whether the franchise should be extended to women (the nays won, of course); the De Mass Family Entertainers from Philadelphia performed on the xylophone, ocarinas, and cowbells and thrilled everyone; all the numbers sung at the Templars of Temperance Choral Society's concert at Town Hall featured "the devil rum" and taught everyone a lesson; the masquerade skating party on Moose Jaw Creek saw "a darkey gent," a clown, and a Chinaman all win prizes. In a lovely ceremony, the freedom of the town was bestowed on the English long-distance walker Edward Holmes and his dog, Boojum, both of whom happened to be passing through. There was never a dull moment.

The Graysons were in the thick of things, of course. On August 2, 1895, the *Moose Jaw Times* reported an especially gala event. "There was an unusually large attendance to Mrs. William Grayson's garden party. Ice cream, lemonade, fruit and cake were served. The children enjoyed the games and clowns and the adults the entertainment provided by guitar, violin, and piano." All that was missing was the Moose Jaw Brass Band, for which the hostess's brother-in-law, John Hawke, served as secretary.

---

*The Moose Jaw Electric Light Company was formed in December 1890, and built a power station on the south side of Moose Jaw Creek; soon, however, blackouts gave it the name of "The Now You See It, Now You Don't Power Co." William Grayson's associate, Arthur Hitchcock, bought the company in 1892 for $4,000, but he soon found it wasn't the milk cow he was anticipating, and he sold it in 1895. The new owner finally suspended operations altogether, leaving Moose Jaw without electricity until 1904.

But the focal point of the Grayson's social life was the Zion Methodist Church. The first service had been conducted in 1883 in the CPR station; William Grayson had organized the event. Twenty-four years later, William Grayson would be instrumental in raising the $80,000 intended to build a truly grandiose church. John Hawke donated one of the three sites. "Moose Jaw Methodists are to have the largest, most commodious and most beautiful church in Western Canada. It will be almost an exact duplicate of Zion Methodist Church in Winnipeg," reported the *Times*. Surrounded by all the town's prominent citizens, and with a beautifully engraved silver trowel in hand, William Grayson laid the cornerstone to applause all round. Built of red pressed brick and trimmed with Manitoba grey stone, with massive stone columns to dramatize its Roman–Ionic pretensions, and with a huge dome made of leaded stained glass, the new church was meant to dominate the town, to serve as a testimonial to Moose Jaw's brilliant future. "It's more a tribute to the Graysons, than God," wrote an anonymous correspondent to the *Times*.

William taught bible class there for years, and John Hawke was often the secretary-treasurer, but it was their wives, Ellen and Adela, who forged the link between the City of God and the Grayson clan. Hardly a day passed that they weren't involved in some social or charitable activity centred in the church.

Ellen Grayson, William's wife, could never have been called a beauty – she was tall and rather stout – but she was kindly and "knew her place," appropriate qualities for the wife of a leading citizen. She was one of eight children of Thomas Babb, who had run a dry-goods store in Mitchell, Ontario, and was an acquaintance of the Graysons when that family lived in London. The Babbs came West in 1880, and in the small town of Sidney, Manitoba, William married Ellen. She was twenty-two and he twenty-eight. The newlyweds arrived in Moose Jaw just as the North-West Rebellion had collapsed. One crystal-clear memory remained with Ellen always – the crowds of people. "Oh, so many half-breeds," packed on the station platform, waiting to catch a glimpse of the prisoner Louis Riel, whispering of when the noose would be firmly placed around his neck.

Babies began arriving right way; eventually Ellen and William would have eight. But, as her granddaughter Joan Bidwell recalls, Ellen always had help – two nannies for the children, a cleaning woman, a washing woman, a maid, a cook. Still, it was often too much for Ellen and she would sometimes return to her parents' home in Sidney, Manitoba, for rest cures. Yet, even when the family could afford Louis XVI chairs, she always insisted on making her own soap, as though that allowed her to claim pioneer status. In much the same way, William regarded himself as a gentleman farmer because he always kept a Jersey cow in the barn behind the Stadacona Street mansion, and even gave a $5 prize for the best-grade milk cow at the Moose Jaw Agricultural Fair. But his passion for flowers was real enough. With only occasional help, he cultivated the "glorious garden" himself. He was picking asparagus when he suffered the stroke that eventually killed him in 1926.

In 1890, another Babb daughter, Adela, arrived to teach school at the small village of Boharm, just west of Moose Jaw. A year later she married John Hawke Grayson. Adela was a sharper, more energetic, version of Ellen. Remembers Joan Bidwell, "My grandmother [Ellen] was a rather pampered woman. She went to church and she supported them, but she wasn't over there doing dishes in the kitchen. But Aunt Dela worked her head off for the church and the ladies aid. They lived right across the street from Zion Church and when there was a banquet, she'd haul half the stuff out of her house over there."

William D. Grayson, her great-nephew, remembered Adela as being austere and unapproachable. She certainly seemed able to manage her strong-willed husband – he never, for example, was allowed to smoke in the house.

In 1896 the Grayson family fortune was given another happy boost. Sir Wilfrid Laurier won the federal election, and political largesse began to rain on the True Grit Grayson brothers.

In 1901 John Hawke was appointed postmaster of Moose Jaw. Even though the post office at that point was nothing more than a seedy little corner in the Fysh Block, this was not only a lucrative job – it paid $880 a year in 1898 – but John Hawke was the first to receive the most interesting and valuable information: the availability of half-breed land scrip, for instance.

~ III ~

Perhaps because so little has been written about it, the unprincipled and calculated swindle that was perpetrated on the Métis of Canada has not sunk very far into our collective psyche. It was the biggest land grab in the nation's history, carried out blatantly and with total disregard for an impoverished people who were defeated, confused, and utterly without resources. It made big banks and small capitalists like John Hawke Grayson very rich. Even honourable people like Tom Aspdin succumbed to the temptation to cheat the half-breeds. And like the rest of society, the Zion Methodist Church of Moose Jaw conveniently turned a blind eye to this massive theft.

It was partly the fact that the vast territory known as Rupert's Land belonged to the Hudson's Bay Company that prompted the union of British North America in 1867. The Fathers of Confederation hoped that, once negotiations with the trading company were completed, the Wild West could quickly be transformed into a vast cultivated garden. They did not overly concern themselves with the French-speaking Catholics who already lived there, the mixed bloods, who seemed so wild and so strange, or with a cocky, studious Métis named Louis Riel, who insisted that the people of Red River had rights both as individuals and collectively as a community.

Since the mid-1700s, the French-speaking Métis and English-speaking half-breeds had been the backbone of the fur trade in the North-West. They not only trapped and hunted, but also worked as interpreters, as suppliers of pemmican for the whites, and as freighters, clerks, and guides. With the amalgamation of the two huge trading companies, the Hudson's Bay and the North West in 1821, a large number of these jobs vanished. Many Métis then settled along the Red River, near present-day

Winnipeg, cultivating long strips of farmland, as well as trapping and working as overland freighters and boatmen. By 1869, with a Métis population of twelve thousand, the Red River was one of the largest, and certainly the most vibrant, settlements west of the Mississippi and north of the Missouri.

The Métis were apprehensive about what was going to happen when their land was taken over by the Canadian government; they didn't like the aggressive English-speaking surveyors who had been sniffing around their territory. So they set up their own provisional government – a Declaration of the People of Rupert's Land and the North-West – to replace the long-moribund Hudson's Bay administration. There wasn't much the Canadians could do, since the official representative, Lieutenant-Governor William McDougall, *en route* to the Red River, had been prevented from taking up his post, and thereby from establishing the authority of Canada. At that point, the Métis provisional government was as legitimate as anyone else's.

Since Sir John A. Macdonald was concerned about keeping Quebec content in the new confederation, he decided to negotiate with, rather than subjugate, the French-speaking Métis nation. Despite outrage from the Orangemen of Ontario – one of their own, the foul-mouthed Thomas Scott, had been executed by Métis firing squad, and they vowed his revenge – a postage-sized province of Manitoba became a province of Canada on July 15, 1870. The Manitoba Act guaranteed two official languages, denominational schools, and land for every man, woman, and child who had been living in Rupert's Land before 1870. Unfortunately for the mixed bloods, the federal government, rather than the new province, retained control of public lands and natural resources.

Whether Macdonald's government ever intended to distribute the millions of acres promised under the Manitoba Act is debatable. Through orders-in-council, a legislative procedure that many now believe was unconstitutional, the Manitoba Act was nibbled away at until, by the mid 1870s, the original intent of the law had been seriously undermined.

Under the act, there were several avenues by which the Métis were to have received their land. Title to the river lots where they had farmed for years was supposedly guaranteed. But after 1870, the federal government decided that Métis would not be given special status but treated like other settlers. They would have to prove that they had previously obtained title from the Hudson's Bay Company, or that they had invested in the land by significantly improving it. The more educated, English-speaking half-breeds readily obtained the deeds to their land, but the French-speakers, those whose lifestyles were closer to the "savage Indians," suffered. The inspectors said that their claims to residency were not satisfactory, improvements to the land weren't adequate, and their devotion to black soil was not obsessive enough, and then they took their land away. In Rat River, eighty-four of ninety-three Métis families were given "writs of ejectment" from the river lots they had thought they had owned for fifty years.

Another way the Métis were supposed to become land rich was through the 1.4 million acres allotted to their children.

The lieutenant-governor of Manitoba, Adams G. Archibald, proposed this distribution be carried out through a quick and simple procedure. Land should be reserved at the back of the river lots around the well-established Catholic parishes, and each half-breed child would get a piece of this territory. He was castigated by his boss, Secretary of State Joseph Howe, and then fired for this outrageously fair idea.

The truth was that Archibald was referring to land that had become too valuable; white speculators wanted it. (Much of it is in present-day Winnipeg, and valued at up to ten billion dollars.) In April of 1872, the government announced that Métis would have to make their selections from the bald prairie, rather than the area around their parishes where they had lived for years. And even this process became snared in bureaucratic red tape. The government's strategy was by now obvious: the Métis land claims would be delayed long enough for white settlers to flood the best prairie land, thereby driving them out.

The Liberals who came to power under Alexander Mackenzie in 1873 were no more sympathetic to the Métis than the Tories had been; in fact they were even more cold-blooded. Under this government, the interpretation of the phrase "half-breed children" as it applied to land entitlement fell into dispute. Did it literally mean children under the age of twenty-one, or did it mean any offspring of a white father and Indian mother, no matter how old? The Liberals chose the former interpretation, and dispossessed four thousand people of their land overnight. Many were the heads of households. Two weeks later, after they took the land away from the mixed bloods, the same government decided to give the original white pioneers 140 acres per head. "Selkirk settlers. . . . were as much pioneers and had suffered as many hardships as the half-breeds," the government said, not noting the racism implicit in their arbitrary decisions.

The Métis, of course, objected to such a blatant injustice, and the lieutenant-governor of Manitoba felt he had to come up with a compromise. He suggested that each head of a half-breed household be issued a piece of paper worth a specific amount – a kind of money – which would be used to purchase any land that was open to homesteading. Thus the insidious concept of scrip was born in Canada.

In 1875, notices appeared in churches, parish halls, trading posts, and land offices, announcing the location and date of scrip-commission sittings. All half-breeds, whether or not they happened to be hunting buffalo miles from their parishes, were expected to show up on that day to swear to his or her parentage, date and location of birth, and place of domicile in 1870.

Some five hundred hungry speculators, many of them agents for banks, were waiting in the wings. Working from the same lists as the commissioners, they descended on these small communities, using any number of devious means to wrest the scrip from the illiterate Métis. This is all a sham, the speculators claimed. The government has no intention of giving you your land. Here's twenty-five bucks and a bottle of whisky. Put your X here (on the money scrip).

If that didn't work, the sharks told the half-breeds that the government wouldn't process their claims unless they retained a lawyer. The Métis would sign a power of attorney, witnessed by a justice of the peace who was either a speculator himself or in the pocket of speculators. Of course, the half-breed would never see the buyer or his scrip again. Virtually the entire issue of money scrip ended up in the hands of bankers and other white speculators.

Even the land allotments for half-breed children under the age of twenty-one weren't secure. Through powers of attorney, often phony, they were passed on to lawyers, real-estate brokers, and other shysters. By 1882, less than six hundred thousand acres of land had been retained by half-breeds, while two million acres had been diverted to speculators.

David Laird, the Liberal Minister of the Interior, understood what it was all about. Métis, he said, knew "something of farming," but he saw no place for them in his vision of Manitoba, where farms were money-making enterprises, exporting wheat for profit. The half-breeds should be evicted from their river lots and encouraged to move north and west, "around the different large lakes which abound with fine white fish." Without land, they would be a source of cheap labour, helping white farmers clear their property and working on road and bridge construction gangs and as freighters. Laird's policy was successful. The first great Métis diaspora began, as half-breed families headed as far away from white civilization as they could get.

They settled primarily south of Prince Albert, in the communities of Duck Lake, Batoche, St. Louis, St. Laurent. For a few years they lived in peace, until the surveyors arrived again.

There was a sense of *déjà vu* about the rebellion of 1885: the characters were the same – Sir John A. Macdonald was again prime minister and Louis Riel had returned from Montana – and the grievance was the same – land rights and government deception.

Sir John A. had recognized in 1878 that the half-breeds of the North-West (who had not yet benefitted from the Manitoba Act) had legitimate land stakes as part of their Indian title, but for five years nothing was done to satisfy these claims. During the North-West Rebellion, a commission had been set up to look into the question. Eventually, 61,020 acres of land and $663,474 in money scrip were distributed to those half-breeds born before 1870 and living in areas where the Indian titles had already been extinguished.

Why this sudden generosity, especially since the Métis had

been so soundly defeated? The government knew very well that by issuing half-breed scrip, hundreds of thousands of acres, formerly designated as homestead land, would be set free. From this vast land the "good ol' boys" could make extraordinary profits. Clifford Sifton, Edgar Dewdney, and Grayson's old friend, James H. Ross, to name but a few, all made fortunes from half-breed scrip.

Two forms of scrip existed – land and money, and most Métis chose the latter because the buyers said it was more convenient. Money scrip could be sold like any other personal property, to pay the tab at the local dry-goods store or to trade for horses, for example. Since the government valued bald prairie land at $1 an acre, and since each half-breed was usually allotted 240 acres, the script certificates bore the amount of $240. They seldom or never received the full value; the swindlers quickly stepped in. One hundred dollars was the going price, but a bottle of whisky or a cow often tempted the impoverished Métis to sign the necessary documents.

Charter and private banks made fortunes on the backs of the half-breeds. They bought scrip and sold it over the counter to farmers who used it to buy out their pre-emptions or other lands, and to speculators like the Saskatchewan Valley Land Company and the CPR, who in turn sold it for large profits to the dry-land farmers who were pouring up from the States.

But there was another, more important, facet of the banks' involvement with half-breed scrip. The late 1880s and 1890s were hard times in the West. The fur trade had dried up, the buffalo hunt was over, the government was stingy about spending money for capital improvements, and private investment for industry or commerce was almost non-existent. "Money at the present time is very scarce all through the country," Thomas Aspdin had written in 1893, a complaint echoed by most farmers.

The Bank Act at the time stipulated that loans made by lending institutions had to be backed by reserves. To overcome this "strangulation," the banks began purchasing huge amounts of half-breed money scrip at greatly discounted prices. But they calculated their reserves on the basis of the face value of scrip they were holding, thereby increasing their ability to make loans. For example, if Métis scrip with a face value of $1,000 was purchased by a bank in Moose Jaw for $350, the bank not only reaped a nice profit on this transaction but also was able to lend more money to white farmers (half-breed farmers were seldom given loans; they weren't considered a good enough risk). Thus the government found a convenient way to increase the money supply in the West and thereby encourage rapid settlement.

Land scrip was another matter. Métis were supposed to present themselves at the nearest land office to personally select their 240 acres. This was a bother compared with the simplicity of money-scrip transactions, and until 1900, when rich American farmers started coming north and land values soared, half-breeds and speculators preferred money scrip. Still there was some speculation in land scrip, especially after it was discovered that the Dominion Lands Office officials didn't particularly care whether the Métis standing before them was the person named on the document or someone the speculator had found on the street. One rancher from White Mud River bragged to the press that his huge land holdings had derived entirely from trading guns for Métis scrip. Small-town lawyers and real-estate brokers who knew where available land was located and could reach isolated Métis communities specialized in this scam. They came to be called "half-breed scrip millionaires," a description that exactly fitted John Hawke Grayson.

Grayson began speculating in land scrip in 1900 after the federal government order-in-council entitled each Métis born between July 5, 1870, and July 16, 1885, to 240 acres of scrip. During that time almost a million acres were distributed through land scrip, of which 85 per cent landed in the pockets of speculators like Grayson. Conditions were ripe. The half-breeds were even more destitute than they had been immediately after the rebellion, and real estate was booming – between 1900 and 1910, land prices in Saskatchewan soared by 201 per cent – making land scrip, which the government arbitrarily set at $1 an acre, very valuable indeed.

Between May 16, 1900, and September 1906, scrip commissioners travelled to isolated parts of Alberta and Saskatchewan, to distribute scrip to qualified Métis. The trick for a speculator was to find out before anyone else where and when a scrip commission would be sitting and sew up deals with the local half-breeds before – sometimes as much as a year before – the procedures began. As postmaster of Moose Jaw and a prominent Liberal, John Hawke Grayson had easy access to this information, which enabled him to set up a system of land-scrip extraction which was amazing.

Jean-Louis Légaré, a six-foot-four French-Canadian with a great black beard, may have been Grayson's entrée to the half-breeds of Willow Bunch. Although Légaré wasn't himself a Métis, he was considered a leader of that community, probably because he spoke French. On first coming West, he had set up a trading post at Wood Mountain – Tom Aspdin knew him well. He had befriended Sitting Bull and then encouraged him to return to the United States in 1881, and he was also the "special constable" who had tricked the starving half-breeds clustered around Moose Jaw in 1885 into pursuing nonexistent jobs on the American border. William Grayson, who was himself instrumental in the deceit, got to know him then. Légaré – there's a Saskatchewan park and a golf course named after him now – was also the dealer who talked the Métis into handing over their land scrip to people like Grayson for a mere song.

Like their friends the Indians, the Métis had lived for years in the valleys around Wood Mountain, hunting and trapping, but also keeping cattle. In 1879 a prairie fire destroyed the forage for miles. Jean-Louis Légaré declared that he was moving to an area about thirty-two miles east, and the Métis followed him. Known as Talle de Saule in French and Willow Bunch in English, the new village was situated in a pretty valley surrounded by sharp hills, deeply lined with coulees. The south side was covered with willows, aspens, and oak, while the north side was completely nude. It's tempting to see in this natural phenomenon a parallel with Métis culture before and after the white man gained power.

At first the community showed signs of prospering. Reverend Father St. Germain arrived in time to baptize the first baby born in the village – Edouard Beaupré would eventually grow to eight feet, two inches and make Willow Bunch famous. He went to school for a while along with the other Willow Bunch kids, helped his father on his scrubby farm, and shopped at Louis Légaré's trading post. But by the time the Giant died in 1904 at the age of twenty-three (while working in a circus in St. Louis), his hometown was in a sad state.

The Métis were trying to survive by hunting small game and by subsistence farming, and, for the few who managed to get their hands on some cattle, by ranching. (Jean-Louis Légaré was one rancher who became quite wealthy, especially after he made money exploiting his fellow townspeople.) Most were illiterate; all were frightened and desperately poor. Maria Campbell, in her book *Half-breed*, expresses the hopelessness that was prevalent among the Métis. Although she is talking about a later time, terrible alienation began to fester immediately after the North-West Rebellion.

I know that poverty is not ours alone. Your people have it too, but in those earlier days you at least had dreams, you had a tomorrow. My parents and I never shared any aspirations for a future. I never saw my father talk back to a white man unless he was drunk. I never saw him or any of our men walk with their heads held high before white people.

It was in this milieu that John Hawke Grayson found it so easy to carry on his swindling.

Grayson might have visited the various places himself a few times, but it was probably the job of an employee, a clerk, to perform the often arduous duties of a claim-runner. For a few years these people were landmarks on the back roads of Saskatchewan. Wearing their big, bulky coats, especially designed with huge pockets to accommodate bundles of $1 bills, they travelled by horseback, ferry, and canoe into the most isolated areas. The really successful scrip-runners understood the mixture of French, Cree, and English that the Métis spoke, and they were always charming, always persuasive. Handfuls of dollars were waved under the half-breeds' noses, temptation to sign away rights for a shockingly small amount.

Competition among the buyers didn't boost the price of scrip at all. W. P. Fillmore was a young law student in a Winnipeg firm who was assigned to a scrip-buying mission at Île-à-la-Crosse in 1905. He was given $5,000 in small-denomination bills, which he carried in a canvas bag in his hip pocket. The trip took almost two weeks, and required that he travel by train, team and wagon, and canoe. When Fillmore got to Île-à-la-Crosse, there was already quite a carnival under way. As he later described, the Indians and Métis had gathered from miles around, mostly travelling by canoe. Each was interviewed by the Indian commissioner, who sat in a large tent; on the spot he decided if half-breed scrip would be issued or not.

The scrip-buyers were eagerly waiting outside the tent. They had already set a method in place to prevent any competitive bidding that would give any edge to the half-breeds. The scrip-buyers, in fact, formed a kind of syndicate, setting the price at $1 an acre (at a time when good farmland was selling for between $25 and $165 an acre); when the buying ended, the proceeds would be divided evenly among the scrip-runners.

John Hawke Grayson's man would sometimes get involved in the complicated manoeuvres that Fillmore describes. But more often, with agents like Jean-Louis Légaré in place, he would have deals with the half-breeds sewn up long before other buyers arrived on the scene.

The individual Métis was supposed to go with the scrip certificate to the nearest Dominion Lands Office to locate the property, although he or she would never set foot on it, because a blank quit deed had already been signed. Sometimes the half-breed named on the scrip certificate showed up, but more often it was a substitute. As Fillmore admits, it would have been too inconvenient to find the genuine holder of the scrip in the vast north: "the practice was for the holder of a scrip to pick out some local Indian or half-breed and take him to the Dominion Lands Office and present him as the person named in the scrip."

John Hawke Grayson had a score of half-breeds on hand who would perform this duty at the Regina lands office. Since the documents were signed with an X, the officials didn't know the difference, and would turn a blind eye anyway. By this time

Grayson was a big shot, and not to be questioned or bothered about such matters.

Between 1900 and 1910, John Hawke Grayson was the chief player in eighty-four Métis land-scrip transactions.* Sometimes Grayson acted simply as an agent, searching for land scrip available and then, for a fee, passing it on to someone who wanted to use it to acquire land. For example, in 1901 he learned that Jean Baptiste Larocque of Willow Bunch was willing to sell eighty acres of land scrip. Grayson then arranged through Légaré for the hotel-keeper John Kern (the same man who had tried to oust Aspdin from his job as liquor inspector) to buy it for $300. Grayson charged $25 for services provided. In the majority of cases, however, he used the Métis scrip to get his hands on the best remaining land in the West. As the Americans began flooding into Canada, this wheeling and dealing proved more and more lucrative.

Some of John Hawke Grayson's land deals were astonishingly simple. On February 2, 1904, his wife, Adela (whether land was purchased in her name for her benefit or because John Hawke did not want the full extent of his speculation uncovered can only be surmised), bought half-breed land scrip from one Ernestine Brière, the eldest daughter (of seven children) of Louis and Josephette, who were farmers living near Willow Bunch. According to the Department of Interior records, the price paid was only $1, although value probably was added in the form of a horse, a bottle of whisky, or the discharging of a family debt. With the scrip in hand, Adela then obtained the southeast quarter-section of 10-16-24 W2, prime farmland located only

---

*These include only those transactions which appear in the Department of the Interior records; Grayson was probably involved in hundreds more, but was too far on the periphery to be officially noted. For example, it was Grayson who discovered that Abraham Beauchamp had land scrip that he was willing to sell to Thomas Aspdin, and it was Grayson who located the eighty acres that Aspdin acquired through the scrip. But it was Aspdin's name, not Grayson's, that appeared in land-scrip records.

three and a half miles from Dougald and Colin Carmichael's homesteads. Four years later, the quarter-section was sold to Laurita Nielson Krogh of Audubon, Iowa, for $2,640. Many similar deals yielded the Graysons a quick 2,000-per-cent profit.

Other land-scrip transactions were more complex, and it was here that John Hawke's talent as an accountant was so useful. In 1900 the Dominion Lands Act was revised to allow companies or businesses to combine the scrip of a number of individual Métis to acquire large tracts of land. John Hawke Grayson quickly discovered he had a gold mine on his hands.

In October of 1900, he purchased 240 acres of land scrip from Louis Ray, a farmer from Willow Bunch, for $200, and the next month he bought another 240 acres of land scrip from Leo Larocque, a twenty-five-year-old farmer from Qu'Appelle, for $140. With these scrip certificates, Grayson made a claim on 480 acres of section 16-16-24 W2, very near where Adela Grayson had located her land. Two years later he bought 80 acres of half-breed scrip from John Archibald Rowland of Battleford for $160, and a few months later he paid Zacharie Chartrand of Willow Bunch $90 for another 80 acres of land scrip. He then applied both pieces, 160 acres, to the same 16-16-24 W2, which meant he had accumulated the entire section in about three years. The cost to Grayson – $590. Three years later, he sold the property to John Hancock Griggs of Granville, Iowa, for $4,480 – a 750-per-cent profit.

In 1901, Dougald Carmichael's homestead, the northwest quarter of 14-16-25 W2, and half of Colin Carmichael's pre-emption, the southeast quarter of the same section, was acquired through half-breed scrip from James Gaudry of Willow Bunch. (Tom Aspdin acquired the other half through Métis scrip provided by Grayson.) Grayson actually paid $250 for the quarter and a half, not a bad price. But less than six months later he sold the same land for $800.

It was not as though Grayson was unaware that his real-estate ventures were fraudulent and immoral. The Métis themselves, and those priests, lawyers, and politicians sympathetic to their plight, had been hammering the government about it for years. Newspapers, especially the Winnipeg *Free Press*, not only covered these stories but in some cases raged against such corrupt practices in their editorials.

Although Grayson was never called to account himself, scandal came close to soiling him on a couple of occasions.

His partner in several scrip deals was the banker and family friend Arthur Hitchcock. In 1904 Hitchcock was alleged to have acquired illegally all the half-breed scrip in Lac La Biche, Alberta. After an investigation, the Department of the Interior agreed not to press charges if Hitchcock would pay the Métis full market value, which he did. Then he continued dealing in scrip.

Also in 1904, Grayson began buying land scrip from a Winnipeg lawyer named R. C. McDonald. A prominent Liberal, McDonald seemed to have had a more direct pipeline into the Department of the Interior than any other speculator. He knew a year before that the government planned to honour the scrip of half-breeds who had fled to the United States after 1885. For months he combed the Dakotas and Montana, wrapping up deals in anticipation of the new regulation, managing to obtain land scrip worth $240 for as little as twenty-five cents. The fraud was so outrageous that the North Dakota Métis launched a lawsuit against McDonald, and the Canadian government felt obliged to set up a judicial inquiry. Winnipeg Judge Robert Hill Myers was to hear evidence in Killarney – in Manitoba on the North Dakota border. *The Winnipeg Daily Tribune* reported what happened next: agents for McDonald bribed every half-breed they could find in the Dakotas and Montana with "large sums of money" not to give damaging evidence at the hearings.

Not surprisingly, few concrete facts emerged, and the inquiry quickly turned into a whitewash, even though a North Dakota court had found that the "scrip had been obtained by fraud." Still, the newspaper stories made it abundantly clear to everyone, including the citizens of Moose Jaw, how scrip was being "finagled, stolen or juggled" from the half-breeds. None of this bothered John Hawke Grayson. He was dealing in half-breed money scrip until the day before he died.

As Grayson's wealth grew, so did his power and influence. In July of 1903, when W. H. Wilson, the U.S. Secretary of Agriculture in Teddy Roosevelt's cabinet, arrived in Moose Jaw in his private railway car, it was John Hawke Grayson who greeted him and his three high-powered capitalist friends and then showed them where the best agricultural land was located in the district. The fact that Grayson was the postmaster didn't deter him in his land speculation. In 1907, when the Dominion Government decided postmasters would become full-fledged civil servants, Grayson shuddered at all the regulations and restrictions that this would entail and quit his position. Just in time, too. A boom of unbelievable proportions was about to explode in Moose Jaw, and every minute of his working day would be devoted to wheeling and dealing in land.

The Grayson wealth was reflected in the houses they built during this period. In August 1904, John Hawke, Adela, and their two children, Garnet and Ellen, moved into a new home at 435 Main Street, right across from where the Zion Methodist Church would be built three years later. Of red brick and Manitoba stone, the Grayson abode was a two-storey affair, very Victorian, with a turret circling one corner. It was a solid, respectable home, but it was to sit in the shadow of another edifice across the street at 30 Stadacona – William Grayson's opulent residence.

Built in 1913, it was an example of what author James Gray described as, "the competition of the new rich to outdo each other in the size and magnificence of their mansions." There was little such competition in Moose Jaw; William Grayson won hands down.

This Grayson house was a huge three-storey affair constructed of South Dakota brick. Inside, it gleamed with highly polished oak – oak floors, baseboards, panelling. A stained-glass window, imported from England, looked onto a landing, from which the stairway grandly swept down on two sides to the huge entrance hall. The living and dining rooms displayed Italian-made crystal fixtures and elaborate sculptured brick fireplaces, and a central vac system, one of the first in Canada, was installed. It was in the lovely solarium on the east side of the house that Mrs. Grayson served tea on her Thursday afternoon "At Homes." Her guests were treated to the best of everything: Coalport china, the best sterling-silver flatwear, music from a baby grand in the drawing room, imported French furniture decorated with gold leaf.

If ever there was a Lord of the Manor, it was William Grayson. Dressed in formal attire, complete with top hat and a gold-headed walking cane, he seemed the embodiment of WASP virtues – industry, temperance, and moral certitude. "He certainly put the fear of God into little boys' hearts," Len Durham, who grew up in Moose Jaw, recalls. That Grayson was Moose Jaw's Crown Attorney for many years may have had something to do with his forbidding image.

Grayson prosecuted every kind of criminal, from the farmer caught stealing his neighbour's tomatoes to a mother who killed her baby. His most famous case, however, involved Hong Wing, owner of a Moose Jaw restaurant. He was charged with having two white women in his employ. That the women were well treated by Hong, received a decent wage, and wanted to work at his restaurant mattered not at all. He was transgressing laws that had just been passed in the Saskatchewan legislature that prohibited white women from being employed by Orientals. Grayson put forth a well-reasoned case, and Hong Wing was found guilty and fined five dollars. The two women lost their jobs.

William Grayson was made a King's Counsel in 1914, and other honours soon flowed: in one year he was elected president of the Saskatchewan benchers, and vice-president of the Saskatchewan Law Society. Rumours circulated that he was about to be appointed to the bench, but this never materialized. Possibly he was never offered a judgeship: he was at his prime when a Conservative government was entrenched in Ottawa, and they certainly would not have appointed a dyed-in-the-wool Grit like Grayson. But it is most likely he turned down the honour. Sitting on the bench would have silenced him politically, and thereby put an end to one of his greatest pleasures.

There were two pillars in William Grayson's life, the Zion Methodist Church – he could see its squat dome from his bedroom window – and the Liberal Party. Indeed William Grayson *was* the Liberal party in Moose Jaw.

"No Liberal gathering would be complete without a few words

from William Grayson," a young Liberal once said. It didn't matter which political pre-eminence the banquet was honouring, Grayson either introduced the speaker, was the speaker himself, gave the thank-you speech, or, at the very least, toasted the king. He sometimes went fishing with Walter Scott, the Liberal premier of the province from 1905 to 1916. Scott's successor, William Martin, stayed at the Grayson home whenever he was in Moose Jaw, as did his successor, Charles Dunning. Grayson presided over a grand banquet for Prime Minister Wilfrid Laurier on his western tour in 1910, and he did the same thing for Prime Minister Mackenzie King eleven years later. And while Moose Jaw didn't always cooperate by electing the Liberal of Grayson's choice, these contacts made him a most powerful player in party politics, not only in Moose Jaw but in the province.

After his one-year fling as mayor, he never again ran for any office except chairman of the school board. That position he held for thirty consecutive years. He did a good job; Moose Jaw was known to have one of the better school systems in the province. Towards the end, however, when teachers rebelled against their pay, which was about what an indentured servant could expect, Grayson was criticized for being too tight with money. "Among the teachers," he admitted, "I have come to be regarded as a 'bad man' of the board, the one who sits on the lid of the cash box." But he added, "the tax dollar can only be stretched so far." Interestingly, year after year, he was the one who screamed the loudest and longest that his property taxes were too high.

Being school-board chairman gave Grayson a soapbox. There wasn't an event in Moose Jaw in which he didn't participate. On the coronation of George V, William Grayson addressed a thousand students, all waving Union Jacks. "There is no British empire today than that which I see on the stand before me now, even though at the crest of the empire the gorgeous coronation spectacle is in progress." In the same capacity he made a similarly fuzzy speech when the governor-general, the Duke of Devonshire, came to Moose Jaw. And at the reception committee for Lady Byng, and at the banquet for Lieutenant-Governor

Brown, and at the dinner for Brigadier-General George Tuxford, and on and on.

Mrs. William Grayson – only a few close friends called her Ellen – was also highly thought of in society. When Mrs. J. A. Sheppard, wife of the speaker of the Saskatchewan legislature, held a formal luncheon for the wives of the lieutenant-governor, of the premier, of the members of parliament, of the members of the legislature, and of the ministers and deputy-ministers and judges, Mrs. Walter Scott, the wife of the premier, poured the coffee first, of course, but Mrs. William Grayson of Moose Jaw poured second.

After each of her eight children was born, Ellen had grown a little stouter, until, in her forties, she was a very substantial woman indeed.

She loved to give teas for any kind of charitable cause: the Red Cross during war time – "We bring our knitting and thimbles and keep our hands busy knitting or sewing for our valiant boys on the front," she told a *Moose Jaw Times* reporter in 1915 – the YWCA occasionally, but most often the Ladies Aid of the Zion Methodist Church. When it became fashionable to join women's committees of political parties, Mrs. Grayson was still relegated to pouring the tea. She was happy to leave weighty matters such as politics to her husband, she declared.

After their children were grown, the Graysons developed a passion for travel. They often visited the Maritimes and the eastern U.S. seaboard. They took cruises to Alaska and Honolulu. They went on grand tours to South America, to Europe, to the Orient. His travels allowed William Grayson to add to his art collection – the third passion, beside the Liberal Party and the Zion Church, in his life.

When he arrived in Moose Jaw in 1883, he had carried with him three watercolours by W. L. Judson, an early Canadian artist. Thereafter, he accumulated an eclectic hodge podge – everything from the massive piece *Highland Cattle* by the British painter Lucy Kemp-Welsh to the Canadian Paul Peel's *Milk Maid*. By the time he died in 1926, he had collected 130 valuable oils and watercolours, which his estate hoped to present to the people of Moose Jaw. But the city was too cheap to provide money for a suitable gallery, and the works were dispersed among his heirs. "That would have hurt him terribly that they didn't care enough to cough up that little bit of money after all he had done for that town," says a relative. His financier's sensibility would have been offended too; today the collection would be worth a great deal of money.

The other Graysons who lived around the corner on Main Street were also influential people in Moose Jaw society, but they displayed a very different style. John Hawke was a power in the Liberal party and he often served as the president or the treasurer of the Moose Jaw Association, but he seldom made public appearances and rarely gave speeches. His work was done in the backrooms of politics.

After the Moose Jaw boom fizzled out, and the real-estate market collapsed in 1913, John Hawke returned to his first love: cattle ranching. By 1930 he owned twelve and a half sections (8,000 acres) of farm and pasture land, including his original ranch at Old Wives Lake, south of Moose Jaw. This made him one of the biggest ranchers in the Canadian West.

In the early days, ranchers and stock men in the Moose Jaw area had trouble making money because of transportation costs; there were no stockyards in Moose Jaw, and all the cattle had to be shipped to St. Boniface, Manitoba. In 1919, the provincial government passed legislation setting up the Southern Saskatchewan Co-Operative Stockyards. John Hawke Grayson was chosen the first president, and was elected to the same job every year thereafter until 1933, the year before he died. It was exactly the right position for him: it gave him power and prestige among the people he liked best – the down-to-earth ranchers and farmers – and he was away from the public eye.

There was a shadow in his life, however, and that was his marriage to Adela. Over the years the two seemed to have become estranged. They lived in different worlds; his centred around cow-punchers and capitalists, hers around the Ladies Aid of the Zion Methodist Church, and the two spheres seldom overlapped. Their agenda of social activities was busy and interesting, but seldom did they appear together at the same event. (Except at church service, of course.) They travelled extensively, but usually not with each other. He would take holidays in places like Florida with an old crony, she would tour Europe with a friend.

Adela Grayson's world revolved almost entirely around the Zion Church. She was a frequent lecturer at the ladies bible class; she went to all the silver teas to raise money for the Women's Missionary Society. She had a reputation for being exceptionally devout, and, as the years went by, she was regarded as something of a biblical scholar, especially after she toured the Holy Land and prepared a two-hour presentation that she would give to any group that asked. Once, speaking at an Old Timers' banquet, she put forth her philosophy of religion. Christianity, she maintained, had rolled westward from Europe, bringing culture and progress in its wake. Prosperity and civilization had become firmly rooted in the prairie soil because the pioneers had brought the gospel with them. She didn't mention that, in the process, the Métis and Indians of the country had been disinherited, that her family's fortune had been made on the backs of people who had been conquered and disillusioned, or that her husband was one of the most unscrupulous "scrip farmers" in all the Canadian West.

THE
FARMERS

Smith

14-16-25 W2

NW	NE
SW	SE
NW	NE
SW	SE

Benjamin Smith
1903-1911

11-16-25 W2

Maybe because he worked harder, he accumulated more land than anyone else in the district. With the machines he passionately loved, he broke, seeded, and harvested more earth than most people thought humanly possible. In later life, his reward for such toil was only a tormenting doubt about whether it had all been worth while.

Benjamin Smith was not an unscrupulous man. "Poverty unimpeached is more to be desired than wealth stained with dishonour," his Methodist faith preached, and he believed the dictum. It was true that he used half-breed script to gain title to the southwest quarter of 14-16-25 W2, Dougald Carmichael's pre-emption, but compared to what speculators like John Hawke Grayson had doled out to the Métis, he'd paid a decent price: $800. That six months later, in order to purchase more land, he had taken out a mortgage with the Trust and Loan Company of Canada for $7,000 on the same one-quarter section, indicating just how much the property was worth – well, wasn't that how one prospered as a farmer in the Canadian North-West?

And it was because he was the quintessential farmer, who believed that industry, thrift, and perseverance, not unearned profits, were what would tame the wild prairie land, that he couldn't be considered in the same category as John Hawke, a man he didn't much like. But while Benjamin Smith honoured the God-given capability of the rich black-brown earth to produce wheat, he was determined to make it profitable – even if he killed himself with work in the process.

Ben Smith had married the right kind of woman for such a dedicated farmer. Sarah Smith was large in body and long in endurance. A few of their eight children took after their father, slight, fair, and tough as guy wire; others were more like her, large, handsome, with dramatic black eyebrows and raven hair.

Ben and Sarah had grown up within miles of each other in southwestern Ontario. Ben's parents, William and Annie Smith, had emigrated from Cornwall, the southern tip of England, in 1849. Their nine-week voyage, steerage class, was something of a nightmare, since their sixth baby was born during a storm at sea. The family often said that Harry's birth was a forewarning of Harry's life.

Once in Canada, the Smiths settled in Newcastle, Ontario, William working as a farmhand and labourer, Annie as an expert tailor. Ben was born there in 1852. Shortly afterwards the Smiths moved. They hewed eighty acres of free land from the bush in Arthur Township, Wellington County. There they milked dairy cows, grew a little wheat, and raised a family of nine children.

The village of Mount Forest, north of Arthur, was mostly a settlement of immigrants from Northern Ireland – Protestants who, as quickly as they built their barns, established lodges of the Loyal Order of the Orange. Indeed, the town of Arthur and the county itself were named after that illustrious Irishman, Arthur Wellesley, the Duke of Wellington. Though the Smiths were English, they shared the same patriotic enthusiasms.

Sarah Wilson's people were among the first group that had arrived from Ulster, and they owned a small farm only a few miles away from the Smiths'. Sarah's grandson, Russell Filson, thinks there remained a bit of Black Irish in his grandmother. "I have the impression that she was close to the old Irish sod, that superstition was deeply ingrained. You know, 'You only cut your daughter's hair by the light of the moon and so on.'"

Sarah and Benjamin were married in 1881 in the tiny village of Moorefield, where one of the first Methodist churches in Wellington County had been built five years before, a building as solid and uncompromising as the religion itself. The couple's first child, George Harry, arrived the following year.

Since there were five sons in the Smith family, the small farm at Mount Forest could hardly provide a future for all of them. Benjamin believed all the propaganda about the North-West and, in 1882, he and his brother-in-law, Richard Wilson, went to Winnipeg, where they were hired by the CPR. They laboured on a work gang as the railway snaked its way westward, but quit as soon as they got as far west as Pile of Bones (Regina). Benjamin had saved $400 – enough, he felt, to start farming. As well, another brother-in-law, Alex Wilson, had already made the trip out west with Ben's childhood friend, Andy Dalgarno, travelling on the railway until it ended at Brandon. Alex and Andy had then loaded their few possessions, including a plough, into a creaky ox-cart and headed west. *En route*, they had run into Moose Jaw's earliest settler, Jud Battell, who told them that the best farmland – no rocks, heavy soil – was located just west of Moose Jaw Bone Creek. Most of the new arrivals from Wellington County, including Benjamin Smith, located their homesteads near a CPR whistle-stop that some-one with great expectations had named Boharm, after Lord Strathcona's magnificent home in Scotland. Boharm was situated to the northwest of Moose Jaw; a diagonal line could be drawn through the town to Pasqua on the southeast, and to Carmichael's place, for he was homesteading at the same time.

Benjamin Smith staked out the southwest quarter of 20-17-27 2nd Meridian, northwest of Boharm, in an area which came to be called the Pioneer School District. He then returned to collect his wife and children in Ontario.

The Smiths were a tightly-knit family, devoted to Methodism, who became prominent in their community – eventually a main street in the town of Arthur would be named after them – by doing charitable work. Saying goodbye was not easy. Ben was particularly close to Harry, his older brother by three years; the two had shared dreams of the great Canadian West since their youth. But while Ben remained determined to pull up stakes, Harry Smith only talked about it. He finally admitted that his wife had refused. "Janet has put her foot down. Says she has no intention of roughing it in the bush, never mind that I've explained to her that there is no bush." Harry opened a butcher shop and bakery in Mount Forest instead, but the two brothers remained close, writing often.

In the spring of 1883 Ben and Sarah Smith and their infant son were able to travel all the way to Moose Jaw on the railway. By April 1 they had built their fourteen-by-twenty foot shack and were breaking the land.

The Smiths suffered all the hardships and all the tribulations that Dougald and Rebecca Carmichael had undergone while they lived on their Pasqua farm. In 1883 Ben Smith managed to clear and cultivate only ten acres of land, and while he sweated, he learned that wheat prices had dropped through the floor. That winter he worked at odd jobs in Moose Jaw and managed to save enough money to buy three cows, a pony, and a pig. In

1884, he broke another twenty acres, cultivated thirty, only to see the wheat shrivel in the August heat. He was saved from financial ruin by a neighbouring farmer who had arrived in the West with far more money than Smith had, and who hired him to help break his land.

Like the Carmichael brothers, Ben Smith carted for Colonel William Otter during the North-West Rebellion of 1885. Unlike the Carmichaels, who returned to farm after Battleford was liberated, Smith realized what a godsend $10 a day was, and continued to haul ammunition for the Colonel, who was recklessly chasing the Cree and Assiniboine northwards. On May 2, 1885, Otter's militia confronted the Indians at Cut Knife Creek. The freighters, including Ben Smith, were crossing the creek when the warriors opened fire.

Jud Battell, who by this time had become a close friend of Ben Smith's, later recalled what happened. "When I heard the shots, I stood up and shielded my eyes to see if I could see anything. Just then Captain French came riding hard back down the hill. 'For God's sake,' he shouted. 'If you don't want to all be killed, get up to the top of the hill.' Even as he spoke, zing, a bullet went past me on one side. Zing, another on the other. I leaped right out on to the wagon tongue and crouched down between the two horses while I laid on the whip from left to right. We galloped to the top of the hill."

One freighter was killed, another wounded, but Jud Battell and Ben Smith arrived back in Moose Jaw safely by mid-June. Benjamin managed to crop thirty acres of wheat. Unlike Dougald Carmichael, he did not spend the money he made carting in the rebellion on making his ramshackle house more comfortable; instead, he bought seven horses, five of them hefty Clydesdales. "Now we can truly begin to farm," he told Sarah.

The spring of 1886 he broke another twenty-five acres and seeded forty, but drought – ten days of hot wind which shrivelled even the gooseberries on the bush and also drove Dougald Carmichael to despair – unleashed utter devastation. "Previously we had managed to obtain water digging holes near the sloughs, but even that failed us," Ben Smith reported home. Many of the early homesteaders, including Dougald

Carmichael, fled the prairie, never to recover from their experience on "the abominable flat land."

Calling it quits was never even discussed by the iron-willed Methodists Benjamin and Sarah Smith. They merely joined the exodus from the Moose Jaw area that winter, herding their livestock south of Mortlach, where a little hay and water were available. They spent a miserable winter, in which blizzards were so frequent they couldn't even collect their mail, in a hastily built and holey – "Certainly not holy," said Sarah – shack.

But the next spring the government supplied free seed, and the Smiths were back at it. It rained that season, but the ground was so dry it soaked up the moisture like an unrepentant alcoholic. The crop was only fair, but there was a crop and some money resulting from it. That fall Benjamin applied for the patent on his homestead.

~ II ~

In 1888 weather conditions were almost perfect; good farmers like Benjamin Smith were getting thirty-five bushels of wheat to an acre, and the price soared to $1.10 per bushel. This was all Smith needed to get on his feet. From that time on, although there would be terrible years of drought and depression during the 1890s, the family prospered.

In the spring of 1888, Benjamin was informed that he had proved up on his 160-acre homestead. Five months later he entered for a second homestead, SW1/4 of 6-18-27 W2, two miles to the north of his first. From then on he acquired land, whenever he had extra cash or could find a mortgage company that would lend him money. Twelve years later he would proudly show anyone who was interested deeds to close to four sections, 2,400 acres; an enormous amount of land for that time, almost all of which he cultivated himself.

Although he was a small man physically, Ben Smith was a farmer made of the right stuff. In 1884, when so many of his neighbours were giving up on the prairies, frightened to death their families would starve, he had performed a little feat that the government's propaganda brochures bragged about for years. "Press of Ontario, please notice. Benj. Smith, of this place, sowed ten acres of wheat on December 2nd. Can your Province do as well? Remember this is the country where [supposedly] the weather is so cold that people cannot put their noses out of doors for six months in the year."

"He would milk out a cow that was just fighting. He didn't put kickers on her or anything. He just put his head down, one hand clamped between her hind legs, held her hind end up and milked her. He knew no fear," recalls Russell Filson, Ben Smith's grandson. He was talking about his father, but, he adds, it could easily describe his grandfather too. "Some years he didn't have enough money to hire a man, so he'd do two men's work. He'd start his outfit at five and work them until noon. We'd take out another team and while he ate his lunch, we'd change horses in the binder. He'd go back at it until dinner and then we'd rotate the horses again and he'd work until it was too dark to see and he was so exhausted he could hardly walk to the bedroom."

All that work meant nothing, if, on an August day just when the farmer decided the kernels were divinely golden and turned to gearing up his harvester, a hailstorm attacked. The terror that came with having no control over one's destiny, of being a small puppet on that vast flat stage, was what had driven Dougald Carmichael from his prairie farm. Benjamin Smith believed he had found the weapon by which he could do battle with a hostile environment – scientifically designed equipment, the bigger, the mightier, the better, was the answer, and Smith, who had a knack for the mechanical, became obsessed with his machinery.

As quickly as his financial circumstances allowed, he snapped up the newest in farm implements: the effective steel ploughs called sulky gangs, pulled by teams of four and six horses; the efficient press drill that dropped the seed and covered it; the wonderful binders that cut and tied at the same time; and "the most astonishing of modern machines," as the Moose Jaw Times put it, "the steam thresher, which moves like some monster with a life of its own from one group of stacks to another, magically separating the wheat from the chaff, spitting out the refuse and then eating it again as fuel."

Machinery was the farmer's future, no doubt about that. When the topic under debate at the Mutual Improvement Society was the value of horses versus machines, Ben Smith said that although he appreciated his huge Clydesdales – they were as much part of his culture as the Orange Lodge and the Methodist Church – he could see a time when the work-horse would disappear altogether. The other farmers laughed and chortled and booed and hissed. "There'll never be a day when my King and Queen won't be more reliable than some finicky contraption," said George Beesley.

When, in 1891, a brass band turned up at the Massey-Harris Implement Shed in Moose Jaw to pipe in the forty-one binders that had been ordered by neighbouring farmers, Benjamin Smith took part in the parade and the "sumptuous spread" laid out at the Brunswick Hotel afterwards. "This may be taken as evidence of the prosperity of the district," said Smith, toasting the future. Everyone joined in.

In 1890, Benjamin Smith and his old friend from Ontario, Andy Dalgarno, had gone into business together. Although born in Wellington County, Dalgarno, a tall, thin, hawk-nosed man, never forgot his Scottish ancestors; a picture taken at the turn of the century shows him proudly attired in an authentic kilt and tam. He had a quick temper – "He had big feet and he used them," his son Ken Dalgarno remembers – but he got over his anger just as quickly. Although he was Presbyterian and a loyal Liberal, while Ben Smith was Methodist and a staunch Conservative, the two men could still agree on everything related to farming. They took every cent they had, borrowed some money from the Hitchcock & McCulloch bank, secured by their land, and bought an L. D. Sawyer, 16-horsepower, straw-burning steam engine for $400. The engine itself was not tractable; it had to be pulled into the fields by horses. But what it did do was run the Reliance Separator, the threshing machine that more than anything else turned the Canadian prairies into the breadbox of the world. Looking like a great puffing dinosaur, it ate up the sheaves as fast as the men could feed it, and then blew the straw, chaff, and dust into barn-sized piles.

Dalgarno and Smith were among the first in the Moose Jaw district to own a steam-threshing outfit, and families from all over came to admire it. Although it was a rather primitive machine, with no blower attached, Smith loved its shiny red, black, and green body. When he could get it running smoothly, it hummed like a cat whose belly was being rubbed. Sitting atop the beast he could feel its strength rumbling, a power that, by his own mastery, he himself could harness.

Harvesting the wheat on Dalgarno's and Smith's own farms was only a small part of the steam-thresher's job; such was the financial investment, that custom jobs for neighbouring farmers, at three cents per bushel threshed from the stack, five cents from the stook, were essential if bankruptcy was to be avoided. (Once, after the steam engine had overheated and been shut down for the second time in a morning, Andy Dalgarno called out to Ben Smith, "I heard there's a special ward in the mental hospital for chaps like us who crack up under the strain of coddlin' these damn brutes.")

The harvesting was done during the day, the travelling by night. As the owners of the outfit, Smith and Dalgarno had to arrange everything: purchasing and delivering fuel, locating good water – if it was too full of minerals it clogged up the machine's plumbing – performing endless, complicated repairs, and, most important, keeping happy their crew of short-tempered, complaining men. Since Ben Smith was something of a mechanical genius, he often acted as engineer, but another half-dozen hired hands were needed: the firemen, the tankers, the hands to haul the water and the straw, the men to feed the sheaves into the machine, others to haul the grain away. There was a shortage of skilled workers around Moose Jaw. Many Easterners who used working on harvest gangs as a way of looking around for some good land at the same time, had given up on the West as a place of prosperity. Smith and Dalgarno had to be as persuasive and patient as diplomats to keep one or another of the hired hands from blowing his stack and quitting. This wasn't such a problem for quiet, even-tempered Smith; but for someone with as short a fuse as Dalgarno – well, his tongue was raw from biting it.

They were, of course, under pressure to complete all their jobs before the first frost. The farmers who anxiously awaited their arrival were all friends, so that the fate of their harvest, and consequently their future prosperity, rested heavily on the two men's shoulders. The case of Mrs. Maria Latham, who owned the half-section adjoining the Smith property to the west, was an example. One of the few women in the area who farmed alone, she was an attractive and rather alluring widow called Queen Lady Farmer by her neighbours. So anxious was Ben Smith to help Mrs. Latham, that "he'd thrash her wheat first even if Queen Victoria herself was in need," as Sarah Smith caustically pointed out. In November of 1891, the *Moose Jaw Times* praised Dalgarno and Smith for their diligence in harvesting Mrs. Latham's crop, pointing out that they had thrashed 8,500 bushels of wheat and 2,000 of oats. Mrs. Latham made $420, Smith and Dalgarno $315.

Despite such satisfactions, the threshing operation was exhausting, nerve-wracking work. From late August to December, the two men often wouldn't sleep for days on end. They'd go without meals, and a bath was a rarity. Ben Smith, who had always been thin to begin with, "could have sat in for the scarecrow out in Mother's garden," according to his daughter. But neither he nor Andy Dalgarno would let up until the hard frost settled in. They were making money, and in a country where "cash was in as short a supply as udders on a bull," what else mattered?

~ III ~

In the winter of 1891, a large package from Eaton's department store in Toronto addressed to the Smith family arrived in Moose Jaw. Since Benjamin had ordered it, he knew what the box contained and hurriedly rode to the CPR station to retrieve it. He had expected his wife to be overjoyed and was a little disappointed when, as the gift was unwrapped, she was strangely quiet. But Sarah Smith knew what the expensive sewing machine – "The New Empress" as Eaton's catalogue described it; "Excellence of Design, Simplicity of Management, Ease of Operation" – would mean: more work, more bother. Not only would her girls now want fashionable frocks, but she knew she would be at the beck and call of neighbours and relatives with curtains or nightgowns or shirts which needed mending on the amazing "foot-treadle machine." And Sarah Smith was already so overburdened.

She had still been breast-feeding Harry when the Smiths came West, and she gave birth to Minnie in 1884, Albert in 1887, Fanny in 1889, Nancy in 1891. (Followed in the next eight years by Norman, Gordon, and Bill.) While the original frame house had been expanded and improved, it remained crowded and chaotic, because there were always extra people around; relatives, farmhands, neighbours. And of course, large-boned Sarah was not one to shirk her farm duties. She kept a garden full of vegetables, which she canned and bottled in the fall; she dutifully looked after her chickens and cows; and she churned butter that was certainly presentable. Sometimes she felt that her Irish peasant roots were as obvious as her big feet; she had not, like Mrs. Mackenzie, won the fancy-sofa-pillow award at the agricultural fair. Nor was she able, like Mrs. Green, to paint flowers on silk, or decorate her table with beautifully embroidered cloths as Mrs. Getty always did. Still, she had placed second in the darning-old-socks competition; her Irish stew with turnips and dumplings was cherished by the often-ravenous harvesting crew; and the bacon she smoked herself was so tasty that she got fourteen cents per pound compared with the eleven cents the butcher managed. But she knew that her most important attribute was her ability to endure her ambitious, driven husband.

Both Sarah and Benjamin were raised on the same uncompromising beliefs of evangelical Methodism. Self-discipline was the key. Man may have been born "altogether corrupt and abominable, full of pride," but he had also been blessed with self-will and was therefore responsible for his own spiritual health, to accept or reject God's grace, to strive unceasingly towards "perfection." It was essential "to overcome one's sensual appetites and desires," which, in the strait-laced Smith household where carnal thoughts would be a shock, meant being lazy and not doing your chores when you were supposed to. It was the proper faith for the pioneer, whose very survival depended on his or her willpower, on his or her faith that the exhausting labours would be rewarded by God. But it wasn't much fun.

One cold December night the entire Smith family crowded into the Zion Methodist Church in Moose Jaw to hear a visiting evangelic preacher rail at them. The Reverend Hunter bellowed all evening. If he was to save their souls, they must banish the three evil Bs from their lives. The *Billiard Room* was to be avoided at all costs, not because of "the actual harm in it but because of its associations." The *Ballroom* too – "How under heaven women can allow dirty, devilish rascals to put their arms around them and swing them around is more than I can understand." But the worst of all was the *Barroom* – "The back kitchen where the devil does all his dirty work, the last station on the road to Hell." Evangelist Hunter concluded his sermon with a thunder from the pulpit: "May God save this city from the curse of strong drink!"

Not only was Methodism the Smiths' religion, it was also the focus of their social life. One rainy evening in May 1901, the little Wesley Church of Pioneer hosted the annual meeting of the Moose Jaw Mission band. Everyone applauded when third daughter, Nancy Smith, sang a duet with her cousin, George Wilson, while second daughter, Fanny Smith, played the organ. First son, Harry Smith, and second son, Albert, both members of the Epworth League of Christian Endeavours, took up a collection "for mission work among the savage Indians." Afterwards, first daughter, Minnie, and second daughter, Fanny, served tea and the delicious raisin buns they had helped their mother bake. The evening ended, of course, with "God Save the King."

Such entertainments in the Pioneer district were innocent enough, but there was a darker side to evangelical Methodism. In his sermons, the Reverend W. C. Bunt (who also administered to Moose Jaw and Caron) was emphatic about the church's goals. "We must throw our whole-hearted support into the campaign to convert foreigners into English-speaking, Christian citizens who will be clean, educated and loyal to the Dominion and to the Greater Britain." He was only echoing the dictates of his church. "The foreigners have brought with them very low standards of morality, propriety and decency." Such Anglophilia naturally bred contempt both for the French language and the Catholic church. And the Orange Lodge, which went hand in hand with Methodism, inflamed the intolerance.

Benjamin Smith chaired the meeting of the Loyal Orange Order, Moose Jaw County, in which a resolution was unanimously passed that no man in that hall would vote for anybody who had a good word to say about the Roman Catholic Church, Frenchmen, or separate schools. And such was the newspaper play about the resolution that every politician in the vicinity took note.

It was only natural that Benjamin would belong to the Orange Order; in Arthur, where he had grown up, almost every Protestant male over twenty-one did.

Founded in 1795 to commemorate the defeat of the Catholic James II by the Protestant William of Orange, fondly called King Billy by his devotees, at the Battle of the Boyne in 1690, the Loyal Orange Order became the main link between the British government and the Irish Protestants, who acted as the volunteer militia during the Irish insurrection of 1798. Orangemen who migrated to Britain and then to North America found the order an effective way to carry on their cultural traditions. In Canada, the Orangeman's orange and black sash became a symbol, in a society that was developing into a cultural mosaic, of unthinking bigotry. As the Conservative MP and dedicated Orange brother T. S. Sproule said, "Canada is today the dumping ground for the refuse of every country in the world."

In 1895 Ben Smith was chosen to represent the Boharm district at the fifth annual meeting of the Manitoba and North-West Territories Orange Order in Medicine Hat. (Travelling with him was the Deputy Grand Master of Moose Jaw County, Tom McWilliams, the man Dougald Carmichael claimed had cheated him on the land with the valuable pottery clay.) As usual, the deliberations were replete with secret passwords and signs, elaborate and mysterious rituals, prayers, and readings from the scriptures. So clandestine was the society that Ben Smith wouldn't even tell his own children what went on, although they were dying of curiosity.

What the Loyal Orange Order meant to them was that wonderful day in July, the glorious twelfth, when the victory of the Boyne was once again celebrated. They relished the parade: fat old King Billy seated on a beautiful white filly; the Stoney Beach band blasting away; young girls and their mothers dressed in gingham and crowded into wagons decorated with garlands of paper flowers and the Union Jack, pulled by horses especially chosen for their magnificent girth. They loved the annual picnic at Caron, with the soccer and baseball games, and the three-legged races, the flirting, and the mounds of food – Sarah Smith was always praised for the scores of blueberry pies she had baked. They not-so-patiently listened to the Rev. Mr. Morrison droning on, "When a man, a society or a nation ceases to care for aught save selfish interests, the doom of that man, society, and nation is sealed." They cheered for "Grand Old British Liberty." Of course, they had little understanding that the celebration was merely a flexing of the muscles of the all-powerful majority, a thumbing of noses at the orthodox Ukrainian immigrant and his ilk, who were just beginning to flood into the prairies. The bigotry of the Orange Order and the intolerance of the Methodist Church encouraged such prejudice and resentment that, twenty years later, a chapter of the Ku Klux Klan would take root and flourish for a brief and inglorious time in the Moose Jaw area.

But the aspect of the Loyal Orange Order that appealed to Smith was not its bigotry but its concern for the welfare of those in the brotherhood. And his Methodism was not that of Preacher Hunter and his banning of the "three Bs." It was the idea of the social gospel. Christianity should concern itself with worldly affairs, as much as with the spiritual matters, he believed. When a visiting preacher from Nova Scotia said, "Public office, the social and political business of the country, must be brought under the Commandments and the Sermon on the Mount," Ben Smith couldn't agree more.

It was natural, then, that he was one of the founders of the Boharm and District Branch of the Farmers' Mutual Improvement Society. It was at the Smith house that the guest expert from the Ontario Agricultural College lectured on "Smut and Its Treatment in England." Afterwards, Benjamin demonstrated his latest invention, a "machine that brings sure death to gophers." It was basically an iron pipe with a lever sticking up from the middle; one end was stuffed into the gopher's hole, the other was filled with sulphur and dry prairie grass. This was lit, and the smoke was pumped into the gopher's burrow, suffocating the animals. As Ben's son Harry pointed out, the farmer's kids could still get hold of the gopher's tail, and so still be able to collect the bounty offered by the government. Sarah urged her husband to patent the gopher-killing contraption, and he went so far as to find an agent to market the device, but somehow it never made the fortune Sarah was hoping for. "You've lent it to so many people, why would they want to buy one of their own?" she chided.

"The real reason these contraptions aren't terribly popular is not only can't the little beasties stand the stink, neither can any human being within ten miles," put in Andy Dalgarno.

Benjamin Smith could be imposed upon to do almost anything in the interest of his community. Although he was a man of few words and hated arguments of any kind, he agreed one February evening in 1891 to participate in the semi-annual Mutual Improvement Society's debate. On the first question, "That mixed farming is more profitable than all grain growing," he argued in the the negative and won. But on the resolution "Total prohibition is preferable to a licence system for the North-West Territories," Smith argued that the demon rum would never be stamped out, and if taverns were licenced to sell liquor, at least there'd be some control. He not only lost the debate, but Sarah was appalled at his performance (which she didn't actually see but later heard about). The Methodist Church had declared that consuming alcohol of any kind was a sin. Why was her husband embarrassing her? Benjamin's reply is not known, but he probably muttered something about being his own man.

For two terms, 1889 and 1890, Ben Smith had served as president of the Moose Jaw Agricultural Society, and he got into hot water because he believed that desperate farmers should be helped. The society had been formed as early as July 1884 "for the purpose of advancing the interest of the farmers in the Moose Jaw district and of agriculture in general." By 1889 its only achievement was to have organized exhibitions – basically competitions offering prize money for the best Herefords, dairy produce, or canned fruits.

Smith felt the society should do more than hold fairs, and during his tenure as president he steered it in a different direction. In 1890 the board voted to loan money to farmers who had suffered such poor harvests that they couldn't afford to buy their own seed. Many members were furious that the society had thus incurred a loss of $274.90, and the North-West Territories Council threatened to cut the Society's grant. Even though the debt had been almost entirely paid back by the farmers during the following year, Benjamin Smith left the presidency under a cloud, although he remained a director of the society for many years to come.

~ IV ~

The year 1891 produced a bumper crop, and over the winter farmers were crowing that the next decade would at last belong to the Great North-West. Once again their optimism was misplaced. The following three years brought devastating drought. "Last year we had the hottest and driest season I have seen, and I have been in this country for thirteen years," wrote someone who signed himself "An Old Settler" in a letter to the *Moose Jaw Times*. "I venture to say there is not more than half a dozen farmers in the Moose Jaw district that have their seed to put in the land that they have cultivated." Old Settler wanted the CPR to provide free seed, because of "buckets of money the railway makes off the farmer in good years."

Not only was there terrible drought during the early 1890s, but freight costs soared and the price of wheat sank to thirty-five cents a bushel in 1894 (from $1.10 in 1888.) The government responded by allowing the farmers to take out seed-grain bonds, loans that were to be paid back with interest. Ben Smith himself was forced to resort to such aid in 1895 and 1896. Not only did the farmer have to put up his land as surety, but he also had to furnish two bondsmen, usually friends or relatives who were ordinary farmers like himself, as collateral security. If someone abandoned his farm, as many did during that period, a bondsman was stuck with a lien against his own property. While the government didn't usually foreclose on the farmer, it was impossible for him to get a patent for a second homestead or to mortgage or sell his land until he had paid off the bond with interest. "And it wasn't even his debt. He simply had feelings of compassion and humanity and came to the relief of his less fortunate neighbour," Benjamin Smith wrote in a petition to the government. He for one was furious at the government's total ignorance of, and insensitivity towards, prairie farmers.

Ben Smith was a dedicated Tory – he had been named a district vice-president when the Moose Jaw association was formed in February 1891 – and probably because of this he had been named postmaster of Boharm the same year, even though his house was located some miles northwest of the town, out of the way for many of the town's residents. During the drought period of the early 1890s, the extra money that this brought in was most welcome. Yet, despite such political plums, Ben Smith came to resent the ineptitude of Sir John A. Macdonald's government. The old party needed a good kick in the behind, Smith decided, and an organization with the strange name of the Patrons of Industry just might do it.

It had begun as an educational society in the United States, but once it crossed the border into Sarnia, Ontario, in 1887, and uncorked the righteous indignation which for years had been brewing against industrialists there, the Patrons of Industry quickly developed into a protest movement. It was an organization attractive to farmers, no matter what their political or religious stripes. Five years later it took root in Manitoba, and soon spread its tentacles into the North-West Territories.

The Smith family had been involved with the Grange in Ontario, an organization formed in the 1870s that attempted to make farmers more aware of their political strength, so the idea of organizing to protest was not new to them. In July 1894, Benjamin was elected the president of the Patrons' lodge in Caron, a town north of Boharm. He outlined the platform at the founding meeting in Moose Jaw. The British connection was to be maintained; government corruption was to be eliminated and spending curtailed; tariffs on farm implements and other equipment was to be removed; the Senate was to be abolished; the sale of liquor was to be prohibited; and – the idea that raised the most eyebrows – women were to be enfranchised. "If only I should live to see that day," retorted Sarah.

The Patrons had ideas more specifically to do with farming, which also appealed to Ben Smith: establishing farmer-owned grain elevators and flour mills; setting up provincial banks that would lend money at 5 per cent; and forcing the CPR to do something about the grass fires started by sparks from trains, an issue which had for years infuriated the people in the Boharm area.

Quickly, CPR-bashing became the Patrons' favourite sport. The farmers resented the fact that the company enjoyed a virtual monopoly in the West, and was free to set freight rates at "preposterously high levels." "Unless we can get our wheat to the eastern markets at reasonable cost, the whole country will be bankrupt," Ben Smith told the meeting. Before they knew it, the Patrons of Industry had turned into a political party.

The 1894 election for the North-West Territories Assembly was marked by a vicious campaign. Walter Scott, who owned the *Moose Jaw Times*, had supported the patrons until they took on one of his own class. Scott was furious that the Patrons would support Mac Annable, the popular rancher, and the man who had often fought the Moose Jaw establishment. Annable was set to run against Scott's friend, James H. Ross, who had sat on the territories' council for the last eleven years. The *Moose Jaw Times* accused Annable of everything from playing party politics (although the Patrons insisted they represented no party, and Ross was a well-known Liberal) to bribing the half-breeds of Willow Bunch. Ben Smith was one of those who nominated Annable and personally visited all forty voters living in the Pioneer district; Sarah held teas for the ladies, impressing them with her new Quadruple silver-plated tea set and tempting them with her famous homemade pies in the hope that they would plead Annable's cause with their husbands.

Since most of the problems that the patrons were complaining about fell under federal jurisdiction, Annable's allies were hard-pressed to uncover grievances with which to castigate Ross. But when he waffled slightly on total prohibition, suggesting the licencing system should be given a chance, the Patrons went on the attack. Ross, they declared, was a "pro-liquor man," a "whisky soak," "one who seeks to place liquor on every table to debauch innocent babes."

Ross's backers, of course, did not quietly sit back and take this. They were the élite of Moose Jaw – Arthur Hitchcock, William and John Hawke Grayson, Walter Scott – and they unleashed their powerful machine. They lashed out at Annable, calling him a "hayseed," "a most dreadful orator," a man whose contempt for "book-learning" made him quite unsuitable to represent the sophisticates of Moose Jaw.

Annable won in most of the rural polling stations, including the Boharm area where Ben Smith had campaigned so vigorously. But the Moose Jaw citizens rejected him by sixty-seven votes, and Ross was elected overall by a plurality of eighty-three. Given the forces lined up against Annable – the next year he would be made to pay for his impudence when Arthur Hitchcock tried to foreclose on his bank loan – Benjamin Smith thought Mac had done pretty well. (Annable did become an MLA in a 1901 by-election – he beat the Liberal Hitchcock.) But by now, it wasn't the election that upset Smith. His great hope for the future, the Patrons of Industry, was in danger of disintegrating. Everyone within the party seemed to be fighting with everyone else.

They fought over the Manitoba school issue, the Catholics supporting the federal government's position that separate schools be maintained in the province, Orangemen like Ben Smith opposing "such interference in provincial business." There were charges that certain politicians who were backed by the Patrons of Industry were corrupt. One had even accepted a free CPR pass, the greatest of all sins. And there were bitter personal feuds: Charles Braithwaite, the Patrons' grand president, slugged it out, verbally and otherwise, with the editor of the Patrons' *Advocate*. By the time the Tories called the federal election in the summer of 1896, Benjamin Smith, and many others, were confused and upset. They didn't much look forward to the campaign.

The Moose Jaw banker Arthur Hitchcock had first accepted the nomination for the Western Assiniboia constituency (which included both Regina and Moose Jaw) but he soon dropped out, supposedly for business reasons but in reality because William Grayson told him no Grit had a chance. His successor, J. A. Grant, manager of the huge Sarnia Ranch Company, also withdrew, fearing a split in the opposition would hand victory over to the incumbent Conservative, Nicholas Flood Davin, founder of the *Regina Leader*. The Patrons of Industry candidate, Jim McInnis, also a newspaper man from Regina, who owned the supposedly independent *Standard*, became Davin's only opposition.

Benjamin Smith was in a dilemma. He disapproved of the Tory record in Ottawa; as far as he was concerned, their much-touted national policy was doing everything for the fat-cat eastern manufacturers and little for the impoverished western farmer. On the other hand, he admired Nicholas Flood Davin as much as Dougald Carmichael did. And Benjamin did not personally like the Patrons of Industry's candidate Jim McInnis, whom he considered a Liberal in sheep's clothing.

By the end of the campaign Ben Smith wasn't saying much, and nobody knew which way he had gone, but certainly his vote counted. After a much disputed and complicated recount, McInnis and Davin were declared in a dead heat. A perspiring returning officer was then required to break the tie. After saying a prayer, he cast his ballot for Nicholas Flood Davin, who was declared the Member of Parliament for Western Assiniboia.

The Patrons of Industry fell apart after that, a victim of internal squabbling, self-interest, and political inexperience. Ben Smith was disturbed and upset by the disintegration of what he thought was going to represent farmer power in Ottawa, yet in his own way, he remained loyal to the Patrons' ideals. He became president of the Farmer's Commercial Union of Pioneer district, one of the first cooperatives in the West. Carloads of binder twine, flour, and apples were bought in bulk, thereby saving the members a lot of money. There was even talk of owning grain elevators and marketing the farmers' produce abroad. The union appealed to Ben's practical side, and he remained one of its chief promoters.

Ben Smith was a fiercely independent man – his very survival depended upon his own hard labour and on making his own decisions – and yet what appealed to him about the Patrons' movement was its advocacy of cooperation. If he had lived long enough, he might have been attracted to the social gospel of J. S. Woodsworth and Tommy Douglas, or he might have remained a radical Tory, a supporter of John Diefenbaker's agrarian movement. He was always proud that the farmers had flexed their muscles, and he wouldn't have been surprised that several such protest movements would rally, and succeed, in the future.

~ V ~

On November 3, 1899, the *Moose Jaw Times* announced, "Postmaster Ben Smith of Boharm has beaten the record so far." His wheat fields, 500 acres in all, had yielded an average of thirty-two bushels per acre, and some fields produced as much as forty-five and fifty bushels. "His oats so far has averaged over 60 bushels, some going as high as the much coveted 100 mark."

By the turn of the century, Ben Smith was considered one of the most successful farmers in the entire North-West. The *Moose Jaw Times* reporter who had been assigned to "Pay a Flying Visit to Rural Districts" was impressed with Smith's spread, which consisted of a huge barn, a stable made of fieldstones, a two-storey house with a wing and annex, a machine shed, a blacksmith shop, and a cow stable. As well as his eldest son, Smith hired three men to work the farm.

There was one stroke of bad luck during that glorious year of 1901. Ben Smith liked to breed horses, and he kept thirty head, mostly Clydesdales. Sarah said he was foolish, because it cost so much, but that spring he had bought from Mac Annable an imported Clydesdale stallion, famous for its sexual prowess and appropriately named Atlas. "Will stand for mares for the season of 1901," Smith advertised in the *Moose Jaw Times*. But only two and a half months later the animal died of kidney infection. Smith thought the horse had had the disease when he bought it, and his friendship with Mac Annable, now an MLA, became a little strained. But Annable was soon vindicated. The following year Robin Adair, another of Smith's famous stallions, suddenly and mysteriously died. He was followed by King of the West, a valuable import from Brandon, which fell victim to a bowel blockage. By the end of the season, three others had succumbed to some disease or another, and since his stock now suffered from a bad reputation, Ben Smith decided to get out of the breeding business. Machines, at least, didn't get mysterious kidney ailments.

On a lovely May day in 1902, there was much excitement in the Smith household, much giggling and groaning. The *Illustrated Toronto Globe* had arrived, and there, spread out on the front page, was a large picture of the Smiths and their home-made steam ploughing machine. Standing in one wagon to the left, looking prim and severe, is Sarah. A gaggle of little kids stand in another wagon. Eldest son Harry, thin and wiry as his father, is feeding coal to the engine, and Benjamin sits under the odd-looking canopy of the plough, which offered protection against the sun, as though he were a king surveying his vast realm.

Years before he had dissolved his partnership with Andy Dalgarno and traded in the old non-tractable steam engine for an up-to-date J. I. Case model. It bothered him that the the 25-horsepower engine usually lay idle outside harvesting time. There must be a way of making it more profitable.

When the wealthy American settlers started flooding into the

Moose Jaw district, it didn't take Ben Smith long to figure how to help them break their land: attach a plough to the engine and go to it.

Sarah Smith was sorry he had ever come up with the idea. It meant that from spring to late fall there was never a respite from the gruelling work. Benjamin and Harry worked continuously doing custom plowing, as did Sarah, feeding her family and the crew. Then harvest time came. By 1901 the Smiths owned so much land that it was a nightmare getting the crop in before freeze-up. It seemed to Sarah that, as their fiftieth birthdays approached, they were working harder then ever.

But as Ben pointed out to her, their wealth made life a lot more pleasant. Elegant chenille curtains, porcelain vase-lamps hand-painted with wild flowers, a fancy upholstered rocker, lovely chromos of German pastoral scenes with agate frames, a cabinet clock in a fine oak case with an eight-day cathedral gong – all had been purchased in the hope of instilling a little elegance into Sarah's chaotic house.

Extra cash also meant the Smiths could travel, and several train trips were made to Ontario to visit Benjamin's and Sarah's families in Wellington County. In 1893, Ben and Sarah had arrived in Arthur in time for the laying of the foundation stone of the magnificent new Methodist church that was to be built at the corner of Smith and Frederick streets. The entire Smith clan was on hand to celebrate, but Benjamin was particularly glad to see Harry. The two brothers were still close; they had even named children after each other.

Harry and his wife, Janet, had seemed to be prospering. They still operated the butcher shop and bakery in Mount Forest, a few miles north of Arthur, and made enough to support their brood of children (nine by 1905). But in the winter of 1898 the building that housed Harry's businesses had burned to the ground. There was no insurance, and the family was close to destitution.

There was no question in Ben Smith's mind that his brother, even though he was already forty-eight years old, should start a new life out West. "I now possess a 27-horsepower steam plow, plows 15 acres a day. Sure be a help to you when you're breaking land," he wrote.

On April 6, 1900, the *Moose Jaw Times* had noted the arrival of "Mr. H. Smith of Mount Forest, Ontario, who has been attracted to the district by the great success of his brother, Mr. Benj. Smith, the well-known postmaster of Boharm. He has brought a carload of settlers' effects."

Harry's arrival meant a lot to Ben Smith. He enjoyed taking his brother into the John Deere dealership in Moose Jaw to examine all the latest machinery; Harry was suitably impressed. They drove over to the farm of F. W. Green, Ben's neighbour, and looked over his fantastic herd of thoroughbred Durham cattle. "Just as good as anything I've seen in Ontario," was Harry's observation. The two brothers were certainly kindred spirits.

Ben had found what he considered was a most suitable homestead for Harry: the southwest quarter of 4-16-25 W2, only two miles from where Dougald Carmichael had started farming. Harry immediately entered for it, and by mid-May all the males in the Smith family had pitched in to build the family's eighteen-by-twenty-four-foot frame house, which Sarah Smith helped furnish, and a barn. By seeding time, Harry had forty acres ploughed, and so was able to benefit from one of the wettest years in memory and the above-average crop that resulted.

The family seemed to fit in nicely. Janet found her neighbours warm and welcoming, and Harry became overseer of the Pasqua Improvement District and vice-president of the Pasqua Grain Growers' Association. There was only one serious problem: school was too far away. However, that was resolved when Petrolia School District was established in 1901, with Harry Smith as trustee.

But then the misfortune that had plagued the Harry Smith family for years struck again. Their eldest son, William, who was twenty-five years old, came down with tuberculosis; the disease wasted him for a year until he died in July 1904. The family was just getting over their grief when Harry became seriously ill. He was diagnosed as having Bright's Disease, an affliction of the kidneys (probably diabetes). Since it was assumed that the best medical attention could be obtained in the United States, the family began to travel back and forth between Spokane, Washington, and Pasqua, a shuttle that went on for years. This meant that Benjamin was often left to manage Harry's farm. Since he was now travelling out that way all the time anyway, he thought he might as well buy the prime quarter-section available just south of Moose Jaw.

In February 1900, Anthony May had entered for Dougald Carmichael's pre-emption, SW1/4 of 14-26-26 W2. (Carmichael had given up the struggle with the bureaucracy at this point, having lost his homestead, and was farming with his uncle in Aldergrove, B.C.) May, who was thirty-eight years old, had arrived the previous year from Castleton, Ontario, with his wife and six children. Since he had so little money in his pocket, he had farmed out for wages, his family living in one rented shack after another. Finally he had managed to build a frame house on Carmichael's pre-emption. But tragedy haunted the family almost from the moment they first set foot on that land.

In September of 1900, Charles May, Anthony's younger brother by thirteen years, who had followed him West, died following an operation for appendicitis. Charles's young wife and two children returned to Ontario. In November of that year, Anthony May himself came down with typhoid fever and was rushed to the Medicine Hat Hospital. While he was there, his two-year-old daughter succumbed to the same illness. Then, a year and a half later, thirteen-year-old Archie, the Mays's beloved eldest child, died, also from an attack of appendicitis. The tragedy was too much for the family, and in the spring of 1903, they returned to "a less savage life" in the East.

Since Anthony May had never received the patent for his homestead, he didn't own the land, and he had absolutely nothing except misery to show for his three years of hard work. It was the ever-vigilant John Hawke Grayson who found out that May was leaving and told Benjamin Smith. And it was Grayson who linked Smith up with Christina McKay Borthwick, a Métis living in Prince Albert, who was willing to use her half-breed land scrip to obtain the quarter-section for him. Smith figured he could oversee Harry's farm and his new land at the same time, and he readily paid the $800.

In March 1906, Benjamin Smith turned fifty-four. He was still skinny "as an underfed mule," but also still strong, "doing the job of a half dozen men," as Sarah said. She was approaching fifty herself, and she felt worn out by all the work.

"It's time we retired," she insisted, "we have boys who want to take over the land."

Ben Smith bridled at this. "We're just as fit as we ever were," he insisted. And as if to prove it, that year at the Moose Jaw Agricultural Fair, he won more ribbons than anybody: a blue ribbon for heavy-draught foal, for shorthorn bull under two years, for boar under one year, for sow under one year; and a second for heavy brood mare, for a boar under one year, for sow and litter, and for Clyde stallion aged. Not satisfied with all that, at the seed-grain fair Ben won champion title in the weed-seed identification contest.

Despite the flurry of honours, Ben Smith's career as a full-time farmer was nearing its end. That year, Sarah became seriously ill with a kidney disease, and doctors were fearful that she wouldn't pull through. When she did recover, Ben no longer questioned staying on the farm. He bought a spacious house on River Street in Moose Jaw. "No more hauling water for you," he told his wife.

This should have been Benjamin and Sarah Smith's golden time, their years of leisure after a lifetime of hard toil. But Ben was discontent and fretful. It wasn't that he missed the farm – he often went to help his son Albert, who had taken over the old homestead. There was something else bothering him; he was out of joint with the times, irritable with ordinary, daily events, inconsolable about misfortune.

His distress increased when Andy Dalgarno announced he was auctioning off everything on his farm. His wife was suffering from ill-health, and they were moving to the gentler climate of Victoria, B.C. Ben knew he'd miss the old sod, even his ridiculous practical jokes. Then the Smiths' daughter-in-law, Nina, Albert's wife, of whom Ben was particularly fond, died of pleurisy at twenty-three. Finally Joshua Annable, the brother of his old friend Mac, was almost murdered.

Joshua Annable later told the court that he thought there was something odd-looking about John Barlow – his eyes darted about all the time – but farmhands were scarce, so he hired him anyway to help with the harvest. After five days, strange things began to happen. A neighbour's shed suddenly burst into flames, and the cause was never determined. The home of Joshua's brother, William, situated a mile away, was broken into, although nothing seemed to have been stolen. Joshua's little cat disappeared. His hunting rifle was not in the place he had left it. But he was so frantically busy – his wheat was "dead ripe" and he was anxious to get it off – that he didn't pay much attention.

On the day in question, Annable was on the binder, while Barlow was doing other tasks. "Gonna make dinner now," Barlow called out. Annable thought this was odd because the cooking was usually his job, but he said nothing, as he was glad to continue working. When he arrived at the shack, Barlow had prepared the meal, but he said he wasn't feeling well, so he didn't want anything to eat. Annable took a mouthful of tea. "God-damn, that's awful," he yelled. The thought crossed his mind that the bitter tea he had drunk might have been poisoned. But he was obsessed; nothing was going to stop the harvesting of his golden wheat. He simply poured the tea out. He did, however, keep the teapot and the liquid remaining inside.

Annable climbed back on his binder, but he had gone only fifty yards when he got off to pick up a stook and noticed with alarm that his limbs were stiff. Still he continued working. He urged his horses on for over half a mile, until he met a neighbour working in his fields. He explained how he felt. "You'd better get to a doctor right away," the neighbour advised.

But Annable was deathly afraid an early frost would destroy his crop. "If I keep going, I'll work the effects of it off," he said to himself. However, by the time he had come around to the shack again he had "stiffened out." His jaw and the cords of his neck were set, his vision blurred. He somehow managed to get his team hitched up, and drove a short distance to a doctor. Fortunately for Annable, Dr. Charlton had an antidote that was effective, and his life was saved.

A day later his brother discovered that something had indeed been taken during the earlier break-in at his home: a bottle of strychnine. The police found Annable's cat, rigid as a weathervane. Tests showed it had died of strychnine poisoning; obviously, someone had tried out the effects of the poison before administering it to Joshua Annable.

Ben Smith sat on the jury that tried John Barlow. He was among those who argued that there was not enough concrete evidence directly linking the man to the crime. Barlow was found not guilty, although many of the jurors believed the opposite. There were two things that disturbed Smith about the affair. First, that Joshua believed his harvest was more important than his life; a few more minutes delay, the doctor said, and he would have been dead. "Doesn't that fool Josh Annable realize you can't cut wheat if you're six feet under?" Ben said to Sarah. Second, there seemed to be no motive for the attempted murder except sheer envy. Joshua Annable had a thriving farm and John Barlow didn't. "Doesn't that crazy man know how many years of drudgery God requires you put in before you get what we have?" The episode was so bizarre and illogical that it put Smith even more out of sorts.

And it didn't help that he worried constantly about his brother. Harry Smith's health had not improved, and he had continued his annual winter trek to Spokane, for medical treatment. On the way back, in May 1910, just as the train reached Medicine Hat, Harry suffered a massive heart attack and died instantly. He was sixty-one.

Sarah always said that Harry's death had a profound effect on Benjamin. He missed his brother more than he would say, and he constantly fretted about how to provide for Harry's wife, Janet, and their nine children. The family tried farming for a few years, but eventually Janet decided she couldn't manage alone and moved into Moose Jaw. A few years later she and several of the children went on to Victoria, B.C.

Once the Harry Smith family had left Pasqua, Benjamin decided to sell Dougald Carmichael's pre-emption, SW1/4 of 14-16-25 W2. In December of 1912, John R. Green, a Moose Jaw real-estate man, agreed to buy it for $7,200. Since Smith had paid Christina Borthwick $800 for her half-breed scrip only eight years before, this added up to a considerable profit. But even the sale made him despondent.

Smith rode his buggy out to Pasqua, to visit the quarter-section just before he sold it. It was such good wheat-growing land, the best anywhere, that he felt a twinge of regret. If he was willing to get rid of such superb land, he knew his days of farming were over.

The completion of the beautiful new Wesley Church in Pioneer district in 1912 lifted his spirits a little. Benjamin had been instrumental in raising the money for it and had donated a good sum himself. Appropriately, his middle daughter and favourite child, Fanny Mabel, and her fiancé, Harvey Filson, a farmer-rancher from Woodrow, Saskatchewan, were the first couple to be married there. The Smiths put on quite a spread in the old farmhouse. Friends and relatives came from all over to wish the newlyweds well and to taste Sarah's superb cooking. Nobody realized that they were also saying goodbye to Benjamin Smith.

Sarah was proud that she had been able to give Fanny a dowry: a cow, a dozen hens, a brand-new sewing machine, and a box of groceries, and that her daughter had arrived at her new home, in reality just a shack on her husband's homestead, in such style. Fanny's brother Harry had driven the happy couple there in his brand-new Ford. It was a symbol, Sarah thought, of the family's progress.

The crop of 1912 wasn't bad. There was a recovery from the partial drought of the previous year, and prices hadn't plummeted as they would the following year. But Ben Smith had developed a terrible cough, and for the first time in twenty-nine years, he didn't help with the harvest. The doctor ordered him to spend the winter in a warm climate, so Ben and Sarah, their youngest son, Bill, then thirteen, and the eldest, Harry, and his wife left for California that fall. They rented a small plot of land near Sarasota; Bill remembered feeding chickens and planting a garden. But Ben fussed all winter; he missed the prairie farm, the community of Pioneer, the Wesley Church.

In the middle of March, the Smith family started back to Canada by train. It was Ben's sixty-first birthday on March 25, and a celebration was planned. "It was to be quite a different birthday party, seeing we were on the train and all," Bill Smith remembered. But that morning, as they sat in the dining car eating breakfast and watching the approach of Medicine Hat, Ben Smith suddenly groaned, and his head fell forward onto the table.

What everyone thought strange was that he had died on exactly the same train, at exactly the same spot – a few miles west of Medicine Hat – of exactly the same cause – heart attack – as his brother had three years before. They were both sixty-one, and both had worked "until it had killed them."

Sarah Smith, who had always lived for and through her husband, lasted only two years longer. On January 28, 1915, at the age of fifty-six, she died of what was then diagnosed as Bright's Disease, a failure of the kidneys, the same ailment that had plagued her brother-in-law for so many years.

In the shadow of a red granite memorial in the Moose Jaw Cemetery, where most of the Smith family is buried, there is one marker on which is written an epitaph. It reads "Life's work well done." Interesting that in his last years Ben Smith should have been tormented by doubt. Was all that toil worth it? Was that really what life was about?

Foote/Slemmon

14-16-25 W2

Robert Foote
1903-1909
John Slemmon
1910-1916

Robert Foote
1903-1909
John Slemmon
1910-1916

11-16-25 W2

A dashing and handsome young man, he arrived just as the golden time in the West was beginning. He was a successful farmer. He married the girl he adored. He had the children he wanted. Yet in the end he was humiliated – by a taste for easy money and a roll of the dice. The land's retaliation? When he was old, he sometimes said as much.

~ I ~

In contrast to the strait-laced Benjamin Smith, Robert Foote was so easy-going, so good-natured, that everybody – his own children, his nieces and nephews, the neighbourhood kids – called him Bob. He'd be talking a mile a minute with his cronies over at the livery, when Eleanor or Thelma or Pearl or Ken would come yelling, "Bob! Bob! Mother wants you to help her wring the wash." He'd smile his resigned smile and saunter home.

"You ever lick those six kids of yours?" Jim Duncan, the implement dealer, once asked him.

"Never could think of any reason for it," Bob Foote responded.

His wife thought that sometimes he made a fool of himself. "I ask him to quiet the children at bedtime," she once complained, "and he starts playing around as though he's one of them."

Bob's brother, Alexander "Sandy" Foote, was just as good-natured. This was quite remarkable, given the Foote boys' rather tragic past. They were born in Brucefield, Huron County, Ontario, of Scottish ancestry. Sandy was three years old and Bob five when their mother died, and their father, a bee-keeper, had to rely on a neighbour named Nellie Snell to care for them. She was not a woman of means, and when Mr. Foote passed away, she suggested that the boys' future might lie in heading West with the rest of the crowd.

The brothers arrived in the Moose Jaw area in 1897. Bob was sixteen and Sandy fourteen. They were quickly hired on as farmhands, and they were both so eager, unassuming, and good-natured, that the men they worked for, including John Hawke Grayson, did everything they could to help them. Sandy discovered that he wasn't much of a farmer; he was interested in working on the railway, and in 1903 he was hired by the CPR on a section crew. Bob, on the other hand, liked to farm, and was exceptionally adept at handling horses and cattle. He planned to homestead as soon as he had saved enough money, but when John Hawke Grayson told him that a prime piece of land close to the railway was available, and that he, Grayson, would be open to easy terms, Bob Foote jumped at the opportunity.

He purchased the southeast one-quarter of 14-16-25 W2, which Thomas Aspdin and John Hawke Grayson had finagled from the Métis, Abraham Beauchamp. He also bought the northwest one-quarter of the same section, which had been Dougald Carmichael's homestead and which Grayson had also acquired through half-breed scrip. Although he was only twenty years old, Bob Foote understood how valuable the rich black soil was, so he readily agreed to the $800 asking price. He put $80 down and signed a promissory note to pay the rest. By the spring of 1903 he had built a frame shack, a stable, and a granary, and could already brag of two bountiful harvests. He had also been able to pay out the debt to John Hawke Grayson in full. The West, he thought, was a fine place, and life was made even richer by the social whirl that never stopped buzzing in the village of Pasqua.

Bob Foote always said that he was lucky to have ended up at Pasqua; it was a place that offered him every opportunity. It was also a place that symbolized the split personality of the new West. It was friendly, priding itself on how warmly it welcomed newcomers like the Foote boys. But it was also a place that had been periodically torn apart by vicious squabbling; beginning, during Dougald Carmichael's time, with Joe Young's attempt to dispossess his neighbours of their land.

In 1884, when the Carmichaels and other early settlers had first arrived, they had great expectations for the place. Just the right distance from Moose Jaw to serve as the first station on the main line eastwards, the town was thought to have "wonderfully bright prospects," as the *Times* stringer, who lived in the village and wrote a column called "Pasqua Dew-Drops," enthused. The opening of Rosine's general store was considered a sign of healthy progress, as was the founding of Pasqua School, with eleven children enrolled. Keeping the school going was a struggle, however; some winters it opened, some it didn't, depending on whether money could be found to pay the teacher. But in 1891 "Pasqua Dew-Drops" reported, "We have just finished the erection of a beautiful new schoolhouse. Mr.

R. Allison [Dougald Carmichael's old friend and partner], who
had it in charge, completed the work in his usual good style."
Two years later, at a public meeting held in the airy schoolhouse,
two of the elected trustees were thrashed, beaten, and punched
by furious farmers. The trustees had announced that because of
hard times they not only didn't have the funds to cover the
teacher's salary, but they were closing the school. Parents were
so enraged by this that they scraped enough money together for
another term, but when the teacher, Miss Glass, returned to
Fort Macleod to marry, the doors of the little schoolhouse
closed forever.

In the 1890s, when drought and depression hit, many farmers
fled in despair, and the village suffered. Even the super-farmer
Ben Smith had to borrow money for seed from the government.
The ex-Mountie Tom Aspdin fared much worse; he lost his land
and livestock. In Pasqua, the post office and general store closed.
The boarding-house operated by Tom McWilliams, Carmichael's old bugbear, the man who cheated him out of the proceeds from the pottery clay, moved to Moose Jaw. The livery
vanished. Pasqua itself might have disappeared altogether if it
hadn't been for an unexpected stroke of good luck.

In May 1892, William C. Van Horne, the president of the
CPR, made an inspection tour of the West (in the comfort of his
luxuriously appointed private car, of course). He subsequently
announced that the junction point of the new "Soo line," which
would carry freight and passengers back and forth across the
American border, and the mainline CPR would be located at a
little village eleven miles southeast of Moose Jaw called Pasqua –
not at Regina, as everyone had anticipated. The railway siding
would have to be shifted one and a half miles west, and with it
the entire town, but that was of no consequence.

The citizens of Regina were enraged that the junction was
located so close to Moose Jaw. The Regina lacrosse team even
reneged from playing in the annual CPR tournament because
the "insufferable" Moose Javians were also competitors. (When
the excursion train, returning home from the tournament,
stopped at the capital, the Moose Jaw players stepped onto the
platform and gave three cheers for the "Regina Defaulters.")

Feelings ran so high partly because the competition between
Moose Jaw and Regina "to become the Chicago of the Canadian West" was still raging, and partly because westerners were
thoroughly fed-up at what they saw as unfulfilled obligations on
the part of the CPR. Once the trans-Canada line had been
completed, it was assumed that the railroad would have built a
web of branch roads radiating from Regina and Moose Jaw. This
would have opened the hinterland to settlement and created
much-needed business for the two cities. But only one such line
had been constructed: the Qu'Appelle, Long Lake and Saskatchewan Railway from Regina to Prince Albert, the road on
which Colin Carmichael had worked. Even then the CPR only
operated the railway through a leasing agreement; it had been
constructed with private money. Finally, in 1890, rumours
began bubbling that something much bigger was in the works.

The CPR was then in a ferocious struggle with the Great
Northern Railway for the freight and passenger rail traffic of the
American Midwest. To compete in the U.S. market, the Canadians badly needed a line from Chicago to Vancouver. To this
end, the CPR had gained control of the Minneapolis, St. Paul,
and Sault Ste. Marie Railroad and planned to construct a
branch line from St. Paul through Minnesota and the Dakotas
to Portal on the U.S.–Canadian border, and from there to Pasqua, where it would meet the main CPR line into Moose Jaw.

The building of the Soo Line created a boom for the entire
Moose Jaw district. Hundreds of labourers were hired; indeed,
the CPR had difficulty finding men for the strenuous work on
the ballasting gangs. At Pasqua, a work train was stationed for
the three years of construction, and once the line was completed, three section crews – one working east on the main
trunk of the CPR, one working west, and one working down the
Soo Line – were stationed at the village. A house was built for
each of the foremen, and permanent bunk-cars were situated
there for the other crew members. Passengers changing from the
CPR to the Soo Line or vice versa had to detrain at the Pasqua
station and, while the wait was usually only a few moments, it
was long enough for some enterprising Pasqua youngster to sell
egg-salad sandwiches or packets of tobacco. There were other

advantages: coal transported via the Soo Line from Estevan ensured fuel for the winter, and most important, the Soo Line quickly became the most popular route for the thousands of American immigrants flooding into Canada's West.

One day in the spring of 1900, the entire community of Pasqua came out to greet a Soo Line special that was carrying twenty carloads of stock and equipment and hundreds of settlers all the way from Kansas City. Most of them were heading for farms they had purchased from the Canadian–American Land Company, and much of this land was located in the Pasqua district. Since the new arrivals had plenty of money in their pockets, the value of land soared. Naturally the village, which now grandiosely referred to itself as The Hub, benefitted from this influx.

In May 1897, the *Times* correspondent (the name of the column had been changed from "Pasqua Dew-Drops" to "Pasqua Chips") had reported; "With the advent of spring, the 'Hub' and suburbs thereof are looming up, not through a mirage but by actual bustle and stir shown by the citizens. Houses that have been vacant for years are being occupied again, and new residences are being created which go to show that Pasqua is destined to yet become of some importance."

Actually, when Bob Foote settled in Pasqua in 1901, the village's appearance hadn't changed that much since Dougald Carmichael's time. It still consisted of a handful of ramshackle buildings strung out directly across from the railroad station; the prairie, as flat as a dough pan, stretched relentlessly on all sides. A few farmers lived right in town. There were two churches, a Presbyterian and an Anglican, both mere shacks, but the most impressive buildings were a post office and the CPR agent's office-house. In a few years the little village, like the rest of the West, would blossom as heartily as a prairie lily. By the 1920s, it would have several elevators, two general stores, a butcher, an implement and lumber dealer, an important post office, a boarding-house, and, of course, a pool hall. Its population at one point soared to two hundred. It even had its town drunks and prostitutes.

Bob Foote arrived just as the good times began, and the

citizens of Pasqua, who were in great spirits, welcomed this charming young man. He was one of those who was at James Slemmon's house on a cold January night in 1901. "The bachelor, the bachelor! Where is the bachelor? We're here to make his life bearable," Bob and his rowdy friends called out as they pushed through the door. Until well past sunrise the next morning, they danced – "The light fantastic was tripped to music by Brubaker and White," "Pasqua Chips" reported – ate rabbit stew, and drank whisky. Actually Slemmon was hardly a bachelor. He not only had a wife – her name was Margaret and she was in Ontario visiting her family – but nine children. What the incident revealed was how popular and high-spirited Jamie Slemmon was. Indeed, if there was a leading citizen of the tiny burg of Pasqua, it was he.

James Slemmon was thirty-two years old and an experienced farmer when he came West in 1889. Eight years before, his father, Sam, who had been a horse-breeder in Ontario, had died. As the eldest son, James had managed the family farm until he decided he could do a lot better out West. He had chosen as a homestead the southwest one-quarter of 6-17-24 W2, in the Leamington district, four miles northeast of Pasqua, six miles north of Dougald Carmichael's homestead. For three long years he worked the land alone, methodically breaking and then cultivating the heavy clay soil and building up his herd of cattle. Finally conditions were secure enough for his family to join him. He returned to Brussels, Huron County, Ontario, to collect his wife and their four kids, and to say goodbye to the Slemmon clan and Margaret's family, the influential Camerons (who were still so Scottish they wore their kilts every Sunday).

That fall, under Margaret's supervision, a solid house with a dry basement and large kitchen was built, and the family settled in.

Despite the hard times of the 1890s, the Slemmons had survived. For one thing, James was a very good farmer. His showing at the Moose Jaw Agricultural Fair in 1899 is indicative: in the heavy draught-horse category, he took first prize for a one-year-old colt and second prize for a spring colt; in the poultry section, he won first prize for Plymouth Rock chickens; but it was growing wheat at which he truly excelled, capturing first prize for White oats, first prize for Red Fife (Benjamin Smith's Red Fife placed second), and second in the Wheat Any Variety category. Two years later, at the International Exhibition in Glasgow, James Slemmon, from the place with the strange name of Pasqua, North-West Territories, Canada, captured first prize for his Banner oats, which weighed in at forty-four pounds to the bushel. The trophy was displayed on family mantelpieces for generations after.

Margaret Slemmon, a most capable woman, was not to be outdone. In 1899 she won top honours for her log-cabin-pattern quilt, her coarse double-knitted woollen mitts, and her crock butter. This was no mean feat, given the brood of children she had to look after. Number five arrived exactly nine months after she was reunited with her husband in Ontario, and four more were born in the ensuing twelve years.

Shortly after he came West, Jim Slemmon had been appointed a justice of the peace by Lieutenant-Governor Joseph Royal, who said Slemmon had a reputation for "usefulness and honesty." The appointment gave him a high profile in the community and involved him in interesting assignments. For example, he supervised the 1898 plebiscite on prohibition in the North-West Territories in Pasqua, which his friends thought was a great joke, since if there was one thing Jamie Slemmon loved, it was his whisky.

The citizens of Pasqua prided themselves on their compassion towards those suffering from misfortune. When the barn of James Watson, a settler who had just arrived from South Dakota, was set afire by a spark from a pipe, and the four horses trapped inside were burned to death, his neighbours took up a collection to replace the animals and helped him build a new barn.

But they could also be cruel and vengeful towards anyone veering from the path of righteousness. And James Slemmon as Justice of the Peace sometimes was required to sit in judgement. Virginia Flack, the daughter of the carpenter who had helped to build the Slemmon house, is a case in point.

Seventeen-year-old Virginia had given birth to a child out of wedlock. The baby had died at birth, and a coroner's jury had been convened to examine the sordid details. Little evidence was produced to show that the girl tried to conceal the birth, then a criminal offence, but the jurors did conclude that the infant had died through neglect. Virginia was therefore hauled before a panel of three Justices of the Peace, including James Slemmon. They ruled she would have to stand trial. She was taken at once to jail in Regina, although bail was arranged a short time later. Eventually she was acquitted; the jury found that at the time of the crime "she was not in a rational frame of mind." Three weeks later, she committed suicide.

This tragedy had occurred at the same time as one of those squabbles that periodically bedevilled the village flared up. And again, James Slemmon was near the centre of the storm.

Alex Dalgetty had met Slemmon in 1884, while he was working on a farm in Ontario. Five years later, the two men came West together, Dalgetty choosing a homestead on the quarter-section directly north of Slemmon's. Dalgetty's wife and seven children arrived about the same time as the Slemmons, and the two families became so close it was hard for neighbours to tell which kid was a Slemmon and which a Dalgetty. They endured the hard times of the 1890s together – Dalgetty almost went under in 1892 when he couldn't pay his debts and had to advertise for a loan – but through sheer hard work, they endured.

James Slemmon considered Alex Dalgetty his closest friend. The two men sat on the board of directors of the Moose Jaw Agricultural Society at the same time, both were dedicated Liberals, and both worked hard to set up the Leamington School District. Slemmon admired his friend's skill with cattle; Dalgetty had devised an effective method of dehorning his cows. Everyone in Pasqua appreciated his talent on the fiddle. But Alex Dalgetty had a very prickly personality. He was opinionated – "pig-headed's more like it," said Margaret Slemmon – especially when it came to politics. Which was why he mounted his vicious crusade against C. A. Gass, the postmaster of Moose Jaw (before John Hawke Grayson).

Dalgetty couldn't abide Charles Gass or his Conservative point of view. "You'd think he'd be satisfied having nabbed the biggest political plum going [the postmaster's job] and keep his big mouth shut," Dalgetty complained endlessly. That Gass operated an implement dealership and charged what Dalgetty considered "outrageous prices" didn't help.

Dalgetty was particularly incensed at Gass's meddling in the 1896 federal election campaign. This was the horse race in which the Patrons of Industry candidate Jim McInnis had lost to the Tory candidate Nicholas Flood Davin by one vote – the one cast by the returning officer. Dalgetty had considered the whole affair an appalling scandal, in which Gass played a leading role.

In the fall of 1897, Dalgetty sent a letter to the post-office inspector, charging Gass with nine serious offences. They were grouped into two main categories; those claiming political influence-peddling – Gass, said Dalgetty, had bribed people to vote Tory during the last election – and those charges alleging corruption in Gass's execution of his duties as postmaster, including a charge that he opened people's letters and withheld mail.

These accusations were so serious that, on September 22, 1897, Post-Office Inspector W. W. McLeod arrived in Moose Jaw to conduct a public inquiry. The makeshift courtroom in the CPR dining hall was packed with witnesses and curiosity-seekers eager to enjoy what they were sure would turn out to be a circus. Gass hired T. C. Johnston, a highly skilled lawyer from Regina, to question witnesses on his behalf. Dalgetty acted for himself. He hemmed and hawed through the questions; on many of his charges he could produce no witnesses; and many of those who did come forward, including William Grayson, gave contradictory testimony. Yet enough evidence emerged to prove that Gass had indeed been heavily involved in political skullduggery. (Three years later he was finally fired, and John Hawke Grayson got his job.)

However, Dalgetty had little success in proving his allegations that Gass was unfit as a postmaster. He could not persuade one soul to come forward with their stories of Gass's transgressions. The inspector raised his eyebrows when he was asked to accept Dalgetty's assertion on his word alone that Gass opened clients' mail. Gass, on the other hand, found people who insisted that

he was a courteous and efficient postmaster. That these witnesses had been slipped a two-dollar bill only came to light later.

Then Jim Slemmon appeared out of nowhere to testify on
behalf of Gass, and against Dalgetty.

Gass's defence was to show that Dalgetty had waged a ven-
detta ever since Gass had sued him for nonpayment for some
farm implements purchased two years before. "Did not Mr.
Dalgetty show up at your farmhouse one evening, his coat off,
his sleeves rolled up, claiming he was after that – ladies and
gentlemen, please excuse the language – sonofabitch Gass?"
Gass's lawyer asked James Slemmon.

"I remember Mr. Dalgetty saying he was going to get even
with Gass, but I didn't think he was responsible for what he was
saying at the time," responded Slemmon.

When the deliberations wound down at 4:20 that afternoon,
Dalgetty ran into Slemmon outside the train station. Dalgetty
was furious. "Turncoat! Turncoat! With friends like you, who
needs enemies," he ranted. Slemmon yelled back something
uncomplimentary. Dalgetty punched Slemmon in the face.
Slemmon immediately laid charges of assault before Justice of
the Peace W. C. Sanders, who was an old friend. Dalgetty was
fined $2 and costs.

The affair split the Pasqua community badly. Some people,
mostly Liberals, felt that Dalgetty's accusations against Gass
were fully justified and that Slemmon, himself a Liberal, should
be ashamed for testifying against his old friend. Others, mostly
Tories, said Dalgetty was a madman, and Slemmon had no
choice but to give evidence.

Alex Dalgetty's wrath did not die down. He not only refused
to speak to James Slemmon but to anyone who had a good word
to say about him. His fury raged on unabated until finally, a few
months later, he rented out his farm and moved his entire family
to southwest Manitoba. James Slemmon was heard to yell,
"Good riddance to the old bugger, even if he is taking his fiddle
with him."

Only later did Slemmon learn that Dalgetty had burned all
the school-district records, a mean act that almost spelled the
end of education in the Leamington area.

By the time the Footes arrived in 1901, the storm had blown over, and James Slemmon was back in everyone's good graces. Bob Foote was immediately attracted to the gregarious farmer for two reasons: first, Slemmon was the president of the Pasqua Football Club, and if there was one thing that Bob Foote loved in life, it was playing soccer; and second, James and Margaret now had seven daughters, two of them approaching marriageable age.

Actually, Bob Foote had spotted Elizabeth Slemmon two years before. He'd been working in the Buffalo Lake area at the time, and had been invited to attend one of Pasqua's famous picnics. He'd enjoyed himself immensely, watching in amazement as the rambunctious Slemmon girls played a game of baseball. "Couldn't have done better myself," he'd called out after Elizabeth had given the ball a good wallop. She just giggled, but he knew he had caught her eye. That was important, because the competition was fierce.

Attractive young women were as rare as tea roses on the prairies, while bachelors were a dime a dozen. (Once when the CPR was arranging for Easterners to come West to help with the harvest, the "desperate" bachelors of Pasqua sent the railroad a letter, half serious, half in jest, requesting that "a large number of nice looking and sensible girls should also be brought to take charge of the bachelor shacks." The petition ended on a rather sorrowful note. "We are afraid being unattached for so long, the old bachelors would be afraid to pop the question anyway.")

Actually, Bob Foote had little trouble attracting the opposite sex, for he was one of the best-looking and personable young men in the district. A photo taken of the Pasqua football team in 1904 shows Foote, the captain, sitting front-row centre, holding the Kern Cup, which Pasqua had won that season. When one young woman saw the picture, she remarked that Bob Foote was as handsome as the ringmaster at the Gentry Brothers Circus, which had recently visited Moose Jaw. "Pasqua Chips" had hinted on several occasions that certain "bachelor girls" would not be averse to receiving Bob Foote's attention. But he only had eyes for Elizabeth Slemmon.

She was certainly pretty. Like all the Slemmons she was small-boned, and under five feet tall. Her glory was her thick chestnut hair, which she gathered like a plump pillow onto the top of her head. Her high cheekbones, definite nose, and serious brown eyes told not only of her Scottish ancestors but also of a strong, determined character. And this was what attracted Bob Foote. "She has more gumption than most ten girls put together," he told his brother.

When she was sixteen, she had fallen from a horse, badly fracturing her leg. With no doctors on hand, her mother had had to set the break herself. It didn't heal properly, and thereafter caused the young woman considerable pain. On bad days, she walked with a slight limp. But that didn't prevent Elizabeth Slemmon, known to friends and family as "Lib," from doing anything.

"There's a picture of her taken when she was young," says her son, Ross Foote. "She's all of ninety-eight pounds. She's sitting atop a harrower or a seeder, and in front of her is a team of six horses. She's managing them as easily as if she was driving a cart and pony."

She was the oldest of the Slemmon's nine children, which was likely why she was so hard-working, so responsible, and so ambitious. Whether Bob Foote saw her only as a sweetheart and future wife, or also as a surrogate mother, was a question many people were to ask. Certainly, from the day they became a couple, she was considered the tough one, the ambitious one – The Boss.

Bob Foote planned to strike up a conversation with Lib Foote at Pasqua's annual picnic in July of 1901. A soccer match was planned between Pasqua and South Moose Jaw, and since Foote was playing for the first time, he was sure he would make a good impression. But he was disappointed. A violent thunderstorm descended just as the entire community of a hundred souls had gathered at Allison's Flats. Everyone scurried home, feeling rather depressed, for this was considered *the* event of the entire year.

They cheered up, however, when a few weeks later, the settlers of Granton District invited the people of Pasqua to their outing. The highlight was the girl's baseball game, the Moose Jaw Clippers versus the Pasqua Daisies. Elizabeth Slemmon was now too old and dignified to play, but she was in the crowd cheering her sisters along. "They did credit to the Boston Bloomers," said Bob Foote, as the Daisies celebrated their fifteen-to-four victory. And thus began the love affair of his life.

Meanwhile, Bob's brother, Sandy Foote, had his eye on the Slemmon's second daughter, Minetta, known as Nettie.

The family still likes to talk about the saga of the two romances. "Sandy and Robert had one horse, so when they went courting Minetta and Elizabeth, they had to take turns riding their mount the six miles to and from the Slemmon farm. The girls used to wait in anticipation until they spotted the lone figure riding across the prairie, then they wondered, Which one would it be?"

The story, however, is apocryphal. According to his homestead records, by the end of 1902 Bob Foote owned six horses and had built a stable to accommodate them, as well as a good-sized house and a granary. He had been on his land for two years, and already he could call himself a genuine farmer.

Although he was young and relatively inexperienced, Foote must have felt the anger, frustration, and outrage of those years as intensely as the old hands did. In 1901, for the first time, the crop was so bountiful, so perfect, that the farmers could dream of the yellowing kernels turning into real gold. But their expectations were cruelly deflated.

The grain-dealers and the CPR – these were the two long-standing scourges that made the farmer's life miserable. The elevator men were part of what the farmers called the "syndicate of syndicates" – the Northwest Grain Dealers' Association, whose tentacles reached from the Winnipeg Grain Exchange to the local elevator agent, and which tightly controlled the "street" price paid for grain. The CPR was in cahoots with this monopoly, the farmers were sure.

For a while the farmers had been able to circumvent the system by not using the grain elevators; they could load their wheat directly from a platform, taking the chance that the price they would receive at the Lakehead terminals would be greater than the "street" price paid by the elevator company. Then, in

1897, the CPR announced that it would handle only grain loaded through the elevators. It was more efficient, the railroad insisted. Wheat could be delivered by boxcars and stored by grade in bins.

The farmers understood at once that the monopoly would be strengthened, that price-fixing and fraudulent grading and weighing of grain would become routine. They complained so loudly that a royal commission was set up by the federal government to look into their accusations. After hearing farmers' concerns at points across the West – in Moose Jaw, Ben Smith's neighbour, Maria Latham, the Queen Lady Farmer, complained bitterly that the elevator men always cheated her because she was a "mere woman" – the commissioners found that there was much truth to what the farmers were alleging. The result was the Manitoba Grain Act, passed in 1900, which restored the farmers' right to load directly over the platform, thereby by-passing the elevators.

The farmers thought they had scored a victory, until the grain blockade of 1901 showed them how easily the rules could be contravened, and their hearts broken in the process.

It was obvious early in the season that the crop of 1901 was going to be exceptionally bountiful. Massive immigration meant many more acres were under cultivation, and weather conditions were near perfect. By August the shortage of threshing machines and men to run them had developed into a serious problem. Then heavy rain fell in September, delaying the harvest even further. By November, it had become obvious that the CPR did not have anything near the number of cars needed to transport the grain to the Lakehead, and by December elevators throughout the West were overflowing. Towns quickly erected temporary warehouses – Indian Head sprouted 120 such structures – and farmers built makeshift sheds, but as the *Moose Jaw Times* pointed out, "any grain so stored will be entirely destroyed by a spring thaw." By January what everybody was dreading became a reality: "The grain blockade is now complete," reported the *Moose Jaw Times*, "buyers having been advised that the elevators at Fort William were filled yesterday. There was storage for only about 3,000 bushels in Moose Jaw elevators and no shipments being made either east or west." At the close of navigation, more than half the crop was still on the farms.

As soon as the elevator companies heard that the Lakehead was filling up, they lowered the street price of grain significantly in an attempt to cover the cost of storing the wheat until it could be shipped in the summer. The farmers' only recourse was to shrug and accept what the elevator men offered. No matter what the government had promised, the CPR, even though it had built loading platforms throughout the West, refused to allocate cars to farmers who wanted to ship the grain themselves. With such a shortage of rolling stock, only the elevator companies had the ears of the CPR spotters who assigned the cars. "The blockade and with it the depression in prices had resulted in a loss to the grain grower almost beyond calculation," a *Regina Leader* editorial concluded.

Pasqua-area farmers were particularly frustrated. They watched as the trains on the Soo Line headed north filled to capacity with immigrants, and returned, a day later, completely empty. The suggestion had been made many times that Canadian grain be shipped via the Soo and American lines through Minnesota to the port of Duluth, where there was storage available for ten million bushels. The CPR refused to cooperate; it was not going to hand business over to a competitor, no matter what dire straits the farmers were in.

Never mind that there had been a blizzard and roads were blocked. The farmers from Pasqua, south Moose Jaw, Petrolia, Granton, Drinkwater, and Coventry still managed to get to the Coventry schoolhouse on a cold night in February 1902. They were there to gripe.

A week before, the first convention of the Territorial Grain Growers' Association, a truly historic occasion for prairie farmers, had been held in Indian Head. Years of frustration and bitterness had spilled over. "No one can deny that the farmer extracts the wealth from the soil by his industry . . . and no one can deny that . . . his rights have been ruthlessly trodden upon by dealers and transporting companies," said W. R. Motherwell. And, he added, the important thing was to be pragmatic, resolute.

The farmers of Pasqua took heart from Motherwell's message and decided to build their own elevator. At the meeting at Coventry schoolhouse, Harry Smith (brother of Benjamin), vice-president of the Pasqua Grain Growers' Association, gave his report: "A 30,000 bushel elevator will cost $4,000 and could be built in ten days after the material is on the ground. Personally I think our difficulties won't be solved until we have our own storage."

There was some controversy in the district, because the idea was so radical and farmers would have to put up money, but in the end the Pasqua Farmers' Elevator Company was incorporated with a capital stock of $10,000 in $25 shares. It was fully subscribed almost immediately.

Pasqua was such a prime location for the storage of grain that nobody was surprised when a large private company, Western Elevator, announced it was also building a thirty-six-thousand-bushel facility.

The two elevators were finished just in time for the 1902 harvest, another record crop. Even though extensive rolling stock had been purchased, the CPR was again unable to cope. "The biggest railway company in the world cannot handle our crop," groaned the *Moose Jaw Times*. So chaotic was the situation in the Moose Jaw CPR yards that freight from Vancouver and points east remained unloaded for as long as six days. At Pasqua, over a hundred freight cars and three engines sat waiting to get into Moose Jaw for weeks. "Last night," reported the *Times*, "the Prince Albert train arrived at Pasqua junction at 10 o'clock and did not get to Moose Jaw until five Sunday morning." The passengers were not amused.

Street prices dropped again as the close of navigation approached. Farmers who had constructed their own elevators like the one at Pasqua were penalized when they couldn't get their grain to the Lakehead on time. But the grain-growers who had to accept the rock-bottom prices offered by the private elevators suffered a lot more. In defiance of government regulations, the CPR was still not allocating cars to individual farmers so that they could load their own grain, preferring instead to assign the available rolling stock to the elevator companies. The

Territorial Grain Growers' Association, flexing its newly developed muscles, decided to do something about the situation.

In December of 1902, a small delegation from the Pasqua Grain Growers' Association – whether Bob Foote or James Slemmon was among them is not known – travelled the eighty miles to the village of Sintaluta. (The Aspdin family was living nearby at the Carry-the-Kettle Reserve, but there is no record of whether Thomas had anything to do with the Territorial Grain Growers' protests. Given the fact that his was a government job, he probably wasn't involved.) They slept overnight in the livery barn, and early the next morning joined scores of other farmers who had flocked into the schoolhouse-turned-courtroom to observe, with some menace, the legal proceedings.

The Territorial Grain Growers' Association was suing A. V. Benoit, the CPR agent at Sintaluta, for not allocating freight cars fairly to individual farmers. After a tense day of testimony, which revealed how arrogantly and rudely the elevator operator had treated the farmers, Benoit was found guilty and fined $50. Red-faced CPR executives, who realized this was a test case, said they would immediately conform to the law.

It was a great victory for the farmers. That they had defeated the mighty CPR and its high-priced lawyers was success beyond all expectations. There would be more fights in the future, but by the following year, the shipment of grain was carried out fairly smoothly.

With the two huge elevators looming, sharp and distinctive against the brilliant prairie sky, the people of Pasqua felt their town had at last put down permanent roots.

They soon had something else to be excited about. A general store opened, selling everything from thread to oats. It didn't have the rich mahogany counters or the shiny brass weighscales of the grand establishments in Moose Jaw – it was really nothing more than a wooden shack – but a farm wife could get bottles of Bovril, boxes of Fairbank's soap and Red Feather Tea, tins of Smith sardines, Supreme netted corset covers, and her husband's Eureka Harness Oil and Fair Play Chewing Tobacco. The proprietor of this popular establishment was John Slemmon, younger brother of James.

In January 1902, James Slemmon had made his first trip in ten years back to Brussels, Ontario. With money in his pocket – "Mr. Slemmon had 5,000 bushels this past harvest," the *Huron Expositor* exclaimed in amazement – he looked prosperous, and he never stopped raving about his prairie farm. His brother, John, was impressed with his brother's bravado. He decided he'd give up teaching school in Ontario and, with his wife, Isabella, and their three children, head West.

John Slemmon bought a quarter-section north of Pasqua, but it was never his intention to do much farming; his health was too delicate for that. He was well-educated and felt he could better make his living out West as a merchant.

Almost from the moment his store opened in October 1902, it was a success. The settlers flooding in from the United States and elsewhere bought many of their start-up provisions from him, especially after Slemmon had established a reputation as a fair man, who wouldn't bilk them at every opportunity. The following year, the post office was transferred from David Dustin's farmhouse to John Slemmon's place, which was also good for business, because his store now became the favourite meeting-place of the village. Hardly a day passed without the entire population of Pasqua district parading through its doors. Sometimes it got a little rowdy, and Slemmon had to post the following ironic list of rules:

1. Drum on the window shelf, as the postmaster likes music.
2. Lean up against the case, as it might tip over if you don't.
3. Shove the delivery window aside and join arms inside the case and help yourself.
4. Stand clear back at the door, or better, go out on the street and holler to the postmaster to bring out your mail.
5. If you get another's letter or paper take it home and keep it.
6. Chew the rag about your mail as much as possible.
7. Have your mail put in the general delivery and don't rent a box. It is too accommodating.
8. If your family got the mail, insist that they lost it and it is the postmaster's duty to hunt it up.

9. If there are a dozen in your family send all of them to the office twice a day, every one alone, so the postmaster will have to look through for your mail twenty-three times a day.

10. If there is no mail, insist that there should be and that the postmaster is keeping it for his own family. Tell him he's a snoozer and pull his nose if you can.

When John Slemmon first arrived, everyone remarked on how much he looked like his brother. Both were small-boned men, with fat moustaches on their upper lips, clear blue eyes, and protruding ears. But they were not so alike in personality; John lacked the gregariousness which made his brother so popular, and yet in many ways he was a more sensitive man.

He was the one, for example, who dealt with the sad case of Mrs. Kapchinsky and her two young sons, who got off the train at Pasqua station one day looking bewildered and frightened and not able to speak a word of English. When the mother tried to explain her situation, all the Pasqua residents could do was shrug and call for Postmaster John Slemmon. Through crude sign-language, he finally unravelled the woman's story. She had travelled all the way from the Ukraine to meet her husband, but because of difficulties, she was two months late. Slemmon asked around and found that the man had worked as a labourer on a farm near Pasqua, but when his family hadn't shown up, he had taken a job on a railroad work gang and had set off for Prince Albert. Slemmon bought a ticket back to Regina for the frightened woman and her children and telegrammed the immigration officials the whereabouts of her husband. A few months later a letter arrived from Mr. Kapchinsky. The family had been re-united, he wrote, and he thanked Slemmon for his great kindness.

It was also John Slemmon who, when a "lunatic" wearing nothing but a loincloth was found roaming the prairie, had had the presence of mind to telegraph the police in Moose Jaw. Constable Wilson arrived by the next train and managed to take the poor babbling man into custody. He had an upper-class English accent, and kept ranting about the gardens of Devonshire. "Sounds like a remittance man gone mad," James Slemmon said after his brother told him the story.

John and Isabella Slemmon were considered refined people – a Hammond organ was among their personal effects. And because John had been a schoolteacher, it was assumed he would take an interest in the educational matters of the district. Certainly they were in a mess.

Since the closing of Pasqua's schoolhouse in 1893, the farmers in the neighbourhood had been in a quandary; either their children had to travel several miles to Eastview School District, one of the few places that had managed to keep its school open through hard times, or else they received no education at all. The latter was most often the case, so Pasqua parents realized that a school would have to be reorganized and rebuilt. Plans were proceeding apace when one of those squalls, which periodically rattled the town, struck again. Nobody could agree on where it should be situated. The trustees wanted it located near their own farms, so their children would not have to travel far in the winter; the other parents, led by John Slemmon, were outraged by this, insisting it should be built in the village. A compromise was finally imposed by the Department of Education that pleased nobody: it was built near the CPR-Soo Line junction, and the noise from the trains was intolerable. It was a strangely bitter fight, especially since only ten families were involved.

It took a man of Bob Foote's good nature and charm to smooth things over. He helped to organize the first Christmas concert held at the school. The drama club, featuring the fourteen students and Bob Foote as narrator, depicted the nativity, Bobby Baird performed on the mouth organ, Ninnie Crosby sang "Away in a Manger," and Minnie Slemmon played a medley of chorals on the organ, which had been loaned for the occasion by her uncle John Slemmon. By the end of the evening, the feud had evaporated and everybody was wishing everybody else Merry Christmas.

With the school established, Pasqua could call itself a respectable town; when its football team won the Kern Cup, it would call itself a remarkable town.

Ever since James Slemmon had become president of the club in 1902, soccer had been a very serious affair in Pasqua. When a Stony Beach player missed the ball and cleavered Len Hicks's leg, "breaking both bones clean in two," as "Pasqua Chips" reported, and making it difficult for Hicks to bring in his harvest, team members passed on their sympathy, but their enthusiasm for the game wasn't dampened in the least.

While competitions were held only in the summer months, from June to September, once a week at six in the evening, every game was relived a hundred times around the stove at John Slemmon's store. Bob Foote was a very good player, and in 1904, he was chosen captain. Lib Slemmon thought he looked incredibly handsome in the team jersey of black and yellow, with number 20 proudly displayed on his back.

Right from the beginning, when the excellent Buffalo Lakers were walloped by Pasqua six-to-zero, the town knew it had a winner. The team chewed its way through Boharm, Stony Beach, and Maple Leaf, and finally, in a tense and dramatic game, beat the CPR team two-to-one. It was a particularly sweet victory because, as the *Moose Jaw Times* pointed out: "THE FARMERS WIN OVER THE RAILWAY."

A week later, at the Brunswick Hotel in Moose Jaw, a lavish banquet was laid on, of oysters, pork with applesauce, mashed potatoes, corn, strawberry pie, and port wine jelly. In a lively ceremony full of tributes and witticisms, the hotel proprietor J. H. Kern presented the team with the Kern Cup, as well as medals for each player. Afterwards, the champions trooped over to Porter's Art Gallery to have their picture taken.

Since Bob Foote had scored one of the goals, he was considered a hero. He was now a well-established member of the community, appreciated as a *bon vivant* and admired as a successful farmer. He was a golden boy in a golden time when the West was booming, and the future looked as limitless as the prairie sky.

Farmers became even more excited as their farms suddenly soared in value. Land around Pasqua was considered ideal, and this became evident, when, in the spring of 1906, H. F. Annable purchased 137 acres in the town at a whopping $58 an acre, and then had the property subdivided into lots. "Pasqua will no doubt be popular on the real-estate market," he said. And John R. Green, the high-powered entrepreneur from Moose Jaw, had also bought a half-section, right behind the elevators. The town's citizens were surprised when he hired a steam plough to break his land, indicating he was going to keep it himself, rather than sell it off.

That summer, James Slemmon reported that he had been offered an incredible $25 an acre for his wheat farm, but, he added, "I turned it down flat." As "Pasqua Chips" chirped, "A pleasing feature of the present land movement is that our old time settlers do not care to sell out . . . we do not know of a single actual settler who has sold out his interests in the district, although hundreds could have done so."

A year later, with so many rich Americans demanding land, prices had soared so high that the temptation became too great, and many farmers did sell out. James Slemmon was among them.

He had extended his original homestead to a full section, with 450 acres under cultivation. His house had also expanded, various extensions being added as more babies came along. As a sign of his optimism, James Slemmon had built a barn so huge it was the talk of the district. But by 1904, he was suffering terribly from asthma, which the doctors insisted was aggravated by grain dust. He decided it was a fortuitous time to give up farming. He sold the south half of his section to Everett "Doc" Eddy of Grand Rapids, Michigan, for $7,000, the north half to another American for the same price, and his second quarter-section homestead to the Luse Land Company for $880. Given he had started fifteen years before with almost nothing, James Slemmon must have felt he was a rich man.

"Pasqua Chips" was happy to report that Slemmon wasn't leaving the district; he invested in his brother's now-thriving business, and opened a lumberyard beside the general store. He also bought three quarter-sections of land, much of it pasture, just north of Pasqua, and there he built another house.

Bob Foote also found himself faced with a difficult decision. Certainly he was satisfied with the two quarter-sections of

14-16-25 W2 – Dougald Carmichael's homestead and the land once owned by John Hawke Grayson and Thomas Aspdin – that he had bought in 1901. Year after year crops had been bountiful, and thirty-five bushels to an acre was not unheard of. "I couldn't have made a better choice," he told his brother one day. Sandy, by that time, had a good job as a conductor on the CPR and was glad to be free of farming, but he wholeheartedly agreed.

Since Bob Foote had purchased the farm at Pasqua from John Hawke Grayson, he was still entitled to free Crown land in the form of a homestead, and on one of his many trips to court Lib, he had come across exactly what he was looking for. In January of 1903 Foote asked the Dominion Lands Office for an inspection of SE1/4 of 28-16-24 W2, just a half-mile south of the Slemmon farm. A few months later, he was told he could enter for it. By 1905 he had broken 125 acres and cropped 35, but had built neither a house or barn. It was not as close to Pasqua as his purchased land, so it meant a longer haul to carry his grain to the elevator.

Lib Slemmon, Bob Foote knew, was not your typical demure, prepared-to-suffer country girl; she had ambition and drive and she had made it clear she would want things for the children, should she and Bob marry. It occurred to Foote that, if he sold his Pasqua farm for a good profit, he could build a first-rate farmhouse for Lib on the homestead he had entered for – and have cash left over.

In March 1905 he sold his Pasqua half-section to James Duncan, a schoolteacher in the Petrolia District, for $2,900. Since Foote had bought it for $850, he realized a 300-per-cent profit in just four years.

Years later Bob Foote admitted to a friend that he wasn't sure he had made the right decision. It had put the sweet taste of fast money in his mouth and had paved the way for disaster – but that was years later.

On June 8, 1906, the *Moose Jaw Times* headed a story: IT WAS A DOUBLE WEDDING:

"A very unique wedding took place in Moose Jaw on Wednesday afternoon at 2:00. Two brothers, Robert Carnochan Foote and Alexander (Sandy) Foote were wedded to two sisters, Elizabeth Eleanor Slemmon and Maggie Minetta Slemmon." Sandy Foote's house, where the ceremony, conducted by Rev. S. Maclean, took place, was packed with excited guests, mostly the Slemmon clan. After the celebration, which went on all afternoon and evening, the two couples boarded the train for their honeymoons in Winnipeg.

The year 1907 should have been the happiest of times for Bob and Lib Foote, but instead, it was full of mishaps and tragedies. The couple's first child, Eleanor, arrived on March 30, but she was a tiny baby who cried constantly and could keep nothing in her stomach. Doctors had almost given up hope when Lib's sister Minetta, who had also recently given birth, said, "Just for the fun of it, give that baby to me. I got enough milk for four." The little girl responded immediately, suckled like "a little pig," and slept for six hours. It saved the infant's life, but it meant that Lib Foote had to drive the buggy into Moose Jaw every morning so her sister could feed Eleanor.

The problem of small babies and inadequate milk continued to plague Elizabeth Slemmon. Of the eleven children she bore over twenty years, five did not survive. Some died immediately at birth, others when just a year or two old. The distress caused by these premature deaths cast a dark cloud over the marriage.

Other afflictions followed. In the early summer of 1907 Bob, Elizabeth, and baby Eleanor were visiting the elder Slemmons in Pasqua. As they returned to their farm at twilight, they noticed grey smoke billowing up in the violet prairie sky. They thought it a lovely sight, until they realized it was coming from their property. They arrived just in time to see their home collapse into a smoking ruin. It wasn't just the destruction of the newly built house that upset Lib; she knew that, with the help of family and neighbours, another would soon materialize. It was the loss of the wedding gifts: the hand-painted silk cushions, the embroidered rocking chair, the fine china soup tureen, the clock. They would probably never be replaced.

But a far greater tragedy occurred that fall. There had been a serious epidemic of typhoid fever in the Moose Jaw district; many children and adults had died of it. James Slemmon, who liked to drink water straight from the slough, came down with the illness in July. Already weakened by his asthma, he died at the Moose Jaw Hospital on August 20, 1907. He was fifty years old.

The *Moose Jaw Times* lamented his passing: "He was widely known throughout the district and was highly respected. . . . In Mr. Slemmon's death, the district suffers the loss of one of its most useful citizens."

His widow, Margaret, still had five children at home. Rather than carry on the business, she decided to farm on the land that her husband had bought at the same time as the lumberyard. She remained in Pasqua, the pivot of a huge close-knit family, until old age forced her to move to Moose Jaw to live with her daughters. She would die in 1952 at age ninety-two. Throughout her long life, she remained fiercely independent.

None of her large family can ever remember her talking about her late husband, James Slemmon. There might have been conflict between them. Towards the end he grew to cherish his bottle of whisky, and she was a devout Presbyterian and a dedicated teetotaller, who was intoxicated by any prohibitionist's slogan.

For John Slemmon, the death of his brother was the last straw. In the ferocious winters of the prairies, his health had deteriorated, and his wife, Isabella, had never liked the West. The vast sky gave her a headache, she said. The winter of 1909 was particularly savage – the cold was fierce, and John Slemmon came down with bronchitis. At his wife's urging he decided to sell the store and retire to Salmon Arm, in southeast British Columbia.

Jim Duncan, the schoolteacher who had bought the northwest and southeast quarters of 14-16-25 W2 from Bob Foote, was interested in starting an implement dealership in Pasqua, so a deal was arranged to exchange this land for the business. John Slemmon thereby ended up owning the quarter that Dougald Carmichael had homesteaded and the land Thomas Aspdin and William Grayson had got their hands on through half-breed scrip. It was a speculative move on Slemmon's part; he would rent the land while watching with delight as its value increased. Five years later the Moose Jaw brick-maker Wellington White bought the half-section for double the price. The following year, John Slemmon drowned while fishing in Shuswap Lake, British Columbia.

Misfortune also plagued the Foote brothers. In January 1911, train No. 205 was approaching Moose Jaw from the south along the Soo Line, six hours late, when it smashed into a locomotive engine pushing a snow plough. The commuter train was completely destroyed, two passengers were killed, and several were badly injured. As a conductor on the ill-fated train, Sandy Foote could in no way be blamed for the accident, but he was dismissed anyway, along with the rest of the crew. "Once you were fired in Moose Jaw you couldn't get a railway job anywhere else in Canada," says Sandy Foote's daughter, Jean Schuster. Fortunately, he had a close friend in Portland, Oregon, who got him a position on the railway there.

Sandy and Minetta Foote were to live happily in Portland for a couple of years – a third child was born there – until misfortune struck again. Sandy tried to grab for a rail at the top of a boxcar, found it missing, and fell fourteen feet to the ground, landing on his back.

His injuries were fairly extensive, and he was advised by his union to sue the railway. He did so, and was awarded a small amount of money, but, as his daughter recalls, "That was the end of that. He lost his job."

The Footes were in desperate straits, and since Sandy had friends in Vancouver to whom he had loaned a considerable amount of money, he travelled there to try to collect and possibly find a job. He arrived just as World War I broke out, and, without saying a word to anyone, including his wife, he enlisted. "It was not so much that he was patriotic. It was a job he badly needed," says Jean Schuster. Minetta and her three children returned to live with her mother, Margaret Slemmon, in Pasqua.

Sergeant Alexander Foote served in the 5th Battalion, 2nd Brigade, and fought in many of the major battles of that gruesome war: Amiens, Vimy Ridge, Passchendaele. He was wounded three times, but never fatally. By the time he finally got back to Canada in 1918, the years spent in the muck of trenches and the exposure to misery had taken their toll. He had developed pleurisy. Three months after his return, he was hospi-

talized at Fort San, a sanatorium at Fort Qu'Appelle, Saskatchewan. In June of 1919 he died at age thirty-six.

The family of Bob Foote, meanwhile, had been experiencing
their own tribulations.

They were still living on the land Bob Foote had taken as a
homestead, after he sold the Pasqua farm. The nearest school
was three miles away, too far for the Foote girls to travel back
and forth every day. Lib Foote was determined that her children
would be educated, and so, in 1913, when Eleanor was starting
grade one, Bob Foote rented out his farm and took a job managing the Saskatchewan Co-operative Elevator in Pasqua. Foote
didn't like the work much, and the family lived in what they
called "the shack," adjacent to the railway tracks, but the school
was only a short walk away.

There were other advantages to living in town. Every Saturday Grandmother Maggie Slemmon took the commuter train
to Moose Jaw to sell eggs and chickens. There was always at least
one Foote grandchild with her, going to his or her music lesson.
"Mother insisted we all study music, and some of us were better
than others," recalls Ross Foote, the youngest of the family.
"Eleanor was very good at the piano but I can still hear my
brother trying to make music on that fiddle. That just about
drove me nuts."

By the the spring of 1917, the Foote family was back on the
farm. There had been an incident in town which had upset Lib:
on her way to school, Eleanor had been accosted by a disturbed
young farmhand who had sworn at her and had alluded to
sexual matters. He did not assault her physically, but the episode was still considered shocking. Lib Foote decided her girls
needed protection from the corruption of town life.

That wasn't the only reason for the family's move. The government was pleading with farmers to put forth a superhuman
effort to feed the Allied troops, and Bob Foote felt it was his duty
to participate, especially as he had a brother on the battlefield.
He also had his eye on wheat prices, which were spiralling
upwards.

Foote missed the bonanza years of 1915, the most bountiful of
all harvests, when farmers around Pasqua got forty bushels to

the acre, and 1916, when the price of wheat shot up to $2 a bushel. The harvest of 1917 was a little disappointing; wheat prices were pegged at $2.21, but still Foote's wheat yielded him a good profit. But 1918 was the poorest wheat crop in twenty years, and 1919 wasn't much better. Drought, hail, and a severe grasshopper infestation did the damage. And, as the war ended, wheat prices began a dramatic downward slide; in September of 1920, a bushel of No. 1 Northern sold for $2.78 on the Winnipeg Grain Exchange: six months later, that same bushel went for $1.76. On top of that, the farmers suffered from inflation – everything cost more, from taxes to land. By 1923, a farmer's purchasing power had shrunk to less than 20 per cent of its pre-war level. No wonder there was a political revolt.

Everybody in the West jumped on the Progressive Party bandwagon in the federal election of 1921, and the farmers' party won thirty-nine of the forty-three prairie seats.

The Progressives sprang from the same seeds of discontent that had produced Benjamin Smith's Patrons of Industry twenty-five years before. Henry Wise Wood told the annual convention of the United Farmers of Alberta in 1917, "We as farmers are downtrodden by every other class. . . . We have grovelled and been ground into dirt; we are determined that this shall not be. We will organize for our protection; we will nourish ourselves and gain strength; we shall strike out in our might and overthrow our enemies." This sentiment had spun into the National Progressive Party.

It was a stronger movement in some ways than the Patrons of Industry – the farmers were much better organized – but it didn't last much longer. The Progressives had four more seats than the Tories, but when Parliament sat in 1921, they refused to act as the official opposition. They deplored the old-fashioned parties and their unscrupulous politics and wanted to play a power game, not become part of the parliamentary process. That was the beginning of the end. If the Progressives were going to evade political responsibility, why should the farmer waste his vote on them?

In the 1925 federal election, two-thirds of the Progressive incumbents lost their seats. In the election of the following year, the party virtually disappeared from the national scene. The farmers' revolt was over – at least for the time being.

Bob Foote had never turned his back on the provincial Liberals (for which, a few years later, he was grateful. When he desperately needed a job, Jimmy Gardiner, the Liberal premier, found him one). It seemed to him that they had always supported the farmers. They had backed the Saskatchewan Wheat Pool, for example, and that had made them heroes in Bob Foote's eyes.

Like everyone else, he had sat mesmerized that warm night in 1923 in Regina, listening to the passionate oratory of Aaron Sapiro. He was an American born in Oakland, California, to an impoverished family. His widowed mother had been left with seven children and eventually four of them, including Aaron, ended up in an orphanage. After a childhood spent hawking newspapers to earn his daily bread, he had had the good fortune to be selected to study at the Hebrew Union College of Cincinnati. There he had become infected with a Judaic philosophy similar to Ben Smith's Protestant social gospel. Doubting that the lofty position of rabbi would allow him to penetrate the real world of poverty, he dropped out and worked his way through law school, obtaining his degree in 1911 at age twenty-six. He developed a passion for grower co-operatives, and he relentlessly organized everybody from the tobacco-growers of Kentucky to the potato-growers in Idaho. The United Farmers of Alberta had heard about his passion for co-operation, and it was they, with the help of the *Calgary Herald* newspaper, who brought Aaron Sapiro to Canada.

His message was simple: prairie farmers must organize pools to sell their wheat and circumvent the speculators. All farmers would receive the same amount of money for the same grade, based on the average price of all grain sold. They would receive initial, interim, and final payments, the price being equal for all growers, regardless of the time of year. The idea caught on like wildfire. The Saskatchewan and Alberta wheat pools were formed in 1923 and the Manitoba arm in 1924. In July of the same year, the Central Selling Agency was set up to market wheat abroad.

In the village of Pasqua, the big elevator was repainted with big black letters: SASKATCHEWAN WHEAT POOL, it read, a symbol of triumph, on the flat, bald prairies. Old farmers like Bob Foote couldn't help thinking this was a natural conclusion to that meeting held twenty-one years before in the little Coventry schoolhouse to gripe about conditions and glory in the formation of the Saskatachewan Grain Growers' Assocation. If Ben Smith had been alive, he would have been amazed at the progress.

After the bumper crop of 1923, prosperity returned to the West, and Foote's farm became a most profitable operation. He was well-off enough to board his four girls at the Academy of Our Lady of Sion in Moose Jaw. It was a Catholic school taught by the sisters of Sion, but many a Protestant farm girl was sent there to enjoy its high-quality education. The Footes were able to enjoy weekends at Manitou Beach, considered *the* fashionable holiday spot in Saskatchewan, and trips to Ontario. Bob indulged in his passion for thoroughbred horses, and Lib bought the odd expensive dress. Some of the family thought she had pretensions of grandeur. "Elizabeth always wanted to be the queen of the ball. She put on any airs she could find," says her nephew, Cecil Champion. "She never got over the idea that Bob was going to be a millionaire."

There's disagreement in the family as to what role Lib Foote played in the disaster that befell them in 1928. Some relatives say she pushed Bob into it; others claimed she was a victim of his poor judgement. There's no question, however, that Bob Foote had for years dreamed of growing rich quickly, but didn't every Westerner secretly yearn to be part of the black gold bonanza?

Oil was first discovered in Turner Valley, near Calgary, in 1914. World War I put a damper on further drilling, but the area's reputation gelled in the national psyche.

By 1925, Turner Valley was again in the news, and Bob Foote followed the thrilling saga in the *Moose Jaw Times*.

Investors had given up on the well, the decision to abandon the hole was made – and then a miracle happened. The last crew, who were to be laid off after the afternoon shift, drilled ten feet more, just for the hell of it. Suddenly there was an explosion. The casing flew apart, and gas and oil exploded into the air.

Thereafter, the road to Turner Valley became clogged with cars, as people flocked to view the spectacle. On one warm Sunday afternoon, Bob and Lib Foote were among the curiosity-seekers. They had driven all the way from Pasqua.

The next year, when an aggressive salesman by the name of Goossens showed up at Bob Foote's farm, slapped down a map, and pointed at the Morley Indian Reserve – "More oil deposits there then Dingman and Royalty put together," he said – Bob believed every word.

He traded his entire farm, a section and a half of the best wheat-growing land in the country, for shares in the about-to-be-developed Morley oilfields. The man he signed his deeds over to was a stockbroker called William Murphy, president, he claimed, of the Wabash Oil and Norcon Oil companies. In a world full of crooked promoters, Murphy was a most notorious swindler.

Eventually the Stoney Indians of Morley did find oil and gas deposits, but not in 1928. Just as the family was about to vacate the farm and move to Moose Jaw, Bob Foote discovered that the stocks were totally worthless. Twenty-seven years of hard work had played the fool to a ridiculous, fast-talking, fast-buck artist.

The Foote family, so proud and independent, had to resort to government relief during the early thirties. Eventually Bob Foote's Liberal connections, and his reputation as an easygoing guy, landed him a job as a dairy-cattle inspector. It was work he grew to like, but, like Dougald Carmichael, he never stopped talking about his lost farm, and about "the sour-lemon" oil stocks that cost him his life's savings. He once said that perhaps if he hadn't speculated on his rich farm south of Pasqua, the half-section 14-16-25 W2, he might never have developed a taste for easy money.

THE
CAPITALISTS

Green

14-16-25 W2

John R. Green
1911-1924

NW	NE
SW	SE

John R. Green
Nov. 8, 1918-
Nov. 25, 1918

NW	NE
SW	SE

11-16-25 W2

No one made more money than he did. He had cast aside his calling as a schoolteacher because it was a poor-paying proposition and got into real estate just as the West was booming. Quickly, he made a fortune. But farming, he said, was his first love, and he collected grain fields as nonchalantly as he did rare coins. Yet there developed a serious split in his personality – the intellectual versus the money-grubber – and in later life he paid for his neurosis. He died a stern, sick old man, who was not at all well-loved.

~ I ~

While the town of Pasqua basked in the prairie sunlight of the first decade of the twentieth century, some seven miles north, Moose Jaw was in an uproar. The years 1901 to 1912 encompass the golden age of that city. The population soared from about a thousand pioneers to somewhere between twelve and thirty thousand people, depending on which pie-in-the-sky promoter you happened to talk to. A new town hall, housing a grand Opera House on the upper floor, a modern hospital, and a Gothic post office were built; Postmaster John Hawke Grayson, lined up with his six clerks to greet the public on opening day, said he felt like a king. Electricity and waterworks and cement sidewalks and even long-distance telephones were installed; that you could talk to your aunt in Winnipeg was amazing, and everybody tried it at least once.

Sniffing profit, the industrialists arrived: the Robin Hood Flour Mills, the Moose Jaw Machine Works, the Western Canada Brush and Broom Manufacturing Company, the Canadian Incandescent Light and Stove Company, the Moose Jaw Hardware Company Limited, the Chemical Soap Company, the Moose Jaw Tent and Mattress Company, the Gordon, Ironside & Fares Meat Packing Company, and, not without controversy, the Moose Jaw Brewing, Malting and Bottling Company. "Good Christians should not become partners in a brewery proposition no matter what the profit," thundered the pastors, as their flock snapped up the company's stock as quickly as it was offered.

Real-estate offices sprang up like prairie thistle, as did loan companies and insurance agencies. Banks, hitherto rather rare on the supposedly unreliable prairies, crowded into any little hole in the wall that could be found. Opportunities to make fortunes abounded – there would never be anything like it again. And among those eager men, dressed in their uncomfortable wool suits no matter what the season, their three-buttoned vests and high wing-collars pinched tight, their bowler hats yanked down over covetous eyes, with their expensive gold watches dangling across paunchy stomachs, none was so cunning, manipulative, or successful, as John R. Green.

He seldom smiled or showed any emotion, but when he started his spiel, he totally mesmerized whomever he had lured into his web. "That man could sell bows and arrows to the Indians," exclaimed one fellow who had just plunked down the profits from his year's harvest on fire, life, and accident insurance, which he had, until that moment, no idea he needed or wanted.

J.R., as everyone called him, had once taught school, and the aura of authority stuck to him like Howitzer's cologne. It was hard not to believe someone who could frame a fancy sentence the way he could. And he was uncannily clever; unlike most others, when the incredible boom began to fizzle, he knew how to cut his losses quickly, and most often, profitably.

His parents had begun life dirt poor. His father, Robert, was one of twenty-six children born to farm labourers in Lincolnshire, England. Robert Green tried his hand at gardening and did a stint in the army before he married a local barmaid, Sarah Elsom, whose lowly station in life did not discourage her from ambitious dreams. With six of the eight children they would eventually have, the couple arrived in Canada in 1874. Robert Green had exactly $6.20 in his pocket. There was little else he could do but hire out as a farmhand. For the next ten years the family lived a peripatetic existence, as Robert Green tried to better himself – renting a small farm with a little shack in Lobo Township in southwestern Ontario, then a bigger place in West Williams Township, where he also made cheese, then a dairy farm in Brooke Township. Finally, in the spring of 1884, the Greens moved to the United States, settling in the small town of Oxford, about sixty-three miles north of Detroit. Robert was share-cropping for a big farmer. "I had been renting all along and I could not see that there was any chance of my getting property of my own," he once said. So he read very carefully the letters which arrived from his eldest son, Fred, who had gone in a quite different direction.

In 1882, Fred W. Green bought a ticket on the CPR as far as the train would go. In Brandon he spent the last of his small savings on a team of oxen and a cart and headed west, eventually finding the farm he wanted three miles north of Moose Jaw. A few years later, he sold his homestead and bought what he considered was better wheat-growing land very close to Boharm, where Benjamin Smith had homesteaded. Indeed, Benjamin and Fred became such good friends that Green's farm was one of the first places Smith took his brother on Harry's arrival in the West.

F. W. Green, as he was widely known, was a very good farmer – in later years he would become famous throughout the West for his innovative and often eccentric agricultural methods – and was respected for his activism; he was a dedicated organizer and then secretary-treasurer of the Saskatchewan Grain Growers' Association. Despite the hard times of the 1880s, his parents were impressed with his vision of the future and decided to follow him.

Robert and Sarah Green returned to Canada in 1887, first renting Henry Battell's farm and then choosing as a homestead the northwest quarter of 2-17-27 W2, just on the outskirts of Moose Jaw. Eventually they purchased another quarter-section from the CPR.

Robert was a quiet little man, whose first love was curling. He was not overly ambitious; it was the big-bosomed Sarah who was the driving force in the family. "She was very headstrong, much like my father," says J. R. Green's daughter and Sarah's granddaughter, Mary Jefferson. It was Sarah who was determined to get the children educated so "the family could come up in the world." Her fifth, John Robert, was considered a brilliant student, and therefore was the apple of his mother's eye. He had been left behind in the United States to complete his school year, but in 1888 he came to Moose Jaw and continued to study at Victoria High School. Both John R. and George, his younger brother by two years, graduated in January of 1890.

Teachers were then as scarce as hard cash in the West, and when the teacher at Marlborough school a few miles north of Boharm left in a huff, John began teaching before completing his high-school studies. (It was agreed he could take the final exams and graduate.) Marlborough was a typical one-room affair, with a heater that didn't work, an outhouse that stank, and eleven students of all ages, of whom never more than seven showed up on any one day. The school was only open from April 1 to September 30, 1890, and Green was paid the royal sum of $35 a month. The school inspector reported, "The present teacher Mr. Green is diligent, but has had no professional training. General tone – fair."

On the inspector's urging, Green enrolled that fall in one of the first normal schools in the North-West Territories, the Moose Jaw Union School, under the firm moral guidance of David James Goggin. In July of 1891 Green was awarded a second class certificate, Grade A. During the following four years, he ruled over a number of one-room schoolhouses; he taught Benjamin Smith's children at Pioneer and Boharm and some of the Slemmon kids at Carmel. He developed into an excellent teacher, strict but patient.

John R. Green was an upright, earnest young man, but not dearly loved. While he would gladly explain the Venezuela territorial dispute with British Guyana at the drop of a hat, he did not enjoy the riotous baseball games he was sometimes forced into organizing in the schoolyard. An enthusiastic Methodist, he would not dance, play cards, swear, or gossip. And he was a prude. In later years he kept a small model farm near his residence and, to overcome the problem of a child accidentally encountering copulation, he banned all male animals, except for one rooster and a gelding.

Mary Jefferson remembers one incident that illustrates her father's puritanism. By the time she came along, the family lived in an isolated area in the outskirts of Moose Jaw. As a small girl, she didn't have much to do but hang around outside the house, and one afternoon she was watching two of her father's workmen tinker with the family's Ford V8. "My crank isn't as hard to turn as this one," one of them joked.

"And I told on him," she says. "I don't know why. He was kicked off the farm that day." Ironically, John R. had a very healthy sexual appetite and would father nine children through two marriages, the last when he was already sixty years old.

In his younger years, J. R. Green was an enthusiastic member of the Royal Templars of Temperance, and had no difficulty sticking to his vow of "never touching a drop in my life." A year before his death in 1938, he was still giving speeches on the evils of drink to the Women's Christian Temperance Union.

In 1893, when John Green first began teaching at Marlborough Primary School, he lived at the home of school trustee, John G. Beesley. Beesley was a gregarious farmer, whose happy house provided a welcome refuge for inhibited John Green.

John and Elizabeth Beesley were among the earliest settlers, having arrived in the Moose Jaw area in 1883; they had known Dougald and Rebecca Carmichael, and had tried to convince them not to give up when times were so tough. The Beesleys came from the same area of Ontario as the Smiths; Elizabeth Beesley and Sarah Smith were sisters. Naturally, the two couples were good friends, and when both began to prosper – by 1900 Beesley could boast of 1,280 acres of land, Smith 2,400 acres, two of the largest landholdings in the North-West – they often went on holidays together.

The Beesley's eldest daughter, Annie Maude, was a much-loved child, pretty and sweet. She was nineteen when she and John R. Green first met. Family legend has it that it took only one glance for Green to make up his mind he was going to marry her. Her first reaction to him is not known, but she did warn her suitor that her father could not abide the "land grabbers that infest this country." Her father's disapproval of Green's wheelings and dealings would become a bone of contention in later years.

Their marriage took place on Christmas Day, 1894, at the Beesley farmhouse. By everyone's account, Annie Maude looked beautiful, outfitted elegantly in a cream cashmere dress trimmed with cream silk and a white veil pinned by a wreath of bright holly. John Green, already rather portly, with a dramatic black beard and heavy black eyebrows framing rather cold eyes, was considered a great catch, because everybody could see that he would go far.

The Beesleys were hospitable and gregarious people, and over a hundred people attended the wedding. The guests danced all night to the music of James Barrie and J. D. Fraser. The table, decorated with thistle, rose, and shamrock, and groaning under the weight of the feast, "would have done justice to the Royal household," as the *Moose Jaw Times* commented.

Annie Maude would live her entire life in her husband's shadow. Outside of some work with the Ladies Aid of the Zion Methodist Church and the Women's Christian Temperance Union, she seems to have had no public persona at all. "She sees to it that John R. is well looked-after, her children well-fed, her house always immaculate but she is rather dull. Dull!" a relative once wrote to the Green family in Britain.

Annie Maude began her married life on Boxing Day by packing her dozens of presents and moving into the fourteen-by-twenty-foot frame house J.R. had had built. It was located on the homestead he had carefully picked out the year before. Although he was now a qualified teacher, Green realized that he must get the patent to his homestead, as the land would surely be worth something one day. The year he entered for his homestead, he broke eighteen acres, and he continued to crop that amount.

It was to be a lonely year for the new Mrs. Green. John R. taught at Boharm School, which was located about thirty miles to the west. He had to live near the school, returning home only on weekends, and only if weather permitted. But there were compensations to being married to so clever, so intellectual, a man.

Annie Green was so proud of her husband as she sat nervously one cold February night in 1895 in the crowded Moose Jaw Town Hall. She was thrilled when he had been chosen to sit on Moose Jaw's debating team, especially considering the eminence of the other members; J. W. Sifton, superintendent of Moose Jaw schools, and J. E. Caldwell, a brilliant young lawyer. Moose Jaw had been challenged to a debate by the famous Boharm Literary Society, which was represented, ironically, by John R's brother, Fred, no mean speaker himself – he was once called "the silver-tongued orator of the golden West" – and two other articulate farmers, James Pascoe and R. Grant Thomson.

The Boharm side went first and spoke in favour of the resolution "That ambition is more harmful than beneficial to man-kind." Human kindness and cooperation would advance society, not cut-throat competition, they argued. The Moose Jaw team then came to the defence of ambition. "If one does not have enterprise, initiative, drive, how can one help one's fellow man to progress?" John Green argued.

"Although," as the *Times* reported, "the audience, in the main citizens of the city, had every reason to be hostile, they rendered an almost unanimous decision in favour of Boharm." It was an early expression of two philosophies which divide the West to this day: free enterprise versus social democracy.

Green lost, but since it was all in good fun, his pride wasn't too badly bruised. Still, as his wife said, "I wish he wouldn't take his own philosophy so much to heart." A year later J.R. announced that he was giving up his teaching job, giving up the farm, and that he and his family were moving to Kootenay District in southeastern British Columbia.

During the drought and depression of the early 1890s, school-teachers could hardly expect to make a fortune, but the average salary of $250 a year (for six months' work) was ridiculously low. With his farm bringing in almost no income, he welcomed the offer to become principal of the public schools in Nelson. The salary was almost double the amount he was making at the Boharm School.

The Greens must have thought the move would be perma-nent, because they auctioned off their farmhouse and all their furniture. (The land itself couldn't be sold, since Green had not filed for a patent as yet, but he told the farmer who bought the house and leased the quarter-section that he would sell to him at a reasonable rate as soon as he had acquired the deed.) He promised his farewell meeting with the Glencourse Chapter of the Royal Templars of Temperance that he would maintain his obligation "not to cease to labour so long as life shall last, or until the evils of intemperance are destroyed." In gratitude, the Templars presented him with a travelling card that would allow him to attend any ban-the-bottle meeting anywhere.

The Greens rode the Spokane Falls and Northern Railway through the "breathtaking mountains" to the mining town of

Nelson, overlooking the west arm of Kootenay Lake. They arrived just in time to witness a fantastic population boom. During John R. Green's first term as principal, he had sixty students under his supervision; two years later, that number had increased to four hundred.

It was a boisterous, bachelors' place, and neither J.R. nor Annie Maude approved of the gambling and drinking that were waged with determination from morning until night. Still, Green learned a fundamental lesson: many people were getting rich on mining stock and land speculation, but it certainly was not the school principal, who had to get by on what seemed now a miserably small income. By 1898 his calling as an educator had lost much of its idealistic shine.

In June, a fever epidemic swept through Nelson, and the public schools were closed early for the holidays. The Greens decided they would return to Moose Jaw for a two-month visit. Upon their arrival, John R. was most impressed by what he saw.

~ II ~

Brother Fred's farm near Boharm was prospering, and brother Harry, who had homesteaded nearby, on land immediately adjacent to Benjamin Smith's, was doing just as nicely. As well, J.R.'s father, always a true Grit, convinced his son that the Laurier government was bringing great prosperity to the West. Moose Jaw, John R. sensed, had the same smell as Nelson – a town about to boom. Huge fortunes would be made, he predicted, and he decided not to go back to British Columbia.

Rather than return to the homestead, the family settled in a comfortable but not pretentious frame house located on downtown Athabasca Street. For a few months it also served as Green's office, for he had given up teaching as a poor man's profession and had turned to the business of making money.

With a little cash in their pockets, farmers had become more interested in what previously had been considered luxuries: insurance policies, for example. Green became the general agent, Assiniboia region, for three companies: Manufacturers

Staff-Sergeant Thomas Aspdin of the North-West Mounted Police. The picture is undated, but it must have been taken after 1886, as Aspdin is wearing the medal he earned for service during the North-West Rebellion. (National Archives)

On the Carry-the-Kettle Reserve after the Aspdin family moved there in 1897. Mary Blackmoon is seated in the middle. Her youngest daughter, Katie (seated), and middle child, Annie, are on the left. The eldest daughter, Alice, stands to the right, beside Clara Williams, a family friend. (Maurice Williams)

A wedding at the farm of the Graysons' friend William Watson in the early 1900s. William Grayson is seated in the front row (the woman beside him, Mrs. C.N. Hopkins, is wearing his hat). Ellen (Mrs. William) Grayson is seated at the left of the centre row, while Adela (Mrs. John Hawke) sits beside her. John Hawke stands beside Adela. (Moose Jaw Public Library Archives)

This picture of the Smith family appeared in the *Illustrated Toronto Globe* in 1902, not long after Benjamin rigged up his steam ploughing machine. Benjamin is seated on the right, Sarah is standing in the wagon on the far left, and the others are all sons and daughters.
(Moose Jaw Public Library Archives)

The Pasqua football team in 1904. Captain Robert Foote is seated, front row centre, holding the cup. James Slemmon stands on the far right. (*Moose Jaw Times-Herald*)

Elizabeth "Lib" Foote (*née* Slemmon) and Robert C. Foote on their fiftieth wedding anniversary, June 6, 1956. (Lorraine and Ross Foote)

John R. Green, shortly after he was elected city councillor in 1903. (Moose Jaw Public Library Archives)

Annie Beesley Green, John R. Green's first wife, shortly before her death at forty-two in 1916. (Moose Jaw Public Library Archives)

Moose Jaw's most glamorous couple, Ollie and Wellington White. The photo is undated, but it was probably taken not long after the marriage in 1898. (Moose Jaw Public Library Archives)

Ollie White's mother, Sarah Brooks, with her four grandchildren. While the inscription on the back of this photo, written by a family member, identifies Isobel and Kathleen (on the left) and Ross (on the right), the little boy on Mrs. Brooks's knee is labelled "unknown child." In fact, it was Frank, the Whites' "adopted" son. (Moose Jaw Public Library Archives)

The White residence shortly after it was built in 1908. On the left stand Kathleen, Ollie, Isobel, Wellington, and Ross (with the family's pet parrot). The names of the two people on the right are unknown.
(Moose Jaw Public Library Archives)

Ollie White at the Moose Jaw silver fox farm in 1927. She is holding five live fox cubs; a sixth, not so lively, encircles her throat. (Moose Jaw Public Library Archives)

The Eberles' wedding photo, taken in Regina, February 21, 1945. Frank's youngest brother, Ray Eberle, acted as best man, and Kay's youngest sister, Rosalie Bishoff, as bridesmaid.

Don Sutherland (far left) just after his first communion at Sacred Heart Church in Regina.

Don Sutherland (on the left) and Ken (on the right) after the two brothers were arrested for killing their grandparents. A few weeks later Ken pleaded guilty to second-degree murder. The murder charges against Don were dropped. (Bryan Schlosser/Regina *Leader-Post*)

Life, Mercantile Fire Insurance, and Dominion of Canada Guarantee and Accident Insurance. The job meant days away from home, combing the bald prairies for potential clients. Weyburn, Prince Albert, Regina, Indian Head, Moosomin, Assiniboia, Humboldt, and Stony Beach were all places he visited within a six-month period. I lis remarkable ability as a fast-talking salesman showed itself at once, and by January 1899 he had drummed up enough business to open an office on Moose Jaw's Main Street, next door to the Union Bank.

Green was a more resolute man when he returned from British Columbia, and to succeed in business, he realized that he would have to break into Moose Jaw's ruling clique. This was the Liberal establishment, dominated by William Grayson, John Hawke Grayson, and the banker Arthur Hitchcock. Agreeing to become secretary-treasurer of the Moose Jaw Liberal Association, a job nobody wanted because it was a bother, was his first step. The president of the association was William Grayson, and Arthur Hitchcock was on the executive.

Green's connections paid off almost immediately. Just as he had done for his friend John Hawke Grayson, Arthur Hitchcock introduced J. R. Green to the fabulous possibilities of half-breed scrip. In the summer of 1900, after receiving a tip from Hitchcock, Green contacted John Roch Blanc, a Métis of Willow Bunch, who agreed to hand over his 240 acres of land scrip for $100. Green located a quarter-section and a half near the village of Pense, smack in the middle of the fecund Regina plain, and took Roch Blanc to the land office to make his entry. At a time when farmers like James Slemmon were being offered $8.50 an acre for unimproved land, Green picked up this prime quarter-section and a half for forty-one cents an acre.

Over the next two years, Green worked through the Prince Albert lawyers Hannon and Lamont, who bought half-breed scrip from an Indian agent, Patrick Anderson. Eventually he was able to assemble large tracts of land near Milestone and other areas southeast of Moose Jaw, which he sold for enormous profits to incoming Americans. His involvement in the half-breed-scrip swindle was not as extensive as John Hawke Grayson's – by the end of 1903 Green had moved on to even more lucrative speculation – yet it laid the foundation for his later fortune. His life-insurance business quickly spawned a real-estate agency. "Scrip for Sale, John R. Green Agency" was a familiar ad in the *Moose Jaw Times* in those days.

With his credibility as a money-maker established, he became a bona fide member of the business élite, a clique which by now was accustomed to running Moose Jaw. Nevertheless, they were not happy with their town's progress. The population was still only 1,158; Regina, with 2,249 people, seemed to be winning the everlasting race to be the Minneapolis of the north. It was true there was some progress – a new flour mill was in the works, a new Methodist church was planned, and a splendid new hotel called the Maple Leaf had been built near the CPR depot, but since the flourish of construction after the fire of 1891, Moose Jaw had not lived up to expectations.

By 1900 the business establishment was rather desperate. They were looking for somebody energetic and clever to help them lift the town out of the doldrums. John R. Green, they soon realized, was just the man. In December of 1900 he was nominated to run as town councillor by the banker Arthur Hitchcock, and in the following election he topped the list of six candidates with 135 votes.

Green used his elected position to climb the social ladder – he was the only one on the Moose Jaw Council, for example, who travelled all the way to Regina in October 1901 to attend the reception for the Duke and Duchess of Cornwall and York. And his business card, proudly displaying "Councilor for the City of Moose Jaw," gave him added credibility as he travelled to Michigan and Iowa selling prairie farmland to eager Americans. Through Liberal connections, he got the job as Moose Jaw's customs-collector, although this lasted only a month, until Green discovered it was far more work than it was worth. He bought and sold houses in Moose Jaw itself. And then he went into partnership with his brother.

Of all the Green siblings, John R. was closest to Harry, older by three years. Harry Green was as smart as J.R., and by 1900 he owned 2,240 acres of farmland, 1,280 of which he worked himself. He had eighteen working horses and the most modern equipment, including a large steam-threshing outfit. But he was tired. "The work's getting to me," he often complained. "And I'd like to feel some hard cash in my pocket." In November 1901, he leased his farm to two of Benjamin Smith's sons and moved into Moose Jaw. The following February, the *Times* announced that John and Harry Green had acquired James Battell's property opposite the town hall. It consisted of three lots on which construction of an office and warehouse would proceed immediately. "We congratulate them for securing such a splendid site for their new enterprise," said the paper.

H. & J. R. Green, Real Estate Owners and Agents, was a mixed-bag of a business. "We own some of the very best wheat land in the West, situated at Rouleau, Drinkwater, Pasqua, Belle-Plaine, Pense, Grand-Coulee," boasted an ad in the *Times*. They also sold fire, life, accident, and sickness insurance. They were land agents for the CPR and the Hudson's Bay Company. And they sold farm implements – Deering Harvester Co., American & Abell Threshing Machines, J. I. Case, anything the farmers wanted. In August the *Times* reported "Already H. & J.R. Green have unloaded three carloads of Deering binder twine. Their business is flourishing beyond expectation."

Yet only four months later, the Green brothers announced they were dissolving their partnership. Harry would continue the business, while John R. planned to team up with a Minneapolis capitalist by the name of Knappen to form the Moose Jaw Land and Investment Company. The reason given for the split was that John R. "wants to devote all his time to that business in which he is largely interested – real estate." But there were hints that Harry did not approve of some of the questionable speculative schemes in which his brother was involved. And by that time John R. Green had also fallen out with the Liberal establishment, but for quite different reasons.

At the 1902 ratepayers' meeting held at the Moose Jaw Town Hall, William Grayson committed an unheard of breach – he attacked a member of the ruling élite, and in public too. He accused John R. Green of "gross and willful extravagance" with taxpayers' money. "Taxes have been increased enormously, and there is nothing to show for it, and since you, Mr. Green, are chairman of the finance committee, you must take full blame."

Ostensibly, Grayson was complaining about a well which had been drilled in an attempt to find Moose Jaw a supply of good water. The casing had not been adequate, and the contractor had refused to continue with the work, with the result that the city lost about $1,200. But almost everybody sitting in the audience that evening knew Grayson's testiness had little to do with drinking water and a lot to do with his own pocketbook.

Under an arrangement conceived in the early 1880s, the CPR and its agent the Canada North-West Land Company, together with the federal government, still owned a good chunk of Moose Jaw, and this ever-more-valuable property continued to be administered by three township trustees. Over the years there had been much haggling and many hard feelings over the trustees' refusal to pay taxes; they would never cough up more than one-quarter the amount that had been assessed. Without these duly owed taxes, the town could not afford to install essential services such as water, electricity, even paved streets. Without them, how could Moose Jaw beat out other western boom towns in the never-ending battle to be the biggest and the best?

In 1900 it was discovered that the title to all the lots comprising the townsite had been invested in the individual trustees from the beginning, rather than in the railway company. This was taken to mean that no tax-exemption could be claimed. There followed a great debate over whether Moose Jaw could collect taxes back to 1882, or whether they would be satisfied if the full amount was paid in the future. Meanwhile, the trustees simply ignored the hoopla and continued to pay one-quarter of what the town fathers claimed was owed.

It was John R. Green's idea to ask the courts to rule on the issue, and shortly after his election to municipal council, he began to lobby Frederick Haultain, the premier of the North-West Territories. By November Green had almost succeeded in persuading the territorial government to make Moose Jaw a test case, and that was why William Grayson attacked him so savagely at the ratepayers' meeting in November 1902. Grayson had been the the Moose Jaw agent for the township trustees for sixteen years, and naturally it remained in his interest to protect their interests. As well, he continued to claim that the property he had bought for himself through the Canada North-West Land Company was also exempt from taxes, and he had paid no more than one-quarter assessed. John Green's exuberance in performing his civic duties, therefore, threatened William Grayson's bank account.

At the ratepayers' meeting Green, looking pointedly at Grayson, said, "I want to live in a town where everybody pays their just share of the taxes and where everybody is on equal footing." He insisted that he had already decided not to run in the next municipal election, but "on account of the turn things have taken, I am determined to stay and fight it out. It will be seen if Mr. Grayson's estimate of me is the right one."

Green had thrown down the gauntlet, and William Grayson quickly snatched it up. The municipal election was a nasty, bitter fight, played out primarily backstage. It was a squabble among the ruling class, and the *hoi poloi* knew little about it. William Grayson quickly called in the debts owed by his cronies. And yet there were enough people who were so angry at the CPR's niggardliness that they were willing to buck the establishment. Grayson's man, the mill-owner, Donald McLean, led the polls with 173 votes, but Green managed 103 votes and last spot on the town council. Still, it was a poor performance compared to the previous year, and J.R. felt humiliated.

The following spring, however, he got even with the Grayson cabal. He did an end-run around them that was so audacious and skilful it was the talk of the town for years after.

In 1900 a commissioner had been appointed to audit the accounts of the townsite trustees. He had found such serious improprieties that the Laurier government became determined to end its real-estate partnership with the CPR. This was accomplished two years later. The question then arose: What was the federal government going to do with the town lots it had acquired? One suggestion was to auction them off to the highest bidders. The other was to simply hand them over gratis to the towns involved, in lieu of the lost revenue from unpaid taxes. It was this idea that prevailed, and in early April 1903, Moose Jaw suddenly found itself with 800 town lots to dispose of as it wished.

While most speculators were frantically jockeying for position to get their hands on this property, John R. Green explored a different path. He began secret negotiations with the other partner involved in town lots, the CPR. On April 17, it was announced that he had acquired a large chunk – a full quarter-section – of Moose Jaw's prime residential land. It ran up a gently sloping hill north of Caribou Street, between 5th Avenue and Main Street, and while it wasn't situated at the heart of downtown, it was well within the city limits. Eventually Green had the property surveyed into the three subdivisions, High Park, Parkside, and Rosemount. Today many of Moose Jaw's lovely old homes are located on avenues like Redland, Grafton, and Chestnut. (Green named one street Oxford, after the town he had lived in in Michigan, and another Ross Street, after J. H. Ross, the patriarch of the Liberal clique in Moose Jaw.) Traditionally it has been the area where many of the town's professionals chose to live, including a future premier of Saskatchewan, Ross Thatcher, and his son, Colin.

The *Moose Jaw Times* seemed surprised at Green's coup. "This property has always been withheld from the market, but somehow Mr. Green succeeded in securing it," the paper reported. Green paid $30 an acre, which seemed an exorbitant sum to many of his critics at the time. But he was smart in the way he handled it. Over the next three years he gradually placed the lots on the market, raising the purchase price as the town spun into its incredible boom period. By 1906, when the last portion, High Park west of Main Street, was sold in an eighty-acre block to a real-estate developer, each lot went for over $900. Altogether Green raked in about $650,000 in three years on an original investment of $4,800. "He bought land by the acre and sold it by the foot," said a farmer of Green, and this became the trademark by which Green was known.

Such a master stroke, engineered by someone so young – he was thirty-three at the time – was both admired and envied by the Moose Jaw business tribe. Many of Green's acquaintances, especially associates of William Grayson, were furious. They snubbed him on Main Street. His application to join the cricket club, newly organized by Arthur Hitchcock, was turned down. Although he volunteered, he was not asked to participate in the debate that year, though he was very interested in the topic: "Resolved that the settlement of capital and labour disputes by strikes should be made a criminal offence."

Apparently Green felt the heat, for in September he suddenly announced he was quitting. He planned to travel on business, he said, "which will prevent me from properly attending my duties." The resignation was a surprise, and the council refused to deal with it. Green was persuaded to remain in office until the December elections, but it was an indication of how fed up he was. A few weeks later he announced that he and his family were moving to Ann Arbor, Michigan.

Supposedly, it was a temporary arrangement; Green was planning to take a special accounting course, he said. But Moose Jaw buzzed with gossip when the family put all their household effects and furnishings up for auction. Rumours circulated that they planned to sell their home.

Once settled in Michigan, however, Green seems to have spent most of his time making contact with wealthy speculators who wanted to invest in the Canadian prairies. Eventually he would cook up a deal whereby 7,000 acres of unimproved farmland on the Arcola branch railway was sold to "Eastern and American capitalists." Over $50,000 changed hands. Moose Jaw was simply too promising a place to forsake, and by April of 1904, he was back in town, nicely settled in a large new office in the Union Bank building on River Street.

Annie Maude Green did not return with their two sons, Wilbert and Alan, until September. Her friends speculated that she was taking a breather from the hectic life her husband had imposed on her. The previous couple of years had not been very happy ones for Annie Maude. In 1902 she had given birth to her third son, Arthur, a lovely child who was robust and inquisitive. One afternoon, when he was eight months old, Annie Maude was preparing to bathe him. She boiled some water, poured it into the tin bathtub on the floor, and then went outside to the pump to get some cold water to add to it. While she was gone, the baby crawled into the tub. He screamed through three horrible days, but then finally died from first-degree burns to most of his body. Annie Maude never forgave herself for her negligence, and mourned the little boy for years.

Relatives claim that she was frightened and upset by her husband's driving ambition. He was no longer interested in the things she had so admired, such as participating in the debating society, or promoting the cause of temperance. There were several old friends of John Green who felt he now cared about nothing but making money. "I've heard he used to laugh and say, 'Well, I made $30,000 today,' and I think everybody got kind of tired hearing it," says his daughter Mary Jefferson.

Certainly, he was attempting to re-establish himself in Moose Jaw society. He lost his bid to be vice-president of the Board of Trade, but after he volunteered to raise money, he was selected to be director of Moose Jaw's first hospital, which was under construction in the summer of 1904. He therefore had a place on the dais that sunny day in July when the cornerstone was officially dedicated. "Blessed be this structure to relieve the sick and distressed," prayed Rev. A. J. Sanders. Green smiled appropriately as the citizens' brass band belted out a gay tune and the Daughters of the Empire secured the flags on the scaffolding. But he wasn't on the speakers' list, which, as usual, featured William Grayson.

John R. could not be snubbed by the élite for long. The Green family was simply becoming too accomplished. The father, Robert, was now considered something of a sage, and his advice on political matters was often sought. F. W. was a leading light in the influential Saskatchewan Grain Growers' Association. Harry's business was thriving, and he had been declared a town councillor by acclamation. It seemed the West had fulfilled their dreams beyond all expectations. Then, once again, disaster struck.

Harry had married the daughter of G. M. Ross, a member of the pioneering family who first staked out Moose Jaw. Barbara Ross was one of the few women who had arrived in Moose Jaw before the railroad had been built; Harry admired and loved her for her strength and exuberance. In January of 1904, she gave birth to the couple's fourth child, a girl they called Elizabeth Christina. Four weeks later, at the age of twenty-nine, Barbara Green died of post-childbirth complications. Two months after that, the baby girl slipped away.

Harry Green was a man who enjoyed life; soccer was his passion, and telling funny stories his art, and he was determined not to become crippled by his grief. He would make a good home for his three young children. He had help from his mother and sisters, of course, and he was able to find a responsible housekeeper. The family was pleased that Harry was able to carry on, and there was even some discussion about finding him another wife. Then in December 1905, he was stricken with typhoid fever. Like James Slemmon, doctors and medicine helped him hardly at all. He grew progressively worse and died within two weeks.

Harry Green had been an immensely popular man. Nobody was surprised to learn that he had bequeathed over $1,000 to the Moose Jaw Hospital and $500 to the Methodist Church – a substantial sum in those days. Most of Moose Jaw turned out for his funeral. The casket was carried from the Zion Church across the street to the Civic Opera House, where it was placed on centre stage. A choir sang "Nearer My God to Thee" as the mourners marched past. J.R. thought the whole thing was in bad taste, like some grotesque musical.

Harry's will gives some indication of how much the Greens had prospered since their arrival, almost penniless, fifteen years before. Besides his implement dealership, Harry Green owned over 2,500 acres of farmland around Moose Jaw, and nineteen separate city lots, some worth as much as $4,000 apiece. (Harry had bought them for $400 each six years before.)

Interestingly, his brother, Fred, was named sole guardian of the three young orphans, which led people to surmise that the breach between John R. and Harry had not been healed. And yet, to untangle affairs left by Harry's untimely death, and to set up sound investments for the children's future, John R. sold property which he and his brother had owned jointly to Harry's estate at prices much lower than the market value.

John R. Green could afford such a charitable act since he too was now a wealthy man. In fact so successful was he at land speculation that the entrepreneurial élite could no longer exclude him. He simply had more energy, more managerial skill, and more cunning than most of them. Moose Jaw was about to engage in cut-throat competition with other boom towns on the prairies, and someone with Green's unrelenting, evangelical boosterism was invaluable.

The *Moose Jaw Times* published a profile of Green about this time, under the heading "PROMINENT CITIZENS." It was a congratulatory piece, of course – "Being of a practical turn of mind, he demonstrated his faith [in the Canadian West] by his works and the result has been most gratifying to Mr. Green and his multitude of friends who are pleased to see him independently wealthy and one of our most influential citizens." What is most interesting, however, is the cartoonist's sketch that illustrates the story. Gone are all hints of the brooding, intellectual schoolteacher. The black beard *à la* Marx and Freud is replaced by a jaunty little moustache, the sombre blue apparel by a loud checked suit. He remains a handsome man, although already his propensity to corpulence is obvious. Every inch the cocksure entrepreneur, he stands casually, with one hand in his pocket and the other extended in welcome to what looks like a horde of speculators rushing towards a large sign that reads MOOSE JAW REAL ESTATE. "I found nothing that appealed to me as a better opportunity for investment than that which Moose Jaw has to offer," J.R. said in a testimonial. It was not surprising that, in 1906, he was elected the president of the Board of Trade.

This organization of the business élite had evolved into a powerful instrument to promote Moose Jaw's growth. First established in the early 1880s, the Board of Trade had faded away during the subsequent depression years and was then rechartered in 1901. At its first meeting that year, members of the board's council, dominated, of course, by William Grayson, were worried about the scarlet-fever epidemic that was raging at the time. It wasn't good for business, they lamented. "If it continues to spread in town it will naturally result in preventing immigration and restricting trade." No motion was forthcoming in aid of the people who were suffering from the sickness. What was needed was not more medicine or health care but more police to enforce the quarantine. No farmer from an infected home should be allowed into Moose Jaw, the board council insisted, even though he might be after medicine for his family.

This attitude prevailed over the years. The Board of Trade was dominated by wealthy businessmen* interested only in boosting their town so they could make fortunes through speculation. Anyone who questioned the lack of decent housing, or drinkable water, or welfare for the down-and-out, or simply wondered whether frantic, unplanned expansion was good for their town, was labelled a "knocker" or a "kicker" – and considered beneath contempt. There was little the underclasses could do. Most did not hold property, and therefore were disenfranchised. And even those who did own their houses were often ineligible to vote, because in hard times they were unable to pay their hefty property taxes, taxes which were being used primarily to promote the speculators' wild development schemes. On the other hand, wealthy men like the Graysons and J. R. Green were allowed to cast ballots in any ward where they owned property. Green once voted five times in one municipal election.

By the time Green was elected president, the Board of Trade was a more powerful body than City Council. Board members often sat in on closed-door council meetings, hammering out such things as where industry would be located, where rail spurlines would go, where housing would be developed. In 1907, when the power plant was not keeping up with the city's growth, the board circulated a petition, signed mostly by businessmen, for an expensive expansion. Council balked at having to raise a debenture for the $90,000, but after a series of in-camera evening meetings with the Board of Trade council, the politicians finally caved in. Such wanton borrowing would

*So was City Council. Between 1904 and 1913, seventy-seven citizens served as aldermen and mayor. Of these, fifty-eight were well-known businessmen.

eventually reap disaster. The city was eventually loaded down with such debt that, in 1937, it would default on its debentures and be, in effect, bankrupt.

The business élite weren't merely concerned with the development of Moose Jaw; their manipulations through the Board of Trade advanced their own personal get-rich-quick schemes more than it did the city.

By 1906, when Green was elected president of the board, the élite of Moose Jaw had pretty good reason to be optimistic about their city's future. Joy and jubilation reigned when a census that year revealed that Moose Jaw was the largest city in Saskatchewan. With a population of 6,249, it boasted thirty-three people more than its arch rival Regina. The gloating that followed was merciless.

Moose Jaw's supremacy had to be maintained at all costs, and one of John R. Green's first duties was to appear before City Council to request an annual grant of $5,000 for promotional purposes. It was a large amount of money at a time when $10,000 would build the town's firehall. The city's businessmen had already subscribed to a publicity fund to the tune of $4,000, and Green felt that now "all ratepayers should contribute proportionally" through tax dollars. The council at first turned down the request – "People have been paying taxes for years and they still don't have sidewalks. Surely it wasn't reasonable to spend money outside for publicity purposes," Alderman J. H. Bunnell reasoned. But at subsequent meetings the politicians reconsidered. Regina council had voted to spend $10,000 to publicize their city and, as Green said, "That will mean that place will surely surge ahead and we certainly don't want that to happen." Handing out taxpayers' money to promote the activities of wealthy speculators soon became a habit, not only with Moose Jaw but with cities all through the West.

Spectacular advertisements appeared in eastern Canadian and American newspapers, praising Moose Jaw in the most extravagantly glowing terms. "It is the gateway of the golden West, the railway hub of the province, the centre of the best farm land in the world, the mecca of international investors, the jeweled buckle on the world's greatest belt of wheat." J. R.

Green, wherever he travelled, never tired of telling people, "Moose Jaw, you know, is the biggest and the best place in Saskatchewan."

Moose Jaw citizens began to feel anything was possible, even snatching away Regina's privilege of being the new capital city of a new province, which was, at last, being formed.

One lovely April day in 1906, John R. Green, suitably attired in a sombre, navy blue, three-piece pin-striped suit and a bowler hat, travelled to Regina so that he could accompany members of the Saskatchewan legislature back to Moose Jaw in a specially chartered Pullman car. A full day had been planned, including a tour of Green's new High Park subdivision, where the lots were selling for $800 a piece, the new Alexandra School, the new Moose Jaw Flour Mills, and the newly expanded CPR stockyards.

The excursion did not include the South Hill, a jumble of workers' houses, where indoor plumbing and adequate ventilation were nonexistent. Nor were the visitors given a conducted tour of May LaVille's brothel, which two days before had been raided by police. Nor did the distinguished guests visit River Street's Royal Restaurant, owned by Qong Sing, Qong Sat, Qong Wing, and Qong Song, which was always crowded with customers – not sipping the wonton soup so much as playing the totally illegal numbers racket.

Green carefully led the legislators into the new Maple Leaf Hotel to enjoy "a Sumptuous Repast and Happy Hour." The fact that only half the members of the legislative assembly had shown up for the excursion might have been a hint to the Moose Jaw clique that proclaiming their city the capital was not in the cards. Three weeks later Premier Walter Scott announced that Regina would remain the Queen City of Saskatchewan.

Moose Jaw's spirits were dampened, but not entirely; it was, after all, logical that Regina should remain the capital. And there was something else in the wind that made the city's heart beat faster; the greatest prize of all, the University of Saskatchewan, was up for grabs. And this battle, General John R. Green was expected to win.

On a Tuesday evening in April 1908, a huge crowd packed the

Moose Jaw Opera House. William Grayson told them, "Sink or swim, live or die, the university must come to Moose Jaw. Our city has been passed over in the past, but she will not this time without putting up a tremendous struggle, which will be felt from one end of the province to the other."

A week later, four carloads of Moose Jaw citizens, mostly Liberals, travelled by special train to Regina. Given the passion of the rhetoric, the MLAs must have expected to confront a crowd that was fighting mad. What they found instead was an intimidated Mayor Richard Bogue (that old friend of William Grayson who fixed Grayson's election to the school board twenty-two years before), who presented a petition with 2,217 names on it, and several spokesmen who were the very embodiment of "admirable restraint and dignity." When Premier Scott told the delegation, as kindly as he could, that it was the university's board of governors, not him, who would make the decision, so they were wasting their time, the two hundred returned home somewhat crestfallen.

The Liberal clique in Moose Jaw had long been unhappy that the sitting member, who was a Tory, had not pushed Moose Jaw as passionately as they would have liked. "If we had someone in the legislature who knew how to put two words together rather than stumbling all over the place, we might have more luck," said O. B. Fysh (who, in the previous election, had run against the stumbler and lost). That someone turned out to be J. R. Green.

Perhaps because Liberal Premier Walter Scott owned the newspaper, the *Moose Jaw Times* never – in public, at least – doubted that Green would win. In fact the paper had still not recovered from the shock of a Conservative victory in Moose Jaw three years before, in 1905.

It had been the province's first election. Before that the vast area of the North-West Territories was administered by a potpourri of politicians who considered themselves nonpartisan. Though they had political affiliations, they supposedly governed as independents, interested only in promoting the welfare of the territories. Chief among them was Frederick Haultain, who served as first minister for nine years.

A morose, shy man, he was also an honest and obsessively hard-working politician. He laboured long and hard to free the territories from Ottawa's apron-strings. Unfortunately, just as this was finally happening, his vision of the future collided head on with Prime Minister Wilfrid Laurier's. Haultain saw one province, vast in size, which would eventually have a population so large as to have great clout in Ottawa; Laurier, also thinking of future power plays, insisted on two provinces, Saskatchewan and Alberta. Haultain thought the new government should have control over education, Crown lands, natural resources; Laurier wanted to ensure that the French-Canadians in the West had access to an education in their own language, and so the rights of minorities were removed from the purview of the new province's legislature. And to promote immigration policies, Laurier insisted that Crown lands and natural resources remain the property of the Dominion government. Even with these serious differences of opinion, most prairie people felt Laurier would be forced to hand over the premiership to the saintly Haultain. Then Haultain made a serious mistake. He attended the Conservative convention in Moose Jaw in March 1903, thereby branding himself as a partisan of Toryism. That was all Laurier needed. Two years later, the feisty newspaperman, Walter Scott, only thirty-eight years old, was named acting premier of the newly created province of Saskatchewan. He was a good friend of William Grayson's, and Grayson wanted a Liberal elected in Moose Jaw.

On December 13, 1905, three months after the elaborate ceremonies inaugurating the new province, an election was called. Haultain attempted to lure Liberals as well as Tories into a group called the Provincial Rights Party. John R. Green's brother, Fred, was among those who decided that Haultain's great reputation and the fear that Laurier and the federal Liberals would hereafter dominate the province's politics were reason enough to vote for the Provincial Righters.

And Scott did indeed get help from his friends in Ottawa. Arm-twisters spread out over the prairies like buckbrush bushes. Every immigrant who was eligible was told where and when he should vote. For whom he should vote was taken for granted, for, after all, Sifton's open immigration policy was likely the reason the voter was on his Canadian farm. More important, with the western economy booming, Scott was able to deliver a message of hope – "peace, progress and prosperity" – Haultain only of chagrin. The voters were in the mood for optimism, and the Liberals won easily.

But not in Moose Jaw. John H. Wellington, a retired CPR engineer, beat Liberal real-estate agent O. B. Fysh, much to the annoyance of the Liberal clique. Hitchcock, Grayson, and company decided to treat Wellington's victory as a mere aberration; after all, he had won by only fifty-two votes. Three years later, in 1908, Wellington announced he was seeking re-election, but the Grayson clique were "utterly confident" that this time a Liberal would take the city of Moose Jaw.

J. R. Green had two major advantages in the 1908 election campaign: the *Moose Jaw Times*, whose devotion to the Liberal candidate knew no bounds – every news story began something like, "No political meeting has been held in Moose Jaw this year in which more enthusiasm was shown than at last night's in the city hall addressed by J. R. Green" – and the achievements of the previous Liberal administration. Railroad construction, a burgeoning population, extensive road building, new schools, all indicated that Scott had managed to set the infant province firmly on its feet in only three years.

Bashing the CPR was a favourite tactic in J. R. Green's campaign; he could claim that Scott's government had finally broken the railway's monopoly and that competitive lines were about to criss-cross the province. What he harped on most, however, was that old melody – the location of the University of Saskatchewan. He never stopped repeating his pledge to "move heaven and earth to see the mighty seat of learning located on the banks of Moose Jaw Creek." Time and again he pointed out that his opponent J. H. Wellington had failed so far in this undertaking.

Wellington was not as sophisticated or articulate as Green, but he too had an edge, which turned out to be more important than the Liberal clique suspected: he was a member of the Brotherhood of Locomotive Firemen and Engineers.

This was an era in Canada when workers had awakened not only to the injustices of the dreadful conditions under which they laboured, but also to the power of their unions. Strikes had flared up everywhere. From the grain-handlers at Port Arthur to telephone-operators in Edmonton, workers manned the picket lines to demand higher pay and better working conditions. The effects of such strikes could be devastating. During the winter of 1906-7, there was such a shortage of coal, a direct result of stop-work action by miners, that Moose Jaw's power plant was only a day away from shutting down. The schools and hospital were on the verge of closing their doors before a relief shipment of wood finally arrived from Prince Albert. Tragedies were common. A Radcliffe farmer was found frozen to death on the prairie beside a sleigh piled high with wood and coal, while his wife and three children suffered the same fate at home.

Despite the bad publicity ladled out unceasingly during labour disputes – "The strikers who are nearly all foreigners are drinking and going around heavily armed, threatening death to all who interfere," was a typical biased account published by the *Times* – Moose Jaw voters (then and now) remained staunchly loyal to their unions – especially the railroad workers.

By 1908 they were the most powerful voting block in the city. And John Henry Wellington, who had laboured on railroad construction gangs during the early 1880s, who had worked his way up to engineer on the CPR, and who had been one of the chief organizers of the Moose Jaw local of the Brotherhood of Locomotive Firemen and Engineers, was regarded as one of their own.

Still, Green was a dynamic speaker, and he was pulling in huge crowds, at least in the affluent areas of Moose Jaw. As the election drew near, the *Times* was confident of a "landslide victory. The city has always been Liberal and to liberalism it shall be redeemed."

When the first results were announced on the hot August election night, the Liberal committee room let out one single shout: "It's skiddo for Wellington and the Provincial Righters." In the City Hall district, where the merchants and professionals were in the majority, Green beat Wellington by 132 to 109 votes.

But it was only the first of six polls, and it was the only poll Green would win. In all the residential areas, where the workers' houses sat cheek by jowl, Wellington scored a significant victory, finally winning the election 763 to Green's 682. (The former Liberal candidate O. B. Fysh had run as an independent and managed 59 votes.)

Both front-runners had the same first name, and campaign slogans had played with this fact. Wellington had been labelled "Honest John" by his supporters; Green "Fighting John R." by his. The voters clearly chose integrity over aggressiveness, which probably was also an indication that pitching Moose Jaw as the "the Minneapolis, St. Paul, and Chicago of the Canadian West," was not so important to the working stiff as his concern that the price of coal had jumped from $7.50 to $8 a ton overnight.

John R. Green was embarrassed by the defeat, especially since Scott's Liberals had done so well in the rest of the province, winning twenty-seven of the forty-one seats. "Personally, I have no regrets," he said. "From the city's standpoint, however, I feel that a serious mistake has been made." In April of the following year, Saskatoon was chosen as the site for the University of Saskatchewan. Green couldn't help muttering "I told you so." That he could have done anything to alter the decision is questionable, especially after one governor was heard to ask, "How could you put the university in a place with such a queer name as Moose Jaw?"

~ III ~

Annie Maude Green hated being in the public eye; she suffered nightmares every time she had to attend a tea or dinner in aid of her husband's cause. The December before the election, her youngest son fell ill with bronchitis, which turned out to be a blessing in disguise. It was decided that Annie Maude and the children should spend the winter with her parents, who had retired to Ontario, California.

On a picture postcard, taken during one of her many trips

south, there is a lovely group photo of Annie Maude, her mother and father, and her sister-in-law. The ladies are dressed in white, pretty in huge flowered sunhats; Mr. Beesley wears a white duster and a golfer's hat. They are sitting in his beautifully decorated automobile, and all are smiling, because he has just been awarded second prize at the Festive d'Ontario. Annie Maude once told a cousin that the only time she was happy in her life was when she was visiting her parents.

After the election defeat, the Greens took another holiday in California. It was just as well that J.R. had a rest, for he was about to face a series of battles that would leave him an emotional and physical wreck.

The first seemed an unlikely thing to get worked up about – electric street railways – but it became a power struggle, a personal quest, which in Annie Maude's mind was blown all out of proportion by her husband.

By 1910 the ultimate status symbol among the newly sophisticated cities of the prairies was street railways. Winnipeg had already constructed one (there had been a violent strike by the conductors) and so had Vancouver; Dougald Carmichael had worked there as a conductor. Calgary, Medicine Hat, and Prince Albert were dreaming of streetcars, but more ominously, Moose Jaw's arch enemy Regina was seriously considering the construction of a municipal railway.

In the winter of 1910 a group of Ottawa entrepreneurs approached the Moose Jaw City Council with a proposal to construct an electric streetcar network. They had built a similar system in the capital, which they bragged was a big success. Immediately the entrepreneurs of Moose Jaw were up in arms. It was their city, and if there was going to be a street railroad, they should build it, not some "outsider." J. R. Green led the forces of protest by presenting a petition of ratepayers' names to the City Council. A two-week delay in awarding the contract was requested, so the Moose Jaw élite could get their proposal together. The councillors agreed but, worried about the race with Regina, only reluctantly.

Annie Maude could never figure out why her husband took the matter of streetcars so personally. Night after night he paced up and down, back and forth, in his study, as though he were solving the world's most serious problems. She became more and more worried about his "nerves." For some reason he perceived the struggle as a violation of his turf, a challenge to his ingenuity, an insult to his very manhood.

Green and associates (including John Hawke Grayson) did manage to form the Moose Jaw and Suburban Rapid Transit Railway Company with a mandate to operate "several lines of tracks, powered by either steam or electricity." The *Moose Jaw Times* was enthusiastic. "We have repeatedly predicted that within the lifetimes of the people who are now paying taxes, the population of the city will be 100,000. That is certainly a reason to raise a debenture for a railway now."

But investors didn't agree. Green and company couldn't get the financing together. At the next council meeting they had no concrete scheme to present, only a request for more time. "The Council is greatly disappointed and much surprised that no proposal has been made," lectured the mayor. The Ottawa group were promptly given the green light.

Green remained in a sulk about the streetcar for years. He even mounted a campaign against the eastern entrepreneurs, pleading with the provincial politicians to cancel their agreement with the city of Moose Jaw. His petition was shrugged off; in his obsession, he became something of a laughing-stock. Yet there was consolation, since the street railway project proved to be a fiasco. The promoters had trouble raising the money, and on the day that railway cars were to start rumbling down Main Street, only a half mile of track was prepared. To save face, City Council decided to go ahead with the inauguration ceremonies anyway.

On a sunny August 19, 1911, the city's establishment (not including J. R. Green, who was fuming in his den) gathered beside the powerhouse, quaintly decorated with green and white bunting and a large moose head. After the usual interminably long speeches, pretty Mrs. Paul, the wife of the current mayor, was escorted to the engine and rather ungracefully yanked a lever. The machine began to cough ominously, but then the 27th Light Horse Band struck up a tune, and the

Moose Jaw Street Railway lurched down Main Street. At Fairford Street, the trolley wires inadvertently came in contact with the city's main power line. Fireworks! The fire-alarm boxes across the city exploded; the switchboard at the city firehall was shorted; a construction gang, working on a building nearby, narrowly escaped death by electrocution.

After such an inauspicious beginning, the electric railway was never much of a money-maker, and by 1932 it was gone.

The streetcars were only one symptom of a strange disease which, by the winter of 1912-13, plagued Moose Jaw and most other towns in the West. It was called the boom-and-bust syndrome.

By 1912, there were thirteen banks in Moose Jaw. All the majors, the Dominion Bank of Canada, the Canadian Bank of Commerce, the Union Bank of Canada, the Merchants Bank, the Bank of Montreal, the Bank of Nova Scotia, and the Bank of Hamilton, had opened offices, and whether they provided better service than Hitchcock & McCulloch, which had operated alone for so many years, was a debatable question. In 1901 there had been four fire-insurance companies; in 1912 there were fifty-four. The number of loan companies had jumped from two to twenty-six. But most dramatic was the epidemic of real-estate agencies. By the winter of 1912-13, they numbered 113. Former bankers, schoolteachers, clerks, photographers, ex-politicians, flooded into Moose Jaw to try their luck at flipping properties, and they often had large amounts of eastern capitalists' money with which to play. Moose Jaw blossomed into a city of pretentiously named subdivisions: Earnescliff, Boulevard Heights, Fairview, Ross Park, Mooscana, Windsor Park, the Highlands, Crescent View, Silver Heights, Morningside, Tuxedo Park, Queen's Park, Hazel Dell, Bannockburn, Strathcona Heights, Connaught Gardens, Richmond Park, Mount Pleasant, Parkdale Boulevard, Hayesmount, Rideau Heights, Mount Elgin, Mount Royal Park, Norwood Heights, Como Park, Kingsway Park, City View, Westmore Prairie Heights, Lynnbrook, George Park, Buena Vista, Shaughnessy Heights, Highland Park, Dunmore, and Coronation Heights. All had been carved out of the virgin prairie.

Travelling salesmen combed the back roads with snapshots showing beautiful landscapes at twilight in early summer and sketches of the lovely garden communities that would soon bloom there. Railway shop-men, washing women, bakers – anybody who could afford the $25 down and $10 a month – bought subdivided lots. Most had no intention of living there; they were waiting for the flood of settlers who, according to the promoters, were sure to arrive at any moment, eager to pay hugely inflated prices for somewhere to live. Many farmers, dreaming of unimaginable wealth, took their hard-earned life savings and bought whole blocks in Ross Park (property owned by J. H. Ross and therefore beyond suspicion) or Tuxedo Park or Coronation Heights. That not a house had been built on these glamorously-named patches of earth; that there seemed to be no one who actually wanted to live there; that the essential services like water, sewers, and electricity had not been installed in one of these subdivisions; that, if on every lot stood an occupied house, Moose Jaw's population would soar three hundred times, mattered not at all. They believed real-estate agent C. M. Wrenshall, who declared with a straight face, "There's absolutely no doubt in my mind that in ten years Moose Jaw will have a population of 100,000 people and in twenty years it will be five times that figure." (In 1991 the city's population stood at 35,000, and had been that for years.)

J. R. Green also indulged in this speculator's game, but with the cunning and hard-headedness of a poker-playing shark. As late as 1909, he was still dabbling extensively in Métis scrip. The land he had bought from the CPR had been subdivided, but, since it was located near the centre of the city, it had been quickly built up, and had yielded Green enormous profits. He was part of a four-man syndicate that developed a 110-acre subdivision called Mooscana. But he considered all of this to be small potatoes compared to his plans for the Moose Creek Valley Estates – a dream that would result in an exhausting struggle with the Canadian Northern Railway.

In 1902 John R. Green had bought a half-section in what was considered the most beautiful part of Moose Jaw. Steep hills heavy with aspen dropped down into a valley, through which

Moose Jaw Creek ambled. The Mountie, Tom Aspdin, had situated his homestead just north of this property ten years before and had tried to farm it until Arthur Hitchcock had seized it as payment for the overdue bank loan. Over the years John R. Green managed to get his hands on Aspdin's property and another three quarter-sections in the vicinity. By 1911, he had a full section and a half of land. There, in a park-like setting, he planned to construct large and elegant homes, nestled among spruce and elm trees, away from the hub-bub of the city, and yet with all the urban services – good roads, indoor plumbing, central heating.

Then the Canadian Northern threw a spanner in the works. The railway was just being constructed into Moose Jaw, and the southern route that was chosen ran down the edge of Green's property. Green claimed the railway was offering a "piddly sum" in compensation, and the dispute went to court.

During the summer of 1913, arguments were heard before a three-man arbitration panel; it was a bitter and, for J.R., a nerve-wracking fight. Green's side claimed that the railway's intrusion had virtually wiped out his investment. A high-class neighbourhood could not be sullied by whistle blasts and dirty smoke. The railway's lawyers said Green was trying to pull a fast one; in an attempt to get the highest price possible for his subdivision lots, he had waited too long to put them on the market. The great building boom was now collapsing, and Green wanted to make good his losses by gouging the railroad.

The panel, two of whom were devoted Liberals and old friends of Green's, awarded him a hefty $43,802, of which $31,833 was for "injurious effect." Since Green had paid only $26,481 for the entire section and a half, he considered the award a great victory.

But the Canadian Northern Railway appealed the decision. By the time the case was heard a year and a half later, the real-estate market in Moose Jaw had completely gone bust; all those communities with lovely names like Boniveen Park and Bannockburn turned out to be mere mirages floating in the salesmen's imagination, and they soon disappeared into the flat prairie whence they had come. All those butchers, and widows, and train engineers, and farmers lost their savings overnight. Hard times followed. By 1913, there were 2,500 men looking for work in Moose Jaw, and the bread-lines stretched for blocks – maybe one reason that the three Supreme Court justices, reviewing Green vs. Canadian Northern, had difficulty believing in John R.'s dreams for his subdivision. They cut the award in half.

Moose Creek Valley Estates was never built. In 1928, J. R. Green, perhaps feeling a twinge of guilt, leased it to the province for a nominal sum, to be converted into a wildlife park, which remains a distinctive feature of Moose Jaw to this day.

In 1913, J. R. Green suffered a severe physical and emotional breakdown. The election campaign of 1908, the electric-railway skirmish, the struggle with the Canadian Northern, all took their toll on him. And there was another set-back as well. In September 1911, Green had worked himself into a fever pitch trying to get Wilfrid Laurier's Liberals re-elected. Green thought Laurier was the best prime minister the country ever had, and he believed in reciprocity, free trade with the Americans. So strong was his passion that he spoke at a number of rallies, and glad-handed throughout the Moose Jaw district – but to no avail. The local Liberal, W. E. Knowles, won, but the Conservatives under Robert Borden took the election. It was another blow that Green took personally.

In May 1913, he travelled to Toronto, where he underwent extensive medical treatment for what was called "nerves." On his return two months later, the *Moose Jaw Times* reported, "Mr. Green's many friends are pleased to note his health is greatly improved." But he did not again take on the hurly-burly world of free enterprise.

~ IV ~

He had already closed down his real-estate business. That year he had moved from his suite in the Bellamy Block on High Street into a small office in the Grayson building, from where he henceforth managed only his own private property. He still owned over thirty lots in Moose Jaw, and he would put much time and energy into fighting City Hall against what he considered were "outrageously" high property taxes. But he basically withdrew from the life of the city and turned back to what he always claimed was his first love: agriculture. In fact, following his practice of never putting all his eggs in one basket, he had over the years amassed a huge amount of farmland – on the off-chance that the city real-estate market might go bust and farming prove more lucrative.

One day in July 1906, he had been visiting the Pasqua district with his good friend Doc Eddy, the farmer-speculator from Grand Rapids, Michigan, who had bought James Slemmon's land. They were passing a particular farm, and Eddy pointed out, "That's a fine field of wheat there."

"Awfully green, though," replied J.R.

The next day Green happened to pass the same spot. He later explained what he saw: "I could hardly believe it was the same field, it was so beautifully headed out. Overnight it had ripened, a remarkable example of rapid growth." That particular field remained a symbol for him of the great expectations he held for the West. It was the SW1/4 of 14-16-25 W2, owned by Benjamin Smith, and in the summer of 1911, when Smith hinted he wanted to sell, Green grabbed the quarter-section, paying $2,400 for 160 acres.

By 1915, J. R. Green owned three full sections, scattered around the south Moose Jaw district, a huge amount of land in those days. Much of it he leased out to tenant farmers on a sharecropping basis, until the Dirty Thirties arrived and his tenants walked away in despair. Other portions he managed himself, always with an army of hired men. As his daughter pointed out, he never actually did field work. "He didn't like getting his hands dirty." Like most things J. R. Green involved himself in, his agricultural enterprise soon became a gold mine. During the First World War, the price of wheat shot up, and along with it the value of farmland. Not only that, Green had found yet another way to make money on land speculation – quietly and without publicity.

The original Homestead Act stipulated that, in every township, sections 11 and 29 were to be earmarked as "school lands" and were unavailable to homesteaders. As mentioned earlier, this did not mean that schools would actually be built there, but rather that the land would be set aside until the neighbouring sections were settled, and when the land was considered at peak value, would be sold at public auctions. The proceeds were then invested in Dominion securities and the interest thereafter paid to the provincial government to support public education. The authorities, quite rightly, were very strict about maintaining this scheme. Thomas Aspdin had run into a brick wall in 1896 when he had tried to acquire a quarter-section designated as school land to supplement his wheat farm.

Until Saskatchewan gained jurisdiction over its natural resources in the 1930s, the federal government's Minister of the Interior administered the school-land program. Usually a set-up price based on value of other unoccupied lands in the area was established, but it was hoped that the bids would merely start there; farmers eager for good land were expected to quickly drive the price up. As early as 1903 some school lands were sold in the Moose Jaw area – both Benjamin Smith and J. R. Green obtained land that way. But it was not until 1918-1919 that this valuable public asset was disposed of in a major way. (In 1915-16, 1,173 acres of school lands were auctioned off in Saskatchewan, compared with 535,065 in 1918-19.)

Almost from the beginning there were accusations that collusion and fraud were the oil that greased the dispensing machinery. Before the school-land auction took place, farmers often got together to decide who wanted what piece and how much that individual was willing to pay for it. The auctioneer would find – not to his amazement – that the bid stalled just above the set-up price. On other occasions, a farmer would be paid a fee, usually by an experienced speculator, to make the highest bid. He would then fail to pay his initial deposit. Under the regulations, the land, having already been offered at auction, could be sold at a lower price to someone else. John R. Green was among those waiting in the wings for choice quarter-sections, which he got for a price much lower than the auction bid. How much he paid the original bidder to do his dirty work was never revealed.

Conspicuous speculation was frowned upon. The scheme, with its favourable terms – 10 per cent down and an annual payment for the next nine years at 6 per cent interest – had been designed so that ordinary farmers could expand their holdings. Speculators showing up at the auction sales could cause a near riot. This didn't bother John R. Green, who worked so effectively behind the scenes. He managed to make considerable money flipping school lands.

Section 11 in township 16, range 25, was situated directly south of Dougald Carmichael's pre-emption and the original farm that Robert Foote bought in 1906. Since this section was designated as school land, the neighbouring farmers had felt free to allow their livestock to graze there, but as the First World War ended, the price of land had soared, and the four quarters of section 11 finally went on the auction block.

On November 8, 1918, John R. Green placed the highest bid for the northwest quarter, paying $28 an acre. He received the patent for it on November 25. That same day he sold it to the flamboyant entrepreneur-farmer Wellington White for $30 an acre, making a $948 profit. Not bad for a day's work.

During the war years, John R. Green had dropped out of the public eye almost altogether. He no longer gave political speeches, seldom went to social functions, and wasn't even much involved with the temperance movement, even though it was at the height of its influence. He may have been too busy with his farm operation, or he may have been grieving.

On August 15, 1916, Annie Maude Green was taken ill and rushed to the hospital. She died the next day of what was termed "strangulation of the bowel." She was forty-two years old. Her brief obituary in the *Times* – "Wife of J. R. Green dies," followed by two short paragraphs – was a reflection of her life. She had existed as a mere shadow of her dominant husband.

By 1919, however, John R. Green was again being seen around town. He lived a bachelor's life – as much as someone who didn't gamble, drink, or fool around with women could. He attended the May Day dance, organized by the bankers in the city at the Bohemia Hall. He presented a set of gold medals to the local football team when it won the southern Saskatchewan championship. He gave speeches to the United Service Club, the Kiwanis Club, the Prairie Club. He was the force behind raising funds for a war memorial. The single women in the city certainly took notice. At forty-five he was still vital and handsome and rich and considered a prime catch.

Green had heard about Alida May Blakely long before he met her. She wasn't beautiful, but she was so elegantly dressed, so smart and vivacious, that she was the talk of the town. Alida had been born in Meaford, Ontario, but raised in Toronto. Her mother believed women should be able to fend for themselves, and she saw to it that her daughter was trained as a milliner. Alida was very good at her job, and in 1918 she was transferred to Moose Jaw to head the millinery department of the Robinson, McBean department store. She was proud when one of her designs was displayed in the store window, and a photograph of one such creation, a concoction of folded chiffon, fancy braid, ostrich tips, and ribbon rosettes, labelled "The Dream," appeared in the *Moose Jaw Times*. Alida May Blakely quickly became known as the most glamorous woman in Moose Jaw.

One day she happened to be walking along Main Street when she saw J. R. Green, whom she had never met but knew by sight, standing on the street corner. He was gasping for breath. "Mr Green, what's wrong?" she cried. With some difficulty John R. made her understand that he had just bought a pain-killer but, rather than rubbing on his sore leg as he was supposed to do, he had mistakenly swallowed it.

Alida rushed him into the nearby soda fountain and poured a full glass of milk down his throat. He was soon feeling better, and had already made a decision – he would marry Alida May.

She had many suitors in the bachelor-ridden town of Moose Jaw, and at twenty-eight she was cunning and experienced enough to carefully weigh the advantages and disadvantages of each. But friends kept telling her, "John R. Green will give you a very fine social position," and when Green wrapped his stick pin with the very large diamond around her finger as an engagement ring, she was convinced. They were married on June 18, 1920, at the Toronto home of Alida May's parents.

Two facts coloured the marriage. First Alida was nineteen

years younger than John R. – he called her "Girlie" because of this – and therefore she had many childbearing years remaining. In ten years the Greens produced four children, the last, a son named David, born when John R. was already sixty years old. "We grew up a family of unwanted children," says Mary Jefferson. "Dad didn't want another family, he wanted glamorous Alida, to end his retirement years with a young, vibrant wife. And Mother considered herself a career woman. She didn't really want us either."

As John R. grew older, he grew less patient and more and more tyrannical towards his sons.

The other thing that shaped the Greens' relationship was Alida's conversion to Christian Science.

Before her marriage, during a visit home to Toronto, she had suffered an attack of appendicitis. In the hospital, she came across the teachings of Mary Baker Eddy. "Mother claimed that this healed her and she became a devoted Christian Scientist ever after," says Mary Jefferson. Alida tried to get John R. interested, and at first he resisted. Finally, because she persisted, he did agree to study *Science and Health with Key to the Scriptures*, the church textbook. Mary Jefferson says that after that her father became even more enthusiastic about the religion than her mother.

It was not difficult to understand why John R. made the leap from strict Methodism to Christian Science: he'd always been a man optimistic that "the right education," or correct thinking, could solve everything. It was the teacher in him. If, for example, he thought that the League of Nations was a good idea, he'd become an expert on the subject, delivering speeches to any service club that would have him. He was a mind-over-matter man – "Self-control will conquer all," he often told his children – and the idea of spiritual regeneration that was so powerful a force that it could heal sickness appealed to him. He became totally obsessed by the religion.

"By that time he no longer had his business and had withdrawn almost entirely from public activities. I think he needed something to stimulate his mind," says Lionel Petrie, whose father was a Christian Scientist and a friend of the Greens.

"And of course, in those days, it was *the* fashionable religion which attracted all those movie stars – Elizabeth Taylor's parents were Christian Scientists, as I recall – and businessmen who considered themselves intellectuals. I think both my father and J.R. had pretensions of being deep thinkers."

By the 1930s John R. Green had become almost totally isolated from the Liberal clique of Moose Jaw. He no longer went to the Zion Methodist Church. He had voted for the Progressives – the farmers' party – in the 1921 federal election. Most Liberals in the West had, but most returned to the fold sooner than he did.

He had moved his family onto the land he owned in the valley south of Moose Jaw. His planned subdivision for the moneyed class had never materialized, so the Greens led a rather secluded existence. And despite their religion in common, the marriage had not turned out to be a particularly happy one.

"It was a cold relationship," recalls Mary Jefferson. "They didn't even share a bedroom. He treated her like a career woman, not a wife. She never called him an endearing name, or even John, always J.R." Their personalities were very different. "She was a very vital little person, always giving teas. Always very interested in art. And she remained very glamorous. People used to visit just to see her hats.

"She liked to gossip and Father absolutely forbade it. I think it was a relief to her after he was gone, that she could just say what she wanted."

J. R. Green had grown more aloof, more introverted with age. "Dad was a very gracious man but he wasn't terribly fond of company. He liked his seclusion, and the older he got the more pronounced this was," says Mary Jefferson. What there was of a social life centered around the Christian Science Church in Moose Jaw.

A distinctive tenet of the faith was self-healing. "There were no visits to the doctor, no check-ups in our family. If Dad got sick he just went to bed for a few days. Fortunately we were all pretty healthy."

However, in 1936, John R. Green became seriously diabetic. "Mother rented him a room up over the Toronto-Dominion Bank [in Moose Jaw] so he could watch the people, and he didn't have to walk back and forth to the valley. He used to sit there day after day drinking root beer – and he was diabetic." He wouldn't see a doctor, and he simply wasted away.

Like everyone else, J. R. Green suffered during the Depression. He still had four sections of land, but he had to borrow heavily to maintain the family's life-style. "We lived just as though everything was the way it had always been. We had a refrigerator, two cars, and a beautifully furnished house. And there was always money for trips to Phoenix, Arizona, in the winter or to Boston, Massachusetts, to visit the Mother Church," says Mary Jefferson. "I think this was hard on him. He was tired, sick and worried, and my brothers were just too much for him."

On July 10, 1938, John R. Green was found floating face up in his outdoor swimming pool. A farmhand rescued him, and a doctor was finally called. He was rushed to the hospital and administered a shot of insulin. But it was too late. He never came out of the coma, and died the next day.

His burial was a reflection of the two lives he had lived. A service, conducted by a member of the Christian Science Church, was held at Broadfoot's funeral home for a few close friends and the family. There was also a second funeral, held at Saint Andrew's United Church, which was attended by over a thousand people, including most of Moose Jaw's prominent citizens.

Mary Jefferson remembers that a blanket of white roses, sent by J. R.'s old Pasqua friend Doc Eddy, covered the closed casket. "I remember picking out two or three roses and was fascinated that each one was set in its own little vial of water to keep it fresh."

Mary Jefferson remembers something else about her father's death. "Mother came home from the hospital the day he died and told me that he had passed on. I started to weep, and she said to me, 'There will be no crying in this house . . . for that man.'"

White

14-16-25 W2

Wellington White
(1916-1942)

11-16-25 W2

His exile to the West had not only brought him success in business, but a fortuitous meeting with the most beautiful, vivacious, and headstrong girl in the district. When he married her, he married someone of determination, a true help-mate, who urged him on as he built his empire. When it all crumbled, she was standing beside him, comforting him. Why then, at the reading of his will, did she feel that she had been humiliated.

~ I ~

Ollie and Wellington White were considered the most sophisticated couple in all of Moose Jaw. She was so fashionable, scintil-
lating, and energetic. If there was a charitable need in the city,
homeless children perhaps, she would organize the church
ladies into doing something about it. Glances of envy were
always cast her way at social events because she was inevitably
the most elegantly dressed. She was a dynamo on the golf
course. And word spread that she actually gave her husband
advice about his business affairs. Annie Maude, the first Mrs.
J. R. Green, considered Ollie White a most formidable, intimidating woman.

Wellington could be gracious too, especially when he entertained the élite – friends such as Lord and Lady Power – but he
was much more aloof than his wife. He could be offhand and
stony-faced towards people he met on Main Street. They understood: he was concentrating on his business. After all, he had
built Moose Jaw. Literally. The bricks from his brickyard had
produced a substantial, solid town, more like the cities in eastern Canada than the ramshackle places on the prairies. The
citizens of Moose Jaw were grateful to Wellington White for that.

In later years, as the Whites' wealth and social connections
grew, when they considered the Vila Riviera in Long Beach,
California, as much their home as College Hill in Moose Jaw,
they liked to talk about their early life in the Canadian bush.
Far from being a *faux pas*, the mention of such a past enveloped
them in a mysterious, romantic aura.

Actually, Wellington White was born in the bustling town of
Erie, Pennsylvania. His father, James White, had immigrated
from County Down, Ireland, to Ontario in 1842, where he met
and then married Kathleen Ross, the daughter of Scottish
immigrant farmers. Brick-making had been in the White family
for generations, and when James was presented with an opportunity to manage a yard in Erie, he grabbed it. Wellington was
born there on April 14, 1867. But the Whites, both Tory loyalists, preferred being part of the Empire, and by 1874 they had

accumulated enough money to return to Canada and start their own business. James opened a brickyard in Owen Sound.

Both of Wellington's parents died when he was relatively young: his mother when he was eleven and his father when he was twenty-one. Eventually the business was sold, and the proceeds were divided among the three male heirs, which was fine with Wellington, because he was already dreaming of heading West.

That same year, he took the CPR to Regina, and then the Qu'Appelle, Long Lake and Saskatchewan Railway to Prince Albert, North-West Territories. There were two reasons he might have chosen this particular frontier town: it was considered the most sophisticated place in the territories at the time, and there was a tradition of brick-making there. A dry-goods store on River Street East had been the first brick building west of Winnipeg. But by the time Wellington White arrived in 1893, Prince Albert's golden years had already passed. It had been an astonishing youth, however. At a time when Moose Jaw was still nothing more than a picturesque meeting place for buffalo-hunters, and Regina a handy spot to butcher buffalo carcasses, Prince Albert boasted four churches, five elementary schools, the offices of four doctors and two lawyers, and many fine houses made of brick.

Good farming wasn't the only thing that attracted people to the northern town; speculators, sniffing out a quick buck, arrived in droves. Since 1872, rumours had circulated that the transcontinental railway would be constructed north from Winnipeg, across the fertile belt of Parklands, where the desert prairie gives way to rolling hills and trees, and through the Rocky Mountains. Prince Albert was on this route, and, since it was already well established, its citizens believed it would surely be crowned the Queen City of the prairies.

As the CPR began its westward trek, a boom erupted. Every square foot around the town was snatched up; a quarter-section on the outskirts, which had been priced at $1,000 in November 1881, sold for $15,000 three months later. The population swelled from 500 to 5,000 in a year. Then the CPR brass spoke. Not only would the railway run far south of Prince Albert, through the drylands of Saskatchewan and Alberta, but the branch lines connecting the town to the main CPR line, which would have been some compensation, were not to be constructed – at least immediately. The town's economy collapsed overnight.

So desperate became the business élite that they would resort to anything to attract the attention of Ottawa – even devising a clandestine plot to provoke the Métis into open revolt. The easterners, dispatched to put down the half-breeds, would have to be housed and fed and provided with ammunition and other services, reasoned the business cabal, which would mean a much-needed infusion of cash into the town's dead economy.

In reality, the Riel Rebellion didn't much help Prince Albert; after the excitement, the town settled into a dull, hand-to-mouth existence as a farm community, population 1,002. The arrival of the railway in 1890 stirred things up a little, but by the time Wellington White got there in 1893, the depression had taken its toll. The Witteman Brothers' brewery was the only thriving business in the place.

The brick-manufacturing, first started in 1876, seems to have disappeared by that time, too. Ample clay was still available, however, and Wellington White got to work at once. By 1897, the year the economy recovered, he produced and sold 75,000 bricks in one season.

He was a handsome young man, heavy-set, with a head of thick black hair and lively blue eyes. Charming and self-assured, he became the darling of the social set, joining the St. Andrew's Society and attending all the dances – he was good at both the square and round – and summer picnics. And naturally, because he considered himself a man who always did his duty, when the call came for volunteers to help round up some rampaging Indians, he was among those who offered their services.

The Indians in question were Swampy Cree of the One Arrow Reserve, four miles east of Batoche. By the early 1890s, disease and starvation had whittled the once-thriving band down to only 109 people, many of whom were suffering from malnutrition. One of the braves, Almighty Voice, decided early on to enjoy his wretched life as much as he was able, and he had been born with the wherewithal to do just that. He was so handsome that he was almost effeminate, with small hands and feet, a fair complexion, and thick wavy hair. By the time he was twenty-one, he had taken two wives and was working on his third, a thirteen-year-old from another reservation, who had quickly succumbed to his charms.

In the summer of 1895, Almighty Voice was on his way to prepare his wedding feast at his father's house when he came across a stray cow. He shot and butchered it and, as a result, the celebration that night was considered the jolliest in years.

Although the Mounties never discovered who owned the cow, they arrested Almighty Voice and locked him up in a small jail at Duck Lake. He was not considered a dangerous criminal, and when the constables on guard duty changed shifts, the keys were left behind. The young Cree walked away.

Something seems to have happened to the young brave after that. Perhaps it was a resurgence of latent pride, a stirring of manhood, a rejection of humiliation. For when Sergeant Colin Colebrook finally caught up with him, and then nonchalantly ignored his warnings to halt, Almighty Voice aimed his Winchester rifle and blasted the Mountie through the chest.

After that, the white community considered the young Cree a "maddened murderer," and the hunt was on. The fugitive managed to elude the manhunt for nineteen months. But, in May of 1897, he and two others were spotted in a bluff of poplars in the Minichinis Hills near Batoche. In the two-day shoot-out that followed, two NWMP officers and one civilian, the postmaster of Duck Lake, were killed. The officer in charge, J. J. McIllree, ordered that two huge brass cannon be put in place and began shelling the poplar grove. Well before the violence ceased three hours later, Almighty Voice and his two companions were dead.

The Prince Albert Volunteers, of which Wellington White was a member, were never in much danger, since they were kept well out of rifle range. Still, they were hailed as heroes by the town citizenry, and when the battle was over, a parade of buggies was sent out to fetch them. When an astonishing young woman beckoned to Wellington White, he jumped into her wagon.

Olive Louise "Ollie" Brooks was wildly, extravagantly good-looking. She stood almost six feet tall, just a bit shorter than Wellington himself. She was big-boned, with big feet and hands and head, thick auburn hair, which had a tendency to come unstuck from her bun and fling itself everywhere, huge brown eyes, and a wide expressive mouth. She was so vivacious, so "full of beans," as her mother said, that people were attracted to her at once. And she was smart. She could read and write by the time she was four. She taught herself to play the piano beautifully – each of her four sisters could sing like a lark. She could ride a horse as skilfully as the native children she played with. In later years, people whispered that she had Indian blood in her; her dark hair and rather sallow complexion proved it, they said. In fact, she was as Anglo-Saxon as they were. She had learned to speak Cree fluently from her childhood friends, and this had given rise to the rumour about her mixed blood.

Ollie's father, Thomas, had immigrated to Toronto from England, where he met and married the beautiful Sarah Gibson, who was of Scottish ancestry. The Brookses had crossed the prairies years before the CPR was built, hauling their goods in a Red River cart. They homesteaded, slowly cutting their farm from the bush. Thomas was also involved in the elusive search for gold in the area, and was at least partially successful. The Brookses had six children, and Ollie was number four.

Ollie's parents' reaction to Wellington White when they first met him is not known. There were rumours that White had been involved in a scandalous love affair with a married woman, and that he had fled Owen Sound in disgrace. And the age difference – he was thirty and Ollie only seventeen – was a disadvantage. Still, Thomas Brooks told his friends that White was the kind of clever young man who would make a success of himself. And most important, as Brooks pointed out, Wellington already had some capital.

By 1898 White was ready to expand his brick-manufacturing business outside Prince Albert. For some time, he had been hearing about a quarter-section on the southern outskirts of

Moose Jaw with a large deposit of clay – "It will last for generations," he told Thomas Brooks – a fine grade of sand, and a river – the perfect combination for making bricks. It was the NE1/4 of 28-16-26 W2, located in the valley of Moose Jaw Creek, directly east of the property owned first by Thomas Aspdin and then John R. Green. The quarter-section had been homesteaded by John Waddell, but he was now working on the CPR as a conductor and was interested in selling his land.

The Indians had made pottery from the clay at that spot for hundreds of years. Early white settlers had talked about the possibilities of brick-making for their bustling town, but it wasn't until 1890 that James Brass, a builder, actually set up a yard, a few miles east of where White's plant would eventually be located. After the fire that devastated Moose Jaw in 1891, much of the city had been rebuilt with his hard, durable brick. "It is the only product of the distinctive red colour [because of high iron content] in Manitoba and the North-West Territories," claimed his advertisements. But after that brief flourish, the depression caught up with Brass, and his business fell off drastically. In 1896 he closed down the Moose Jaw operation and took off for Slocan, a booming mining town in the West Kootenays, not far from Nelson, where J. R. Green had also been lured that year.

On June 17, 1898, the *Moose Jaw Times* whispered that a certain Wellington White from P.A. was registered at the Windsor Hotel and was conducting secret business negotiations. A week later, the newspaper announced that the Moose Jaw clay property had been bought. "Mr. White has at present a force of ten men on and will be able to supply the public with a first class article in a few days."

White's brickyard went into operation just as the economy was recovering and Moose Jaw's expectations reviving. He immediately built two beehive kilns beside the river and ordered a new press from Michigan. Most of the work was done outside, so the Moose Jaw yard operated only seasonally, opening on May 1 and closing in mid-October. White intended to run both the Prince Albert and the Moose Jaw operations. Therefore, throughout the summer he was continually travelling between the two cities. That year he turned out half a million bricks and, as he reported to Tom Brooks, "This is not sufficient to meet local demands never mind outside orders."

By early October, Wellington White was exhausted, and suffering the first manifestation of the bronchitis that would plague him for the rest of his life. Badly in need of a rest, he took off for Banff to "test the efficiency of the health-restoring hot springs." White's trust in "curing waters" would have important business repercussions years later.

By mid-October he was back in Moose Jaw, closing his brick plant and preparing to return to Prince Albert. By mid-November he was getting ready to marry Olive Louise Brooks, who, at the ripe age of eighteen, was considered old enough to take on the responsibility of a husband.

Ollie's wedding outfit, a travelling dress of grey silk trimmed with fur, was as elegant and unconventional as she was. Her sister, Josie, had chided her on the choice. "It is neither pretty nor feminine enough for a wedding," she said. But Ollie insisted it was practical. After the celebrations at her parents' Merryfield Farm, she and Wellington boarded the three a.m. train bound for Winnipeg.

Extensive travel became a feature of the Whites' married life. Hardly a year went by that Ollie wasn't packing their clothes for months away at one place or another. On their honeymoon, they went to Toronto and points east, eventually landing in Owen Sound, where, during the winter, Ollie got to know Wellington's family. (An in-law hinted at his scandalous past. Her reaction is not known.)

The Whites were back in Prince Albert in time to open the brickyard there, but Wellington had already decided that Moose Jaw had more of a future than Prince Albert. He told Ollie they were moving there.

~ II ~

Wellington White always felt a little out of joint with his environment, for the very weather that brought ripening wheat fields, and therefore prosperity to Moose Jaw, was bad for the brick business. The farmers wanted rain; he needed as sunny and dry a climate as possible. In June of 1899, the first fifty thousand bricks taken off, all still green, were attacked by a late frost and destroyed. Rain followed, and the orders rushing in were seriously delayed. Yet, despite the weather, by mid-August the Moose Jaw yard had broken through the half-million mark. Bricks were being shipped as far away as Medicine Hat in the west and Brandon in the east.

In 1902 White bought two new down-draft burning kilns, state-of-the-art technology, for what was then the steep price of $1,000 each. He also began manufacturing the specialized fire bricks, able to withstand extremely hot temperatures, which were used to line boilers and furnaces and kilns.

The rare clay needed for these was taken from the very place that Dougald Carmichael and T. E. McWilliams had discovered while they were out looking for abandoned shanties some fifteen years before. It was located at Claybank in the Dirt Hills, twenty-five miles southwest of Moose Jaw. As Carmichael later wrote, the two men had agreed that they would share any benefit resulting from the claim, but when McWilliams made a deal with a group of businessmen, including banker Arthur Hitchcock and hotel-owner J. H. Kern, Carmichael's interest had been conveniently forgotten.

Wellington White got access to the valuable clay and began making fire bricks. "The output of Mr. White's yard has been tried, tested and pronounced superior," crowed the *Times*. About one hundred thousand of these were manufactured each year, but this was only a small part of his operation. The 1902 season saw over a million ordinary bricks produced at the Moose Jaw yard alone.

White always said that, although he worked like a mad dog, this was the time in his life that gave him the greatest sense of accomplishment. But they were not particularly happy years for his young wife. Ollie's first child, James Wellington, had been born a month premature on August 18, 1899. He was a sickly, colicky baby, and Ollie's time was taken up nursing him. Then, shortly after James's birth, her husband suffered another serious attack of bronchitis, and it was decided he should spend the winter in the health-inducing climate of southern California. Ollie returned to her family in Prince Albert to await his return that spring. Her mother and sisters had helped her nurse the sickly baby. But it was to no avail. A few days short of his first birthday, James Wellington died.

The fact that Ollie was pregnant again eased her grief a little. On February 8, 1901, Kathleen (after Wellington's mother) May, had been born. She was a healthy and vibrant baby, who would grow up to become the apple of her parents' eye.

By this time the Whites were building their splendid home. Perched on top of a high hill just on the southern rim of Moose Jaw, it overlooked the valley where Cree Indians had traditionally camped. Ollie always remembered her first impression on looking down towards the river where the brickyard was situated. "We called it Snake Hill. There were thousands and thousands of reptiles swarming along the river bank." The new house, a solid, gabled affair, was spacious and made of brick, of course. Ollie breathed a sigh of relief when the family finally moved in before the birth of her next child, Isobel Gertrude, in November 1902.

Despite having such a young family to care for, Ollie White helped out in the brick business. Over the years she would be the driving force behind many of her husband's enterprises. She looked after the food supplies for the twenty men working in the brickyard, and if the cook didn't show up or was sick, Ollie prepared the meals. "Could she work! She wanted to be moving all the time. There wasn't a moment she'd sit down," remembers Frank White.

In April of 1904, Ollie gave birth to her fourth child, a son, Ross Gibson. A few months later, another infant, Frank Russell, suddenly appeared in the White household. He was presented to the curious of Moose Jaw as an adopted son, but he now says, "Nobody would say where I came from." When he was drafted into the U.S. army in 1943, Frank sent away for his Canadian papers and discovered that his father was Wellington White. He suspects his mother was Mary Feltis, the family's Polish-born cook, who remained with the Whites almost her entire life.

Frank White says he was treated well in Ollie's household, but in pictures taken of the Wellington White family over the years, he is usually missing. In one photo, he is about fourteen months old and is sitting on Ollie's mother's knee, with the other three children gathered around. On the back of the picture, the names of Kathleen, Isobel, and Ross are noted; Frank is referred to simply as "unknown child." Few people knew the truth of Frank's birth, but it was a heavy burden that Ollie had to bear over the years. Interestingly, after Frank's arrival, she did not become pregnant again.

Meanwhile, Wellington White was hard at work laying the foundation of the family fortune. The list of new buildings made from his red brick was impressive: the three-storey Maple Leaf Hotel near the CPR depot, which, as the *Moose Jaw Times* reported, "Greatly improves the appearance of our town from the passengers' point of view"; the Brunswick Hotel, which became famous throughout the West because of its extra-long bar; the City Hall, which housed not only the council chambers but the Opera House and the fire department; the Bank of Montreal, with its two huge stone pillars flanking the solemn main entrance. But it was the splendid "Union Bank and White Block" located at Main and River streets, the very heart of Moose Jaw, that sent a message to the town's business élite: Wellington White was certainly a most successful entrepreneur.

White had bought the property for a song in the spring of 1902 from a Thomas Baker who, realizing he was deathly ill, was hastening to liquidate his assets. White went into partnership with the Union Bank of Canada, and constructed the three-storey building the following year. "It is by all odds the largest and most substantial business block in Moose Jaw and one of the largest and best in the North-West Territories," bragged the *Times*. "Classy," was how Moose Jaw citizens described it. The doors of the main entrance were solid oak with bevelled plate glass, the Union Bank's fixtures were of American quarter-oak in Flemish finish, and the tellers' cages were a network of brass. There was a huge vault made of Wellington White's bricks, containing a burglar-proof steel chest. Wellington White occupied a suite of offices, as did C. W. Milestone, the manager of the

Alberta and Railway Coal Company, lawyer W. B. Willoughby, real-estate agent J. R. Green, and M. J. Jacobson, a land-dealer from Wheaton, Minnesota. The Moose Jaw Club, of which White was a charter member, also laid out its elegant rooms there.

White might have given the appearance of being a solidly established entrepreneur, but he was also a gambler, a poker-player who would grab at any opportunity without considering the consequences. His brief flurry into the clay banks of Irvine, Alberta, was a case in point.

In 1904 Wellington White finally gave up on Prince Albert and sold his brickyard there to Horace H. Ittner, newly arrived from Omaha, Nebraska. A month later, the *Times* reported, "Mr. White has secured a splendid deposit of fine brick clay within the village limits [of Irvine, Alberta] and hopes to manufacture a million bricks for the Kootenay market." What he apparently didn't investigate was the water supply; by July the ground was so cracked and dry it made White think of a dead person's veined hands. He closed the brickyard, losing money in the process.

The Irvine brick venture wasn't entirely a fiasco, however. While he was in Alberta, White heard rumours that the huge Oaler, Hammond and Nanton cattle operation (CY Ranch) might be up for sale. He made inquiries, but was told it was simply a rumour. The following spring, however, he was presented with an offer he couldn't resist. Did he want to purchase the 40,000 acres that constituted the CY Ranch? Asking price $200,000. White was as eager to jump into land speculation as anyone else at the time. He approached an old acquaintance W. F. Smiley, a land-dealer from Minneapolis, and his brother William White, and the three men formed the Taber Alberta Land Company.

The community of Taber (from the first part of the word tabernacle) was not much more than a post office for the few Mennonites who had farmed there, and a few shacks surrounding the Canada West coal mine, ugly mushrooms squatting on the flat prairie. But the drylands were quickly opening to homesteaders, and Wellington White was sure the land prices around

Taber would soar. "LAST CHANCE TO GET IN ON THE 'GROUND FLOOR'" screamed the full-page *Moose Jaw Times* advertisement. "NO STUMPS, NO STONES, NO GUMBO, NICELY UNDU-LATING PRAIRIE."

With such promises of nirvana, the Taber Alberta Land Company syndicate was amazed to find no line-ups outside their Main Street offices. They got a few nibbles, but that was all. Fast coming due was a payment of $40,000. Financial ruin was threatening. Wellington White finally insisted that Mac Annable be brought into the consortium so they could take advantage of his incredible ability as a salesman.

George "Mac" Annable was one of Moose Jaw's great characters. A *bon vivant*, he was the man who years before had fought with Arthur Hitchcock and the Graysons over a bank loan and had gone on to defeat Hitchcock in a territorial by-election. Since then he had made a name for himself as a politician, land-speculator, and horse-trader, *par excellence*.

The White syndicate offered Annable $1,000 in shares if he'd go out and sell the Alberta land. He immediately headed for Winnipeg, where he knew some land agents with big bucks in their pockets. He managed to get a price of $7 an acre, and since White and company had paid $5, he thought that would satisfy them. But the offer involved only a small amount down, subsequent payments to be made over ten years. The White brothers and Smiley wanted their equity out at once, and so refused the offer. Annable was "sore as hell" and marched down to the railway station to purchase a ticket to Victoria, where his wife was already on vacation. Wellington White ran after him. "White and the others begged me to continue in my endeavour to dispose of their holdings. The coming payment was hanging heavily over head," Mac Annable later recounted.

Annable finally agreed, but by the time he got back to Winnipeg, his prospective buyer had disappeared.

The situation was now quite desperate; Wellington White's telegrams were shrill. Mac decided that he'd better head for Chicago.

There, Annable managed to sell the entire 35,000 acres (5,000 acres of the original ranch had already gone) *en bloc* for $7.50 an acre or $262,500 to Harvey & Barnum, Chicago land-dealers. Wellington White and the others bragged about their windfall – until Harvey & Barnum began getting $10 and then $20 an acre for the same land.

Meanwhile, Moose Jaw had tripped into its fantastic years of prosperity and growth. Wellington White's brickyard, now running much of the year and employing forty-eight men, was creating the city's skeleton. The Union Hospital, the Empress Hotel, the backside of the grandiose Zion Methodist Church, the lovely St. John's Anglican Church, famous for its stained-glass windows, all used the red blocks imprinted with the initials W.W. MJ.

In 1911, White expanded into cement, forming the Moose Jaw Construction Company. He paved twelve miles of Moose Jaw sidewalks, laid the pipeline for the city's water supply, and constructed all the retaining walls and concrete walks for the magnificent legislative buildings in Regina. "Mr. White has obtained some of the largest contracts in the province," announced the *Moose Jaw Times*.

There were enormous profits flowing during these years, but, as Frank White says, "My father didn't like money lying around; he seldom had more than $50 in the bank. He'd put cash into anything that was going." Some of these investments were disasters.

In 1910 he bought a quarter-section, SE1/4 of 28-16-26 W2, which lay directly south of his brick plant, from a farmer, James Gilbert. The asking price, $8,000, was a huge amount in those days, but like the rest of the citizens of Moose Jaw, Wellington White had swollen dreams. He had the quarter-section surveyed into hundreds of lots, a subdivision that he called City View. Four months later a Winnipeg land-developer, Herbert Hurtubise, bought the property for a whopping $30,000. Champagne flowed in the White residence high up on the hill that night, with toasts of congratulation. "It's a windfall almost too good to be true," enthused a guest, and, as it turned out, she was right.

The terms specified that Hurtubise would make a down-payment of $2,000, twice-yearly payments of $2,500 each for two years, the remaining amount, $18,000, by October 1913. Hurtubise, of course, was supposed to be pushing the lots as only he knew how, but, by the fall of 1911, only a handful had been sold. He couldn't make the payments, and the entire mess was back in White's hands. By January 1913, the property was considered so worthless that White didn't even bother to pay the $39.12 he owed in back taxes and almost relinquished the land to the city. City View eventually reverted back to farmland, and White sold it years later for less than he had originally paid.

But other business ventures were decidedly more profitable. Land speculation in the land of milk and honey, for example.

Wellington's severe bronchitis – and his deathly fear of contracting tuberculosis – meant the Whites had to escape Moose Jaw's harsh winters. They tried Tampa, Florida, but Frank White says they found it too humid and the insects too bothersome. They had friends in southern California, and after visiting them, the Whites "followed the birds south" every fall, leaving Moose Jaw around Christmas each year and returning in March (their season in California got longer as they got older). In 1909 the Whites bought an elegant Spanish-style house that they called Vila Riviera in Long Beach, a tourist city on San Pedro Bay, twenty miles south of Los Angeles.

Ollie White loved the time she spent in California. She organized the Long Beach Canadian Club, and through its myriad of social and philanthropic activities over the years, she befriended glamorous people like Douglas Fairbanks, Junior, and Mayor A. E. Fickling. Once a month a picnic was held at Santa Monica Beach, and usually at least forty vacationers from Moose Jaw showed up. The link between California and the Whites became so strong that three of their four children moved there permanently after graduating from university, and Ollie eventually retired there.

When Wellington first went to southern California in 1900, he was impressed that almost one-third of all farms in the state were irrigated, which had resulted in bumper crops of apples, apricots, peaches, and pears. On one trip to a San Francisco agricultural exhibition, Wellington came across a giant lemon, some twenty inches in circumference. He thought it so amazing he brought it back to Moose Jaw. For a month, the fruit freak sat on display in the Main Street window of Kent and Brown's store.

He was also impressed by the "milk factories" that had been set up in California by dairymen who had immigrated from Holland and Switzerland. In the winter of 1909, White heard that about 100 acres of land was for sale near Lancaster, a small town forty-five miles north of Los Angeles. Because it was located in the Mojave Desert, albeit in the Antelope Valley, it was cheap. "He was going to start a dairy herd," remembers Frank White, "but he ran out of money or something and that never happened. Then, of course, as Los Angeles got bigger, the land became too valuable to herd cattle on." Finally in the early 1930s, the United States Air Force bought it for fair market value, and incorporated it into a bombing and gunning range which, in 1949, was named the Edwards Air Force Base. Today, among other things, it serves as a landing site for U.S. space shuttles.

Money passed through Wellington White's bank account as though it were caught in a revolving door, so he was always geared up to make as much of it as he could. No matter what his circumstances, though, he always had enough cash to indulge his wife's pleasures. "And she spent money as quickly as he did," says Frank White. Her great passion was her wardrobe. "She was so tall, and until she reached middle age and started to put on weight, she had a fabulous figure. And she liked to show it off," says Vi Pruitt. Mrs. Pruitt was only a young girl in Moose Jaw in 1915, but her mother was one of Ollie White's close friends.

In 1912, Ollie was one of the organizing forces behind the Saskatchewan Music Festival, held that year in Moose Jaw. As the *Times* pointed out, it was "the paramount topic of conversation in the city for weeks." Since she was on the committee preparing the all-important reception for Lieutenant-Governor G. W. Brown (at which time he would present the prizes), she, of course, had to dress for the occasion. And when she walked into the auditorium, there was a collective intake of breath. As the *Moose Jaw Times* reported, she looked stunning in a gown of the most exquisite sea-green silk eolienne, trimmed in rich gold appliqué and gold ruffles. Her great circular hat was of gold-lace straw, decorated in green velvet poppies. "That was Ollie all right," says Vi Pruitt. "She would out-dazzle anyone."

Ollie White's life wasn't all parties, however; various charitable organizations were subjected to her inexhaustible energy. She collected contributions for the newly established Children's Aid Society. And some people whispered that Ollie White thought she owned St. Andrew's Presbyterian Church. "She worked so hard for that church. She'd get down on her hands and knees and scrub if she thought the floor was dirty. Nobody could keep up to her for work," remembers Bart Meadows, who for years was Wellington White's right-hand man.

For ten straight years Ollie was president of St. Andrew's Ladies Auxiliary. Since this was a most prestigious position for a society matron in Moose Jaw, now and then someone would aspire to topple her from her throne. They never got far. Ollie simply invited the entire auxiliary to her house for tea, always planning something special. One time Wellington arranged for the ladies to take boat trips along the creek in rented launches. "A most lovely and unusual afternoon was provided by the audacious Mrs. Wellington White," the *Times* babbled.

Ollie White loved to involve the often trembling, fearful ladies in various physical events. "Once she organized a track-and-field meet. She had races for fat ladies, races for thin ladies, for girls under twenty-five years, for women over sixty-five. Of course the last thing many of them wanted was to broad jump or be forced into a relay race, but she made them do it. At the end of the afternoon, everybody's face was dirty and everybody was laughing. Ollie, I think, got a reputation as a bully and some of the women were really frightened of her. On the other hand, absolutely nobody wanted to miss her parties," recalls Vi Pruitt. "I think my mother thought of Ollie White as one of the Valkyries. She was in awe of her till the day she died."

In 1908 the Whites built a new house, right in front of the old one, high on College Hill, with Moose Jaw spread at its feet. (Today Aldersgate College is located in the same building.) If it hadn't been quite so squat, its bricks quite so red, and if it had boasted a gothic column or two or a solarium, it might have been included on the roster of grand mansions built by the *nouveaux riches* of western Canada in those days. It was not as grand as William Grayson's mansion, but it was a beautiful home, replete with heavy Victorian furniture of solid oak and walnut – Ollie particularly loved a fumed-oak wine cabinet, originally owned by Wellington's parents – Persian rugs, rolltop desks, massive leather armchairs, rich velour curtains, and eventually an electric fireplace with brass rails and fire irons. Ollie's favourite piece, however, was a Gerhard Heintzman cabinet-grand piano.

Wellington had happened to be in Toronto at the time of the Canadian National Exhibition, and had come across the piano, which had won first prize for tone. He bought it at once for Ollie. Says Frank White, "I don't think a day went by that she didn't play on that piano. She had never taken a lesson in her life, but she could play as well any maestro." Until a throat infection and the subsequent operation gave her a whisky voice, she could also belt out a song. Remembers Bill McWilliams (grandson of T. E. McWilliams, who owned the fire-clay property), "Mrs. White was the greatest piano-player for a dance you ever heard. She was in an orchestra at the Odd Fellows Hall. Alex McLean played the banjo, and Jack Messer, who farmed at Stony Beach, played the fiddle. I liked his playing better than Don Messer's, who was his brother. Mrs. White was so big that she shook that old piano from one end of the stage to the other. She had terrific hands that could fly about that keyboard. Oh, she was wonderful."

The Whites entertained in a more sedate manner in their new home; as the years passed the guests sometimes included British aristocracy or rich American industrialists or Canadian prime ministers, but they weren't pretentious people. Farmhands and labourers who worked for them would be invited to stay at the Moose Jaw house while they enjoyed the sights of that city, and they were treated like honoured guests while they were there. Wellington's two closest friends were locomotive engineers. Ollie White was an imposing, often intimidating, figure, but she was not a snob. "She'd talk to anyone," says Frank White, "and if she found them interesting, she'd invite them home for dinner."

Fortunately Wellington liked people, because his social butterfly of a wife dragged him everywhere. Once Ollie even got him to dress up as an oversized sunflower for a masquerade party. The Fireman's Ball, the Hospital Ball, the Law Students' Ball, the annual "At Home" of the Moose Jaw Club – the Whites went to them all. "They loved to dance," remembers Vi Pruitt. "Although they were both big and rather heavy, they floated around that floor as though a cloud was at their feet."

Although Moose Jaw was really just a puddle of a town, there were rigid and distinct social groupings. For instance, the Whites and Graysons never attended the same functions. "They were like oil and water, they never mixed," laughs Vi Pruitt. "I don't think Ollie liked the Grayson women. She thought they were insufferable prudes." There was more to it than that. The Grayson brothers were competitors with Wellington White in business, and there had been bad blood involving a speculative venture. As well, the Graysons represented the Liberal establishment, while White was part of the Conservative clique. And then there was the matter of the churches.

The Methodists were the first to be dissatisfied with their run-of-the-mill church. Built in 1901, six years later it was already considered too small, too pedestrian, for a town with the potential of Moose Jaw. In 1907 a huge new church rose right on Main Street. Of Menomenee red sand brick, it was a massive, squat affair, capped by a huge dome. In 1902 the Presbyterians had also built a pleasant little church on Main Street, but they too soon had visions of grandeur. Their monument to booming Moose Jaw opened its doors in 1913. Made of white tyndall stone, St. Andrew's is the very embodiment of Gothic, an elegant structure with huge stained-glass windows and a lofty steeple on which sit delicate corner steeples.

It was said that the architecture of St. Andrew's and Zion were as different as the people who went there. The Methodists saw themselves as pious, industrious, no-nonsense people. The Presbyterians considered themselves – or at least some of them did –

more sophisticated, more enlightened and intellectual. The Grayson family was the embodiment of Zion Methodist; the Whites nicely represented the St. Andrew's type, and their paths seldom crossed. They didn't even attend the same funerals.

The fairy-tale world of Moose Jaw society was shattered on August 4, 1914, when Britain's ultimatum to Germany demanding their withdrawal from Belgium expired, and the British Empire, including Canada, declared itself at war.

~ III ~

Moose Jaw reacted to the news like every other prairie town – with ecstatic excitement.

The band of the 60th Rifles gathered at the post office at about ten-thirty the night the dispatch was received. Belting out "Rule Britannia," they started off down Main Street and were soon followed by a thousand cheering citizens, many of whom had gotten out of their beds to participate. The makeshift parade paused in front of the Maple Leaf Hotel. It was here that the young men were already lined up, hoping to enlist before the night was out. Members of the Legion of Frontiersmen, who were overseeing the recruitment, stepped out onto the hotel's balcony, waved grandly as though they were foreign princes, and were greeted with a joyous roar. Someone yelled "Boots to the Kaiser" and "Let 'em have it!" Then a French-speaking Canadian, who on any other night would have been snubbed like all foreigners, began reciting the words of the Entente Cordiale. Somebody carrying a Union Jack stood to attention beside him. The band struck up "The Marseillaise," and two beefy British immigrants lifted the astonished man onto their shoulders and proceeded on their way down Main Street.

Over the next week and a half all of Moose Jaw held its breath in anticipation. When would the 60th Rifles be mobilized? When would they be off to fight the Hun in Europe? Their commanding officer, Lieutenant-Colonel Herbert Snell, sent a telegram to the military district office in Winnipeg on behalf of his impatient men. "All ranks keenly enthusiastic to go. Early reply would be most welcome." They were told to be patient, their time would come.

On August 24 the Moose Jaw contingent – 255 volunteers for the 60th Rifles and twenty-five for the 27th Light Horse Brigade – made ready for their march down Main Street from the Exhibition Grounds, where they had been billeted, to the CPR station. There they would catch the train to take them to Valcartier mobilization camp.

Wellington White had seen to it that he and Ollie and the four children had been allotted a spot on the balcony of the Maple Leaf Hotel. It was the perfect place from which to watch the spectacle below. Nobody could contain their excitement, especially the *Moose Jaw Times*. The paper reported that the troops had to pass through a solid mass of humanity, "which packed Main Street from building to building and overflowed on the hotel verandas up on the steps and roof of the CPR freight sheds, at all the windows of the station and over the roofs of the freight and passenger cars in and around the yards."

After immense cheering from the crowd, the train carrying the troops finally left. Among the soldiers was Bob Foote's brother, Sandy.

Few questioned the unthinking embrace of "this most necessary of wars," or whether the courageous boys who had hitherto been unemployed were grabbing at uniforms for the dollar-a-day pay or for "a righteous cause – the glorious British Empire." The ever-more-pompous William Grayson presumed he spoke for everybody. He had just returned from a tour of England, and thus was able to report on the world situation. As usual the *Moose Jaw Times* reported almost every word of his speech. "Canada is one of the greatest plums on earth and what is there to stop it dropping into the mouths of Germany, Russia, or Japan?" he asked. The answer, of course, was Britain, "our flesh and bone, the seat of civilization."

When the slaughter got under way, when the *Times* began listing the dead and wounded, when Moose Jaw tallied the consequences of its unquestioning patriotism, there were people who hissed at William Grayson as he passed them on Main Street.

On the surface, life for the White family in the big house on the hill seemed hardly affected by the war. Ross and Frank were ten years old, too young even to be thinking of enlisting. Wellington spent even more time in his office armchair, studying every stratagem, every battle, through any newspaper he could get his hands on. He grew excited every time he passed the windows of Hembroff, Coppin and Smith, for there was displayed a magnificent Ross Rifle, which had been donated for the benefit of the Patriotic Fund. White desperately wanted the rifle, and when the auction took place, he out-bid a dozen others, paying an exorbitant $150 for it. It was proudly mounted above his huge oak desk.

Ollie embroiled herself in various charitable works, donating clothing to the Soldiers' Aid, singing "My Own Canadian Home" and "Laddie in Khaki" at the Red Cross talent night, stationing herself for the entire day at Victoria School to collect eggs for the Children's Aid Society's Easter program, organizing the homemade cooking sale at the Robinson, McBean department store to raise money for the YWCA.

However, the war didn't hinder the Whites' travel plans; in 1915 they went on an extensive two-month tour to Chicago, Miami, Tampa, New Orleans, Houston, Phoenix, and Los Angeles (the children being looked after by Mary Feltis, the cook and housekeeper). On the surface everything seemed quite normal; in reality Wellington was having to scramble to keep his family in the style to which they were accustomed.

As soon as the war began, the Moose Jaw City Council announced that it was unable to sell its bonds on the international market and therefore was discontinuing all public works. There would be no more money for street pavement, roads, new schools, or any government buildings. Even the band concerts in the park were to be discontinued. All Saskatchewan cities and towns were faced with a similar situation, which meant that Wellington White's Moose Jaw Construction Company was left with almost no work. White immediately laid off his twenty or so employees. Actually the company's economic situation had been rather desperate ever since the fabulous building boom had burst in 1913.

It was the construction of a railway network, as detailed and extravagant as a spider's web, which had fired the prairie windfall, and it was the collapse of railway building that dissipated it. Real-estate values sank; the construction industry flattened. The annual value of building permits issued in Brandon, Winnipeg, Moose Jaw, Regina, Saskatoon, Calgary, and Edmonton had been $23 million in 1912. By 1914 that figure had plummeted to $3 million, and remained below $6 million in each of the war years.

The economic downturn was felt at once in Moose Jaw. The CPR and other industries laid off their workers, until there were 2,500 unemployed, and soup-kitchen lines stretched for blocks.

With the economy nose-diving, there was no new construction, and therefore no demand for bricks. To add to Wellington White's frustration, there had been severe electrical shortages – Moose Jaw's power situation had always been something of a scandal. He finally decided to pack it in. In the spring of 1915, the kilns of the Moose Jaw Brick Company were not fired. Not another brick would ever be produced there. Frank White remembers that the surplus bricks sat in piles, like a giant child's red building-blocks, until, bit by bit, the citizens of Moose Jaw spirited them away for their own use.

White kept his construction business going, but there was little work during the war years. The only significant wartime industry, munitions manufacture, bypassed not only Moose Jaw but the entire prairies (which received less than 1 per cent of the $1 billion spent on that industry). Unemployment soared, and many of the city's skilled workers left for work elsewhere; in 1915, scores of machinists returned to Britain or else moved to Minnesota or Ontario.

Fortunately, like John R. Green, Wellington White had found something far more lucrative: the ripening grainfields of Saskatchewan.

Not long after he had arrived in Moose Jaw to make bricks, White obtained entry to a homestead, the SE1/4 of 18-16-24 W2, about a half-mile south of Bob Foote's farm, near Pasqua. In 1907 he bought another quarter-section, NE 28-16-26 W2, adjoining his Moose Jaw land. On these properties he was able to raise hefty mortgages, with which he purchased more and more farmland. Ironically, he was helped in this by the depression.

The economic collapse had hurt farmers. For years they had poured money into machinery, and had bought more land, but by 1913 banks were refusing to extend their credit, mortgage companies were threatening to foreclose. Three years of continuous drought, coupled with low wheat prices, spelled disaster. The Dominion Minister of Agriculture received one letter in which a family had enclosed a recipe for the stew they ate every day: "boil the gophers with the Russian thistle and add a little salt." Desperate for work, farmers, their hired hands, their sons, poured into the cities, where the ranks of the unemployed were already swollen.

White and others who had cash available took advantage of the hard times. Either they bought out a desperate farmer at rock-bottom prices, knowing that a year later the land would triple in value, or they waited until he couldn't pay his taxes. Once the land was seized, they could usually get it for a fraction of what it would be worth sixteen months later. The speculators were smart; with Britain and France cut off from Russian supplies, grain quickly became worth its weight in gold.

In 1915-16 came the bonanza. The winter was snowy; spring and summer were sunny and hot, punctuated with heavy downpours; the autumn was warm and dry. These were perfect conditions for growing wheat. The crops on Wellington White's land were so thick and full that they choked his binders; he ordered his workers to cut narrower swaths. He got as much as forty bushels an acre, and so did many of his neighbours. It was a mammoth crop, by which all other harvests would be measured for thirty years.

Wellington White used his profits to expand his empire. In February 1916, he successfully bid on the school lands, NE1/4 of 11-16-25 W2; this was the quarter-section located directly south of what had been Dougald Carmichael's pre-emption. Ten months later he bought the SE1/4 of 14-16-25 W2 from John Slemmon, who was still keeping store in Salmon Arm, B.C. White also bought another half-section from Slemmon directly north of this quarter – the homesteads of Dougald and Colin Carmichael. In November of 1918 he purchased the NW1/4 of 11-16-25 W2 from J. R. Green, who just weeks before had successfully bid for it in a school-land auction. Finally in June 1925, he bought the SW1/4 of 14-16-25 W2, the land which Benjamin Smith had bought with Métis land scrip and which John R. Green had subsequently purchased. All of this cost him approximately $27,200; by 1927 it would be valued at more than twice that amount.

By the time the soldiers returned – all exhausted, many crippled – from the nightmare which was supposed to have been a quick, glorious victory, Wellington White owned 2,400 acres of land, almost four sections of the best wheat-growing land in the world – an enormous spread for that time.

During harvesting, White's operation turned into an exhausting fourteen-hour-a-day marathon, with thirty to forty horses in teams of four to six, and thirty men to run the huge, irascible steam-threshing machines. A handful of employees whom White trusted were kept on year-round to oversee the operation. "Wellington White was a good boss," remembers Harold Mulligan, who worked for him for years. "Anything he wanted done, he'd never say, 'Do this!' He'd wander around with a cigar in his mouth about yay long and he'd remark, 'Perhaps you might look into fixing this [piece of machinery].' You got the message, but you also felt good."

"Father was never fond of the routine work of farming," says Frank White. "It was nothing more than a business to him. If he could manage from his office on River Street, that was fine with him."

The strange and exotic did appeal to Wellington White. He kept parrots because he enjoyed coercing them into saying something, and he was inordinately proud when, in 1911, he took first prize in the talking-parrot category of the Moose Jaw Poultry and Pet Stock Show. His blue-ribbon winner was a bird called Victoria who screeched "Rule, Britannia" whenever given the opportunity.

The weed-slayer was also an oddity that caught Wellington's attention. There was some argument over whether it was he or his friend Neubert Baldus, a mechanic he had met in Long Beach, who had thought up the idea, but the stubble-, weed-, and insect-burner that they had created was going to cure the prairie farmer of most of his headaches. Since it took them two years to put the contraption together, its debut on Wellington White's farm near Pasqua, on a lovely July day in 1922, was awaited with great anticipation. Early in the morning, a crowd of spectators had gathered to watch the strange mechanical object being pulled along by six straining horses. Basically, it was an eight-foot-high blowtorch. When a lever was pulled, great jets of flames, fed by crude oil, sprouted from its underside and beat the ground. "It looks more ferocious than St. George's dragon," joked farmer Hugh McKellar.

"It'll do a hundred acres a day," claimed White. "And it will kill everything in its path, from Russian thistle to stem sawfly eggs." And the strip through the field of mustard seed over which the monster had been pulled was certainly as bare of growth as a grid road. The problem was that it also destroyed the land. Farmers were just beginning to realize that burning off stubble, instead of converting it to trash cover, was a major cause of soil-drifting on the prairies. The stubble-, weed- and insect-burner sat unused on White's farm until the Second World War, when it was gathered up during a scrap-metal drive.

While Wellington was getting rich from the war, Ollie was living up to her social obligations. There was the farewell dance for the 128th Battalion, the Great War Veterans' Association Picnic, the Patriotic Club Ball, the many silver teas to raise money for the comfort of returned soldiers, and so on. Ollie White could not be called a feminist; she never participated in the exciting drama being played out by women's rights advocates in those years. When asked by Vi Pruitt's mother, she refused to go to meetings of the Women's Christian Temperance Union advocating prohibition, nor was she interested in the Equal Franchise League, which was fighting for women's suffrage. Yet the suffering she saw in the faces of the returning veterans did have an effect on her; she became more involved in serious charities, such as the Red Cross, the Returned Soldiers Welcome Committee, and the Halifax Relief Fund. But it was the Spanish flu epidemic that dramatically brought out Mrs. Wellington White's organizational abilities – and they were formidable.

The epidemic, which struck in the fall of 1918, was a particularly vicious one. Within the first forty-eight hours, twenty-two people in Moose Jaw died from the flu. After a few days the bodies began piling up, as grave-diggers, frightened of catching the disease, refused to go to work. The columns of the *Moose Jaw Times* were filled with short obituaries, which, along with the "killed-in-action" announcements from the war front, made for morbid reading. In many homes every member of the family was ill, so there was no one to attend to anyone else. A state of emergency was declared, and the Citizens' Health Committee was organized, with Ollie White as one of the mainstays. She set up a soup kitchen to feed the ill in the basement of St. Andrew's Church and proceeded to talk farmers in the area into donating beef, vegetables, and eggs; she organized a car pool to get soup and medical supplies to the ill; she was the convener of a committee to canvass for volunteer nurses; she helped arrange for the distribution of 15,000 cotton masks, which all Moose Jaw citizens were required to wear; she managed a team that linked calls for help with doctors and nurses. By the time the epidemic had subsided, Ollie White had slept about ten hours in two weeks. As the *Times* pointed out, "Mrs. White's genius as an organizer has been given full scope and her untiring devotion to duty has had a wonderful effect upon the general situation."

Ollie White was a woman of such common sense, of such amazing energy, and of such natural managerial ability, that in another era, she would have become the executive director of a charitable foundation, chairman of the board of a large company, or a senior civil servant. In Moose Jaw in 1919, her talents were given full rein only as long as she did all the work but didn't covet the prestigious titles. "I don't know how much advice Ollie was permitted to give my father about his business affairs. He might have listened to her without indicating he was doing so. Probably if he listened to her more, he wouldn't have gotten in the jam he did," Isobel White once wrote.

Wellington White still carried on his business from 8 River Street West, the office building he and the Union Bank had built in 1906. He liked to get out for some air and to talk to people, and so, often at noon, he'd stroll across Main Street, along River, and straight into the city's sinful, seamy underbelly.

White would eat lunch at the Savoy Cafe, which not only served a fairly decent chicken chow mein, but was a front for a numbers racket that operated across the province. Down the street, the Paris Cafe specialized in Canadian roast beef and opium dens at the back of the kitchen, which stayed open twenty-four hours a day. Yip Foo's was a multi-faceted business; a grocery store faced onto the street, poker games were played in the basement, and a dozen harlots plied their trade upstairs. Next door was situated the Elk Billiard Parlour, which had to compete with the other River Street establishments of a similar nature situated within three short blocks – Elmo Billiard Parlour, Colonial Billiard Parlour, D'Jazz Pool Hall, Riley's Pool Room, Cecil Pool Room, Veterans Billiard Parlour, Russell Pool Room, and the Queen City Barber Shop, which had a couple of chairs in the front and a half-dozen tables at the back.

It wasn't just the thrill of having your money lifted by some out-of-town shark that was the attraction of the billiard joints; these spots were the operating centres for Moose Jaw's notorious bootleggers. Also on River Street sat the dance halls, the most popular known as "The Academy" in polite society, and as "Gonorrhea Race Track" by those who frequented it.

Lined up on the north side of River from Main to Fourth were the hotels – the Alexandra, the City Hotel, the Brunswick, the Empress, the American, the Plaza (almost all built of Wellington White's bricks). From these grimy windows, the infamous Bad Girls of Moose Jaw would wink and nod and smile and wave at passersby. Catch an eye and Maria or Leona or Bertha would flash a young farmhand a five-buck sign. He'd wave back three. With her nod, a deal was struck, and if he looked shy, she'd meet him on the second-floor landing.

Ken Serviss grew up working in his father's pool hall. "Most of the girls came from poor prairie farms. They weren't educated and not very good-looking. They didn't like to do housework, and their places were a mess." But, he says, they did indeed have the proverbial hearts of gold. "They were terrific people. They were good people. They and the bootleggers donated hundreds of dollars to the old folks' home and the children's shelter. They kept that house going." Ollie White never said no when contributions to the Children's Aid were offered by a madam.

Moose Jaw had always had a split personality: the genteel, often pretentious, face it showed to the world, expressed in the city's ridiculous number of grandiose churches, and the wicked underside, thriving in a jungle of brick and wooden slums that spread out like ragweed from the railway station.

Wickedness thrived because Chief of Police Walter Johnson wanted it to. He was getting rich off River Street; on a rather measly salary he managed to build up a thousand-acre farm north of Moose Jaw, which was a model of its kind, and he owned a very fine home on 1st Avenue N.W., opposite the police station. The madams and bootleggers and casino-owners didn't mind paying him his weekly tribute if it bought the protection of the entire police force.

When he was first hired in 1905, Chief Johnson had struck on a *modus operandi* – out of sight out of mind – which would work brilliantly for the twenty-two years he was chief. He ensured that the wickedness would be contained on River Street; vice that spilled over into other areas of the city was promptly stamped out.

The burghers of Moose Jaw rarely complained about Johnson's methods, because many of them, like the chief himself, were making money from the bedlam on River Street. William Grayson owned the buildings containing, among other businesses, the Bamboo Cafe, the Nippon Barber Shop, the Chinese National League, and the offices of David Gellerman, the brother-in-law of Harry Bronfman, who dominated the mail-order whisky business on the prairies in the early twenties and made a fortune in the process. Grayson also held mortgages on many properties on River Street, including the notorious Yip Foo block.

The degree of corruption in the Moose Jaw police force came to light in 1924 when seven cops were jailed for theft and possession of stolen goods. While supposedly protecting the business establishments on Main Street during the night, they were systematically robbing them blind. The policemen were particularly fond of the merchandise in Robinson, McBean department store, but they didn't play favourites; every kind of retailer from hat-maker to hardware-dealer was hit. When the policemen were arrested, a truck was needed to carry away the loot from their residences. When their cases finally came to court, some of those who pleaded not guilty were acquitted. One man who had stolen the most received the harshest punishment – twenty-seven months in the penitentiary, a most lenient sentence in the days when horse thieves were sentenced to fifteen years hard labour. And Chief Johnson? Once again he walked away unscathed, his reputation intact, at least to some degree. He simply hired a new police force and continued to preside over his River Street fiefdom.

Wellington White watched all this more with amusement than moral outrage. Although he was a regular at St. Andrew's Presbyterian Church, he lived by the philosophy "live and let live," especially when making a buck was involved. His house was far enough away from the seamy underside of Moose Jaw that he could enjoy the civilized existence his wife arranged without concern over boozoriums or brothels.

Wellington considered his personal life a remarkable success. His daughters, Kathleen and Isobel, had done well at high school in Moose Jaw, and their father had sent them on to the University of Toronto. Isobel had graduated with an honours degree in the arts, and was teaching high school at Smithville in Ontario. Kathleen had been one of the few women to study medicine, graduating from the University of Toronto in 1924. She had interned at the Ogdensburg Hospital in New York, passed her American medical exams, and then moved to California. But it was the Whites' son Ross who was the most brilliant of all. He also had studied medicine at the University of Toronto, as well as playing the violin in the Varsity String Quartet. Only Wellington's "adopted son" was something of a problem. "I loved horses and hated school. I couldn't sing worth a damn, and I was a rabble-rouser," says Frank White. Instead of going to the western United States like the other White children, Frank headed for Florida, eventually setting up an IGA store in St. Petersburg.

By the mid-1920s Ollie White was at the peak of her influence in Moose Jaw's society – a surprisingly hectic and sophisticated social whirl. In the summer of 1924 Ollie did the following: lent her home for a musical to raise money for St. Andrew's Ladies Aid; went to the Regina Agricultural Fair with her daughter Kathleen; donated cakes and sandwiches at a picnic for the children's shelter; entertained her mother, who was visiting from Prince Albert; spent a lovely weekend at the Manitou Beach resort with family and friends; cut the ices at an entertainment for Mrs. James Lee, a visitor from St. Leonard's-on-the-Sea, England; organized a home-cooking sale to raise money for the CGIT (Canadian Girls in Training); organized a silver tea to raise funds for the fancy-work circle of the St. Andrew's Ladies Aid; was put in charge of the "tea equippage" while attending a reception for that year's graduates at Moose Jaw College; entertained a group of missionaries, including Rev. Dr. J. Taylor from China; gave a veranda tea for Mrs. Hincheym, who was celebrating her eighty-seventh birthday; was once again a judge for the prettiest-baby competition at the agricultural show; helped arrange the flowers and welcome the guests at the annual Moose Jaw Golf Club Dance. There was never a dull moment.

"Ollie developed a passion for playing golf," says Vi Pruitt. "I can still see her with the club raised as though she was going to slaughter the ball. . . . She was so determined and so big and formidable in that golfing outfit she wore, she scared the living daylights out of anyone who happened to run into her on the fairway."

The Whites were at the opening gala of the Temple Tea Gardens and Dancing Hall in August 1921. Actually, Ollie helped organize the benefit because money raised went to her favourite charity, the Children's Aid Society. As the *Moose Jaw Times* reported, "On every hand there were enraptured comments about the new hall." Moose Jaw could now claim the most elegant ballroom found anywhere in the West.

The hall's architecture was a combination of a Moorish fort and a California bathhouse. The dance floor was made of the finest B.C. hardwood, designed to stand the strain of the Charleston, the shimmy, and the black bottom. The orchestra platform, called the Crystal Tunnel, was eight feet above the ground, surrounded by full-length mirrors and infused with subdued lighting. There were the regular bands: Budd's Blossoms, Sigurd Larsen's Orchestra, the Tantalizing Toe Ticklers, but it was the big, out-of-town attractions that got the crowds. Mart Kenny and his Western Gentlemen, Bert Niosi, Bobby Gimby, and even the famous Tommy Dorsey all appeared at Temple Gardens in its heyday.

The Whites went often. Recalls Vi Pruitt, "Ollie, as big as she was, loved to do the Charleston, and there'd be nothing stopping her. She even entered one of the dance marathons one night, though she only stuck with it for a couple of hours."

In the Roaring Twenties in Saskatchewan, summer weekends were spent at Manitou Beach. The chemical properties of Lake Manitou were much like the famous Carlsbad Spa in Germany; the high salinity made the water so buoyant that it was almost impossible to drown. The Indians were the first to discover its healing ability, claiming that it even cured smallpox. But it was its exotic quality – mounds of salt spray which looked like small Arctic icebergs floated around the lake in the heat of summer – that made it so popular with the holiday-goers.

As the 1920s approached, Manitou Beach had developed into a bustling resort community with seventy-seven cottages, two hotels, several boarding-houses, a moving-picture show, two drugstores, three grocery stores, a barber shop, four ice-cream parlours, and two hot bath-houses. There were plenty of bootleggers and at least one brothel, but they were accepted as necessary evils by the local populace.

In 1918, Wellington White's construction company had been hired to install a water-supply system for Watrous, located five miles south of Manitou Beach. However, times were tough for farmers, and the town, with so many taxes in arrears, ran out of money before White could finish. He was stuck with a heap of pipes and other materials. "I'm going into the swimming-pool business," he announced. Not only his wife, but everyone at Manitou Beach, thought he was crazy. "Build a swimming pool beside a lake! That was a pretty stupid thing to do – at least that's what we all thought," recalls Harold Mulligan.

Wellington went ahead anyway, and he didn't pinch on expenses. When it first opened in June of 1922, White's Pool was fantastic. It was more like a Hollywood bathing pavilion, with ninety-eight individual cubicles, each with its own little door, where the bathers changed – "We had mirrors in each one until they all got stolen," remembers Mulligan. There were freshwater showers, a restaurant, and a spectators' gallery. But it was the pool itself that was the most amazing. Twenty-five-by-sixty feet, it held 253,000 gallons of salty lake water, which was pumped in and heated to eighty degrees. A sunlit fountain was built in the shallow end, and bathers could luxuriate in the fine spray of fresh well-water that spurted from its top. Floating barrels and logs, diving boards, and various platforms were installed for the rambunctious. But it was the trapezes that the young-at-heart loved. Remembers Harold Mulligan, "There were these rings hanging on chains, five on one side and seven on the other. The idea was to grab one, swing, grab another, down the whole length and back up. If you fell in the water you were considered an amateur." People became expert at it, but it was Mulligan who established the record; he swung back and forth twenty-one times without stopping.

White's Pool was a resounding success. "The season was short," recalls Vi Pruitt, "but during the two and a half months it was open, it was one continuous party." There were no set hours; the pool opened when the first bather arrived, usually about eight a.m., and closed when the last one left, always after midnight. Admission was twenty-five cents a swim, thirty-five cents with a towel.

In 1928 White invested considerable money in the Rainbow Danceland, a fabulous ballroom. It was built right on the lake edge – the orchestra leader used to park his boat underneath – right across from White's Pool. "The dance floor was really something special," says Harold Mulligan. "There were only four like it in North America. It was called a spring floor, because underneath the wood there is a layer of horse hair, ten inches thick. In the twenties and thirties when you had five hundred people in there bouncing and jumping to those crazy dances, well if you got out of step that floor was wheezing so, it'd trip you. It certainly was easy on your legs, though."

Stars like Mart Kenny and Norma Locke and the Silver Tone Seven played there often. The Art Harmony 6 broadcast by remote control from Rainbow Danceland over CFQC each Friday evening, but the regular band was a seven-piece orchestra led by a blind musician named Guy Watkins. Only the men paid – ten cents a dance or three for a quarter; while the couples circled the floor, the floor-walker Del Van Buskirk went around and collected the jitney tickets. The place opened every night except Sunday. The highlight of the year was the Tit-Pullers' Ball, so named because it ended only when the farmers left to milk the cows.

For the Whites, Manitou Beach was not only a money-making enterprise, but a place for them to entertain. Guests would arrive by the car – and train – loads. Harry and Bertie Henderson from Long Beach made the trip, as did several other Californian friends. Wellington's good friend Walter Simington, a railway engineer, and his wife, Jean, came up from Regina. And from Prince Albert came a young lawyer, whom Wellington in particular found interesting, by the name of John Diefenbaker.

The Whites and their guests spent every evening on the spring floor of Danceland. "I can still see them twirling about," says Vi Pruitt, who visited the resort when she was a teenager. "Wellington was a good-looking man, a man who stood out in the crowd, although by age fifty he had become rather heavy. And while Ollie wasn't getting any slimmer either, she was still graceful. They made a striking couple."

They were Moose Jaw's most glamorous couple, and Wellington White decided to take advantage of the fact. In August 1925 he was nominated to run in the federal election as the Conservative candidate in the Moose Jaw district constituency.

~ IV ~

It was something of a surprise. Unlike the Graysons or Green, White had not participated in the political life of the city before this. Sitting on the boards of hospitals and charities did not interest him at all. Provincial politics were so dominated by the Liberals, especially under Walter Scott and later Jimmy Gardiner, that a staunch Tory like White had little influence. He had, however, cultivated powerful friends among the federal Conservatives. The party's leader in 1925, Arthur Meighen, was a personal friend of the Whites and stayed at their home the few times he visited Moose Jaw.

Robert Borden, Canada's prime minister from 1911 to 1920, was a hero of White's, and White had actively promoted a single candidate for both the Tories and Liberals of Moose Jaw in the 1917 election, when it was thought that the war effort needed a Union government. In Saskatchewan 71 per cent of the population voted for Borden's government that year, including the citizens of Moose Jaw.

But the Unionists barely got to enjoy a honeymoon before the wrath of the prairie farmer descended on them. Just two weeks before the election, Borden had promised that farmers' sons would not be conscripted; four months later, as the new crop was being seeded, the exemption was cancelled. Instead of tariffs being lowered, as the farmers had demanded, the Union government raised them, both for American and British goods (tariffs on gas tractors were removed, but neither the farmers nor the tractors were ready for widespread use). Instead of lowering freight costs, the government suspended the Crow's Nest Pass rate on grain and approved a general freight increase. Instead of making credit more readily available, interest rates shot up. By the time an election was called in December 1921, prairie farmers had developed not just disapproval but a passionate hatred for the Unionists – read the Conservatives.

The Tories were humiliated by the election results of 1921; no previous government had ever been rejected so resoundingly by the voters. Not a single government candidate survived in the West, but then again, the Liberals didn't do very well in that region of Canada either, although they won the election nationally. The national Progressive Party swept the West, electing sixty-five Members of Parliament. Even in Moose Jaw, an Eastview farmer, R. M. Johnson, won the seat for the farmers' protest party, knocking out the Graysons' favourite son, W. E. Knowles. The Conservatives came a poor third. (In 1923 Johnson lost his seat for alleged "corrupt election practices." A by-election was held, and another Progressive, E. N. Hopkins of Moose Jaw, won it.)

Wellington White had been asked to accept the nomination in the 1921 election. He wisely refused. "Owing to my health, I'm afraid I will not be able to stand the strain of the campaign." By 1925 Wellington must have been feeling better, because he said he was ready to serve his country.

The meeting of the Moose Jaw Liberal-Conservative Association was held in the Rose Room of the McIntyre Hotel. Actually, seven others ready to serve had already been nominated before Wellington White's name was put forward, but once that happened they withdrew. As the *Times* reported, "Thunderous applause broke forth [when White's name was mentioned] which was only equalled by the cheering that broke out when Mr. White stood up and made his bow as the duly nominated candidate of the convention."

Wellington's acceptance speech was short. "I've devoted my life to working and not to speech-making," he said. "Although I've lived in Moose Jaw for twenty-eight years, I've never taken a prominent part in politics, but I am satisfied to make a sacrifice for the country." In fact, he hated speaking in public and was not very good at it. Vi Pruitt remembers her mother saying, "Ollie was far better on the speaker's platform than Wellington was. She was far more gregarious. It was she who had made the White name in the community. If it hadn't been for her, I don't think anybody would have given him a thought."

Ollie worked "like a fiend" in Wellington's campaign. There wasn't a tea she didn't attend; she lavishly entertained the "difficult" Arthur Meighen at her home; she even got involved, for the first time, with the Women's Conservative Association; she had "private chats" with her myriad friends. "Even if their husbands vote Liberal, doesn't mean I can't convince them to use their own heads," she told Vi Pruitt's mother.

Wellington White would need all the help he could get. Moose Jaw district was a Liberal fiefdom. The riding had been dominated by Liberals, except for the Union candidate, whom even the staunch Grit William Grayson supported (not one Liberal ran in the 1917 election), and the Progressives, who had infringed on the territory in 1921. But the farmers' party was in such a weakened condition that Grayson and company assumed most would return to the Liberal fold. And their candidate was a pure Liberal blue-blood: J. Gordon Ross, a handsome young rancher-farmer from Caron, was the son of James H. Ross, the man who had, in 1883, nursed William Grayson when he had scarlet fever. James H. had enjoyed a long career as a Liberal politician, and by 1925 he sat in the Senate. During the 1925 campaign, the voters of Moose Jaw would be continually reminded of Gordon Ross's bloodlines.

But Wellington White had several advantages going into round one of the election. Prime Minister Mackenzie King had accomplished almost nothing during his four-year term; none of his previous election promises, including the introduction of unemployment insurance and old-age pensions, had materialized. King had hoped that the Progressives were now in such disarray and so weakened that they would disappear as a political force and he would be able to rule in Ottawa with a clear majority. But the farmers' party wouldn't give up that easily; E. N. Hopkins was nominated again in Moose Jaw. Wellington White's camp hoped Hopkins would split the Liberal vote, and that their candidate would sail up the middle. White's third advantage lay in his own reputation. By that time his success in business and farming was considered phenomonal. Words like "shrewd" and "forceful" were used repeatedly in his campaign literature. "I might say I expect you to elect me," White told a rally, "and I am going to handle your business the way I have handled my own."

It was a difficult campaign for the inexperienced White. Many of his platform planks – higher tariffs and an end to the Crow's Nest Pass freight rate – had been anathema to prairie farmers for years. Still, Wellington White was a much stronger candidate than the Grits had anticipated. He might not have been much of an orator, but on a person-to-person level, he could be overwhelmingly charming. "Wellington was uncannily honest," recalls Vi Pruitt, "which is probably why he never ran for political office before. He said exactly what he thought, and lots of farmers liked that." Realizing that they had a horse race on their hands, Liberals mounted a gossip campaign. However, the worst thing they could come up with was that White had made his money in California. Frank Wright, a Tory journalist, came to his defence, pointing out that, "if the Conservative candidate does make money in the United States, he brings it back to Canada for investment."

Wellington White lost the election, but by only 317 votes (out of 13,784), the best a Tory had done federally in twenty-five years. He garnered 5,351 votes, winning a small majority in the city. But in the rural areas, the issues of tariff and freight rates defeated him. His one compensation was that the Pasqua district, where his own farm was located, voted solidly for him. Part of the problem was that the Progressive candidate, E. N. Hopkins, managed only 2,765 votes; many of the farmer's party supporters had, indeed, returned to the Liberal fold.

The Whites were exhausted by the ordeal, and the day after the election they left for California. They were not allowed much respite. Less than a year later, the now-infamous "King-Byng Affair" erupted in Ottawa, and another federal election was called.

Arthur Meighen was actually victorious in the 1925 campaign. The Conservatives had nearly doubled their strength, winning 116 seats in Parliament to the Liberal's 99. But the Progressives held the balance of power. Although they had lost two-thirds of their Members of Parliament, they still managed to elect 24 (and there were 6 independents). Since many Progressives were Liberals at heart anyway, King didn't have too much difficulty in convincing them to support his party. Mackenzie King therefore ended up prime minister, not Arthur Meighen.

Naturally, Meighen was upset about this turn of events, and he wrote in 1926: "This is a shameless, brutal assault not only on the most sacred principles of British constitutional government but on common honesty."

Almost immediately after the election, a scandal was uncovered that sent shock waves through Ottawa. Canadian customs officials were apparently involved in a smuggling ring in the eastern part of the country and implicated were a senior customs inspector and a former Minister of Customs and Excise – and therefore, the Liberal administration. The Progressives suddenly found themselves in the awkward position of supporting a party that epitomized the kind of corrupt government they had been complaining about for years.

Arthur Meighen then decided to sponsor a vote of censure in Parliament. But before Meighen could make his move, the crafty Mackenzie King did an astonishing end-run, which would go down in history as the King-Byng Affair.

King realized that it would be better if an election was called than to have his government face censure and defeat in the House, so he asked the governor-general to dissolve Parliament. As John Diefenbaker, who had been trying to get elected in Prince Albert during these years, later wrote in his memoirs: "Never before in Canadian or in the whole of British parliamentary history had such a request been granted to a Prime Minister facing the censure of the House of Commons. Lord Byng rightly and properly refused King's request." Byng asked Arthur Meighen to form a government instead. Meighen agreed and committed the biggest mistake of his career.

Meighen was not as crafty as King, and he did not have the Progressive support solidly in his pocket. His government lasted less than three days, before it was defeated in the House by a fluke vote. An election was called for September 14, 1926.

Wellington White had come so close to winning the year before that it was logical that he would stand for the Conservatives in this election as well. But it was an exhausting, bitter fight.

In the previous election there had not been an all-candidates meeting; Wellington White, who was not fast with words, had quite wisely refused to meet the articulate Gordon Ross head-on. This time Liberals insisted that such a meeting be held, and so much publicity ensued that the Conservative camp could hardly say no. It was held at a school in the small town of Pelican Lake, on a very hot August evening early on in the campaign. Wellington White was not there. His strategists had decided he would be represented by two well-spoken Tory doctors. J. Gordon Ross, the Liberal candidate, spoke for himself. Although the debate was uneventful and rather boring, White was labelled a coward.

The Tories tried to make as much hay as they could out of the customs scandal. "If Canada should return Mackenzie King to power, it would be winking at the worst scandal ever revealed in Canada," Wellington White said on the hustings. But the Liberals effectively dismissed the issue as a red herring. More important, the Grits claimed, was the Constitutional crisis tearing Canada apart, which had been precipitated by the leader of the Opposition. They maintained (quite falsely) that Lord Byng had been acting on instructions from Downing Street and Buckingham Palace when he had asked Arthur Meighen to form a government. Only Mackenzie King, they claimed, could save Canada from colonial domination.

There was one other serious challenge facing Wellington White. Good times had returned to the West, and the Liberals kept reminding farmers that they now had money in their pockets. "Prosperity was on the way. Westerners will see it is not side-tracked by Meighen and his minions," Ross's campaign literature emphasized.

On many days of that gruelling campaign, the temperature reached ninety degrees. The Whites were finding it increasingly difficult to muster the energy to fight the Liberal machine. Campaign meetings were not as well attended as the previous year, although, as Ollie pointed out, "It's harvest time so what can you expect?" Even the arrival in Moose Jaw of the Conservative leader on August 25 did not generate as much excitement as his previous visit. The Liberals kept harping on the Tory policy of high tariffs, and Wellington White couldn't seem to convince farmers that the cost of a binder had actually gone up during King's administration. A huge cartoon, which appeared on the front page of the Liberal *Moose Jaw Times*, the day before the election, was headlined "The Wrong Toys for the West!" In it, Wellington White is portrayed as a little boy, wearing short pants and a middy blouse. He is holding a doll that looks like Arthur Meighen in drag. At his feet are strewn some toys. A train flies a sign "Higher Freight Rates." A child's book is titled *High Tariffs*. Little boy Wellington is bawling his eyes out because, as the caption read, "The boys won't play with me" – meaning other farmers. The satire so unfairly displayed on the front page of the *Moose Jaw Times* probably did him in.

More people actually cast their ballots for White than in the previous year's election, but that was because the Progressive support had collapsed, thus freeing up a good number of votes. In 1925, Gordon Ross's majority over the Tories was only 317 – in 1926, he beat Wellington White by 2,422 votes. It wasn't just Moose Jaw that felt this way. The Liberals were returned to Ottawa with a comfortable majority.

Ollie was more disappointed than Wellington. By this time she had developed a genuine interest in politics, and she had seen herself as the powerful doyenne of Tory wives, a trend-setter, western style, in the social world of the capital. "At least we won't have to endure winters in Ottawa," Wellington pointed out, trying to mollify her. Besides, as he added, his business affairs were piling up.

That winter in California he actually seemed relieved that his descent into politics was over. He had been like a duck out of water, and now he could get back to the business of making money.

~ V ~

Wellington White was a creative entrepreneur; he had always liked to invest in new and different enterprises, not minding the risk that this involved. The silver-fox farm was a case in point.

In August 1925 Wellington had attended a Rotary Club luncheon, and the speaker had explained in great detail the business of farming silver fox, which was then popular in Prince

Edward Island. The idea fascinated White. "He was sure there was a gold mine in it," says Frank White. A few months later the Moose Jaw Silver Fox Company was formed, and three hundred animals were shipped from Prince Edward Island.

Actually, it was Ollie White who ran the business. In a fascinating picture of her taken in 1927, she is dressed in the wool culotte suit she often wore when she did manual work. A black satin tam-like hat, decorated with a sporty feather, sits jauntily on her head. In her arms she carries five fox cubs, all looking lively and cute. Around her neck is a furpiece, the tail clipped into the mouth of the fox, who is dead and looks very sombre.

Although large huts made of galvanized steel were built on the outskirts of Moose Jaw, the fox farm lasted there only a few years. The Whites decided that California would provide a better environment for fox-breeding, and so the animals were transported to Long Beach. But, according to Frank White, the business didn't exactly thrive there either. "What wrecked it was the oil boom. When those creatures were whelping, they couldn't stand the ruckus that was going on. So they died out."

The oil boom might not have been good for the fox business, but it certainly was for Wellington White's prime money-making activity: playing the stock and commodities markets. His specialty was oil; he bought stock in Signal Petroleum Company of Los Angeles, Home Oil of Calgary, Prudential Oil of Moose Jaw. "For every three dollars he made, he invested five," says Frank White. "My father tinkered in everything." General Electric shares that he bought rose from $130 to $396 in a year. International Nickel and Brazilian Traction Light and Power had similar records.

As a farmer, Wellington also liked to play with grain futures. When the family was in Moose Jaw, he would drop in every day to chat with his brokers at James Richardson & Sons on Main Street (later Richardson Greenshields, which would be similarily frequented by Frank Eberle). The first page he turned to in the *Times* was the Winnipeg Grain Exchange quotations; unlike most investors, he had even made money on the great bull market of 1924-25, selling just before wheat prices dropped drastically. By 1928 he was listing his profession as investor, declaring that he had retired from farming.

In November 1927, Wellington White sold his Pasqua farm; four sections, including the entire 14-16-25 W2, the west half of which had once been Carmichael's homestead and pre-emption and then had been owned by Benjamin Smith, and the east half, once the property of Thomas Aspdin, John Hawke Grayson, and Bob Foote. Also included in the deal was the north half of 11-16-25 W2, the land that had been previously owned by J. R. Green and John Slemmon and had once been school endowment. One family, William, Margaret, Arnold, and George Fox bought the entire acreage for $230,555. Farm implements worth $15,000 were included. The Foxes did not put much money down; they were to pay for the farm by handing over to White half the crop profits each year. The Foxes settled in just in time to seed for the 1928 season, which produced one of the most bountiful harvests in the West's history. White thought he had made a "very good deal."

Wellington and Ollie planned to enjoy a more leisurely life; they would spend more time in California. Three of their four children would be living there: Isobel had married Dr. Albert Campbell, a medical student she had met at the University of Toronto, and they had moved to Long Beach. Kathleen was practising psychiatry and planned to marry Leon Delbridge, a businessman. Ross, too, was engaged to be married the following year.

In June of 1929 the Whites travelled from California to Toronto to attend their son's convocation ceremonies at the University of Toronto. He was graduating after a brilliant career at medical school. He was to intern at Luther Hospital in Los Angeles, but planned first to travel with his parents to Moose Jaw to say goodbye to his friends. The Whites got back to Saskatchewan just in time to vote in the provincial election and to celebrate. A coalition of Tories, Progressives, and Independents had finally beaten the Liberals who had been in office since Saskatchewan had become a province. The Whites knew the new premier, J. T. M. Anderson, personally, and they expected great things from his regime.

It was a pleasant, relaxing summer for Ollie. Several guests came to stay, including her good friend Jean Simington, the wife of Wellington's railroad engineer friend Walter. Ollie attended the usual showers and teas and bridge parties, and since she had been elected to the executive of the Moose Jaw Women's Conservative Association, there were meetings to attend and political work to be carried out. The highlight of the summer, however, was her impressive showing in the women's section of the Patterson Cup Golf Tournament. The Whites were leaving for California a little later than usual, in the first week in November.

On October 29, Wellington White sat in his big armchair down in his office, listening to the news over the radio. It was four o'clock in the afternoon, and he had just lost a fortune.

He knew the economy had been a little skittish in the past year. While in California, he had heard complaints that retail sales were down, people weren't buying like they usually did. On the other hand, stocks had continued to rise on Wall Street, at least until Labour Day, when the market seemed to be running out of steam. White thought that the sharp drop in stock prices that followed was to be expected and that a "correction" would soon follow. On October 24 the price of wheat on the Winnipeg Grain Exchange plummeted, and that did scare him. Still, he was not prepared for the total disaster that occurred five days later – but then few people were.

On Black Tuesday, October 29, the New York Stock Market had begun its plunge the moment the morning gong had sounded. Like every other investor in the world, as soon as he heard the news on the radio, White picked up the phone and screamed, "Sell! Sell! Sell everything!" At the end of a day of pandemonium on Wall Street, grown men were openly weeping, and Wellington White was no longer a fantastically rich man.

There was no thought in his mind of suicide or anything equally drastic, not with his stiff-backed wife there to buck him up. But what bothered White almost as much as losing his shirt, was that his boasting during the elections of how successful and clever a businessman he was – "I'm going to handle your business and the business of the country, the way I've handled my own" – now seemed utterly ridiculous.

It was Ollie who rallied. Their stock holdings might be worthless, but they still owned their property: several residential lots in Long Beach, plus a half-section of farmland in North Angeles County, their home in Moose Jaw, and, of course, White's Pool. It and Rainbow Danceland had done very well for them during the 1920s; after the market crashed, the Manitou Beach business became the White's main source of income.

By 1930 Little Lake Manitou had become the liveliest, most popular summer resort on the prairies, a rival even to Harrison Hot Springs in Banff. On any particular weekend, two thousand autos would be parked in fields surrounding the village; more people arrived by train, getting off at the nearby town of Watrous and taking one of the shuttle taxis to the resort.

For many years, White's Pool had been the centre of activity, but in 1929-30 the Chalet Swimming Pool was opened on the wealthier and classier west part of the beach. Lionel Sproule, who grew up at Manitou Beach, puts it bluntly, "The Chalet was where the Jewish people went, because they weren't welcomed anywhere else." Still, it represented real competition, and Ollie White fought back by mounting a sensational promotional campaign: WATROUS WATERS WORKS WONDERS AT WHITE'S read the handbill, which was distributed in movie theatres from Calgary to Winnipeg.

By 1928 Ollie was pretty well running the place. The previous manager had been discovered with his hand in the till, and she had stepped in until someone else could be hired. But after Black Tuesday, the Whites needed all the income they could get from the business, so Ollie took over the running of the operation.

Ollie White was called "Boss" by her employees. "She reminded me of Queen Wilhelmina [of the Netherlands], same build, same walk," recalls Harold Mulligan. "She was a very nice person, but you knew she was in charge." Mulligan says the pool was "making money hand over fist." He knows of one typical two-day weekend in 1927 when the cash receipts were $6,000, a goodly amount in those days.

During the summers Ollie White lived in a cabin behind the

pool. Mulligan said there wasn't much to it, just three rooms, but "Ollie had a old-fashioned stand-up organ in there that she banged away on all the time." Wellington would come on weekends, sometimes with friends. Still, it was a decided change in lifestyle for Ollie White. Gone were the leisurely summers full of teas and veranda parties. She was now a "working woman." "I have no doubt," says Vi Pruitt, "that without Ollie's incredible hard work, the Whites would have been in bad shape in those days."

Of all the provinces, Saskatchewan was the hardest hit by the Depression of the 1930s. As drought and grasshoppers and poor wheat prices ravaged the farmers, it became obvious that the Anderson government in Regina or the Bennett administration in Ottawa were not up to the task of effecting a recovery. This too-obvious fact tormented Wellington White. He believed firmly that government spending should be pared to the bone, taxes lowered, and the free market left to provide for the workers. He, like Arthur Meighen, did not believe in welfare programs such as old-age pensions. With such "socialistic" legislation in place, it would only be a few years before communism enveloped Canada. But as the Depression deepened, and this philosophy appeared totally inadequate, White became confused – especially as he himself was suffering. He had sold his four sections of farmland to the Fox family on the understanding that they would pay the purchase price of $230,555 by half-crop sharing. But since 1930 they had not had one decent harvest, and so not a cent of the principal or interest had been forthcoming. The Foxes were threatening to walk away from the place, and since this would have created a worse headache for White, in 1932 he forgave the interest owing.

The Depression deepened and 1934 was the worst year for the Whites. Ollie was now president of the Saskatchewan Women's Conservative Association, and she returned from California in March, a month earlier than Wellington, to work for the election that would soon be called. She must have realized the Anderson government was in terrible trouble when the speech she was scheduled to give the night before the election was cancelled because only twenty people showed up. Not a single

Conservative was elected to the legislature; the Liberals took a massive fifty seats, and the Farm-Labour group managed five. "The people have become fed up with rigid-thinking, hidebound, do-nothing politicians," wrote a commentator.

On their drive to Watrous that summer, the Whites were horrified at the terrible toll the four years of the Depression had taken. They saw the heads of households dressed in tattered overalls, their wives in flour-sack dresses, their children often in hardly anything at all. No painting had been done for years, and barns and houses were grey and peeling. Everything from tractors to tea kettles had been patched and patched again, until they were hardly functional. The dry ground lay useless, also a dreary, unyielding grey. Wellington knew there would be no payments from the Foxes that year.

The only compensation that awful summer was that the temperature soared so high – to 110 degrees – that everyone who had a few coins in their pockets came to White's Pool to cool off and relax. It became so hectic that Wellington and Ollie were looking forward to the time when the busy season would be over and the cooling breezes of fall would arrive.

They were planning to return to Long Beach on October 16, but, at the last moment, they decided to delay their trip for a few days. Their good friend Walter Simington had just bought a DeSoto automobile, a new Chrysler design called an Airflow, which very much interested White, and he and Walter decided that they and their wives should take a test run to Saskatoon.

October 15, 1934, was a lovely fall day when the Whites and Simingtons started out. Showing off a little, Walter was driving at between forty and fifty miles per hour, a fairly fast clip given the fact that Highway Number 2 was a secondary road and not in top-notch shape. Just after one that afternoon, coming down a hill where Number 2 meets the main highway to Saskatoon, the foursome were laughing about some remark that Ollie had made when a huge boom suddenly rang out. Simington stepped hard on the brakes, which was exactly what he shouldn't have done. The vehicle careened to the side of the highway, flipped over, and then rolled not once but twice, landing on its roof in the bottom of a deep ditch, wheels spinning in the air.

Ollie White had been thrown free of the car, and although she suffered cuts and bruises, she was not badly hurt. She immediately thought of her husband. "Wellington, where are you?" she screamed. She found him lying unconscious fifteen feet from the auto, blood trickling from the corner of his mouth. Jean Simington had been pitched from the car on its second roll, and she lay in the ditch among rocks. She was alive, but unconscious. Walter Simington was jammed behind the wheel of his car. "Help me get out of here," he called to Ollie. She managed to pry him from the vehicle, and although he was badly hurt, with a broken arm and other injuries, he was soon mobile.

Ollie White was trying not to panic. She had heard a car whizzing by, but because the DeSoto had crashed in a deep ravine, the driver had not seen them, so she climbed to the roadway. She had to wait what seemed like an eternity – actually only about twenty-five minutes – before another car came in sight. James Neal, a railway mail clerk, his wife and children, and two friends, were on their way to Saskatoon. As soon as they saw Ollie frantically waving, they screeched to a halt. Taking off their coats, they tried to make the injured as comfortable as possible. Meanwhile, another car was flagged down. Fred Snooks immediately rushed to the nearest town for medical help. Just moments before, the doctor had left, but his nurse was available. At the scene of the accident, she found Jean Simington and Wellington White still alive, but unconscious. She administered to them as best she could.

Finally, an ambulance arrived and the badly injured were rushed to Moose Jaw General Hospital.

It was soon apparent that both the Simingtons would recover, but Wellington White's condition was much more grave. He never regained consciousness, and at six-thirty on Tuesday morning he died. The Royal Canadian Mounted Police who were investigating thought it ironic that, when he had been thrown from the car, he had hit his head on some rocks and on an old red brick which had been imprinted with the letters W. W. MJ.

They also found that the right rear tire of the DeSoto had been punctured by a railway spike, and the blowout had spun the car out of control. The RCMP wondered how a railway spike could have found its way into the middle of the road, and for a while they suspected foul play. The investigation yielded no clues, however, and the matter was dropped. The man didn't have enemies, they were told.

Wellington White's will was read on the evening of the funeral, after the children arrived from California and Florida. It revealed the rather depleted state of the White family fortune. Wellington had exactly $1,715 in the bank. He held two mortgages and several outstanding promissory notes. These totalled about $18,000, but there was some question about whether any of it would ever be paid. There were some stocks, all worthless, and then the properties in California, Moose Jaw, and Manitou Beach.

Ollie White was to be provided with an annual income of $2,000 in monthly or quarterly instalments. After her death, whatever estate remained was to be divided equally among Wellington's four children, including his "adopted son," Frank. There was a stipulation in the will that said everything about Wellington White and his relationship with his wife. If Ollie should ever marry again, she would be cut off without a cent. Never mind that it had been her hard work that had built the business at Manitou Beach, had helped to establish the successful brick-making plant, had launched the silver-fox farm, and had assisted White in assembling his farming empire, or even that her managerial abilities had made the Moose Jaw home and the Vila Riviera the ideal place to entertain Wellington's business associates. She was deemed to have no direct ownership in any of it.

Primarily because of the California connection, White's will became entangled in legal snares and took over a year to be probated. By 1936 the Fox family had still not been able to pay a cent on the $236,000 owing on the farm south of Pasqua. Eventually, the four sections of land reverted back to the Wellington White estate. Ollie then took over the management of the farming operation, cultivating some sections with the help of hired men, renting out others. During the Second World War, when the value of farmland began to rise, Ollie, who by this time badly needed cash, sold off a large part of her Pasqua holdings, including one section that would be farmed by Frank and Kay Eberle.

Ollie's income came primarily from White's Pool at Manitou Beach. She managed the business for another fourteen years until finally, in 1948 at age sixty-eight, she sold the pool and her interest in Rainbow Danceland and retired to the Green Hotel in Pasadena California. St. Andrew's Church threw a huge farewell party for her that September. "I won't say goodbye. I don't ever want to say goodbye to Moose Jaw," she told the crowd. "Moose Jaw will always be home to me." Ollie White died in 1971 at age ninety-one. Her son, Ross, had predeceased her by four weeks.

Ollie had been only fifty-four when Wellington was killed, and she was still a most attractive and vivacious woman. During her summers at Manitou Beach, "gentlemen friends" would often arrive. Harold Mulligan remembers a professor from the University of Saskatchewan; Vi Pruitt was told about a politician who lived in Regina and a wealthy businessman from Los Angeles. On that special ballroom floor of the Rainbow Danceland, she would whirl round and round in the arms of some admirer or other, but the dance never evolved into anything serious. Ollie White never remarried. Whether she never found anyone to replace Wellington, or whether she was abiding by the stipulations in his will, remained her secret.

On one occasion she went to stay with Frank White, who was running his IGA store in St. Petersburg, Florida. It was during a hot, muggy spell, and the house was a small bungalow, without much privacy. Frank felt that Ollie was not very comfortable. She never complained, though, and willingly went on all the excursions the family planned for her. "She'd go into a store," recalls Frank's wife, "and every clerk would stop what they were doing and come and wait on her. I don't know if it was her regal bearing or if they could smell that she was going to spend money." Frank's two sons called her Mrs. White. But the Polish cook, who worked for so many years for the Whites and came to visit Frank's family on several occasions, was known as Grandma Mary Feltis.

THE "ALIENS"

Eberle

14-16-25 W2

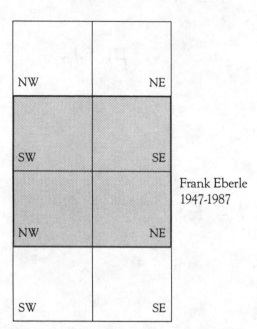

Frank Eberle
1947-1987

11-16-25 W2

They lived on the land for forty years. He understood everything about farming, and was good at it; she loved her home and her garden, and loathed to leave them, even for a short vacation. On the surface, theirs seemed the most ordinary of lives, models of hard work and frugality, of dedication to their daughter and grandchildren. Yet tension and malevolence rippled the surface, until it exploded in a brutal act of violence.

~ I ~

The settlers were not overwhelmed by the vastness when they first arrived on the Canadian prairies in 1891; they had already conquered similar wild lands, had transformed them into flourishing wheat farms – and not too many years before.

The Eberles originally came from a small village called Blankerborn in the Rhineland-Palatinate, a German state which bordered on Alsace-Lorraine. During the Napoleonic wars, the village was continually harassed by soldiers marching back and forth to battle. In their wake, the French wreaked havoc: crops were destroyed, trade disrupted, oppressive taxes levied, and young Germans conscripted to fight in foreign wars. And there was little religious tolerance. To escape the chaos of daily life, several families of Eberles accepted an offer of farmland from Czar Alexander I and set off for the southern Ukraine.

Actually, the czar offered far more than 162 acres of free land; he also promised exemption from military service in perpetuity, complete religious freedom, the right to speak German, and the authority to control the schools and the judiciary.

In 1809 the Eberles travelled overland through Austria, Czechoslovakia, Moravia, and Galicia, until they reached the town of Radziwillow, on the Russian-Polish border. From there they headed towards the fertile grasslands of the southern Ukraine near the Black Sea, to a region northwest of Odessa on the River Tichikleya. The Russian government had insisted that the Germans gather in communes – the free land would be owned communally – which was fine with the settlers, since the vastness of the Ukraine steppe terrified them. In the spring of 1810 the Catholic colony of Rastadt, so named because the majority of settlers had come from Rastadt, Germany, was established, population 469. (It is likely that Rastadt is now called by the Russian name, Mostovoe.)

Situated on a terraced knoll, the colony consisted of two thoroughfares, Main Street and New Street (which were exceptionally wide so that vegetable gardens could be grown down the centre), and seven residential cross-streets. The houses, almost all constructed of fieldstone, some of them very fine indeed, were enclosed by massive stone fences, which indicated that perhaps the commune was not really a commune in spirit at all.

The Russian authorities had insisted that a rather unusual system of entail be adhered to by the Germans: to avoid the division of land, the original grants must be bequeathed only to the youngest son, a system known as ultimogeniture. It was expected that to provide for the remaining male heirs, the German settlers would be forced to buy land, mostly from the Russian gentry. This they did, and as a result they assembled vast estates. In certain areas around the Black Sea, for example, the Germans constituted about 6 per cent of the population, but they owned 23 per cent of the land. Russian envy and animosity grew, fanned by the Germans' insistence on isolating themselves from the Russian culture around them. So oblivious were the Germans to the world outside their towns, that it was unusual to find even the smallest symbol of Russian culture, a samovar or icon perhaps, in their homes. Intermarriage with neighbouring Russians was almost unheard of. All of this resulted in bitter resentment and demands that the German settlers be deprived of their special status.

After 1871 the German settlers lost their exemption from military conscription, Russian became the language of the schools, and separate local courts were dissolved. The Germans who had settled earlier along the Volga were the first to flee, followed by the Protestants living in the Black Sea area. The Catholics, however, hung on a little longer. In 1881 Alexander III, a strong nationalist and virulently anti-German, ascended the Russian throne, and intolerance was given royal approval. Talk in the German colonies revolved around little else except who among them would leave.

Those in Rastadt eager to emigrate had decided to go to the United States. However, an acquaintance who had left for Canada in 1886 and was homesteading near Vibank, North-West Territories, wrote of the Canadian government's generous offer of free land and the potential wealth from farming. The vision of paradise was reinforced by a fast-talking Canadian agent working out of Odessa. In 1890 five families and two single men decided to try their luck on the Canadian prairies. Among them were Johannes Eberle, born in 1852 in Odessa, his wife Elizabeth, their seven children – aged seventeen years to two months – and Johannes's brother, Meinrad Eberle.

All the Rastadt families except the Eberles came via New York City directly to Winnipeg, and then on to Regina. On the advice of the immigration agent in Odessa, who told Johannes he could make a fast buck working in the mines, he and his family made a detour to the small village of Saltcoat, Minnesota. It must not have been a pleasant experience; by the spring of 1891, they had joined the others in Canada.

The Rastadt families got off the CPR in Regina and then headed seven miles southeast to the small town of Kronau. The railway hadn't yet arrived, so there wasn't much there other than a few ramshackle buildings facing onto one main street, but it was the gathering point for another group of Russian Germans who had recently arrived. In fact, the town was named after their colony in southern Russia. That they were Lutherans didn't matter; they had similar histories and were German-speaking.

The Catholics from Rastadt were leery of the heavy gumbo they found near Kronau; it froze solid in the winter and was hard to work. Northeast of the town, the earth was lighter, which made it easier to plough. That it was also sandier and laced with stones didn't matter so much to the farmer straining to break the tough earth with a team of horses or oxen. Only years later, when drought hit and the soil drifted away so easily, did they realize their mistake in not choosing the heavier, blacker, and more productive gumbo.

The settlers from Rastadt chose homesteads as close together as was possible. "They were very clannish," says Father Isadore Gorski, who grew up in Odessa, Saskatchewan, another Russian-German settlement. "They tended to look down on us Austro-Germans, and they were very upset if one of their sons or daughters married outside the Russian-German orbit." Following suit, a week after he arrived, Johannes Eberle filed for a quarter-section north of Kronau, very near the other Rastadt settlers.

The early 1890s was a desperate time for farmers throughout the North-West – it was during this period that Thomas Aspdin lost his farm – and Johannes, like Benjamin Smith, had to resort to government seed-grain loans, of potatoes in particular. Yet, through gruelling work, he managed. In 1898, when he filed for the patent on his homestead, he had sixty acres under cultivation and owned six horses and ten head of cattle.

The Germans had not been able to liquidate many assets because of the political unrest in Russia, and most arrived in their new country flat broke. To raise a little cash, they took any kind of job. They cut and hauled hay, and were lucky to show a two-dollar profit; the young hired out as farmhands for seventy-five cents a day; the older men worked as labourers in Regina, which was just beginning a construction boom equivalent to Moose Jaw's.

By 1896 the Rastadt colonists, twelve families, had collectively acquired enough money to buy a quarter-section a few miles north of Kronau from the CPR for $2.50 an acre (paid in instalments). They chose this area because they thought it was so pleasant; a little wooded valley, through which Many Bone Creek meandered, broke the monotony of the flat prairie. There they established a colony, which, since they were all from Rastadt, was naturally called Rastadt. (It was a difficult name for Anglo-Saxons, so the residents obliged them by also referring to it as Seven Colony, because it was located on section seven.) The southern portion was divided into lots on which homes were built. They were huts, constructed of rough logs mortared with mud, smoothed over with clay, and then white-washed – dwellings that were remarkably cool in the summer and warm in the winter. The northern portion, through which the creek wandered, was left as pasture land.

Although the heads of three households had purchased the land for the entire colony in trust, Rastadt was not a commune; farmland, machinery, and livestock were not held in common, except occasionally among family members. In fact, it was far from being a Tolstoyian paradise; bitter disputes, some of which raged on for years, soon bubbled to the surface. Many of these arguments had to do with money, which, to these immigrants, was synonymous with power.

Yet, despite the squabbles, the colony managed to do what it set out to – provide a refuge to nourish a specific and insular way of life. It wasn't the German culture that provided the binding glue, so much as their intense Roman Catholic faith. Every time Mike Fahlmann stopped his rounds to fill the seeder box, he prayed to God for a bountiful harvest.

The first immigrants had hardly untethered their oxen when an Oblate priest from Regina arrived to say mass. In 1894 a little sod hut with a roof of hay was built to shelter the worshippers from the weather. In 1903, after fierce arguments over its location – the parish included two other German-Russian settlements, Katharinental and Speyer, both of which wanted the church located in their villages – St. Peter's was built in Rastadt Colony. The church, a white wooden structure still standing today, seems too refined and delicate for the fierce prairie landscape. The one thing that anchors it is a slender tower, on top of which is perched a silver dome like a brilliant white onion, the only hint that the settlers had come from Russia. Unpretentious as it was, it dominated the colony of Rastadt.

"The priests told you how to behave, how to dress, how to think. And especially they told you who to vote for," says an Eberle descendant who still lives near the colony. "They had far too much to say about your personal life in those days." This perceived arrogance and power of the clergy would eventually have serious repercussions for the Eberles of Rastadt Colony.

The bumper crop of 1899 – experienced farmers like Benjamin Smith bragged of fifty bushels to the acre that year – firmly rooted the German-Russian immigrants in the Canadian prairie. Johannes Eberle's operation was no exception – there was talk of adding to the house and buying more land. But the family had hardly had time to taste their new prosperity when tragedy struck, not once, but twice.

In the summer of 1901, the Eberles' eleven-year-old son Jakob, born just before the family left Russia, was gored to death by a maddened bull. The following year Johannes suddenly grew ill, and he died on November 15, 1902. He was fifty years old.

Elizabeth was left with four children still at home; the youngest, Anna Marie, was only six. But fortunately for Elizabeth, three older sons, who had already married, lived nearby. "They were a great help to their mother," says Elizabeth's grandson Frank Eberle, who still lives in Rastadt. When it was time to do the heavy chores, the annual butchering or the making of blood sausages, the Eberle boys would perform this work for their mother before they'd do it for their own wives.

At the time of his father's death, the fifth Eberle child, Thomas, was twenty years old and still living at home. He was a dour, ambitious young man, who on the day he turned nineteen, the legal age for obtaining a land grant, entered for a homestead. Situated closer to the Speyer Colony than it was to Rastadt, his land was not only inconvenient to get to but had soil that was swampy and hard to work. He broke forty acres the first year, but no more after that. Like many of the German-Russians, he soon sold his original homestead and bought better land. In 1905 he also held a third interest with his two brothers Joseph and Frank in a quarter-section much closer to Rastadt. It was flat country, but there was a gentle roll to it, especially near the creek, and it was dotted with heavily wooded copses.

Thomas Eberle was a hard-working and painstaking farmer. "Any stone was not too little for him to pick up," remembers Anton Herauf, who grew up nearby. By 1910, with many good crops behind him and his homestead sold, Tom was able to buy another quarter-section, adjoining the property he and his brothers owned. Over the years he would acquire another four quarters, a large amount of farmland for those days.

In November of 1904, Thomas was married in one of the first wedding ceremonies conducted in the newly built St. Peter's Church. His bride, Catherine, was the daughter of Michael and Clara Seiferling, who had immigrated from the Crimea, southern Ukraine, to the Rastadt area. An older sister, Helen, had married Thomas's eldest brother, Joseph, seven years before. "The Seiferlings were very smart people, more sophisticated and

outgoing than many of the German settlers. I think the Seiferling women who married the Eberles really suffered, especially
Thomas's wife, Catherine," says a former Rastadt settler.

"Thomas Eberle was a very rough man," says Clara
Fahlmann. "He was the boss, and he was determined to get his
way." Catherine, on the other hand, was quiet and rather
refined.

The year after Thomas and Catherine were married, the
babies began arriving: Helen in 1905, Mike in 1907, Andrew in
1909, Fred in 1911, Frank in 1913, Clara in 1914, John in 1916,
Ray in 1919, and as a surprise after-thought, Mary in 1929. The
Eberle family lived in a roomy two-storey frame house, located
out on the farm, not in Rastadt proper. Not only was there no
more room left in the colony, but Thomas Eberle, like most of
the offspring of the original settlers, no longer needed the security of close neighbours – nor could he endure the squabbles
that were continually breaking out, mostly to do with stray
chickens and pigs.

Thomas Eberle's generation had become Canadianized, but
only to a degree. "The Germans from Russia were individualists
and ambitious. They thrived in a culture where you could work
yourself to death if that's what you wanted to do," says Tom
Hodel, an American historian. They learned enough English to
deal with the society around them – to be able to communicate
with the man who ran the grain elevator was very important –
yet they continued to speak German in the home and in the
schoolyard, so that their children, although born in Canada,
had pronounced accents. It marked them as aliens, and in
difficult times, during World War I for example, the colony
would shrink inward again, sheltering its own from a hostile
world.

Thomas's father, Johannes Eberle, had suffered enough political trauma in Russia to hunger after stability; on the day he had
resided in Canada the required three years, he had begun the
legal procedures to become a British subject. This stamp of
approval on the documents is dated October 29, 1894. Because
they were naturalized, the Eberles were never in danger of being
swept into concentration camps during the war years as others

were, particularly the hapless "Galicians," a term applied to almost anyone who spoke "a strange, European language" and came from somewhere around Russia. Still, life could not have been very pleasant for the German-Russian settlers. Every day the Reinhards and Dielschneiders and Schmidts suffered from the bigotry that was rampant at the time. In the fall of 1914, for example, the Moose Jaw City Council assigned extra men to patrol its reservoir after a guard reported that he had seen "Galicians and Austrians go to the water which was intended for consumption of the city and wash their dirty, filthy clothes. . . . A large number of Germans round there make the water pools their convenience" – meaning the foreigners had peed in Moose Jaw's drinking water.

While the German-Russian farmers suffered from the nativism that ran rampant in Saskatchewan during the war years and after, they also prospered from bumper crops and high grain prices. As one member of the Alberta legislature put it, "It makes one feel too sad to visit the West now. You see the country being cleared of our fine Anglo-Saxon stock and the alien left to fatten on war prosperity." Thomas Eberle was one of those trying to produce as much wheat as he possibly could for the Allied cause.

By the end of the war he had established himself as a man of influence in his community. Although he wasn't as prominent as his elder brother Joseph, who sat on the Rastadt district school board for years, he did serve as chairman in 1916. He was active in St. Peter's Church. But his prestige stemmed from his reputation as an innovative, successful farmer. "Uncle Tom was the most prosperous one around here," says Frank Eberle of Rastadt. "He owned the very first combine and the first big truck, so he must have been doing good." In the early 1920s, he sold some twenty horses and bought the first gasoline-powered tractors in the area, an event considered so progressive that the *Regina Morning Leader* ran a story about it.

Thomas Eberle also had a reputation for being particularly tight with money – something of a feat among people who were famous for their frugality. "I think it hurt Uncle Tom Eberle to have to spend one cent," says Frank Eberle. The oldest boy and the oldest girls were the lucky ones in the family. Now and then, they experienced the thrill of wearing a pair of new shoes or a new coat; the others knew nothing but hand-me-downs. At the beginning of each school term, Thomas Eberle would buy one or two pencils and break them into pieces for each of his children. Patrick Gleason, the teacher at Rastadt School, finally wrote the Department of Education complaining about him.

Thomas Eberle was extraordinarily strict with his children. "I can still hear that loud gravelly voice of his," says a former neighbour, "ordering his kids around as though he were a sergeant-major." The uproar used to torment Thomas's wife, Catherine, so much that she would go upstairs to her bedroom and put a pillow over her head in an attempt to drown out the racket. "Uncle Tom was a very stern man, but so was everybody in those days," says Frank Eberle of Rastadt. "You went to school, came home, and did your chores on the farm, and that was life."

The Eberle brothers, all six of them, were big, handsome boys, bright and hard-working. "It was hard to tell who was who," recalls a neighbour. "They looked quite a bit alike, and they basically had the same personality – they were slow-speaking, you might even say plodding, yet they were very clever; they could fix anything that was mechanical. And they were always polite."

None of the Eberle children went beyond grade eight, except the youngest, Mary, but that was the norm in those days. The law insisted you go to school until age fourteen; the day of your fifteenth birthday, you were out working in the fields. "The Russian-Germans didn't place much value on education," says Father Gorski. "The important thing was to help out on the farm, to make even more money, to buy another quarter-section of land."

Cousins of Frank Eberle, Thomas's fifth child, who were at Rastadt school at the same time, say he was a particularly bright student. "He always seemed to be so sure of himself, as if he already knew he'd succeed in life. He wasn't disobedient, yet he never seemed frightened of the teachers, as so many of us were," recalls Maria Grimmer, who was born at Rastadt Colony. He had a passion for practical jokes. Recalls one cousin, "We had this Irish teacher, Pat Gleason. He wanted us to speak German to him so he could learn a few words of the language. Frank, who was almost ready to leave school, he was about fourteen, yelled out in class 'Schweinhund! Du bist ein Schwein!' The kids all laughed their heads off. The teacher went over to see Father Metzger and asked him to translate. It means 'Pig-dog! You're a boar,' the priest was obliged to tell him. It wasn't a nice thing to say at all. Frank got into trouble, but he didn't seem to mind too much."

Frank's father, Thomas, possessed another character trait which would mark his sons profoundly – he was incredibly bull-headed. Says Alexander Eberle, "When it came to dealing with people, Uncle Tom could be rough. He stuck to his ideas, and that was that." No one would intimidate the proud Thomas Eberle, not even the all-powerful parish priest.

In truth, Henry Metzger, with his fine, aristocratic features, his round, wire-rimmed glasses, and his flyaway hair playing about the sides of his bald head, looked as though he should be sipping aperitifs on the boulevard du Montparnasse instead of overseeing the spiritual welfare of unpolished prairie farmers.

Metzger was born in 1877 in Grendelbroock, Alsace. In early childhood, he started painting, inspired by the medieval castles that dotted the landscape of that part of France. By age eighteen, he was studying at the École des Beaux-Arts in Paris and, according to a biographical sketch that he wrote himself, doing well. By that time he had heard his calling and entered a seminary in Munich. The church allowed him to continue his artistic studies, which included courses at the Julian Academy in Paris and working tours to Italy, Egypt, and Palestine. In 1901 he was ordained, and settled into a parish in Paris.

Why he decided at thirty-two to come to Canada was never explained, although he does seem to have had a sense of adventure and a love of the outdoors. He arrived in Saskatchewan in 1913, and since he could speak German almost as well as French, he was assigned the German-speaking parish of St. Joseph's in Balgonie. His duties included a weekly trip to say mass and hear confession at Rastadt Colony.

The farmers in the area were amazed at this sophisticate in their midst and overjoyed when, in 1915, Metzger convinced the archbishop that St Peter's should have it own parish priest, namely Father Metzger himself. The delight with which the parishioners received the news was dimmed a little when the bills started coming in: each family was assessed $25 to clean up a church debt and $65 for the building of Father Metzger's rectory, which turned out to be something of a mansion.

Father Metzger often talked about how homesick he was for the hills and dales of his native Alsace; in the numbing emptiness of the vast prairie, only the valley that sloped down sharply to Many Bone Creek bore any resemblance to the landscape of his youth. There, he decided, would be built a shrine to the Blessed Mother, as civilized and tasteful as any that might be found in a European village.

Father Metzger's flock didn't hesitate to give him what he wanted. In the spring of 1917, right after seeding, they began digging up the fieldstones on their land. Day after day they hauled them to the hill on Many Bone Creek near the church. "It was an exciting time," says Clara Ferner. "People still remember the rumble of the horses and the clanging of the harnesses as the wagons drove back and forth loaded with fieldstone." The women and girls mixed the mortar and set the rocks in place. At the end of each day they got a reward for their labours: one glass of Father Metzger's homemade wine to wash away the dust.

In two months the Grotto of Our Lady of Lourdes, for which Father Metzger hoped he would be immortalized, was completed. To this day, annually on the second Sunday in August, pilgrims, often in the thousands, descend on the village of Rastadt to take communion at the stone altar sitting in a cave of rocks. The aura of mystery surrounding the grotto remains so strong that villagers still believe that not one soldier in St. Peter's parish was killed during either world war because Father Metzger had called on the Blessed Virgin to protect them.

Henry Metzger had brought the cultured life with him. He owned a fine collection of linen, china, and crystal, looked after by his sister, who served as his housekeeper for many years and who was every bit as aristocratic as he was. It was Miss Metzger, in consultation with her brother, who decided which of the women parishioners would be allowed to serve at one of the elegant dinners of at least five courses, French service, given for the bishop, some influential politician, or the lieutenant-governor. "It was considered a great honour to be chosen," says Clara Ferner. "Everything had to be just so so. Miss Metzger made sure every fork, every glass, was set in the right place." Meanwhile, the rest of the parishioners were eating their chicken dinners in the parish hall.

The back part of the rectory had been turned into a large studio, and there Metzger produced the paintings and photographs which would bring him some fleeting fame. The Stations of the Cross lining the walls of St Peter's Church were painstakingly created by him, although much of the elaborate design was obviously carried out with benefit of a stencil. The lifelike figures may have been Father Metzger's creations; if so, they are remarkably flat and unemotional. Jesus appears to be facing his death on the cross with little more than annoyance. More successful were Metzger's portraits of Indians – such paintings as those of Day-Walker, the Cree medicine man, and Muskeg, a 103-year-old Cree, are drawn with great precision, although they are rather subdued in expression. If nothing else, they represent a colourful record of native dress and customs.

Among his most interesting paintings is a remarkable self-portrait. In it he is immaculately groomed, his cleric's collar a dazzling white, and he sports a dainty, pretentious, monocle. But it is his gaze that is so revealing; the viewer feels caught that very moment in some terrible sin, possibly the seduction of a spouse's best friend.

From 1915 until he died on his birthday, July 15, 1949, Father Metzger ruled his little fiefdom of St. Peter's parish with an iron hand. "The parishioners were all farmers, people of the land. Father was the learned one. He was their spiritual advisor, at times their lawyer, their financial consultant. And he could be very abrupt with anyone who argued with him." He had no hesitation in dictating to a young parishioner whom he or she should or should not marry.

In his sermons from the pulpit, Father Metzger would drop

hints as to whom his flock should vote for. For decades there was hardly a ballot not marked with an X for the Liberals in the entire parish of St. Peter. The German Catholics had never forgotten that it was the Liberal Party that had allowed, indeed encouraged, them to immigrate to Canada. But their loyalty was based on more than that. The German Catholics had come to fear the Tories in Saskatchewan. They knew, for example, that some Conservative politicians had supported the Ku Klux Klan.

The KKK had first popped up in the province in 1926, and three years later could boast of a hundred local chapters, with a membership of between ten to twenty thousand. The climax of the movement was a hysterical revival meeting in Moose Jaw, attended by some eight thousand people. When the sixty-foot cross at the top of Caribou Street was set on fire, frightening hooded figures – imperial wizards, exalted cyclops – could be seen for miles. "One flag, one language, one race, one religion [Protestant fundamentalism], race purity, and moral rectitude," speaker after speaker roared.

Although they were an offshoot of the American movement, the KKK in Saskatchewan was not out to persecute blacks – they would have had a hard time finding any. Rather their victims were the "ignorant, garlic-smelling, foreign-speaking Continentals," particularly "Catholics of Hun background."

While the KKK faded away in a few years, the Tories continued to alienate the Catholic population. In 1930, the government introduced amendments to the School Act which prohibited the display of religious symbols and wearing of religious dress in public schools. The crucifixes were removed from the walls of Rastadt School, the Ursuline nuns (who, by that time, had a contract to teach there) showed up in ordinary skirts and blouses, and the German Catholics of St. Peter's parish were traumatized. They still talk about it to this day. From that time on, Father Metzger faced no political dissension among his congregation. As much as the Eberles would sometimes disagree with the priest, they too were imprinted by the experience, and most, including Frank Eberle, voted Liberal for their entire lives.

Henry Metzger had one serious fault: he played favourites. In the scramble to seek his approval, one family was often pitted against another. It was one way of ensuring that the flock did his bidding. Father Metzger particularly liked the easy-going and malleable Joe Herauf, the patriarch of a family which had been feuding with the Eberles for years; the priest did not like the stern and proud Tom Eberle.

"My father and the priest were in cahoots," says Tony Herauf, "and it made life easier for us." The children of St. Peter's parish were required to learn their catechism; mothers prided themselves in drilling their offspring until they could recite the answers at lightning speed. "Father Metzger never quizzed us Heraufs unless it was an easy question," say Tony Herauf, "But the others, particularly the Eberles, he'd ask them the hard ones, and if they didn't know the answer, he'd take them by the ear and make them kneel by the altar."

It wasn't just the way Metzger favoured the Herauf children that irked Thomas Eberle; he thought the priest was vain and arrogant. He was incensed when a delegation of Heraufs and Obrigevitchs (another Rastadt family) came asking for donations to buy the priest a car. "This was in the Depression, and Tom Eberle didn't think it was right," recalls a former neighbour. "He said, 'I'm not able to drive a car. Why should the priest?' And he refused to give them money. This not only made the Heraufs mad, but I believe Father Metzger, too."

One Sunday, as the entire community sat in St. Peter's Church, Father Metzger said something from the pulpit – nobody can remember exactly what – that Tom Eberle and his sons considered disparaging of them, and insulting. "I was a young boy," says Bernard Ferner, "but I still remember people suddenly standing up and leaving the church." Outside, a brawl erupted, which raged up and down the main street of Rastadt Colony for what seemed like hours.

The priest's remarks represented the final straw for Thomas Eberle. He swore he would never step into St. Peter's again and, says his nephew, Frank Eberle of Rastadt, "I don't believe he ever did."

But it wasn't just Tom himself who was alienated from his

religion. His sons and daughters were as infuriated with Father Metzger as their father was, and remained lukewarm towards their church for their entire lives. Tom Eberle's long-suffering wife, Catherine, however, was a deeply religious woman. Her husband's repudiation of his faith left her depressed and disconsolate, and she died only a few years later.

~ II ~

Nine consecutive years of drought, crop failure, and uncertain grain prices devastated the Rastadt Colony during the Depression as much as any area in Saskatchewan. "The soil was light, so it drifted easily," recalls Alexander Eberle. "And our land was too high, so we had no sloughs, so we couldn't raise horses and cattle."

"Cultivation methods were their downfall," says Bernard Ferner. "Russian thistle thrived in the drought and grew yay high. They didn't have the implements to work the weed into the soil. So what did they do? They burnt it off. The stubble blew away, and the soil went with it."

One indication of how cash-poor people became during the Dirty Thirties was the fee charged for membership in St. Peter's Ladies Auxiliary: in 1929 it was $1.25 per year; by 1939 it had dropped to ten cents. So few parishioners could pay their church dues that Father Metzger was forced to sell his Indian paintings to keep the parish alive.

And yet, few of the Rastadt settlers abandoned their farms as so many others in Saskatchewan were forced to do. They were able to hang on because that old spirit of cooperation had reasserted itself once hard times hit. "When the going was good, there was some rivalry, a keeping-up-to-the-Joneses, that could be really upsetting," recalls Bernard Ferner. "But when the going got really, really tough, they stuck together like glue. And they got through that terrible time."

For the frugal Eberles, the Dirty Thirties meant a serious setback, but it was never a matter of survival. "My Dad always had a few bucks. He even bought a car," remembers Frank

Eberle of Rastadt. "We always had enough to eat and we never took relief. The same could be said of Uncle Tom."

But even Thomas Eberle was not wealthy enough to provide a livelihood for each of his six sons, who, as the Depression began, were heading into their twenties. They were big, strong young men, with not enough to do. "The father couldn't possibly afford to start them all on their own," says Alexander Eberle. "They were just sitting around doing nothing. One guy would go out and do this chore and the next guy would sit around and wouldn't even help him. Squabbles developed because there just wasn't enough to do."

In 1933 the four eldest, Mike, twenty-six, Andrew, twenty-four, Fred, twenty-two, and Frank, twenty, rented a section of farmland near Craik, Saskatchewan, fifty-two miles north of Moose Jaw. Their father gave them some used equipment, basic things like a tractor, an old disk harrow, a seed drill, to get them started. The implements were in good condition – Tom Eberle's machinery was always in good condition – and some of the Craik neighbours were envious; after four years of pitiful income, with no money for anything new, everything from cooking pots to tractors were so patched and repaired that they were hardly worth keeping.

The first year the Eberle brothers farmed, the rains came, at least in southern Saskatchewan. Everyone prayed for the first good harvest in five years. But their hopes were quickly dashed. An outbreak of stem rust, the worst since 1916, decimated the crops; farmers could only stand hopelessly by and watch as the ugly reddish-brown pustules formed on the stem and leaves, sucking the water and nutrients from the plants. It's estimated that Saskatchewan farmers lost $100 million that year. The next year was so hot and dry, the average yield was only seven and a half bushels to an acre in an area that commonly could boast of twenty-five bushels. But it was 1937, the eighth year of drought, that was the true heart-breaker, the worst crop failure in prairie history. Two and a half bushels an acre was all the Saskatchewan farmers got off their parched fields. It was a nightmare of dust, heat, and grasshoppers, swarms of them, so thick that at high noon they obscured the sun. Not only did they devastate the wheat crop, they ate the lace curtains in the sitting room. To add to that summer's general misery were wild, frightening hailstorms, and then an infestation of army worm which chomped its way through any crop that might have been left. By fall, two-thirds of Saskatchewan's rural population was on relief.

The Eberle brothers might well have been disheartened, except that they had already decided they were not going to sit around and wait for the weather to improve to make their fortune.

Nobody is quite sure who made the initial contact with Canada Permanent Trust, but it was likely the second eldest, Andrew, who had a good head for business. He worked out a deal with the company which, in a half-dozen years, while every other farmer was growing poorer by the harvest, would make the Eberle brothers rich.

As the Depression deepened, thousands of farmers threw up their hands in despair, declared themselves bankrupt, and abandoned their land. In the ten years after 1931, an estimated quarter of a million people moved off the prairies. Since Canada Permanent Trust had held many of these defaulted mortgages, the company ended up owning huge tracts of land. Much of it was on the verge of reverting back to a wasteland of sand dunes and weeds, the virgin prairie with which Dougald Carmichael had wrestled. If Canada Permanent Trust was ever to sell it as valuable farmland, it would have to remain "black," the soil turned over, the weeds controlled. A handsome fee would be paid to those willing to travel the backroads of southern Saskatchewan, Manitoba, and Alberta, to minister to the wreckage of what had once been prosperous farms.

The Eberles formed a company in which all six brothers – the two younger, John and Ray, soon joined the enterprise – had an equal share. Helen, the oldest Eberle sister, who had looked after her young siblings for so long she was called Mom, had moved to Craik to keep house for her brothers. There she met Chris Buch, who, with his sister Pauline, had immigrated from Poland in 1929. A romance ensued, and Helen and Chris were married in November of 1933. Buch joined his brothers-in-law in their growing business.

From the beginning, the endeavour was a lucrative one, and by 1938 enough money had been accumulated to buy a section of land near Lake Valley, twenty-two miles north of Moose Jaw. The old farmhouse on the property became the headquarters for the custom-farming enterprise.

The Eberles owned some of their own equipment, but, as they became more seriously involved in line work, Canada Permanent Trust offered to bankroll the operation. The brothers eventually paid the company back from the proceeds earned and ended up owning a fine line of state-of-the-art farm machinery. They had one-way drills, combines, and powerful tractors. "We had a big, big tractor – a Minneapolis, one of the biggest you could get in those days," recalls Clifford Gentner, a hired hand.

By the time Gentner went to work for the Eberles in the early 1940s, they had three separate crews, all with their own outfits. "We'd all go out, one tractor following the other, and turn a field black in a matter of hours. . . . We worked twenty-four hours a day. One guy would sleep, the others would till a field – we had big lights on the tractors so we could work at night – and another would cook. We'd finish, we'd load up our machinery, and then the guy who had been sleeping would drive two hundred miles in a different direction. Then we'd start all over."

The farm equipment was transported on huge flat-bed trailers, while the workers travelled in housetrailers fitted with kitchens. "It made quite a caravan going down the road."

During the drought years, the travelling could be hazardous. Hired hand Albert Slywka remembers hitting a "black blizzard," of blowing dirt just south of Maple Creek, Saskatchewan. "It'd be two in the afternoon, the sun be shining – all of us sweating like pigs because it was 103 in the shade – and you couldn't see a foot in front of you. That black dust just whirled around like something straight from hell. Terrifying, I'll tell you."

It was also depressing. "Those little ramshackle houses? The owners had fled long ago. Maybe they were homesteads. I thought about all the work that had gone for nothin'. Saw nothin' but people's broken dreams all day long." Slywka could never make up his mind whether he should consider the Eberles heroes for their part in turning back the desert or opportunists for taking advantage of other people's misfortune. "Just smart, I guess," he concludes.

About once a month the crews would return to the Lake Valley farm so that the machinery could be serviced. "We needed the break to clean up," says Gentner. "Out on the road we just take our work clothes and swish them in gasoline. It was a very fast cleaner." As long as the laundry was immediately hung out in the air to dry, it didn't smell, he added.

At Lake Valley, the hired men were put up in bunkhouses; the Eberles lived in the main farmhouse nearby. "There were always women working hard in the kitchen there, Eberle sisters and cousins, so you always got a good meal, plain food not fancy cooking, but there was lots to eat and it was very tasty," says Gentner.

The hired hand could always relax after work; someone had a mouth organ and another a saxophone, and decks of cards could be pulled from back pockets. But not the Eberles. They were too busy working. And yet they weren't dour men; there was a sense of fun among them. They were all practical jokers: a wrench missing from a toolbox would be discovered in the cookie jar; a much-longed-for bottle of booze would be found to contain coloured water rather than rye. Brian Eberle remembers his father, Andrew, many years later: "He'd be sitting back watching television or reading a newspaper, and all of a sudden he'd start smirking. You knew he was reminiscing about what he did to Mike or Fred – hiding their pants or whatever. And from what I understand, Frank Eberle was the biggest joker of all."

Frank was also the one who kept the machinery in order. "He was very quiet, a gentleman," says Gentner, "and he was a very busy, busy person. He always seemed to have his fingers in doing something. He was a good welder too, could fix anything."

"With Frank Eberle it was nothing but work, work, work," says Albert Slywka.

All the Eberle brothers laboured in the fields along with the hired men, but, Gentner says, they also had specialized chores. The head of the operation was Andy, who acted as the accountant-bookkeeper and "ran the whole show." Ray was the youngest and looked after the Lake Valley spread. Gentner worked primarily for Fred, the third oldest. "He was a likeable chap, but a little more on the strict side."

Cliff says that Fred would not hesitate to get rid of someone if he wasn't doing his job. He even fired a hired hand who had been recommended by his girlfriend. The other workers had complained that he wasn't pulling his weight. "What was a little hard, though, was that the Eberles wouldn't even take him to the train station. He started walking across the field and I said to Fred, 'Jeez, I should give the guy a ride to town.' He let me go, but he wasn't pleased."

Although a war was approaching, Gentner can't remember the Eberles ever talking about it. "I don't know if they even listened to the radio or if all they did was work." They may simply have been sensitive to criticism. While they were all Canadian-born, they still had heavy German accents and a distinct German name. (Some Eberles added a y, giving the surname an English flavour.) Raymond Laird, who would become a Lake Valley neighbour, recalls one incident that occurred while the Eberles were shopping in Moose Jaw. Laird spotted one of the brothers coming out of Joyner's department store just as "a couple of young guys yelled, 'Kraut! Nazi! Go back to where you belong.' Suddenly three Eberle brothers – and they were big and strong – appeared out of nowhere. When those guys saw them walking towards them, they took off as fast they could."

"It wasn't unusual for us to be called square-heads in those days," says Alexander Eberle. "We had to be very careful." He knows of few German-Russians who actually volunteered for service. "They couldn't see fighting a war for the Russians. There was still such a hatred for that country." They also heard stories about the mistreatment and humiliation of the few who did join the army. Their German accents in particular were ridiculed.

None of the Eberle brothers enlisted; after conscription was implemented in November of 1944, John, the second youngest, was called up, but he never went overseas. "I think the Eberles felt they were doing their duty by farming twenty-four hours a day, producing the food which the Allies needed," says a niece.

Perfect weather conditions in 1942 produced the biggest wheat crop in history. The problem was getting it off the land. Young people had either enlisted or left the province for jobs elsewhere in munitions factories. The labour shortage was so acute that high-school boys and girls were recruited to help with the harvest. "The uncles' answer to the labour problem," explains Fred's son Brent Eberle, "was to rig up these self-propelled combines before there were self-propelled combines. They devised a shaft for the steering and installed a series of cables, so that one man was able to operate the tractor and the combine together." The John Deere company was so impressed that they had film shot of the Eberles out in a field running John Deere Number 9 combines and five John Deere tractors. (The Eberles also owned Minneapolis tractors, but these were conveniently hidden.) It was a time when people were fascinated with the new farm machinery, and the film was shown in movie theatres across the country.

The handsome and self-confident Eberles cut quite a figure in small-town Saskatchewan. One of their neighbours at Lake Valley remembers running into them at various local hotels. "They liked their smokes and they liked their rye and they liked to argue. They all talked with the same peculiar German accent, very slowly. They all had voices that seem to rumble from the bottom of their bellies." The neighbour says they were impressive men and "they obviously had a few bucks, so the ladies were attracted to them – no doubt about that."

The weddings began in the early forties. Andrew married Peggy Vogt, the daughter of farmers of Prussian origin who had settled in Odessa, Saskatchewan; Fred took as his wife Blanche Wallace from Brownlee; the two youngest Eberle brothers married sisters, Hilda and Hertha Siebert, whose father had homesteaded in the Southey area. (The youngest Eberle sisters, Clara and Mary, married the Moser brothers.) Mike, the eldest Eberle brother, remained a happy bachelor, everyone's favourite uncle. With the exception of Blanche Wallace, whose family was of Scottish origins, the young women all spoke a dialect of

German. All seemed well-suited to the rural life the Eberles would offer. But of all the brothers, it was Frank who ventured the least far outside the German-Russian circle to find his bride. When his engagement was announced, family and friends gasped in shock: he had fallen in love with his first cousin.

Katherine "Kay" Bishoff was working as a cook at the Eberle brothers' farm when her romance with Frank began, but they had known each other all their lives. Kay's mother, Anna Marie, was sister to Tom Eberle, Frank's father, and youngest child of Johannes and Elizabeth Eberle, the original immigrants who had come from the Ukraine to settle in Saskatchewan's Rastadt Colony. She had been only six when Johannes passed away in 1902, and her sisters and brothers, including Thomas, had watched over her, especially after her mother died suddenly of a burst appendix in 1910.

In February of 1916, Anna Marie had married Wendelin Bishoff, who was from an area north of Maple Creek, very near the Saskatchewan–Alberta border. This was another large community of German Catholics from Russia, but they had come to Canada later than the Rastadt families, about 1908, and therefore had to travel much further west to find suitable homesteads. Unlike the Eberles, Wendelin Bishoff was a rather luckless farmer. He applied for a homestead near Maple Creek, but for some reason quickly abandoned it. After his marriage he tried farming at Montmartre, not far from Rastadt, but the soil there was too light and sandy and the family soon pulled up roots again. They headed west, finally settling near the spot where Bishoff had originally applied for his homestead. "I don't think Wendel Bishoff made out too well there," says Frank Eberle of Rastadt. "There was a lot of rocks on his farm. He wore himself out working day and night." On November 29, 1930, at age forty-three, he died after a short illness and was buried at Saint Anthony's Roman Catholic Church at Mendham, Saskatchewan. Anna Marie was left with eight children (a boy had already died at age eight), aged six months to fifteen years.

She soon realized she couldn't work the farm on her own. In the summer of 1931 she moved with her children to Regina, where she would be closer to the Eberles.

That July was terribly hot in the Queen City, but it was the fierce thunderstorms that struck like revelations from God which were so frightening. Buildings burst into flame, power stations were knocked out, street paving was ripped apart. The violent weather foretold the frightened, desperate mood that would soon settle over the city, for by the end of that year, 30 per cent of Regina's wage-earners were out of work. Anna Marie Bishoff's family was only one of thousands who relied on public relief for their survival.

"Auntie Annie had a tough time," says a niece. "She had nothing, and there was a large family to support. It was very, very hard for her." She was supposed to rent a house for $20 a month, heat it for $10, feed her brood of eight on $36. But more than the lack of cash, it was the terrible shame of being on the dole that haunted people for years after. Relief did not come in the form of cash, but was grudgingly doled out: food rations consisted of a box of groceries filled with beans, rice, macaroni, tinned tomatoes, and a small roast. Each baby was allotted six cents per day for milk, although the amount required for good health cost seven cents. Used clothing was distributed at a central depot, but the garments were often so tattered and torn that needle and thread were supplied on the spot to repair them. Each person was allowed only one pair of underwear. It was a degrading enough existence for the Bishoffs, but it would have been worse without the help of Anna Marie's brothers and sisters.

"My mother used to always feel sorry for Aunt Annie," says Frank Eberle of Rastadt Colony. "There wasn't a week went by when I didn't have to drive up and bring her a chicken or a few eggs." Other brothers contributed anything they could: vegetables from the garden, beef and pork after the butchering, clothes. The younger children often spent the summers at the farms of one or other of their uncles. "That got them out of the city and out of Aunt Annie's hair," says a niece. "While all this help was appreciated and really needed, I think it gave them all a sense of inferiority. 'The poor Bishoffs,' that's how they were talked about."

Katherine was the eldest in the family. Already sixteen at the time her mother moved to Regina, she was considered too old to continue school. She was needed at home, anyway. She helped her mother and took jobs to earn some cash – cleaning houses, babysitting children. For one year she worked as a domestic at the Grey Nuns' Hospital. "I think the Depression and her mother's circumstances left an indelible imprint on Kay," says a family member. "There was a sense of insecurity that was almost pathological."

"Kay was very strange about money," remembers a sister-in-law. "She didn't like to spend it at all, and whenever anybody bought something new, like a car or some furniture, she would have something to say about it, something very critical and disparaging. It was very odd."

Kay was always of fragile health, and in the late 1930s she contacted tuberculosis. She spent some months at Fort San, the provincial sanitorium, but by 1940 she was well enough to go to work at the Eberles' Lake Valley farm operation as a cook, and well enough to be courted by Frank. The fact that they were first cousins didn't seem to worry them, but it shocked others. "It didn't bother me," says Alexander Eberle. "but it bothered some people, because the church was against it. Some priests had refused to marry first cousins, and they ended up going before a Justice of the Peace."

However, Frank and Kay had no difficulty in obtaining dispensation from the church. On February 21, 1945, they were married by Father Walsh, the first couple to be wed at the newly built St. Cecilia Roman Catholic Church in Regina. A story in the *Regina Leader-Post* described the wedding. "The bride accompanied by her brother entered the church to strains of the Bridal chorus. She was charming in a gown of winter white satin and a sweetheart head-dress. Her bouquet was of roses. A gold locket, a gift of the groom, was her only ornament." Kay looked radiant in photographs taken that day. She's much shorter than Frank, tiny-boned, almost birdlike, with rich auburn hair and dark eyes. He looks handsome in his pin-striped suit, a boutonnière in his lapel, and a bright blue tie. With his slicked-back hair, his longish side-burns and a little moustache, he appears a debonair man. And Frank, indeed all the Eberle brothers, had more than good looks and nice personalities to offer their brides – by the time of their respective marriages, they were all prosperous farmers with substantial land-holdings.

As the Eberles had roamed the back roads of Saskatchewan doing custom harvesting, they had carefully noted farms for sale. They wanted good land, heavy clay gumbo, well-drained, as frost-free as possible, and in districts that were not prone to drought. In the 1940s, Andrew and Mike, on behalf of the other brothers, began buying up whole sections. Much of the land was owned by Canada Permanent Trust, and the Eberles were able to purchase it through a crop-sharing scheme: each year a percentage of the harvest would be paid to the trust company. "But if they didn't get a crop, maybe because of drought, the company didn't get any money. And there was no interest. So it was a very good deal," says Brent Eberle. By the mid-forties the Eberles had paid off all debt owing to Canada Permanent Trust.

But there was other property, not owned by the trust company, which the Eberles bought outright for cash. This was usually excellent land which, for one reason or another, was going for bargain prices.

In the early 1940s, the Eberles had heard rumours that Ollie White wanted to sell land she owned around Pasqua. There were legal complications with Wellington White's estate; death duties were outstanding, a signal that the land might sell cheaply. In February 1942, one section, consisting of the northwest and northeast quarters of 11-16-14 W2 and the southeast and southwest quarters of 14-16-25 W2, was sold to Allan G. Cook, a real-estate broker in Regina. He paid $17,800. On July 3, 1943, Andrew and Mike Eberle bought it from him for $20,800. They paid cash; no mortgages have ever been placed on that section, and in 1988 it was conservatively valued at $224,000.

As the end of the war approached, land values revived, so that the trust company was able to sell much of its holdings; custom farming services were no longer needed. The Eberles were tired of it anyway. "Once they got married, they didn't want to be traipsing around the countryside. They needed to have a place to call home, to settle in one spot," says Judy Dixon, Fred

Eberle's daughter. The company was dissolved, and the assets divided. "They had put together so many sections of land. This was divvied up depending on who had put in the most work and time. I think maybe there was a dollar value involved, one would have more equity in the property than the other," explains Brent Eberle. Most brothers ended up with two sections, although interestingly they never worked more than one. They were exhausted from working so many hours, day after day, and their health had suffered. "All they wanted at that point was a small farm that they could manage well," says a relative. The other section was either rented out or sold.

Frank Eberle ended up owning two sections, one kitty-corner to the village of Lake Valley, and the Pasqua land, previously owned by Wellington White. "The land around Lake Valley was light, with a fair number of rocks, while the land around Pasqua was heavy gumbo, and you'd have to import stones, if you wanted them. No question which any good farmer would choose," says Brent Eberle. The Lake Valley land was rented out and then sold to Kay's sister, Genevieve, the youngest in the Bishoff family, and her husband, John Finiak. Frank considered the place at Pasqua to be ideal, a gem of a farm, and in 1947 he and Kay moved there.

~ III ~

Since the days of Bob Foote and the Slemmon brothers, the town of Pasqua had experienced its ups and downs. During the 1920s, most travelling was still done by train, so the fact that Pasqua was the junction point between the main CPR and Soo lines was significant. Mail and passengers coming from the United States switched trains at the little town. "The CPR was almost like a bus service in those days," says Walter Champion, the grand-nephew of Bob Foote, who has lived in Pasqua for over thirty years. "You could catch a train going one way or the other every hour." The train station, the three section-houses, the bunkhouses – "There must have been twenty-five guys in each car and they managed to make their own breakfast every

day," recalls Champion – the Western and the Pool grain elevators, and a stockyard where cattle waited to be loaded into
trains, all made for a bustling town. There was still a blacksmith,
as well as a meat market, a general store, and a post office. James
Duncan had opened his lumberyard in 1910. When gasoline-
driven tractors came into vogue, he started selling farm implements, and by 1929 he was doing a roaring business as an
International Harvester Dealer. He also pumped gas – he had
one of those gas pumps, round and slick as cucumbers, which
were seen in every little town on the prairies – and Jim or his son
or nephew could do a grease job on your truck in no time. The
Presbyterian Church transformed itself into a United Church
after union in 1925. And although the rectory had been vacated, a minister came from Moose Jaw every Sunday. "He'd get on
the 8:00 a.m. train and arrive in time to eat his breakfast at our
place. He'd hold a church service at 11:00 a.m., eat his dinner at
our place, and hold another service at night. And he'd oversee
Sunday school in between," remembers Jean Schuster, whose
mother was Minetta Foote, the widow of Sandy, Bob Foote's
brother. Minetta ran a boarding-house in those days.

Like all small towns in Saskatchewan, Pasqua suffered during
the Depression. The church was the first to go; there was so little
money available to pay clergymen that a town that was as close
to Moose Jaw as Pasqua became the first victim of budget-
cutting. Jim Duncan bought the building, tore the pretty steeple
off, and, to the dismay of the local residents, turned it into a
machine shed. Since there was no cash around, especially for
gambling, the pool hall soon disappeared. The CPR whittled
away at its operation, and some of the farmers who lived in the
district left town – Darcy Dennis moved out in the middle of the
night, leaving all his debts behind. But most Pasqua people were
determined to endure the hard times. "It was their home; they
had homesteaded it," says Gertie Aitkin. "Where would they
go? Everybody was in the same boat, no money, so they helped
each other out. They got by. That was about it, they just got by."

By the time Kay and Frank Eberle moved there in 1947,
Pasqua was bustling again. A new school had been built that
year, which doubled as the social hall where Christmas pageants

and fowl suppers were unrelentingly organized. Jim Duncan's gas station–implement dealership had somehow survived the Dirty Thirties and was now in good health. Bill Best had converted the front of his house into a grocery store–post office. Once a day the entire population of the Pasqua district dropped by to pick up their mail, including Frank Eberle. People remember two things about Frank: how much he liked to talk and how slowly he talked. "He'd pick and choose every word he was going to say," says Brian Stirton, a neighbour. "If you didn't know him, you'd think he was slow. But he was really intelligent." People noticed that his bundle of mail almost always included a stack of magazines and newspapers, mostly business journals like the *Financial Post*.

Kay sometimes came along, but most of the time she preferred to sit in the car and wait rather than face a bunch of chatting neighbours. What everybody remembers about her was how serious and quiet – painfully so – she was. "She was very nice, but hard for me to talk to," recalls Walter Champion. "The conversation never got very far. It was probably my fault, but we seemed to be on different channels."

In the 1940s, many descendants of the Footes and Slemmons still lived around Pasqua, and the town had maintained its predominantly WASP flavour. "I sometimes think it was a mistake for Kay and Frank to have moved there," says a nephew. Other than Andrew, who had contracted tuberculosis and lived near the sanatorium at Fort San, the other brothers continued to farm around Lake Valley. While they remained close to each other in this community, over the years Kay and Frank became more and more isolated. They didn't participate in community affairs; Kay, in particular, shunned things like the ladies' group, which was very active in the town.

The Eberles' home was situated not far from where Dougald Carmichael had built his original homestead sixty-five years before. Although he had help excavating the basement, Frank constructed the rest of the house himself – in a most ingenious manner. He used lock staves – two-by-sixes made with tongues and grooves, which interlocked at the corner of the buildings. In the 1930s and 1940s, granaries, garages, and other outbuildings were built in this method, but very few houses. The material was expensive, although Frank may have got a deal on it, and difficult to work with. But because it was so thick, it was sturdy, durable, and provided insulation. "Such a building should be able to withstand cyclones, or even stop bullets," says Regina architect Ken Scherle.

It was a modest house, much like the wartime homes that popped up everywhere at the time. A one-and-a-half storey, it had a small living room, a rather large kitchen, Frank's office, and one bedroom all on the ground floor, and two small bedrooms upstairs. Later, Frank built a sitting room over the garage. It was a pretty house, with its face of red-brick veneer, a wood-shingled roof, white siding, and red-and-white striped aluminum awnings framing two picture windows. In the early 1950s, it was considered modern and rather grand for the country.

As Dougald Carmichael had found out to his sorrow years before, there was no usable water on the land; it had to be hauled from Moose Jaw. But Frank installed big cisterns, and eventually set up a dug-out system. "There was running water and a flush toilet in the Eberles' house," recalls Joan Pawelchuk, whose family lived nearby. "They were the only ones in the district who had such a luxury. Everybody came to gaze at this wonder." There was also no electricity, and Frank built a large windmill to provide power. This, too, was considered very modern. "It was a very nice house," says Doreen Meadows, a neighbour, "but you never felt it was a home."

No children came of Frank and Kay's union. Whether they realized this was a permanent condition, or whether they felt a sense of obligation, in 1950 they adopted Kay's sister's baby.

Rosalie was considered the beauty among the Bishoff sisters – "a black rose," was what her fiancé once called her – and she was more outgoing and vivacious than her older sister, Kay. The sixth child of Annie Bishoff, she also managed to get a better education than her older siblings. In 1944, at age eighteen, she began working as a steno-bookkeeper for the Regina News Company. Nobody seems to remember how she met Bob Burns, who was from Toronto, but they had a whirlwind courtship and were married in 1947. On February 10, 1948, their daughter, Carol Anne, was born. Two years later an epidemic of tuberculosis swept Saskatchewan, and Rosalie was one of the victims. She would spend the last two years of her life at Fort San. Her marriage did not survive the ordeal.

Rosalie was particularly close to her eldest sister; she had been maid of honour at Kay and Frank's wedding. It was natural that, when she realized her chances for recovery were slim, she turned to the Eberles. She asked them to adopt Carol Anne, and they readily agreed. "This gave her peace of mind because she knew they were well-off and responsible," says a relative. On February 27, 1951, Rosalie Burns died at the age of twenty-six.

The Eberles were delighted to have the little girl. Pictures taken at Christmas dinners and children's birthday parties when the Eberle brothers and their families were still closely knit show Carol Anne to be a beautiful child, with fat cheeks, huge brown eyes, and lovely dark-auburn hair. In one photo, although she is only four, she's dressed nicely, if a little severely, and she's sporting a watch and a little necklace. Some of the relatives thought Carol was being given too many things. Says a cousin, "Uncle Frank and Aunt Kay had the resources. They obviously loved to give and tried – possibly too hard – to buy Carol's love. In my opinion she was very spoiled and selfish when she was growing up."

But there was a darker side that only a few members of the family acknowledged. The Eberles were inhibited, unemotional people, set in their ways. Says a niece, "I don't think that Frank and Kay were easy people to live with. They weren't geared to the way things go when you're raising kids. Certainly I don't think they should have been designated as the guardians for a child."

Such opinions would have profoundly shocked Frank and Kay's friends and neighbours. In the early years, the Eberle farm seemed to embody everything that was ideal about rural life.

Frank was a very good farmer like the rest of the Eberle brothers. "They were very particular, very picky," says Brent Eberle. "They had a lot of pride in what they did."

Vi and Jim Foote – he is Sandy Foote's youngest son, born while his father was working on the railway in Portland – were among the closest friends Frank and Kay Eberle had. Said Vi, "Frank never left a piece of machinery sitting in the yard, never neglected anything. His combine, when it was finished, it was all swept off, all washed off and put in the machine shed. Same with all his equipment."

Frank Eberle disliked using chemicals, not because of a sensitivity towards the environment but because they weren't cost-effective. "He'd sit down with a pencil and paper," says his nephew Brent Eberle, "and he'd figure it out from ten, twenty different angles. He'd say, 'I can't convince myself nor can anyone else, that fertilizing makes economic sense.'" Pesticides were used only when grasshoppers were heavy; herbicides very rarely. In later years, he tapered off on chemicals altogether and some of his neighbours frowned on the broad leaf and wild oats that they saw growing, especially in Frank's south half-section. His habit of ignoring a weed here and there was one reason alarm bells didn't go off at once when the Eberles suddenly disappeared; when the fields weren't being worked, the neighbours merely thought Frank was laying off a little.

People in the district admired not so much Frank Eberle's farming techniques as his mechanical inventions. "Frank just loved to get into that machine shop of his," says Jim Foote. "He could fix anything, and he could make anything." Neighbours would show up with broken knives that needed welding or broken parts that needed soldering; Frank was delighted to take on a new challenge, no matter how small. "And always without charge," Foote emphasizes.

Frank once bought an old bomber, World War II surplus, that sat on his property until after his death and became a symbol of both his ingenuity and his eccentricity. Bill McWilliams recalls that, in the two years between the period Frank started farming at Pasqua and the time when he had completed the house, he used the airplane as a place to cook and sleep when he couldn't be bothered to return to Lake Valley for the night. "It struck everybody as so funny to see him get out of that plane and onto the tractor."

"It was terrific fun for us kids to play in," recalls his nephew Brian Eberle. Even though it didn't have wings, Frank still idled it around the yard, and his nieces and nephews thought it looked like a huge, maimed duck. But slowly it was stripped, until it sat incongruously, a gawky skeleton, in Frank's field. He used the miles of wiring and tubing out of the framework, the thousands of nuts and bolts, the fuel tanks, the tires, in his various inventions.

"He was a very intelligent and very ingenious person. He developed many things to make farming easier," says his nephew Brian Eberle. "He didn't bother to patent any of it. Should have. He might have become even richer."

These homemade devices were often quite simple, made from discarded junk. Walter Champion gives an example: "Frank would buy an old oil-burner at some auction. He'd take a hot-water tank that was blown, and he'd cut a hole in it, make a smoke pipe for it. Then he'd install the old oil burner. And he'd heat a building with it."

But it was his grain-storage system, built bit by bit over years, that was the talk of the district. "It was just like an elevator," says Jim Foote. "You backed up and dumped your grain in the hole. From there a leg with a spout off the top ran up and down into any of the three granaries. They were big steel bins built into the barn." It meant less work, saved time, and was considered so ingenious that representatives of Pioneer Grain Company came out to take a look one day – and were impressed. Frank Eberle was proud of his granary system and welcomed anybody who wanted to inspect it.

During the 1950s, the cash income from wheat farming rose steadily, but costs soared much more quickly. In 1946, 1,938 bushels of wheat were required to buy a combine; by 1958, that figure had risen to 5,593 bushels. Frank Eberle was a master at keeping his expenses as low as possible. There was no mortgage on his house or land – he never got into the debt that plagued so many others – he seldom used hired help, he could afford to pay cash for machinery, and since his equipment was state-of-the-art, he could make a good living on one section of land while other farmers were forced to expand. Consequently, when the bumper crops of 1952, 1953, and 1954 choked the elevators, his profits piled up as high as the wheat in his granary.

Yet despite Frank's hard work, despite his dedication and ingenuity, the farm was merely a hobby. He made his real money elsewhere. "Most farmers lose their shirts on the stock market," recalled Vi Foote. "But not Frank. He was as smart as they come. He could turn a ten-dollar bill into a thousand in nothing flat."

The custom farming business had not only left each of the Eberle brothers with good land and farm equipment but also with some cash. All of them began playing the stock market. "When the boys got together, that's all they talked about – investments. Which was the better way to make money," remembers one of the wives. "I used to get so tired listening to it, I'd go out of the house."

Andrew, the second-eldest, owned land near Belle Plaine, between Moose Jaw and Regina, but he was too ill to farm it himself. Frank worked it for him for several years until it was finally rented out. But this did not yield a lot of money – the family lived on Andrew's investments.

Ray, the youngest, was also sickly, another victim of too much hard work. He died in 1967. His securities provided a nice income for his widow, the lovely and ebullient Hertha, who rented a suite at the Harwood Hotel in Moose Jaw and lived there for twelve "interesting" years.

Mike Eberle, the happy bachelor, constructed huge charts, three feet by four feet, which he nailed to the walls of his dining room. On these he listed each of his investments, and every day he painstakingly mapped out their performance on the stock market. When Mike Eberle died in 1988, he left an estate of over $1 million, which he bequeathed to his fourteen nieces and nephews.

Frank, however, was the shrewdest of all.

His investments were varied, but in the late 1940s and early 1950s, he made a bundle on flax. This is quite a different crop than wheat, and many farmers don't like to handle it. The seeds are smaller, which means it must be planted at a shallower depth. It often takes a long time to mature, and many farmers don't have the patience to wait for the harvesting. In addition, the stubble is difficult to get rid of: as it takes years to decompose, it can't be ploughed back into the soil and must be burned, which is bad for the land. Most important, unlike cereal grains, which are pooled at a fixed, guaranteed price, flax is sold on the commodity market. It appeals to farmers with a gambling instinct.

"Most farmers would sell their flax crop as soon they got it off because they needed the money right away. Frank could afford to wait," says Brian Stirton. Wait, that is, for the right price.

Sometimes he would hedge. If the price was high enough at seeding in the spring, say $8, he would agree to deliver so many bushels at that price after harvest. If, in the fall, the price had dropped to $6, he would have made a good profit; if it had increased to $10, he would spend restless nights worrying about the money he hadn't made. Sometimes he would store his flax crop in one of his huge granaries, where it would sit until he could sell it at the right price. Frank also played the futures market as an ordinary speculator – nothing to do with growing flax. Brent Eberle remembers Frank saying, "Well, I lost $30,000 on flax futures today. But that's how it goes. You win some and you lose some and just hope you win more than you lose."

Actually, Frank did not take outlandish risks. A good 80 per cent of his portfolio – and this grew larger as he grew older – was tied up in fail-safe investments, such as Canada Savings Bonds, various mutual funds, secure corporate stock. But it was the remaining 10 to 20 per cent, the money he used to speculate on the stock market, that provided his *raison d'être* in life.

Several times a week he'd drop in on his brokers, Richardson Greenshields in Moose Jaw (the same firm whose services Wellington White had used in the 1920s), where he kept an active account – in 1986, $100,000 was lodged there – so he could conveniently buy and sell. He had a preference for risky gold and oil offerings but he'd invest in anything he thought might make a profit, from battery factories to mink farms. "He was a good listener," says his long-time broker, Arthur Stow. "But you could go to the bank on what he said because it was always right." Art Stow and his wife became close friends with Frank and Kay and on a few occasions visited them on the farm. "Frank was one of the gentlest, kindest individuals I have ever had the pleasure of knowing." Of Kay, Art Stow simply says, "She was very shy."

The Eberles spent a large part of the day immersed in the business of the stock market. Frank read the *Financial Post*, the *Western Producer*, the *Wall Street Journal*. If for some reason he wasn't home, Kay would sit at the kitchen table and carefully take down the stock quotations which were broadcast on CBC Radio's noon market report. "Playing the stock and commodity markets became the single most important activity in their lives," says a nephew. "They wouldn't take a vacation in case something went awry at Richardson Greenshields."

Yet Kay and Frank were frugal people, obsessively so. "If your shoelace broke, you just tied it together and that saved you thirty cents – but then all the brothers were like that," says a nephew. "They were into recycling long before recycling was fashionable." Nothing was thrown away. Pork-and-bean tins were used as containers for nuts and bolts. Every part of every machine, no matter how old and decrepit, was set aside to be utilized in some far-distant future. Even worthless stock certificates were kept as scrap paper.

Frank did have one extravagance. Every two or three years he'd walk into Central Motors in Moose Jaw, slap the necessary cash down, and drive away with the "biggest, fanciest" Cadillac on the lot. "That car was very precious to him," says Brian Eberle. "I guess it symbolized his success."

"The funny thing is," says neighbour Brian Stirton, "I don't remember seeing him in it more than a couple of times. He always drove his old half-ton truck. The Caddie was left in the garage back at the farm." It would be taken out and polished up for special occasions. In 1953 Frank Eberle of Rastadt asked his first cousin, Frank Eberle of Pasqua, to be his best man at his wedding. The Eberles didn't object to attending the ceremony at St. Peter's Church – Father Metzger had died four years before. "The guests were pretty impressed with Frank's big black Cadillac," says the Rastadt Frank Eberle, "so he took them all for little rides around."

Kay engaged in no lavish expenditures at all. If Frank was often tightfisted with his money, Kay was neurotically so. "She was very, very frugal. I can't emphasize that enough," says Brent Eberle. "You didn't run the tap unless there was a good reason."

"There'd been such a long period in her life when there wasn't any money that she lost the ability to spend it. I don't think she ever got her hair done at a beauty parlour the whole time I knew her," says a sister-in-law.

Her clothes looked as though they had been bought at the Army and Navy discount store. "She wore these nylon dresses with flowers on them that were so out of style in the 1960s and 1970s," says a family friend. "And yet, after her death they found a cupboard full of really good clothes that Frank or somebody had bought her."

Kay loved to garden – not for the love of flowers, but because she saved money by growing vegetables and fruits. She canned and preserved, even during those times when she wasn't well, taking great pride in the family's minuscule grocery bill. If she cooked a chicken, every part of it, including the feet, went into the pot. "If it wasn't for Frank, I think she would have starved herself to death," says Les Winter, a family friend.

If Frank's work-shirt had a hole in it, Kay would mend it, even though most people would consider it beyond salvage. "Get another three or four months out of it," she'd say, as she added a patch that was of a different colour plaid than the shirt. Kay and Frank liked to smoke, but there was the expense to worry about; she felt less guilty when he bought a giant make-your-own-cigarette machine. She would wear heavy-duty socks and Frank's sweaters in the house so she wouldn't have to turn up the heat.

Because she never threw anything out, Kay's house was always in disorder. There was only one small cupboard in the big kitchen, and the counters and the floor were always cluttered with pots and pans, canned goods, and containers of every imaginable kind. A sewing machine that sat in the kitchen was always piled high with bits of clothing, newspapers, letters. While the appliances, which had been purchased when the house was new, were of good quality, they were never replaced. A visitor to the Eberles in the late 1970s remembers: "The fridge was one of those old rounded types, the stove looked like it had been there for a hundred years, and the pots and pans were enamel, something you'd see in a magazine advertisement of the 1940s. The bathroom fixtures were also ancient.

"After you saw their house, you'd never think they had money. They looked like they were poor. "

Everyone who visited noticed that, despite its many large windows, the house was kept in near darkness. "She had these heavy, heavy drapes on the front windows, which she always kept closed," recalls Doreen Meadows. If a beam of sunshine did manage to filter in, the furniture was protected. Kay covered everything with sheets of paper and blankets.

Carol Anne's room, says Doreen Meadows, was not like a little girl's room: it was cold, and rigidly neat. Frank's office was the only place in the house with real warmth. "It was beautiful, with lots of leather, a large swivel chair, a great big desk, and an adding machine, which in those days was considered very modern, like a computer nowadays. But it was always locked up. We kids were forbidden to go in there."

The Meadowses were one of the few families with whom Kay and Frank would visit. "The Eberles used to come and play cards until 2:00 or 3:00 a.m. They were never in a hurry to get home. In the winter they'd come on a tractor because of the snow, and Frank would keep it running all night so it would start.

"We kids all liked Frank a lot," Doreen adds, "but Kay always looked kind of frightened, with big sad eyes, and she'd say 'Egads!' all the time. The world, for her, was a very dangerous place. When we were driving, Frank would comment, 'You're going too fast. Kay's nervous.'"

Kay Eberle never learned to drive herself, which is most unusual for a farm wife. She relied on her husband far too much says a sister-in-law. "She would ask Frank's opinion before she would do anything, even start the dinner. 'What do you think about this, Frank? What do you think about that?' All day long."

"I've dealt with mental illness for twenty-seven years [in a professional capacity]," adds Doreen Meadows, "and I would have to say she was obsessive, phobic. Like she was afraid to live."

This timidity naturally was reflected in how she raised her daughter. Most of the neighbours and friends who watched Carol Anne grow up felt she was made to lead a much too restricted life. "Frank and Kay, but in particularly Kay, were always frightened something was going to happen to Carol Anne. She led a very protected life, and as a result I think she had a very lonely childhood," remembers a cousin. "She would sometimes come to play at our place at Lake Valley. She was supposed to stay for two or three days, but she'd never get through the first twelve hours without becoming homesick. Frank would have to come and get her. I don't think she had a lot of confidence in herself, even then."

Carol Anne went to Pasqua school for her entire elementary education. It was a typical one-room country schoolhouse with a furnace room that doubled as a cloakroom, hardwood floors stained indelibly with ink, large windows on the west side to catch the afternoon sun, blackboards on the east and front, and desks in rows from grades one to eight. Outside there was an acre of playground with a baseball diamond and running track.

"I think it was a better education than we would have got in town," says Bruce Champion. "You got individual help, not only from the teacher but from the kids in the higher grades." The teacher ruled over her domain of between sixteen to thirty students with discipline. "She could whip out the old strap and also she knew your parents. You didn't get away with anything."

The social activities in Pasqua – the Hallowe'en dance, the fowl dinners, the pot-luck parties – were organized by the ladies' group. "We had a lot of fun," said Vi Foote, "but we could never get Kay Eberle to join. She would say she wasn't feeling well, or something like that."

The major event of the year was the Christmas Pageant. "It was a big production," recalls Bruce Champion. Every kid had to play a part, even if it was only an angel in the nativity scene or singing Christmas carols. Bleacher-like seats, stored for most of the year in a shed, were set up, and everybody in the district came, including Frank and Kay Eberle. It was one of the few events in which they actually participated.

Her school chums remember Carol Anne as a very pretty girl,

with shiny auburn hair tied back with a bow. She was obviously well looked-after, but there was something odd about her. "I think her clothes told the story," says a classmate. "They were very expensive, they cost far more than any of us could afford to spend on our stuff, yet they were very old-fashioned – long woollen kilts when flared skirts with crinolines were the style."

Says Doreen Meadows, "Carol Anne did not have an easy life. She was very withdrawn. I think she would have liked to have been accepted by the other kids, and she wasn't, partly because of the way she was dressed."

The Academy of Our Lady of Sion in Moose Jaw was considered the ideal high school for girls. Located in a huge convent on North Hill, overlooking the city, it was full of rich oak and soft lights. The Sisters of Our Lady of Sion had come to Prince Albert from Maine in 1904. In a primitive log cabin they opened an academy for girls, where not only academic subjects were taught, but French, piano, and petit point. The sisters came to Moose Jaw in 1914, but it wasn't until 1924 that the impressive convent was constructed. It quickly became a refuge for farm girls, Catholic or Protestant, whose parents sought something better in life; Bob Foote sent his four daughters there during the 1920s.

By the time Carol Anne Eberle attended Sion academy, the sisters were losing control of the school; in 1966 it became the co-educational, government-funded Vanier High. But in 1962, Carol's first year, Sion was still a private school, financed by the parents of the students. The nuns and lay teachers, all female, prided themselves on academic excellence, on "turning out scholars." "If you went to Sion in those days you were considered more or less the élite. And we all wore uniforms, which made you stand out," says Judy Dixon, who attended Sion for her last year of high school.

There was a sense of innocence and exuberance about the place. "Racing down the floor double-dribbling or travelling, we merrily strive for baskets. In our striking black and gold vests, the Obeds were a terrific team," wrote a budding reporter in the yearbook. But there was also firm discipline.

Carol Eberle boarded at the school. One classmate remembers that she chafed at the regulations that were imposed. "She was a very personable girl, always smiling, but, as I remember, she hung out with an older group, not connected with the school. She didn't participate much in school activities."

She was a mediocre student; "She wasn't academically oriented," says a cousin. She played volleyball but wasn't active in much else. The yearbooks hint at her interests in those days. While other students were described as "the industrious type," "accomplished pianist," "outstanding at sports," "definitely artistic," Carol Eberle was a "fun-loving Sionian." While Joyce Peepeetch's motto was "one good turn deserves another," and Linda Dunn "dreams of playing her clarinet in Carnegie Hall," and Carol Craigen, "lends willing support to all school activities," Carol Eberle was described as a social butterfly. "If she isn't on the phone, it's because she is waiting in line," said the yearbook. By the end of her second year, she was in open revolt both against Sion academy and her parents.

"Mrs. Eberle thought Carol should be in her bedroom studying. Carol found it was easy to climb out the window and run down the road to some friend's house," says Val Lewis, a neighbour. As an adolescent, Carol was reined in very tightly on her weekends home from school. While friends were sometimes welcomed at the Eberle house, she was often not allowed to play at the homes of others. "They were always afraid something would happen. They were always trying to protect her," says a cousin. But they also wouldn't put themselves out to provide a social life for her. Dances were held at Pasqua school, with music provided by a local band. They were great fun, and everybody from grandfathers to babies went – except the Eberles. Carol Anne would have loved to take part in these events, but she gave up even asking her mom and dad.

The years 1964 and 1965 were difficult ones for Carol Anne and the Eberles. Against Frank and Kay's wishes, she dropped out of high school. "She defied them in everything," Vi Foote said. "Frank would come to us and say the more we tell her one thing, the more she does the opposite. She was hot-tempered, and Kay would try and soothe things over." It was an emotionally stressful time for everyone. Says a neighbour, "Kay was just beside herself. She had no idea of what to do with a rebellious teenage daughter. How do you cope?" At one point, Carol was rushed to the Union Hospital in Moose Jaw after she took an overdose of prescription drugs. "I think Carol was desperately trying to find herself," says a friend. "She was tired of being lonely."

By the fall of 1966, Kay and Frank had persuaded Carol to return to school. She moved in with her grandmother, Anna Bishoff, in her house on Garnet Street in Regina's central-east end and enrolled in grade eleven at Ursuline High School.

Located in the basement of Sacred Heart Church, it was founded as a Catholic school by the Ursuline Sisters in 1954. By the time Carol arrived, the courts had ruled in favour of tax funding for parochial schools in Saskatchewan, so that tuition fees were lowered and enrollment mushroomed. There were about two hundred students, boys and girls, crammed into a rather limited space. But it was a school full of spirit; "It was very close-knit, everybody socialized – parties, barbecues, picnics, we went to them all," says Terry Lean.

Ursuline was noted for its excellence in sports. In the sixties, the volleyball team won the Southern Saskatchewan Championship almost every year, including 1966. "We had a good shot at the provincial championship, but they were held in Saskatoon, so we got to stay at a hotel. We all got drunk the night before and bombed on the courts," recalls Joe Welsh, a Saskatchewan writer. The baseball team was also renowned. "There was a guy called Ron Hildebrand, who was just a great left-hander and got us into all the baseball playoffs."

Ursuline students bowled, curled, played hockey. They also received an excellent academic education provided by the Ursuline sisters and a few lay teachers, including a man, who was hired to keep the boys in line. "He usually ended up with a nervous breakdown after the first year, and I have to admit I was probably in on that," says Les Winter. "Ursuline was pretty relaxed, informal," recalls another student Steve Durnin. "Of course you were expected to do your studies. There was discipline, but it was all productive discipline. Writing lines, cleaning up, going to the convent to help the nuns." Dances were held every Friday night in the church basement. Friends who knew Carol Anne remember that she would attend these infrequently, and that she had a very strict curfew that she "sometimes" adhered to.

Diane Fuller [a pseudonym], who would become Carol Eberle's best friend during her time at Ursuline, remembers that she seemed shy and withdrawn when she arrived a few weeks late for term, but as soon as a few students befriended her, she blossomed. "She was very quiet but popular; everybody liked her." Remembers Joe Welsh, "All the boys were in love with her. She was one of the most beautiful girls in the school. I remember she had gorgeous auburn hair, a great set of legs, a nice smile. She seemed a genuine person."

Yet Diane Fuller recalls there was an odd side to Carol. She never talked about the past, never mentioned that she had attended Sion academy at Moose Jaw. "She said that she was raised on a farm, but never told us anything about her parents. And I don't remember them visiting the school." Diane was invited to lunch at Carol's grandmother's on a couple of occasions. The house, she remembers, was clean and tidy, but furnished with only the basics. The blinds were drawn, so that, even in the middle of the day, the house was dark and gloomy. Carol introduced Diane to Mrs. Bishoff, but the old lady disappeared immediately. "Her head peeked around the corner a couple of times," Diane remembers, "but she never appeared again." Carol was obviously anxious to leave, urging, "Let's get out of here." Diane thought that, in a strange way, Carol lived only in the present – with no past or future. And although Carol was generally popular, Diane believes that she was her only close friend.

Carol was attracted to Gerry Sutherland right away. "I remember her standing on the sidelines watching a volleyball game, and she kept saying, 'Oh, isn't he cute? Isn't he handsome?'" He was one of the most popular students in the school. "Gerry was a real nice guy. Quiet and shy in a way, yet really good-natured, fun-loving. And, boy, did he like to party," remembers Terry Lean.

Gerry Sutherland had grown up in Rosetown, in the west-central part of the province. His mother died when he was just entering his teens, and his father decided to move to Regina and continue his business selling life insurance for Metropolitan Life. "His dad was never home," remembers Les Winter. "He had no control over his kids. Gerry spent more time at our house than he did at his dad's apartment."

"He and his brother Ron and me and my brother, we took to each other right off the bat," says Joe Welsh. "Their dad bought them identical cars, '54 Fords, so, of course, that made them popular."

Welsh says that Gerry was "a lousy student," but smart enough to get 70 to 75 per cent without trying. Although the yearbook states that Sutherland planned to become an engineer, Welsh says there was little talk about the future. "I don't remember us being serious about anything really. Just trying to get money to put gas in his car and buy a case of beer here and there." Adds Les Winter, "I don't think we ever thought too much about the future. We knew we didn't have the families to back us up to pursue further education. We thought we'd work for a while to save the money to go to college. None of us ever went though."

The one trait for which Gerry Sutherland is remembered is his even temper. "I only saw him mad once," says Joe Welsh, "but then I was mad, too." The Welsh and Sutherland brothers would take on short-term jobs, manual labour, through temporary manpower agencies to make extra money. During one Easter holiday, Joe and Gerry were hired to set up shelving in a factory. "We got paid on the Thursday afternoon, and we asked our two brothers to buy a whole bunch of beer because we were going to party after working on Good Friday. We got back at midnight and these guys had drunk all the beer. Gerry was mad and he said, 'You dirty, rotten son-of-a-bitches, you drank all our fucking beer.' We were going to take those two guys and beat the hell out of them but, of course, we never did."

Gerry Sutherland was in his senior year, dating the most attractive girls in the school, when he met Carol Eberle. "Carol really went after Gerald," says Diane Fuller, "and she was so pretty, he could hardly resist." By the end of the year, they were "a number." "I was a little jealous," admits Joe Welsh. "He was going with the best-looking girl in the school." Joe says that by this time Gerry was devoted to Carol. "Lots of times we'd say 'Let's go and play pool.' He'd answer, 'No, Carol and I are going to do something.' If it had been any other guy, his buddies would have called him an asshole – 'You're tied to her apron strings,' that kind of thing. But nobody gave Gerry those kinds of gears. He was too well liked. He was a prince."

Gerry was graduating at the end of the term and Carol decided to quit school. Through her sister, who was working at Foodmart grocery store, Diane Fuller got Carol a job as a cashier. But Carol showed up for only two days; nobody could find her after that. The store manager was angry, and Diane felt responsible. "Our friendship ended abruptly."

A few months later, Carol announced to the Eberles that she was pregnant with Gerald Sutherland's child. The young couple had gone to Ursuline High's pastor, Father Isadore Gorski, to ask him to officiate at the wedding. He was fond of both of them but thought them very immature. "I said to them, 'Listen, it strikes me that the only reason you want to get married is that Carol is pregnant. The reason for getting married must be much more serious than that. You should wait until the child is born and then make a decision.'" Father Gorski said that Carol and Gerry thought about it, but then decided to go ahead anyway.

"Forlorn" was how the pastor described their wedding ceremony. It took place on a cold and windy fall day at St. Joseph's, Father Gorski's parish church in Balgonie, not far from Rastadt Colony. The heat had not been on all week and, although the priest tried to get the church warmed up before the wedding party arrived, it was damp and chilly. There were no flowers, no music, and the only people attending were the parents of the bride and groom and two official witnesses. Father Gorski's impression of the Eberles was that they were very plain people, not given to much talk.

The marriage only added to an already stressful time for Frank and Kay. In December 1965, the daughter of Andrew and Peggy Eberle had died of leukemia at age twelve. In February of

1967, Ray Eberle, the youngest of the brothers, succumbed to the same disease after a three-month illness. He was forty-eight.

The two deaths and her daughter's forced marriage were too much for Kay Eberle. Just days before Ray's funeral, she suffered a severe stroke. When she was finally released from Moose Jaw Union Hospital, she was partially paralysed in one leg and one arm. "She was pretty young – fifty years old," said Vi Foote, "so she came back pretty good, except for her memory. She had to start keeping track of everything in her life. She had to write it down." She began writing notes to herself about everything; when she had purchased a tin of tomatoes, the date she had washed the drapes, what the temperature was at a specific hour, when Frank went out and when he returned. When the police searched the Eberle house ten years later, they found hundreds of such notes, scattered everywhere. Pieced together, they constituted a detailed diary of Kay's life over twenty years.

The stroke also affected Kay's personality. She became even more withdrawn, more reclusive. "We used to drive by the farm and she'd be sitting out in the yard," Doreen Meadows remembers. "Dad would wave at her, and she'd just get up and walk in the house." Because he was so devoted to Kay, Frank also became more isolated. Says a neighbour, "I'd meet Frank at the Co-op and, of course, we'd stop and chat – I always pictured Lawrence Welk whenever Frank opened his mouth. My wife would have done all the shopping and gone through the checkout counter and he'd still be talking. I got the impression he was very lonesome."

~ IV ~

But there was also some joy in Frank and Kay's lives. On July 28, 1967, Carol gave birth to her first child, Donald James, and less than a year later, on July 1, 1968, to her second son, Kenneth Gerald. Kenny was a typical Bishoff, rather chunky, with huge brown eyes, fat cheeks, and darkish hair, while Don was more slender and fair, like his father.

The Eberles doted on their grandchildren. Frank saw his

longed-for dream coming true: his grandsons, he was sure, would grow to appreciate, even love as he did, the black, fertile soil; the farm would remain in the Eberle family, and nothing meant more to him.

Frank was also pleased to discover that he and his new son-in-law were compatible. Friends often joked about how much the two men were alike. Both talked slowly, and both liked to tell long and convoluted stories to make a point. Both liked their rye. Les Winter, who became a very close friend of the Sutherlands after their marriage, used to run into Frank at Gerry and Carol's. Winter remembers how much Frank liked to talk, making points in the air with his roll-your-own cigarettes.

"He was a very clever man, a very clever man. To meet him, you'd write him off as an immigrant who was unable to sign his name. Once you talked to him more than five minutes, you realized there was a lot of knowledge in that man." Les says that Frank Eberle also had a well-defined code of ethics but that he didn't impose this on anyone else.

Winter realized that Frank Eberle was a wealthy man, and it wasn't because he drove a Cadillac. There was something about him that spelled success.

"It was the quality of the man. You knew that, if he was wearing a fifty-dollar suit, he could afford a five-hundred-dollar suit. He'd look good in anything, and he wasn't all that attractive. He was clumsy and awkward, all the things you wouldn't invite him to a cocktail party for. Yet once he was there, the group would be in awe of him. He had a magnetism."

Les found Kay Eberle a very different person. "She was naïve, prudish, with very little understanding of anything she didn't know or was uncertain about. . . . She came from a different era, and she still lived in that era even though times had changed."

Gerry Sutherland loved the outdoors, and he was eager to help his father-in-law around the farm. And as far as Frank was concerned, there was nothing that he liked better than hearing his grandsons' voices as they romped about in his farmyard.

The Sutherland boys were hard to handle right from babyhood. "Don was the most difficult person in the world, from the time he opened his eyes coming out of the womb. He was a crabby baby, obstinate as hell, right from the start," says Les Winter. Ken was a sweeter kid, but he was also hyperactive.

One Sunday, in the spring of 1971, the Sutherlands had spent the day at the farm so that Gerry could help Frank with some chores. When they finished supper, the two men decided they'd haul a truckload of grain to the Pool elevator at Pasqua. Kenny, who had just turned three, began to whine – and whine. He wanted to go on the drive with his father and grandfather. Frank finally agreed, but said the child would have to sit in the truck and wait while the loading was going on. They were almost ready to start when Frank realized he had forgotten his quota book and went back into the house to get it. Gerald Sutherland followed him. Meanwhile, Ken had spotted his brother, Don, and decided it would be great fun to hide on him. He climbed down from the truck and ran into the barn. He had just crawled into the granary and was about to call out to Don, when his father came out of the house. In order to move the grain from the granary into the truck, he turned on the auger. As the shimmering wheat moved downwards, a funnel rapidly formed. Kenny's foot was sucked into it. He felt a horrible tug and reached down, desperately trying to pull it out. The whirling blade of the auger caught his small hand, his arm. Then there was a terrified, high-pitched scream.

Kenny remembers nothing of the ambulance that rushed him to the Moose Jaw Union Hospital; remembers only slightly the frantic activity as doctors and nurses fought for his survival. So much blood had been lost for someone so tiny. In the end his life was saved, but his left arm was severed above the shoulder joint, the left leg above the thigh.

Kay Eberle turned to her relatives that night and said, "If there was a God, this would never have happened."

It was nobody's fault, a freak accident, yet, "There wasn't a day went by that Frank didn't feel guilty. He blamed himself because it was on his farm and it was his machinery," says a neighbour.

"Frank said he was going to do everything he could, no matter what the cost, to get that kid fixed," says Jim Foote. "And he damn well did."

Years of hospitalization and treatment followed. Kenny was sent to hospitals in Toronto and Winnipeg to be fitted for, and trained to wear, various prostheses. Every time he grew an inch, it meant being fitted yet again. Any new innovation was tried. When the police searched the Eberle property years later, they found a pile of artificial limbs, in all sizes and shapes, piled in the corner of an outbuilding.

The young boy's rehabilitation was something of a struggle; while he became very agile using his artificial leg, he rebelled against wearing an arm. He said it was uncomfortable and that the kids at school were frightened by it. They called him a freak, he said. Since he could do most tasks, writing or drawing for example, with his good right hand, eventually the idea of making him wear an artificial arm was abandoned. "Carol and Gerry went overboard in protecting Ken. They did everything possible for him," says Les Winter.

There were serious fallouts from the tragedy. As Kenny grew older, he spent so much time at hospitals and rehabilitation centres that his schooling suffered. "He was always trying to get caught up," a social worker would later write. "The school was very good, but I think it was hard on him." Les Winter claims that neither his parents nor his teachers would impose any discipline on Ken because of his handicap, and this would have serious repercussions in the future.

The accident and its consequences left emotional scars on both brothers. "Afterwards, Kenny got all the attention," says a close friend. "Everybody felt so sorry for him, gave him so much sympathy, naturally, that he began to hunger after the limelight. Meanwhile, Don suffered because not enough attention was paid to him. The whole thing was very, very hard on the family."

Yet, on the surface at least, the Sutherlands seemed to be coping. A third son, Sean, was born on March 28, 1970. The new baby might have been a financial burden, but Gerry had nailed down a secure job: he worked for CP Telecommunications servicing telex machines. His salary wasn't huge, but he also made a few dollars fixing cars in the backyard. And the Eberles helped the young family out.

Frank provided the house they lived in. Located on Elphinstone Street in north-central Regina, it was small but comfortable – a bungalow with a modest living room, a master bedroom and one other small bedroom, a kitchen, and a bathroom. Since it sat on a lot and a half, it had a fair-sized back yard, where Gerry would tinker with his cars. Carol's grandfather Thomas Eberle had built it when he retired from farming and moved to Regina in 1952. He had died about a year after he moved in. Frank had purchased it from the estate and rented it out until Carol and Gerald married in 1967.

The Eberles also supplied cash when needed. Relatives recall how Kay and Frank were visiting them one day at their home in Regina when Frank excused himself, saying he would return in an hour. Kay explained that he had gone to pay Carol and Gerry's telephone bill, which had mounted into the hundreds of dollars. Yet, the relatives say, Kay didn't seem annoyed; it was merely the well-heeled parents helping out the struggling young family.

The two oldest boys attended kindergarten at the nearby St. Luke Elementary School, Don in 1972 and Ken a year later. They were rambunctious kids, a little naughty, but full of life. Remembers a schoolmate, "Kenny seemed a happy, smiley kid. We called him Hopalong Cassidy 'cause he walked with a limp, but that didn't seem to bother him."

Adam Eberle, a first cousin of Frank's, was the custodian of St. Luke during the time the Sutherland kids were there. He remembers both of them as polite, but Ken was particularly outgoing. "He called me Uncle Adam. I thought he was a very nice, sweet kid."

According to Father Gorski, the Sutherlands were "cavalier" in their church attendance, but they made sure they raised their children as Catholics. At their first communion, friends remembered how well-dressed they both were. In fact, they were usually as well-scrubbed as energetic youngsters could be. Ken's sweet smile also distracted adults from noticing that he was often self-consciously hiding his false left arm.

The boys would often visit their grandparents' farm on weekends. Another snapshot, taken in 1974, shows Frank's "flivver," a couple of boards equipped with wheels and a small engine, which was used to carry gas to the machines on the farm. The kids loved riding it. In the photo, Don is sitting on the contraption and he is smiling, while Ken stands beside him, looking chagrined, probably because he's not in the action seat. In another photo, probably taken on the same bright summer day, the sky a cobalt blue so intense that it's painful, Carol stands holding her youngest son's hand. Sean is strangely unlike his brothers in appearance; his little thin face is sharp-featured, and his hair is fair, a mass of curls. He is looking at his mother. She is smiling, but curiously her expression is cold, almost imperious, as if she doesn't see the glory in the day around her.

In fact, the picture of the Sutherlands as a happy, normal family was an illusion; early on, the marriage had begun cracking, and by 1978 it was beyond repair.

Even before Ken's accident, the Sutherlands had temporarily separated; Carol had had gone to live in Calgary. With the help of Father Gorski, who counselled them on several occasions, the couple had reconciled, but the marriage remained rocky. "You have to understand that Carol was raising those three boys by herself," says Les Winter. Gerry worked every day, he liked to tinker with cars, he liked to hunt, and he liked to party. "I'd come to town," says Winter, "and have a pocketful of money and a hell of a thirst, and off Gerry and I'd go – a night on the town. It was hard on Carol, damn right. And in the early years, I didn't think there was anything wrong with it. I was single, it didn't matter a rat's ass to me.

"And those kids, they were terrible from the start." Les says his sisters refused to babysit them after a couple of bad experiences. Once they broke into the padlocked medicine cabinet, locked themselves in the bathroom, and threatened that they were going to kill themselves if they didn't get what they wanted.

Carol developed health problems; a malignant growth was found on her neck. "I used to kid her," says Winter. "You don't have cancer; you had to have that throat operation because you yell at those kids all the time." Although it was successfully treated, the encounter with cancer badly frightened her. Friends thought it brought Carol and Gerry together and kept the marriage going for a few more years. But as the seventies progressed, and the idea of women's rights became prevalent, Carol began cultivating a wider circle of friends outside her marriage, many of whom frequented the swinging bars in Regina. Gerry grew resentful that she was away from home and the children too much.

Says Father Gorski, "There was a whole breakdown of communication in that marriage. And looking back at Gerry Sutherland or even Carol, I wonder if they have an innate incapacity to communicate. Some people are stuck in neutral as far as communication is concerned. They don't even work at it."

The atmosphere in the Sutherland home became more and more poisonous, and it was exacerbated by the alarming behaviour of the two oldest boys. Although they were only eight and nine, they began to have run-ins with the police. Les Winter says Gerry was never a disciplinarian and, if the boys had done something exceptionally bad, "like rob the community centre," he would merely sit them down and talk to them. "He would say 'Now, we're going to have to discuss this, 'cause this has hurt me quite a bit.' Don's like, 'Oh yeah, how long's this going to take?' and Ken's saying, 'Oh no, I won't do it again,' when already he's planning the next scam.

"Gerry meant well. I think he felt that his father was never close to him, had never been there, and he wanted to be close to his sons. . . . So there was no discipline."

In a report filed with the Court of Queen's Bench several years later, Dr. Charles Messer, a psychiatrist, described Gerry Sutherland as "a wife and child abuser." Friends rush to Sutherland's defence on this, claiming it isn't true. "There were lots of times I felt that, if he would have spanked the boys or even reprimanded them for the things they did, it would have helped, but no, he was too easy-going," says a close friend.

Carol was desperately unhappy in those years. And there seemed nothing Gerry could do to relieve her misery. He bought a new home in the middle-class suburb of Normanview, but for some reason they never moved in, and it was sold. She said she wanted to be more independent, to go to work, and she took courses to complete her high-school education. She got her diploma, but never found a suitable job. Finally she felt her situation was intolerable; her marriage was beyond saving. "There was one more hill to climb, and Carol and Gerry didn't have the right boots," is the way Les Winter puts it.

In April of 1979, Gerry was on a three-week training course in Winnipeg. Les was staying at the Sutherland house to help out with the kids. One day, shortly after Sean's ninth birthday, Carol Anne called the two oldest kids to get up for school. When they were ready, she hugged and kissed Don and Ken. "I love you," she kept saying over and over.

"Gosh, Mom, we're only going to school," Don replied, as he and his brother marched out the door. Carol then packed her bags and left the family for good.

She took only one child with her – her youngest. "It was good that she took Sean with her," says a friend, "because the two oldest had often picked on him. He wasn't as good in sports as they were, and they considered him a sissy. His life would have been hell if he'd been left with them."

Carol told friends, "I've looked after these kids with little help from Gerry for all these years. Now it's his turn." It was left to Les Winter to phone Gerry Sutherland and break the news.

He was devastated, and so were the Eberles. "They couldn't believe that Carol would leave those little boys like that," said Vi Foote. Kay, in particular, blamed Carol for the marriage breakdown. On one of the few trips they ever took, Kay and Frank drove to Victoria to try to talk their daughter into returning. It was an emotional and difficult encounter, but Carol remained adamant. She told them she was making a new life for herself, and that she intended to get a divorce as quickly as she could. They were upset, of course, because even though they weren't strong church-goers, they were still Catholic. There was other shocking news. Carol was not striking out on her own in pursuit of independence. She was already living with Garfield Ostrander, whom she had met after she left Regina. He worked for the Department of National Defence as a painter of ships. Within two and a half years, Carol would give birth to two more children, both sons.

When the Eberles returned from their futile mission to Victoria, they had a will drawn up which reflected their displeasure towards their adopted daughter. While they didn't cut her out of an inheritance, they painstakingly drew up a scheme that they hoped would provide a future for the grandsons, especially Kenny. In the end, their well-intentioned plans would dramatically backfire.

Carol's desertion would often be blamed for the nightmare that would afflict the Sutherlands a few years later, but people who knew the family well said the seeds of disaster were sown well before she left. A friend who saw Gerry during the trying time right after the marriage breakup says the house on Elphinstone Street was scarred by the chaos and unhappiness that had reigned there. "It was very run-down. It was not painted, it was dirty, it was falling apart. The walls were gouged, the doors had holes in them, as though they had been pounded with fists. It looked as though nobody had cared for years, as if the kids had terrorized the place."

Gerry was very resentful about being left with the two children. "He was bitter, certainly, but he had no right to be," says a friend. He had no trouble attracting the opposite sex. Within four months he had met the woman who would become his second wife.

Donna was a few years older than Gerry. A mother of four, she too was in the midst of a marriage breakup when she met Sutherland. She thought he was pleasant and easy-going; he thought she was responsible, solid. By the fall of 1979, she was living in the Elphinstone house as a full-time homemaker, and when both divorces were finalized, she married Gerry Sutherland in April 1981.

Donna attempted to make the Elphinstone house into a home; she scrubbed and painted and landscaped – the front lawn and back garden had not seen grass for several years. And she tried to nurture the boys. She felt that, at ages eleven and twelve, they were still young enough that she could have some influence on them. "But it was tough, because they were tough kids."

At the beginning Donna thought Ken was a nice boy and liked him. As a friend of Donna's said, "He was a lovable little devil. He liked your arm around him; he liked you to spend time with him." This impression was reinforced by another family friend. Alice Laird (a pseudonym) was seeing Gerry before Donna settled in, and she continued to see the boys after the marriage. "I enjoyed Kenny. He was my sweetheart. I'd go out of my way to spend time with him. He was the one kid I really cared for."

Alice's son, Dwayne, also became friendly with Kenny. It was at a party for Dwayne's twelfth birthday that he realized how out of place Ken felt. "Girls found him different [because of his disability] and treated him different. I think he was starting to realize the significance of that."

Dwayne remembers that Ken used to kid around about his artificial leg. "He would sit on the stairs and release his leg and let it fall down the stairs. 'Oh my goodness, my leg fell off!' he'd yell. It would freak out those people who didn't know he was joking. He was comical and outgoing unless somebody made a big deal about his handicap. Then he would clam up, isolate himself."

By this time he steadfastly refused to wear his artificial arm, and his leg often gave him trouble. In the hot summer months, painful red blisters would develop on his stump, which he would have to keep clean and powdered. Often he would have to go to Wascana Rehabilitation Centre to have his prosthesis readjusted. Yet he never complained. Friends say he was embarrassed to talk about his handicap, and they knew enough never to mention it in front of him. But he was so agile that they soon forgot about it. He was an excellent baseball player, a left-fielder for the Pepsi Pete's, and played just as well as the other kids. Gerry and Donna would often go and watch his games.

Gerry owned a trailer at Sherwood Forest, a private camping-ground just outside Regina, where the family would spend summer weekends, swimming and playing golf. Remembers Dwayne Laird, "Kenny golfed too, but he would get angry because he couldn't do much. He was a natural athlete, and not being able to go full-out was such a frustrating thing for him."

There remained serious problems in the family. Much of it had to do with Ken's relationship with his older brother. By everyone's account, Don was the dominant one. "I don't know if Ken worshipped Don or if he was afraid of him. But if Don said jump, Kenny jumped," says Alice Laird. "And if Don did something wrong, which was often, he blamed it on Ken."

Says Les Winter, "Don didn't have the guts that God gave him to stand up and do things himself, so he would plan and have Kenny execute it. And of course, Kenny was blamed for it." This was a characteristic that many people noted about Ken, even as he grew older: he was willing to take the punishment for mischief that either Don had committed alone or the two brothers had committed together. And by the time Donna Sutherland arrived on the scene, their childish mischief had developed into serious behaviour problems.

They stole money whenever the opportunity arose. They lifted $101 out of their Grandmother Sutherland's purse; they pinched $5 in quarters from a friend's piggy bank; they picked up anything they could get their hands on at the local 7-Eleven. "They would look you in the face and be picking your pocket at the same time," says Les Winter. "Ken would sit on the couch beside someone, and while he was talking to her, in that cute sweet manner he had, he'd be rifling her purse with his one good hand. I watched him do it, and I would go in the bedroom and get the money back afterwards." Gerry was making a fair wage, but he could hardly afford to pay back all the cash his kids had swiped.

Money was always missing in the Sutherland household. Donna got in the habit of not keeping any cash in her purse. Every night, Gerry hid his wallet under his underwear in a drawer. When Donna's son, Kelly, came to stay with the Sutherlands, his ghetto blaster, his leather jacket, and a ring his father had given him were gone within a week of his arrival. When he confronted Ken and Don, they just laughed in his face.

In later years, the stolen goods would be quickly cashed in for money to buy drugs and alcohol. But Ken's dependency problem began when he was quite young. His stepmother was cleaning up the backyard one day when she happened to look into the doghouse and spotted several vials under a pile of discarded paper bags. Ken was still small enough to crawl in with the family's Irish setter, and there he would sniff glue.

Gerry would accept little responsibility for his sons' increasingly obnoxious behaviour; he blamed it on the company they kept. Elphinstone Street was the westerly border of a residential area that used to be called Parkdale, until the racists in the city renamed it Moccasin Flats (because so many Native Canadians live there). In reality, it is a mixed neighbourhood of welfare recipients and solid working-class families; there are tiny, run-down houses sitting tooth by jowl to substantial homes with well-kept lawns and yards. It's the kind of area where you have to choose your friends carefully. "As far as Don and Ken were concerned, if there was a bad kid, a really bad kid, they were attracted to him at once." Many of the Sutherland brothers' chums have been continually in and out of jail since they turned sixteen.

As they approached their teenage years, Ken and Don often skipped school. Day after day, teachers and principals would phone their house, reporting their absence. Gerry would try and talk to them: You have to go to school; you'll have no future; you won't be able to get a job. He was especially concerned about Ken, because he was disabled. But after his father left for work in the morning, Ken would walk out the door and head for the nearest shopping plaza. He had a passion for video games.

With the boys' truancy becoming ever more of a problem, the Sutherlands finally decided to move to another neighbourhood. The new house that they had built was a spacious, three-bedroom ranch-style, with a fireplace and large partially finished basement. Donna decorated it beautifully, with off-white rugs and fine furniture. Friends say that perhaps it was a little too elegant for teenage boys to feel comfortable in. The new house was situated on Hopkins Crescent in the northwest part of the city, in what is called McCarthy Park, a very middle-class neighbourhood. In September 1981 the family moved in, but it quickly became apparent that the change in environment would not solve the problems. As Donna Sutherland put it at the time, "When they were young they got into little-boy trouble, but as they grew older it got to be very scary."

One evening in 1981, not long after they had moved into the new house, Donna, Les Winter, and a friend were out for the evening. When they returned, they noticed that a car belonging to Gerry's brother was missing from where it had been parked in front of the house. It turned out that the boys had taken it without permission – they were legally too young to drive – but in a short while they pulled up in front of the house. The adults knew immediately that Don was high on something – alcohol or drugs. He was standing outside on the patio, waving one of Gerry's hunting rifles, threatening to kill the people inside. "The women were very frightened," recalls Les Winter. "Basically, Don and his friends were trying to take us hostage." The police were not called. Gerry was away on an errand to do with his work, and Donna and Les decided to wait for him to see if he could do something with his kids. But by the time he returned, the boys had disappeared. "He couldn't see what our problem was," says Donna Sutherland. "Gerry didn't do anything about it, not a thing," says Les Winter.

Actually, something did come of the incident. Sutherland put bars on the windows, iron lattice-work – not to keep the boys in, but to keep them out.

About this time it became obvious that Ken was developing into a deeply disturbed and angry young man. Donna's daughter, Michelle, who was fifteen when her mother married, was also living with the family. She and Ken took an instant dislike to each other, and unceasing battles raged between the two. Michelle claimed her personal belongings were stolen from her room all the time. "I used to set up traps, like putting the ironing board at a certain angle, to try and catch them. They went through everything."

She found her sanitary napkins stuck to mirrors with nail polish staining them the colour of blood. Her underwear was discovered in Kenny's waterbed. He had masturbated in them.

Donna used to nag Gerry, "Why don't you try and talk to the boys? Why don't you get help for them?" His answer was always the same: "It won't do any good. I don't have the time." Sometimes he would get angry. "What am I supposed to do?" he'd demand. "I've tried everything." Donna replied, "Get them some help before they do something that they are not going to get out of."

Carol seems to have had little involvement with her sons during this period. Donna told friends that Carol did not phone more than two or three times during the entire three years that she lived with the Sutherlands.

When the pressure became unbearable in the house, the boys would escape to their grandparents. No matter what trouble they got into, Kay and Frank always stood by them, tried to help. Donna Sutherland felt they were closer to Frank than they were to their own father. "They liked their grandparents and respected them, if nobody else. And Frank and Kay obviously loved them."

People who knew the Sutherlands at that time remember being a little shocked at how much talk there was about Frank's wealth. They say the boys would joke about how much money their grandpa had and how they were going to inherit it one day. Frank himself often told his grandchildren that the farm would be theirs once he was gone.

In the country Ken in particular thrived. Frank let him drive the old truck around the farm and got him to help out with the chores. "If only he could have been kept on that farm, away from his brother's influence, I think he would have straightened out. But as it was, Don always showed up," says a friend.

Surprisingly, for someone so timid, it was Kay who would insist that the boys behave. Remembers a family friend, "They were fooling around at the supper table, and she didn't feel they should be doing that. Then, when she told them they could watch television, they started horsing around in the front room. She went tearing in and yelled at them to stop. Kay didn't hesitate to get after them."

Once they stole the keys to the Cadillac out of their grandmother's purse – she had hidden them there, away from temptation – and then drove the car into into Moose Jaw. They were both too young to have a driver's licence. Surprisingly, Kay actually called the police but, as usual, the repercussions were not serious. "Kenny would smile and con his way out of it," says Les Winter.

Still, the Eberles continued to do everything they could to help their grandchildren. For a short time the boys attended school in Moose Jaw (by that time the Pasqua school had closed down and children were bussed to Lindale School in the city), but they quickly rebelled against the rules imposed and hitch-hiked back to their father's house in Regina. Says Les Winter, "They liked Frank a lot when they were younger. When they were in the eight-to-thirteen range, they shied away because of the strictness. When they got a little older, they realized that the farm was their breadbasket for the rest of their lives, so suddenly they got close again."

Gerry's second marriage was in serious trouble by this time. "Donna had a heavy load put on her. She did everything that was humanly possible," says Les Winter, "but those boys created an intolerable situation."

"Gerry can't handle it any more," Donna Sutherland told a friend at the time. "The boys are controlling him, not the other way around; I think he's afraid of his kids. I know my daughter and I sure are."

The final straw came when Gerry and Donna went away one weekend, and Ken and Don threw a party for two hundred of their favourite friends. With the bathtub full of booze, it quickly turned into a riot. On their return, the shocked Sutherlands viewed the wreckage with disbelief; the new house had been trashed. There was huge hole in the dining-room wall; the off-white carpets were a filthy black, not from dirt, but from grease – the guests had brought a Harley-Davidson into the living room; there were burns in the furniture.

Ken was the one who was shipped off to a foster home. "It was Don who had organized the party, not Ken. Ken took the blame, just as he had for everything that he and his brother were involved in," says Brian Tooley. "Don would say to Kenny, 'You're handicapped, you're crippled. They'll go easy on you. They will be hard on me.' And this is what Ken always did. He took the blame for every wrong-doing that Don committed."

Ken spent over a year with Brian Tooley and his wife, along with six other teenage boys in foster care. "When he lived with us, Ken was always a good kid," says Tooley. "He didn't get into

376 Siggins/Revenge of the Land

serious trouble, and I don't think he was into drugs." The Tooleys were amazed at how he coped with his disability: "He could tie his shoelaces faster than anyone."

There were problems, however. For one thing, Ken still refused to go to school, even though his teachers insisted he was smart, and could do the work if he tried. The Tooleys thought it would be a good idea to enrol him in Cochrane high school, a type of vocational school. Ken was a superb artist, and they thought he might get some graphics training there. "We phoned the principal at Cochrane, who got hold of Ken's I.Q. tests. He said he didn't think Ken would last there because he was too smart." They finally enrolled him in Miller Comprehensive, a Catholic high school, but he simply refused to go. "He just hated school," says Brian Tooley. "We'd make sure he caught the bus in the morning, sometimes we'd even take him. But he'd walk in the front door and out the back." Right to the nearest mall or bowling alley.

Brian Tooley says that, to his knowledge, Ken's mother never phoned once to enquire how her son was, even at Christmas. "His father didn't come around too much, either. Once in a while he'd take Ken home for the weekend, but not too often." Only his grandparents seemed to be deeply concerned about him. "They would phone every week. They'd ask how he was making out, how he was doing in school. On a Saturday night, they'd come into town and take him out for supper. I think they really thought a lot of Ken."

In the spring of 1983, Ken began associating with Don and his brother's friends. "We knew there'd be trouble," says Tooley. "I didn't like Don from the first time I met him. He was ignorant, obnoxious, a leader of his group. You could see Ken change when Don came around."

That spring, the Sutherland brothers stole a car and raced out to British Columbia to seek refuge with their mother. In less than a month, Ken was returned to Regina by the Saskatchewan Social Services. A year later, after running away from another foster home, he again joined the Ostranders in Victoria and enrolled in Esquimalt Secondary School. Carol was determined to make one last attempt to help her second son. At a court hearing two years later, lawyer Clifford C. Toth succinctly explained what happened. "His mother's common-in-law husband did not like the influence [Ken] had on the other children. As a result he was returned to Saskatchewan."

From that time on, Ken's anti-social behaviour intensified. He was becoming more and more belligerent, harder to handle, angry at everyone around him. He began running with his brother's crowd, and by that time they were into crime in a serious way. Ken's juvenile record shows he was caught stealing only twice, but friends who knew him then say that was only the tip of the iceberg. "He had only one arm and one leg, but he could break into a house and steal a hi-fi or television, just as fast, or faster, than the other guys." Says Les Winter, "Kenny's no longer the cripple; he's the guy who pulled it off – part of the crowd. A hero."

Once they turned sixteen, breaking the law became a more serious business for the Sutherland brothers; convictions would lead to jail sentences. About a month after his sixteenth birthday, Don was picked up in Regina on a theft charge. It was a minor matter and he was given an absolute discharge, but it was a harbinger of what lay ahead.

Lying just under Regina's commercial belly is a strip of some twelve blocks of huge, once-elegant houses, many built during Regina's boom at the turn of the century. Here live the derelicts, the impoverished, the families of hopeless alcoholics. So do the city's toughs. Sometimes they work at day jobs, or they scrounge off their pathetic girlfriends, who pull the odd trick and receive welfare cheques. More often they live on what they can steal. Don Sutherland fit in nicely with this crowd.

By the summer of 1984, he was sharing a house with several young men at 1044 Atkinson Street. A friend who knew him at the time says he was a frightening figure – dark, brooding, and absolutely determined to get his own way. "No question, he was the leader; and some of those guys were really tough."

On July 6, 1984, Don Sutherland and two friends, Denis OConnor and Hugh Keeffe, walked into the the 7-Eleven convenience store at Broad and 2nd streets in Regina wearing ski masks. All three had knives, which they brandished under the nose of the terrified checkout clerk. It seemed a dramatic gesture for what they ended up with – a couple of packages of cigarettes. Don would later claim that they were falling-down drunk. They were picked up by police later that night. Gerald Sutherland reluctantly put up the surety, and Don was released on bail. His trial on this crime would not come to court for over a year, and by that time he was into more trouble.

Sutherland had finally run out of patience with his son, and so Don turned to what was always his last refuge in the storm, his grandparents' farm. In the summer of 1984 Ken went to live there as well. The boys promised there would be no more trouble. "We're here to work on the farm," Ken insisted.

Two months later, Bob Woodrow, who owned a farm near the Eberles' place, was sitting in a bar having a drink. Some guy approached him and asked him if he'd like to buy a cheap VCR. Since his had been stolen from his house the previous September, along with his hi-fi equipment, he was mildly interested. It took only one look for him to realize that it was his VCR. By threatening to call the police, he extracted the identity of the thieves from the would-be salesman. He was not surprised when Don and Ken Sutherland were named.

Because he liked and respected the Eberles, Woodrow decided not to go to the police right away. He wandered over to their place instead. Frank was in the hospital for a minor operation on his back, and Kay was all alone. She asked Bob not to tell the authorities, but instead to take Don out behind the house "and beat the daylights out of him." Woodrow got the impression she was sick to death of both her grandchildren. He certainly was not going to assault Don, and so finally called the police, who were furious that he had not done so earlier.

Don and Ken were eventually charged with three counts of break and enter. They had not only stolen Woodrow's electronic equipment, but three days later, they had rifled the woodshed of the nearby Woodley farm, and on September 28, 1984, they broke into Gaudry's Texaco station and got away with $50 in cash. They pleaded guilty, and both were sentenced to jail terms – terms consisting of the time they had already spent in prison awaiting their trials. They were also placed on probation;

Ken for three years and Don for two years, which included a midnight curfew, and reporting regularly to a Moose Jaw probation officer.

It was obvious from a pre-sentence report that Ken had very serious problems. As part of the probation order, he had to seek treatment for alcohol and drug addiction and undergo counselling to cope with his physical disabilities. And he had to remain within a ten-mile radius of Moose Jaw, unless he obtained written permission from his probation officer. Frank was in court when Ken was sentenced. He again took on the responsibility of trying to straighten out a very disturbed sixteen-year-old.

"Mr. Eberle was well aware of all the trouble these boys had been in in terms of the criminal law," says Crown Prosecutor Walter Wall. "Yet he was prepared to help them. I thought it was remarkable, because they had put him through a lot of grief already, but he was still going to help in whatever way he could." Helping included buying Don a motorbike.

"Those boys got anything they wanted," says Bob Dixon, the husband of Frank's niece. "Anything that Frank thought would keep them on the place, keep them from running around."

Family members were becoming alarmed that Frank and Kay had taken on such a responsibility, particularly Frank's brother Mike. "Those kids are getting awfully hard to handle for those old people. I can't figure out why those boys are allowed to be there," he kept saying.

"But if you told Frank that," says his nephew Brent Eberle, "you'd be wasting your time. He'd listen to you but he'd likely not take your suggestion."

"The simple fact was Frank and Kay loved those kids," says a niece. "They were the only ones who didn't give up on them."

In November of 1984, Don's preliminary hearing on the charges of robbing the 7-Eleven store the previous July was heard, and the judge, not unexpectedly, sent it to trial. Don was still out on bail, and by December 1984, he was living back at his father's place in Regina. Gerry Sutherland's marriage to Donna had by this time disintegrated, and she had moved elsewhere. But, rifling through a drawer one day, Don found some old cheques on which her name and address were printed. It was too good an opportunity to ignore, and within a few weeks he had cashed so many phoney cheques on her bank account that he had wiped out her small savings. No charges were laid at that time.

Don decided at that point that he couldn't face his trial for armed robbery, which was fast approaching, and once again he headed for his mother's place in Victoria. His stay this time was a short one, for by mid-April Victoria police discovered he had violated his probation order and he was shipped back to Saskatchewan. Once again he moved in with his grandparents.

One August evening, Don was enjoying himself at a party, when he stumbled across a misplaced wallet. Inside he found a $500 cheque belonging to Gerald Wykes, a member of the Canadian Armed Forces, stationed at Moose Jaw. The next day, having forged Wykes's signature, Don showed up at the Money Mart in Regina, waving the Treasury Branch cheque. The manager took one look at Don's long hair, dirty black T-shirt, and jeans and realized that no military person would dare go out in public like that. He immediately locked the entrance and exit doors and called for help. Don was just about to throw a chair through the window to escape when the police arrived. During the investigation, not only were the forged cheques on Donna Sutherland's account uncovered, but so was a cheque for $200 made out to Frank Eberle's bank. Don had forged his own grandfather's name. It was a practice run for future criminal deeds that would prove far more appalling.

Don was sentenced to thirty days for theft, forgery, and uttering. But by this time he was already in jail. His long-awaited trial for the armed robbery of the previous summer had begun. By this time the police had uncovered yet another stick-up of another 7-Eleven store, so Don was faced with two counts. Judge W. L. Meagher sentenced Sutherland to two years less a day in a provincial correctional institute, a heavier sentence than was meted out to either Keeffe or OConnor. Says his lawyer Tom Dore, "I think that if Don had kept his nose clean before his trial, the judge might have been more lenient with him." Don served less than a year of his sentence. He was paroled on September 24, 1986.

Meanwhile, Ken Sutherland was living a dismal existence. After returning from his mother's place in Victoria, he drifted from one rooming-house to another, sometimes hanging out with his brother's friends, often on his own. "He'd show up at your door with no place to go," says a friend at the time, "so you'd have to let him in. But then he would get teed-off at you for no particular reason and do something stupid like slash your tires. He was a very angry young man."

On October 22, 1986, Ken was asleep in a car with Alberta licence plates, parked at 900 Block McTavish, when a policeman happened to wander by and, peeking in the window, noticed a Winchester .243-calibre rifle lying on the back seat. When the cop searched the car, he found a sawed-off Cooey .22 single-shot rifle in the trunk. It was enclosed in a sling made from a pair of nylons, which made it easier for the disabled Ken to use. The police officer confiscated the guns and charged him with possessing a prohibited weapon. His buddies didn't know whether to laugh or to cry. They claim he was supposed to be keeping watch while they were scouting out someplace to rob. Instead he had fallen asleep, likely because he was dead drunk. Without the aid of a lawyer, he pleaded guilty and was sentenced to six months in the Regina Correctional Centre. It was a tough sentence for someone who had no adult criminal record.

~ V ~

By late spring of 1987, both Ken and Don were back at their grandfather's farm. A strict regime had been laid down: no more trouble with the law; no partying and getting drunk every night; and they were to work responsibly on the farm. They were street-wise enough by this time to realize that the farm was their only hope for a future. Anyway, when their grandparents were gone, it would be theirs and they might as well learn how to manage it.

Frank was now seventy-four and feeling more vulnerable. In the early 1980s he had developed back problems. Recalls Harvey Brentnell, an old friend from the days when Frank farmed his brother's Belle Plaine land, "He was at an auction sale, and he was in such pain he was having trouble following the crowd around, so he had to go and sit down. That's where I ran into him. 'I don't know what to do about this damn back of mine,' he complained to me." His back problem made him a little slipshod in his farm work. Chores didn't get done as quickly as they might have. Neighbours noticed a lot of wild oats growing in his fields. Bill McWilliams dropped in one day to find Frank tinkering as usual with his old trucks and his antique farm equipment. "Come over here and help me," Frank yelled. "I want to start these old things up and run them for awhile. There's lots of work should be done on these things. And I'm running out of time."

And yet, in the spring of 1987, friends thought he looked better than he had in some time. "I met him at the John Deere's spring open house," recalls Harvey Brentnell. "I asked him how his back was and he said, 'Pretty good.' He was in a real good mood."

He might have had a new lease on life because he believed that Don and Ken were at last taking their careers as farmers seriously. Says Bill McWilliams, "Frank bought all this new equipment – tractors, combines, swathers – that he didn't need. You see, he made a desperate attempt to try and get those grandsons to farm." After Don had been swathing on a chilly spring day, he complained to his grandfather that he had been cold in the field. Frank picked up the phone and ordered a new tractor – an International 784 model, with a cab attached to it. Don helped him build a large new outbuilding and renovate the upstairs of the house to make the boys more comfortable. They used a machine Frank loved to work with, a Dewalt radial-arm saw, to do the finishing job, the baseboards and window casements. While he forbade Don and Ken to use the Cadillac, especially after Don was found guilty of drunk driving and spent a couple of months in jail that spring of 1987, the boys were mobile – Don had a motorcycle and Ken was allowed to drive the half-ton. The few friends and relatives who saw the reclusive Eberles during that spring felt that the situation with their grandsons might be improving, that the boys might at last understand what their grandparents were doing for them. It was an illusion. Under the surface, dangerous tensions were rippling.

Part of the problem was Ken. As he grew older, and particularly after his release from the correctional institute, he developed into a bitter, frustrated young man. He had lost much of his sweetness, his charm. Friends feel that as he grew older he realized that, with his disability, his poor education, and his own lack of willpower, his future was very limited. He was at the mercy of his grandparents and their farm, and that bred resentment and an increasing addiction to alcohol and drugs.

He couldn't do many of the jobs his brother was able to do around the farm, and that also resulted in frustration. And his grandfather, despite his years, was still something of a perfectionist in his farming. "I don't think Frank would be the easiest person to get along with," says his nephew Brian Eberle. "I don't mean he would be mean or anything. But there would be a lot of, 'This is the way you do it, my way, and there is no other way.' I don't mean he was hard to get along with, he would just want things done right."

But it was not his grandfather but his grandmother who was driving Ken to distraction. "In her own way she was rather strong-willed, and quicker to state her opinions than Frank was, even though she was a nervous woman. A little bird without feathers – that's the way I thought of her," says a relative. "But she wasn't afraid to nag those boys when she disapproved – which was often. She hated their drinking and their taking drugs and she let them know it."

Her habit of scribbling down everything that happened in life drove Ken "bananas." She never failed to record the exact time he and Don left the farm and when they returned. When Ken found one such note in a flowerpot, written on a cut-up cereal box, stating the last time she had watered the geranium, he ripped it into shreds. But it was her constant nattering at him to do this, do that, that drove him particularly crazy.

His lawyer, Clifford Toth, would later tell a judge, "He did not feel at all welcome on the farm. He was not able to do a lot of things around the farm. His grandmother, who wanted him to do things, was critical towards him. Ken perceived that she was riding him. He perceived, and I think correctly, that she did not want him on the farm. He didn't have any place else to go. He didn't have any particular work skills or any other place to turn. He became increasingly moody and edgy and depressed."

In early July, Carol came back to the farm where she had grown up to visit her parents and to see how her sons were making out. She did the rounds of various relatives, including Kay's sister Genevieve Finiak, and she talked with her cousin Judy Dixon during her visit. Although the two women had once been close, they hadn't seen each other for years, and they decided they'd get together. But an injured horse owned by the Dixons required immediate attention, and by the time Judy telephoned, about five days later, Carol had already left.

Judy talked with Frank, and she felt a little concerned. "Frank didn't sound like he normally sounds. He talked about the crops and the garden coming in. He sounded a little bit frustrated, as though everything was coming in all at once and there wasn't enough time to get it all done. And for somebody who had really nothing but time, it was odd. He seemed frustrated over something."

August was a cold month, and harvest was a little late. As usual, it was a frantic time for everyone, and it was only around the second week in September that Eberle's relatives and neighbours noticed that his fields of wheat lay untouched. He had been tardy in past years – as Grant Babich says, "He had the machinery for three sections of land; he didn't need to rush" – so this wasn't considered too unusual. But when harvest was nearing an end, and threshing on the Eberle farm had not even begun, Babich says, "We thought it was pretty funny." Grant also noticed a lot of activity, a lot of traffic going back and forth. He finally drove into the farm and asked where Kay and Frank were. "The boys told us they were away, and I guess we had no reason not to believe them."

"Different people kept coming up to us and asking, 'What's going on at Frank's place? Do you know there's nothing being done?' We didn't get too excited at the time; we were harvesting ourselves and we didn't have time to bother," says Judy Dixon.

The Dixons and many other relatives and neighbours phoned the farm. Ken would usually answer and deflect the questions. Kay and Frank had been called away to Calgary for a funeral; they'd be back soon. Kay and Frank had gone to Hawaii on a holiday; they'd be back in a month. Kay and Frank had decided to visit Carol in Victoria; the date of their return was uncertain. The explanations seemed plausible at the time, although when people later thought about it, they realized how ridiculous it was that they should even for a moment have believed them. Kay and Frank would simply not leave the farm at harvest-time. Brent Eberle says that, when he phoned, Ken told him that Frank was having problems with his investments and he and Kay had gone to Calgary to check on the situation. "The newspapers were full of the Principal Trust scandal, so I thought there was some logic to it. When I think of it now, I realize that Frank would have just picked up the phone and called his lawyer or broker and dealt with it that way."

Brent's father, Fred Eberle, had lost his wife not long before and was distraught. Still, he became more and more concerned about Frank. "I know something is wrong. I know something is wrong out there." Finally, at the beginning of October, his son-in-law, Bob Dixon, and his granddaughter, Lesley Dixon, decided to take a drive out to see what was going on. It was about five o'clock in the afternoon as they turned onto Highway 39, on the way to Pasqua. Bob had previously bought a cultivator from Frank but had never gotten around to picking up the narrow shovels that went with it. He used that as an excuse to go and check out the farm.

The moment they drove up to the farmhouse, they knew something was wrong. "Lock your door," Bob told his daughter. There was trash everywhere – beer and liquor bottles, papers all over the place. Grain was strewn all over the yard. The big machinery was sitting out: the tractor had a flat tire and the combine was all plugged up. Bob drove up to the back door and Ken came out, a bottle of beer in his hand, followed by his buddy Frank Bell. Ken told Bob that they had finally finished harvesting.

"Looks like you had a rough time here," Bob said.

"Yeah, we had a couple of breakdowns," was Ken's reply. "But some people stopped by to give us a hand getting going."

"Well, what's holding you up now, then? You got sixty or eighty acres of flax there to do."

"Oh yeah," responded Ken. "We're just chilling out for a couple days, then we'll get back to it."

"Chilling out, man?" Bob asked.

"Yeah, chilling out."

Bob then asked Ken where Frank was. "He's out in Alberta," said Ken.

"Where in Alberta?" Bob asked.

"At a funeral somewhere. Not sure whose funeral. A cousin or something. Be back next week some time."

Dixon told Ken that he'd better clean the yard up before his grandparents came home and then left. By that time he had already decided to go to the police. But he thought he would make one last check, phone around to relatives to see if the Eberles did perhaps have cousins in Calgary or Edmonton.

At three in the morning on October 3, Betty Ray Day, a nurse at Moose Jaw Union Hospital, was on duty when a young man dressed in a stained Harley-Davidson T-shirt and hat stumbled into the hospital. Doubled over in pain and bleeding badly, he could barely walk and was supported by another man. Nurse Day took a quick look, and saw what looked like four stab wounds: one in the abdomen, two under the arm in the left chest, one in the back. She realized this was a life-threatening situation and began preparing the wounded man for the operating room.

Dr. George Miller immediately performed surgery that saved Andy Muntean's life. He was soon able to tell his story to the police.

Muntean was a friend of Ken Sutherland's; four weeks before he had been taken on as a hired hand at the Eberle farm. Sutherland, Muntean, Frank Bell, and another friend, Ed Racette, had managed to get something of a crop off and had decided to throw a mammoth celebration, complete with a disc jockey who specialized in heavy metal. It was called a yuk-a-futz party, named after the punch that was served. A bar was set up in one of the Quonset huts and two huge garbage pails were filled with this rot-gut, consisting of equal parts rye, vodka, and rum. As guests arrived, they contributed booze to the mixture. There were also several kegs of beer. It didn't take long for the party to become a falling-down drunk.

Ed Racette happened to have a shotgun in his car and, supposedly as a joke, he took it out and began brandishing it. One of the guests became angry at Racette's nonsense, picked a fight with him, and beat him up.

Andy Muntean had not appreciated Ed Racette's hi-jinks – for one thing, he didn't want any police involvement; he already had matters before the courts. When Andy saw Ed Racette's brother, Aaron, he complained to him about Ed's behaviour. "Aaron thought it was a kind of joke. So I called him an idiot and walked away," said Muntean. Racette claimed Muntean then threw his drink in his face and that Muntean punched him and broke his nose. Muntean denied this. Whatever the case, a knife suddenly appeared from Racette's sleeve. Muntean was stabbed four times. Dr. Miller testified that, if Muntean had not received immediate medical treatment, three of the four wounds would have proved fatal.*

Corporal Keith McGillivray and Constable David Butler of the Moose Jaw RCMP arrived at the farm about three-thirty that morning. The party was still in full flight. "There were so many drunken people around, that it was impossible to make any sense of them," says McGillivray. The two policemen decided to leave but to return at dawn. Back on the farm, it didn't take them long to spot a hunting knife with a brown handle in the Quonset-hut-cum-bar.

They questioned the dozen or so survivors of the ordeal, who were sleeping off hangovers all over the place. They asked Ken Sutherland where his grandparents were. "Gone to Calgary to visit relatives," they were told.

---

*On January 28, 1988, Aaron Racette was found guilty of aggravated assault and sentenced to sixteen months in a provincial correctional institute.

During the turmoil of the previous evening, one of the guests, Brenda Bell, had gone to Jim Boyle's nearby farm to ask for help. Boyle had been feeling uneasy about the situation on the Eberle farm for some time; he had watched the parade of long-hairs coming and going every day, knowing that Frank and Kay would have strongly disapproved. After the rowdy party, he phoned several of the Eberle relatives to express his concern and then phoned some officers he knew in the Moose Jaw police force.

Meanwhile, Bob and Judy Dixon had decided to file a missing-persons report. On October 5, Bob Dixon drove to the RCMP detachment in Moose Jaw and was surprised to learn that Judy's cousin, Roseanne Chamberlain, the daughter of Kay's younger sister, had done the same thing only minutes before.

The following day the police asked Kay Eberle's brother, Adam Bishoff, her sister Genevieve Finiak, her niece Roseanne Chamberlain, and Bob and Judy Dixon to return to the RCMP depot. There they grilled them about why they were filing the missing-persons report. Ken Sutherland also arrived at the detachment that day. His father had got wind of what was happening and had told him to go to the police. He gave a written statement that Frank and Kay were in Calgary. "They phoned us on September 4 from Calgary. They wanted us to pick them up," he told the police. Ken said he had written down the address, but had since lost the slip of paper. He agreed to let the RCMP search the farm.

By this time Sergeant Ken Burns of the RCMP's general investigation services in Regina had been called in. He was sure that foul play was involved, and he carefully organized the search.

On October 7, Bob Dixon, accompanied by a half-dozen police officers, drove out to the Eberle farm. Dixon was given an escort and told to walk around the outbuildings to see if he could spot anything unusual. "Stay clear of the house. There're people in there," he was informed.

The two men walked north to the pond and were circling back through the yard, heading towards Frank's southern fields, when Dixon spotted a police officer coming out of the house.

The policeman stooped over and lifted what looked like a wooden lid. Then he yelled for his colleagues to come.

Kay Eberle's body was floating in the septic tank.

Bob Dixon was told to go immediately and sit in the car, because arrests were about to be made. Four young men were paraded out of the house with their hands on their heads. As he was being led away, Ed Racette spotted a wagon beside the storage building, jumped up on it, and said, in a silly tone, "No, they're not in here, officers."

Ken Sutherland's German shepherd was on the loose, and when they first arrived at the Eberle farm, the police had ordered Ken to contain the dog in the garage. Just as Sutherland was getting into the police car, the dog got out and jumped into the driver's seat. Ken had to lock it up again, and as he was doing so he spotted Bob Dixon. "He looked at me and I looked at him and he said, 'Well, we'll see you.'" As he got into the police car, he started to laugh. Later that afternoon he was charged with first-degree murder.

A massive police search got under way that day. Police dogs, scuba divers to search the sloughs, helicopters, front-end loaders, and three dozen police officers were used to comb the farm. They were looking for Frank Eberle's body.

The boys had trashed the place. Garbage and liquor bottles were strewn everywhere. Farm implements were plugged up and misused. The house looked as though it had been the field of a major battle. Walls, doorways, and floors were gouged. The plumbing system had broken down and there was no water and no flushing toilet. The place stank.

After two days of searching, the police still had not discovered any clues as to the whereabouts of Frank Eberle. At that point, Sergeant Burns became very interested in some information he had received from the provincial correctional institute where Ken Sutherland was being held.

Ken was in a most agitated state of mind. He had heard two rumours that day that had upset him: one, that his grandfather's body had been discovered (which was untrue), and second, and more important, that his brother, Don, was soon to be charged with first-degree murder. He actually made several confessions – to inmates he knew, to the prison guard, and, finally, to the police.

On the evening of Thanksgiving Sunday, October 11, Ken confessed to the RCMP that he had murdered both his grandmother and grandfather.

On the evening of August 12, Ken and Don had been carousing around the countryside, drinking, until finally they ended up in a bar in Moose Jaw. There they had met some friends and had a wonderful time, returning to the farm early in the morning. They were both drunk, and neither could face what they knew would be a tongue-lashing from their grandmother. They decided to spend the night in the half-ton truck.

The next morning both the Sutherlands woke up with hangovers, and they shuffled into the house to get a cup of coffee. Kay was waiting, and she started right in on them. Don immediately went outside to work, but Ken remained. His grandmother continued nagging at him. "You're wrecking your life. If you don't stop drinking you can leave. You are good for nothing."

Something snapped. All the anger and frustration exploded in his brain. He walked out to his grandfather's workshop and picked up the .22-calibre rifle that was used to shoot gophers. When he walked back into the house, Kay was standing with her back to the sink, facing him, looking right at him with accusing eyes. He pointed the rifle with his one good arm and blasted his grandmother right between the eyes.

She died instantly, the blood already an ocean, even from so tiny a woman. Ken stared at the horror for a few seconds. Then turned around and walked out of the house.

He knew that there was one person who would soon come face-to-face with the terrible deed, and that that person would know immediately who had perpetrated it.

Frank was working north of the farmhouse, adjacent to the field where he had often planted his money-making flax crop. There was something wrong with the tractor, and he was fiddling with it. Ken drove up in the Studebaker truck, but Frank was so engrossed in the mechanical problem that he didn't look up. Ken walked up behind him, said softly, "Sorry, Grandpa," and shot him once in the head. Frank Eberle died instantly.

Ken was then faced with the daunting task of getting rid of the bodies. With his disability, he couldn't easily dig a grave. But then he remembered the front-end loader. Although it was difficult to shift gears, he had used it before, and with the big machine he managed to peel back a layer of stubble. He then dragged his grandfather's body into it, covered it with five pieces of tarp, threw in some tools and the rifle he had used to murder Frank, and then, using his one hand, covered the grave with a thin layer of dirt. Finally, with an old rag, he cleaned the blood off the tractor.

Getting rid of his grandmother's remains posed an even bigger challenge to someone without an arm and a leg. But driving back from the field in the old truck he figured it out. In the house, he took a blanket and wrapped it around Kay's small body. Then, using it as a sling, he dragged her out the back door. The septic tank was located thirty feet away on the west side of the house. He lifted the small wooden lid and dropped her body into it.

The next hour and half were spent cleaning up. Blood had splattered on the tank's concrete top and on the grass. Ken then tackled the inside of the house; since the body had been dragged, blood was smeared everywhere. Once that task was finished, he took the rags he had used and his own bloody shirt and burnt them in the fire pit out near the chicken coop.

Whether he suffered any anguish or guilt for the terrible deeds he committed that day he never revealed, but obviously he felt a sense of freedom, of relief, from the strictures that his grandparents had imposed. At noon on the day of the murder, he and Don went to pick up a friend, John Soika, in Moose Jaw and drove him back to the farm. "Why don't you come and live here with us? There'll be good times," they promised him. Soika thought that was a little strange since, just the day before, when he and his buddies had come over to meet the Sutherland brothers, Ken had rushed out of the house and told them to hush up as his grandparents were at home. Soika said he'd think about their offer. The three then piled into the pick-up truck and headed for Regina. They spent all afternoon and evening partying and drinking at Delbert's nightclub. They got back to the farm at seven in the morning. "And goddamn, there was nobody there to nag."

There was only one problem – the Sutherlands were running out of cash. The next day, August 15, they drove over to the farm of Don and Norman Wright. The brothers were surprised when Don told them that everything on the farm was for sale, since they hadn't heard Frank talk about retiring. The boys took Frank's Dewalt radial-arm saw off the truck. "A steal at $60," they said. The Wrights realized it was worth at least $500, and so snapped it up. Don then told them he'd sell Frank's new tractor, complete with a front-end loader, and the Wright brothers agreed to come over to the Eberle farm and have a look.

When they got there they were astonished at all the garbage and debris scattered all over. "Where's Frank and Kay?" they asked.

"Gone on holidays," was the reply. The Wrights thought this was odd because Frank and Kay never went anywhere. Ken and Don said they'd sell the tractor for $1,500. In the Wrights' opinion, the machine was worth at least $8,000. "We realized something was fishy, so we backed off."

Ken and Don had thought up a better way to get their hands on some cash, anyway. On August 15, Ken wrote out a cheque for $200 on his grandfather's account at Guaranty Trust in Moose Jaw and forged Frank's name. Don cashed it so easily that the boys laughed for hours over the fast one they had pulled. Three days later Ken forged a similar cheque, only this time for $550, payable to Ed Racette, who by now was supposed to be working on the farm. Again the teller cashed it without blinking an eye. Three days later they followed the same process, only this time the cheque was worth $1,200.

It was so easy that Don decided they would go for the big fish. On August 24, he walked into the Guaranty Trust Company, spotted a cashier he recognized, and explained to her that he and his brother had decided to buy a house in town, and their grandfather had agreed to give them the down payment. With little hesitation, she handed over $12,000. Four days later, another cheque for $6,000 was cashed at the Royal Bank in Moose Jaw.

With so much money in their pockets, the Sutherlands were able to live out their lifelong dream – to get smashed on booze and drugs every night, and at last to drive their grandfather's big, black Cadillac.

During this time, on August 18, Ken, John Soika, Ed and Aaron Racette, Dale Breese, and a girlfriend, Angie Nelson, spent the evening drinking in Regina. A gaggle of drunken teenagers was not the typical possessor of a sedate black Cadillac, and when the car was spotted careening down Broad Street, the police stepped in. Ken was driving, and he did not have a driving licence. As well, open bottles of liquor were discovered. The ownership checked out to Frank Eberle, and the police, suspecting something fishy, impounded the car. Ken had to phone Don at the farm and ask him to come and collect the crew.

Two weeks later, Don and Ed Racette convinced a friend in Regina, an old man in his sixties, to forge Frank's signature and sign the Cadillac out. The elderly man was given Frank's driver's licence as identification and $100 for his trouble.*

The Eberle farm, meanwhile, was the scene of many rowdy parties. A cousin of Ken and Don's, who hauled asphalt to the United States, was surprised when a trucker in South Dakota described a corn-roast he had gone to on the Eberle farm. But the fantasy world of drugs and booze turned into a nightmare after the October 3 yuk-a-futz party.

The day after his confession, Ken was taken to the Pasqua farm, where, step-by-step, he re-enacted his crime for the police. They found Frank's remains in the shallow grave, but the corpse was so badly decomposed it would take three days before it

---

*There is speculation that the old man may have been Bev Kerney. Kerney was a caretaker at one of the run-down apartment buildings that Sutherland and the Racettes frequented. On December 3, 1989, his body was found stuffed inside the freezer where he kept the rent money he collected. He had been strangled to death. Aaron Racette was charged with second-degree murder, but in May of 1990 a jury acquitted him of the crime.

could be positively identified. Although the body was not ready to be handed over to the funeral parlour, the double ceremony at Sacred Heart Church went ahead anyway. The priest alluded to how reclusive the Eberles had become in later years, how "they preferred each other's company to the company of others." A large crowd gathered to mourn, friends, close and distant relatives, many of whom chided themselves that they had not paid more attention to the disappearance of the Eberles, had not gone to see them when they suspected something was wrong. Carol Ostrander was there, looking worn, pinched, and old. What she said to her second son when she visited him in jail is not known.

Ken Sutherland's preliminary hearing was scheduled for two weeks in January, which would likely have been followed by a lengthy trial. Ken told his legal-aid lawyer, Clifford Toth, that he wanted to get the ordeal over as quickly as possible. If a deal could be worked out with the Crown to drop the charges from first- to second-degree murder, he would plead guilty. Prosecutor Walter Wall had already decided he couldn't prove that Sutherland had carefully and deliberately planned the murders, which was necessary if a first-degree murder charge was to stick, so he agreed.

On November 30, 1987, Ken Sutherland appeared before W. R. Matheson, a judge in the Court of Queen's Bench in Moose Jaw. In a hearing that lasted less than an hour, Ken Sutherland pleaded guilty to two counts of second-degree murder. Pale and shaken, in a voice so quiet the recording device in the courtroom did not pick it up, he blamed his terrible deed on "one moment of blind rage." Neither his mother nor father was in the courtroom that day.

The sentence for second-degree murder was life imprisonment, but the judge had some discretion in the sentencing: it was he who determined the amount of time Ken would serve in prison before he was paroled – ten years the minimum and twenty-five years the maximum. Given Ken Sutherland's age – he was only nineteen – and his not-too-lengthy criminal record, some leniency would be expected. Walter Wall had concluded that fifteen years was an appropriate time for Ken Sutherland to be imprisoned before being released on parole. He outlined his reasons to the court: there was not one murder but two. Although there was no planning and deliberation within the context of the law, so that it was not first-degree murder, some measure of thought went into the murders, especially Frank Eberle's. The victims did not contribute to or precipitate their own deaths. The accused was involved in concealing the bodies, and in an extensive cover-up for almost two months. There was little, if any, remorse shown by the accused. His main motivation for making his confession was concern that his brother might be implicated in the murders. Finally, "There appears in this case to have been no passion involved, just a cold-blooded killing in each case."

Sutherland's lawyer, Clifford Toth, sketched, in the briefest terms, the tragedy of Ken's life. The horrible accident at age three, which resulted in his severe handicap, his poor performance at school, primarily because of time lost in rehabilitation. "Both of those contributed to how he approached the world. He was disabled and angry and uneducated." Toth went on to tersely describe the bitter separation of Ken's parents; the arguments with his father; his sojourn in foster homes; his hope that he might start a new life with his mother in British Coumbia, which was thwarted by his stepfather. "The morning of the shooting," said Toth, "what happened was that all the anger and the frustrations and everything else in his life just exploded. In his statement to the police, he used the word snapped. I think that's a correct assessment as to what, in fact, happened to this young man. It all just came to a head and he snapped."

Toth submitted a report written by a psychiatrist, Dr. Charles Messer, which gave more detail on Ken's psychological state. It was in this report that Dr. Messer reported that Gerald Sutherland was a child- and wife-abuser.

Mr. Justice Matheson, emphasizing that "both killings were of a rather cold-blooded nature and, if not cold-blooded, then certainly these killings were committed dispassionately," sentenced Kenneth Sutherland to life imprisonment, with no eligibility of parole for fifteen years. He would serve his time in the federal penitentiary at Prince Albert.

If anything, Don Sutherland proved more of a problem for the Crown attorney than his brother Ken. Ken's statement placed him on the farm on the morning of the killings. What role, then, did he play in the murder?

Don Sutherland told police that, on the morning of August 13, he and Ken had been sleeping off an all-night drunk in the Eberles' truck, which was parked in the farmyard. After waking, he had followed his brother into the house. At that point his grandmother told him that she and Frank were going to Calgary to attend a funeral. When Ken and his grandmother began to quarrel, Don left. He then went into the farmyard to carry out some chores Frank had assigned him. He said that Ken later joined him on the job. During the morning, Don heard no shots, nor did he see anything unusual. Later in the afternoon he went to the field to continue the job of rodweeding, which his grandfather had begun earlier on. At no time did he see Frank in the field. The tractor had been acting up – Frank was fixing it when he was shot in the head – and by six p.m. it had broken down entirely. Don then returned to the Eberle farmhouse. Tacked to the door was a note from his grandfather saying he and Kay had gone to Calgary for a funeral.

His story, and the statements made by his brother and friends, were full of contradictions. Ken Sutherland told the police two stories: first, that his brother had hitchhiked to Regina the day before the murders and had returned to the farm a day and a half later; second, that his brother had been on the farm the morning of the murders, but had left at ten a.m. and returned three or four days later. Their friend, John Soika, had an entirely different version of events: Ken and Don had picked him up at noon on the day of the murder, brought him back to the farm, and suggested he could live there; at about one-thirty that afternoon the three of them drove into Regina to party at Delbert's nightclub.

Don insisted that he knew nothing about the murder of his grandparents until two RCMP officers told him on October 8. But one wonders why he wouldn't have asked some questions. Why would his grandmother tell him she was going to a funeral early in the day? Why, when Kay and Frank did go to Calgary, did they not take any personal belongings? Even Kay's purse was left behind. Why did he tell the Wright brothers that all Frank's farm machinery was for sale if the Eberles had simply gone to a funeral? Was he not worried when he hadn't heard a word from the Eberles for several weeks and harvest-time was approaching? As someone said, Frank would not let Don rodweed half a field without telling him how to do it.

One thing was certain: Don was not on the farm the night of the famous party nor the day the police found Kay's body. He was sitting in a Calgary jail.

On September 5, three weeks after the murders, Don and Ken and some friends had gone to Calgary in Frank's big black Cadillac, their first stop on their way to visiting Carol Ostrander in Victoria. They had just come out of a bar when they were pulled over by the police, who did a quick check and discovered the Caddie belonged to Frank Eberle. Don gave a false name and a phoney excuse as to why he had the car. At that point the policeman decided that Don would have to go to the station, though the others were to be let go. But Ken, who was blind drunk, was getting more and more belligerent and mouthy. The police finally had enough of him and slapped him in jail for the night. The next morning, Ken was released, but the police had discovered Don's true identity, and charged him with breach of probation – travelling outside of Saskatchewan. Ken returned to Moose Jaw with the Cadillac and Don remained in prison. By the time the Moose Jaw RCMP caught up with him, he had been in jail in Calgary for over a month and was just about to be released. A warrant for his arrest was quickly issued, and he was shipped back to Moose Jaw. He was then charged with first-degree murder.

Despite much contradictory evidence as to Don's where-abouts on the day of the murder, the murder charges against him were dropped on December 23, 1987. The prosecutor, Walter Wall, says he had no choice. During all the times Ken Sutherland had been questioned, he never once implicated his brother in the crime in any way. Says Wall, "Ken's confession was very specific and was backed up with the circumstances in which the bodies were found. And he was quite adamant that

Donald had nothing to do with the killings." There were no witnesses to the tragedy and no forensic evidence linking Don to the crimes. Don Sutherland was still not completely off the hook, however. On December 30, he pleaded guilty to three counts of forging cheques on the Eberles' bank accounts and one count of attempted theft – his effort to sell off Frank's farm machinery.

When Don made his court appearance before sentencing, the Crown asked for the maximum sentence – two years in a federal penitentiary. Wall told the judge that this was a case where "rather than appreciate and respect his grandfather for the efforts that Mr. Eberle had made over the years to assist him, instead of appreciating that, he took advantage of Mr. Eberle's death and his absence by stealing from him. If indeed he knew that his grandparents were dead, then it would appear to be a particularly cold and mercenary activity on his part."

Lawyer Ken Cornea responded by admitting that Don had indeed profited from his grandparents' death. It was certainly a tragedy, he said, since, "they were two of the people he loved the most in this world and had been the only stable influence in his life."

Mr. Justice G. Maurice sentenced Don Sutherland to fourteen months in a provincial correctional institute. Within a year, he was back on the Eberle farm.

During the court hearings, irony hung heavy in the air. The Crown suspected that since such a long time – eight weeks – had passed between Kay's murder and the discovery of her remains, the forensic evidence linking Ken to the crime would have been weak. Although Frank's body would probably have been found – his hand was already sticking out of the shallow grave, and police dogs likely would have sniffed it out – there were no fingerprints on the murder weapon found in the grave. And finally, there were no witnesses to the murders. If Ken had not been so concerned about his brother's well-being, if he had kept his mouth shut, he might have gotten away with the crime. He might not be spending his youth, perhaps his entire life, in Prince Albert's federal penitentiary.

~ VI ~

At the time of his death Frank Eberle was worth $1,140,000. Of this, about $410,000 was connected to his farm operation – the estimated value of the land, the machinery that had been auctioned off, the grain on hand, 15,600 bushels of wheat, 900 bushels of flax. The remaining $730,000 was either invested in stocks and bonds or sitting in bank accounts. Kay Eberle left an estate of $172,346, all invested in bonds, mutual funds, and bank accounts. When news of Frank Eberle's worth circulated in the district, neighbouring farmers, many of whom were up to their ears in mortgages and other debt, scratched their heads in puzzlement. How could a farmer with only one section, not much land in the days of mammoth agri-business, leave so much wealth behind?

Frank's and Kay's wills were written in May 1979, just after Carol had left her husband and two eldest sons, and the terms reflected the Eberles' disapproval. Carol was to receive the interest from the money invested, as well as any income derived from the farming operation during her lifetime. But she did not gain control of the assets; she could not cash in any stocks or bonds or sell the land. If she needed extra cash, she would have to apply to Guaranty Trust, the executor and trustee of Frank's and Kay's estates. The company would have "uncontrolled discretion" in deciding if Carol could impinge on the capital. If Carol should die, the income would then be distributed among the grandchildren once they were twenty-one years old. Only after Carol was dead and her youngest child reached the age of thirty-five would the estate be divided among the heirs. (Guaranty Trust brought a motion before the courts that had the effect of disinheriting Ken Sutherland. In Canadian law, a criminal cannot benefit from his crimes. Don Sutherland's fraud charges were considered too minor for this law to apply to him.) The will was a desperate attempt by Frank Eberle to keep his farm in the family. Since Carol's youngest son, Dylan Ostrander, was only five at the time of Frank and Kay's deaths, it would be thirty years before the land could be dispersed. Surely in that time someone would become as devoted to it as Frank Eberle had been.

The first task faced by Guaranty Trust and Carol Ostrander was to find someone to work the farm. Frank's will had stipulated that Gerry Sutherland should be given first choice to rent the land, but he turned down the opportunity.

After the funeral, Carol Anne and her husband, Garry Ostrander, had supper with Judy Dixon and her husband, Bob. The conversation quickly turned to the wonders of life in Victoria. "B.C. has everything going for it," said Garry Ostrander. "We have horses, and we can fish, and we can grow anything we want. It's paradise." According to the Dixons, Garry Ostrander did most of the talking; Carol seemed dominated by him. The two couples enjoyed a pleasant evening, and Judy Dixon was not surprised when she and her husband were asked if they wanted to rent the Eberle farm.

Judy's brother, Brent Eberle, wanted a piece of the action, so he leased the north half, the Dixons the south half. The Dixons and the Eberles view farming as a business which must be carefully planned, so the terms of the lease were very specific. They were to rent the land for three years and have access to the buildings on the property, including the house, the Quonset huts, the barns.

In 1988, Saskatchewan was hit by a drought so severe it was reminiscent of the Dirty Thirties. Bob Dixon watched a dust storm, black as night, fierce as a tornado, sweep across Frank Eberle's yard. The south half of Frank's section was not in the best condition; the land was very dry, and there was evidence that the topsoil had been blowing. Bob Dixon got a very poor crop that harvest, and therefore counted on the second year to make up for his losses.

At Easter of 1989, in the second year of their lease, Judy Dixon received a telephone call from Garry Ostrander. He told her that he and Carol had decided to leave Victoria and to move onto Kay and Frank's farm. "I said, 'I beg your pardon?' and he went on: they wanted to start a new life, their life had been in shambles, they couldn't get anything to work out right, this was the only place they could find peace and quiet. I answered, 'I don't know if that's going to be possible because we have a three-year lease with you, unless you want to break that lease without compensation. We can't afford to throw up our hands and walk away from it. That's not how it's done.'"

Maria Reed had had her home on Calypso Drive in the new Moose Jaw subdivision of Sunningdale custom-built. Everything was done to Maria's specifications: the huge, airy sunken-living room with fireplace, the mushroom wall-to-wall carpeting, the spiral staircase reflecting in a wall of smoked glass, the kitchen with its $18,000 oak kitchen cabinets, the exercise and jacuzzi rooms, the huge deck overlooking the prairies. However, by the time Maria and her husband had finished the place, their marriage had disintegrated, and the house was for sale, asking price $235,000, a great deal of money in town where good resale houses can be had for $32,000. There were many lookers but no takers, so Maria Reed finally took it off the market. A week later, she was pulling up to her driveway when she saw a half-ton truck with B.C. licence plates sitting in front of the house. It pulled away, but in a few hours she got a phone call asking if the house could be inspected. Garry Ostrander took a cursory look around, phoned Carol in Victoria, and bought it on the spot.

Neighbours and relatives of Frank's and Kay's were aghast when they heard the news. Carol hadn't lived in the Moose Jaw area for twenty-three years; she had seldom even visited. "And she returns after one son is convicted of murdering the grandparents and another has danced on the grave."

By this time, relations between the Ostranders and the Dixons were strained. Garry was insisting that he wanted to farm; the Dixons were determined the lease would not be broken without some compensation. Says Judy Dixon, "We managed to scrape through the second year, but it wasn't very pleasant. We were on constant alert because strange things were happening around the farm. Every time we went out to the farm we saw campfires, beer bottles, other garbage." As part of the agreement, the Dixons had the use of the outbuildings – the big barn, the metal Quonset huts, and the Eberles' house, in which they stored machinery. "Every time we went out there, something was gone. The snowmobile was stolen, a section of harrows off the draw bar went missing. And what possible good that would do anybody was absolutely beyond me, but it was like a message and that's how we took it."

The Dixons were so alarmed at the situation that they bought a cellular phone so Bob could stay in contact with his home the whole time he was out on the Eberle farm. Finally, after the harvest was in, the Ostranders agreed to pay out the lease. The Dixons breathed a great sigh of relief and quickly wrapped up their farming operation.

By that time, money was available to the Ostranders because Frank's and Kay's wills had been overturned by the courts and Carol Anne had gained control of their wealth.

Frank and Kay had tried too hard to manipulate the future from their graves. Their wills were improperly drawn and offended the rule against perpetuities – a set of arcane laws designed to prevent people from tying their estates up far into the future. There was a distinct possibility that at least two of the clauses in the will were invalid and that Carol Ostrander might be able to have Frank Eberle's will declared void by the courts. That would have meant that the grandchildren would be left with nothing.

In February 1989, the Public Trustee for Saskatchewan worked out an arrangement with Carol Ostrander's lawyer. Each of the four heirs named in Frank's will (Ken Sutherland having been disinherited) would receive $36,000. Since Don and Sean Sutherland were over eighteen, they would get the cash immediately; the Public Trustee would invest the money for the two younger grandsons, Garry and Dylan Ostrander. It was also agreed that a $12,000 life-insurance policy would be purchased for the benefit of any more children born to or adopted by the Ostranders. The remainder of the estate, valued at approximately $1.2 million, including the precious farmland, passed to Carol Anne Ostrander. These terms were agreeable to Carol Ostrander, her sons, the Public Trustee, and the court. Guaranty Trust, Frank's executors, didn't intervene. What the Eberles feared the most had happened: the grandsons were left with no compelling link to the land.

The Ostranders bulldozed Kay and Frank's little house and the wooden outbuilding which Frank had built himself, and then they burnt the remains. The barn with the ingenious grain-storage system inside was kept, but the proud sign that said FRANK P. EBERLE was yanked down. Within a week, there was little left on the property to indicate that Frank and Kay Eberle had lived and worked there for exactly forty years.

May 1990

A rich cream colour, it shimmers on the prairies like a pearl. It's called a Cape Cod and it's an exceedingly grand house for an ordinary farm, with its spacious living and dining rooms, its sunken fireplace, its two full and two half bathrooms, its huge double garage, and its lovely bay windows overlooking the vast prairies. Rebecca Carmichael, Mary Blackmoon, Sarah Smith, and Lib Foote would have been awed by this palace. Annie Maude Green and Ollie White would have savoured its charm. Even Adela Grayson might have appreciated its modern lightness. How Kay Eberle would have regarded this house that so recently replaced her little home, well, others must think about that. Their husbands would probably have had a different reaction. They might wonder what future revenge the land would inflict, and on whom.

Note on Sources

Dougald Carmichael

Many of the direct quotes and personal information in this section come from the Dougald Carmichael homestead file (Saskatchewan Archives Board), which consists of more than forty pieces of correspondence, dated from between 1886 and 1911. Other personal memoirs that were used include, "The Road to Caron (The Story of Ase Hurlburt's Prairie Days)," "Life Story of Edward J. Heath," "Memories along Moose Jaw Creek" by Fred Wilkes, "The Memoirs of Henry Dorrell," and "The Memoirs of Sam McWilliams," all unpublished, and *Judd Battell's Story of the Early Days of the West*, by Evangeline Chapman. Kings County Historical and Archival Society, Sussex, New Brunswick, provided background material on the Carmichael family. Keith Allan Foster's M.A. thesis, "Moose Jaw: The First Decade 1882–1892" yielded much valuable information, as did the *Moose Jaw News* (1883–1886) and the *Moose Jaw Times*. Interviews: Helaine Folkins, Vancouver, B.C., and Colin Seibert, Saint John, New Brunswick.

Thomas Aspdin

The Thomas Aspdin service file in the National Archives outlines in detail his career in the North-West Mounted Police. Extensive correspondence pertaining to his land difficulties are found in his homestead file, Saskatchewan Archives Board. Dan Kennedy's autobiography, *Recollections of an Assiniboine Chief*, relates conversations with Aspdin. References to Aspdin's experience as an Indian agent were found in the "Reports of Superintendents and Agents," Department of Indian Affairs, annual reports, 1900–1907. Information was also obtained from various correspondence provided by the family of Thomas Aspdin. The letters of John O'kute-sica, Saskatchewan Archives Board, gives valuable information about Mary Blackmoon and her family, as do various materials from the "Sitting Bull and Sioux Indians" file of the Saskatchewan Archives Board. The *Moose Jaw Times* was also a valuable research source. Interviews: Maurice Williams, Cherry Creek, South Dakota; Eleanor Thompson, Cherry Creek, South Dakota; Bill Mackay, Saskatoon; William Lethbridge, Wood Mountain.

William and John Hawke Grayson

The research on Grayson's dealings in Métis land scrip began with the valuable work done by Ron Bourgeault for the Gabriel Dumont Institute, Regina. Using National Archives files, Bourgeault was able to trace the name of the Métis person to whom the scrip was sold, how much it was sold for, and the land acquired. Through the Moose Jaw Land Titles records, the next transaction involving the land could be tracked. It was therefore possible to ascertain the amount of profit a speculator such as J. Hawke Grayson made on specific land.

Other sources used include the homestead records, Saskatchewan Archives, of Albert, Charles, John Hawke, and William Grayson, as well as Andrew Hardie. The *Moose Jaw Times* was an invaluable source, as the paper seemed to publish every public word the Graysons uttered. Many of the memoirs cited in the Carmichael section also mentioned the Graysons. Mac Annable's memoirs, written by George Green, were particularly interesting. Cecil Tannahill's pamphlet, Hitchcock & McCulloch, Moose Jaw, has some interesting documentation of the workings of that bank. Garry Andrews' M.A. thesis, "The Commercial Elite in the Development of Moose Jaw, 1882–1914," was a valuable resource, as was Heather Robertson's *Grass Roots*. Interviews: William D. Grayson, Regina; Joan Bidwell, Moose Jaw; Ron Bourgeault, Ottawa; Larry Heinemann, Regina; Leslie Thorpe, Toronto.

Benjamin Smith

The Saskatchewan Archives Board was a particularly valuable source for the section on the Smith family. The homestead papers of Andy Dalgarno, Albert May, and Benjamin and Harry Smith reveal much interesting information, as do the files on the Moose Jaw Agricultural Society, the Patrons of Industry, the Loyal Order of the Orange, and the Pioneer School District. Correspondence among family members contributed insight into Smith's later years. Benjamin Smith and his family appeared in the *Moose Jaw Times*, until the paper's focus shifted from the farm community to the town's land boom. Benjamin Smith's estate inventory (Surrogate Court, Judicial District of Moose Jaw), May 1913, was a source of much information. Interviews: Russell Filson, Regina; June Woodley, Moose Jaw; Ernie Smith, Moose Jaw; Bill Smith, Moose Jaw.

Bob Foote and James Slemmon

Archival sources used in this chapter include the homestead papers of Alex Dalgetty, Robert Foote, and James and John Slemmon, and the *Moose Jaw Times*, 1900–1911. The files of the Pasqua and Leamington School Districts (Saskatchewan Archives Board) contained much interesting correspondence, as did the records of land transfers and certificates of title found at the Moose Jaw Land Titles Office. The Glenbow Museum in Calgary assisted in providing information about oil exploration on the Stoney Indian Reserve. Much of the detail for this chapter, however, came from interviewing descendants of the Footes and Slemmons. They include: Jim Foote, Moose Jaw; Vi Foote, Moose Jaw; Lawrence Champion, Riverhurst, Sask.; Leo and Gerty Aitken, Moose Jaw; Jean Schuster, Regina; Ross Foote, Regina; Evelyn Evans, Calgary; Cecil Champion, Moose Jaw; Walter Champion, Pasqua, Sask.; Darlene Foote, Moose Jaw.

John R. Green

Details of John R. Green's speculative real-estate ventures come from several sources. The Gabriel Dumont Institute in Regina has a record of his Métis scrip transactions, which were further traced through records of land transfers found at the Moose Jaw

Land Titles Office. His real-estate deals involving the CPR property in Moose Jaw can be tracked through the *Moose Jaw Times*, Moose Jaw tax assessment records (Saskatchewan Archives Board), and land transfers (Moose Jaw Land Titles Office). Details regarding his acquisition of school lands was obtained through land transfers (Moose Jaw Land Titles Office) and through National Archives records. Early history can be found in the homestead records of F. W. Green, Harry Green, John R. Green, and Robert Green, and in the *Moose Jaw Times* (in particular, "Married on Forty Cents a Day and Saved his Passage from England," June 28, 1913). Letters of the Beesley family provided some detail on John R. Green's first marriage. Donald Stuart Richan's M.A. thesis "Boosterism and Urban Rivalry, Regina and Moose Jaw, 1882–1914" revealed details about Moose Jaw's land boom, as did the transcripts of the arbitration hearings and appeal, Canadian Northern Railway Company, and John Robert Green, Supreme Court of Saskatchewan, 1913. Green was also a favourite of the *Moose Jaw Times*, and many of his activities from 1896 to 1938 were recorded. An interview with his daughter, Mary Jefferson of Moose Jaw, provided a valuable perspective on his life.

Wellington and Olive White

For years the *Moose Jaw Times* was fascinated by the Whites, particularly Ollie, and detailed the couple's social activities from the time they arrived in Moose Jaw to Wellington White's death in 1934. The paper also reported on White's business activities. Other sources include his homestead records (Saskatchewan Archives Board), land transfers and certificates of titles (Moose Jaw Land Titles Office), and Moose Jaw City Council minutes, 1911-1913 (Saskatchewan Archives Board). Mac Annable's memoirs had several references to White. The National Archives provided information on White's school-land transactions with John R. Green. White's will and the listing of his assets (Surrogate Court, Judicial District of Moose Jaw) yielded many pertinent facts. While written records formed the skeleton for this section, interviews provided the flesh. These included: Frank White, St. Petersburg, Florida; Vi Pruitt, Toronto; Bart

Meadows, Moose Jaw; Harold Mulligan, Manitou Beach, Sask.;
Lawrence Mulligan, Saskatoon; Lionel Sproule, Manitou
Beach; Bill McWilliams, Moose Jaw.

Frank P. Eberle

The material on the migration to Saskatchewan by the Germans from Russia is contained in the Dr. A. Becker Collection,
Adam Shortt Library of Canadiana, University of Saskatchewan. The comprehensive collection includes speeches, pamphlets, articles, and books, including Father Henry Metzger's
"Historical Sketch of St. Peter's Parish and the Founding of the
Colonies of Rastadt, Katharinental and Speyer." Information
about Father Metzger was supplied by Leo and Clara Fahlman,
who have a collection of his paintings and memorabilia. The
family tree that has been produced by members of the Eberle
family was also helpful, as were the homestead records (Saskatchewan Archives Board) of the early Eberle settlers. The
Rastadt School District records (Saskatchewan Archives
Board), which include correspondence, gave an interesting history of the colony. Histories and yearbooks of Our Lady of Sion
Academy in Moose Jaw and Ursuline High School in Regina
shed some light on Carol Anne Eberle's teenage years. Court
documents played an important role in this section. The wills of
Frank and Kay Eberle and the hearing involving the Public
Trustee for Saskatchewan and Carol Anne Ostrander yielded
much information. Provincial Court and Saskatchewan Court
of Appeal documents sketched the criminal careers of Don and
Ken Sutherland. However, much of the information for this
section was obtained through some sixty-eight interviews.
Because of the circumstances surrounding the deaths of Frank
and Kay Eberle, many of the interviewees wished to remain
anonymous. For that reason, and because the list is so lengthy, I
have not included it here.

Bibliography

GENERAL
Archival Sources
Glenbow Museum, Calgary
Moose Jaw Public Archives
National Archives of Canada
Regina Prairie History Room
Saskatchewan Archives Board
Newspapers, Periodicals
Moose Jaw News, 1883-84
Moose Jaw Times, 1885-1935
Regina Leader
Regina Leader-Post
Saskatchewan History, The Saskatchewan Archives Board, 1952-1983.
Published Sources
Archer, John H. *Saskatchewan: A History*. Saskatoon: Western Producer Prairie Books, 1980.
Berton, Pierre. *The Promised Land: Settling the West, 1896-1914*. Toronto: McClelland & Stewart, 1984.
Francis, R. Douglas. *Images of the West: Changing Perceptions of the Prairies, 1690-1960*. Saskatoon: Western Producer Prairie Books, 1989.
Friesen, Gerald. *The Canadian Prairies: A History*. Toronto: University of Toronto Press, 1987.
Harrison, Dick. *Unnamed Country: The Struggle for a Canadian Prairie Fiction*. Edmonton: University of Alberta Press, 1977.

Hawkes, John. *The Story of Saskatchewan and Its People*, vols. I-III. Chicago and Regina: S. J. Clarke Publishing Co., 1924.

Knight, Leith. *All the Moose, All the Jaw.* Moose Jaw: Moose Jaw 100, 1982.

Voisey, Paul. *Vulcan: The Making of a Prairie Community.* Toronto: University of Toronto Press, 1988.

Wilson, Barry. *Beyond the Harvest: Canadian Grain at the Crossroads.* Saskatoon: Western Producer Prairie Books, 1981.

CARMICHAEL
Archival Sources
National Archives of Canada
  Hyttenrough Mills file MG29 E10.
Saskatchewan Archives Board
  Dougald Carmichael homestead file
  Colin Carmichael homestead file
British Columbia Provincial Archives and Record Service
  "Inquisition into the death of Edward Carmichael, March 23, 1911" file 20233.
Kings County Historical and Archival Society, Sussex, N.B. Census and other materials.
Unpublished Manuscripts
Dorrell, Henry. "The Memoirs of Henry Dorrell." Moose Jaw Public Library Archives, 1967.

Foster, Keith Allan. "Moose Jaw: The First Decade, 1882-1892." M.A. thesis, University of Regina, 1978.

Heath, Edward J. "The Life Story of Edward J. Heath." Moose Jaw Public Library Archives, n.d.

McWilliams, Sam. "Reminiscences of Sam McWilliams, 1884-1893." Moose Jaw Public Library Archives.

Wilkes, Fred. "Memories Along Moose Jaw Creek," initiated by the Petrolia Congregation. Saskatchewan Archives Board, 1958.
Published Sources
Berton, Pierre. *The Last Spike: The Great Railway, 1881-1885.* Toronto: McClelland & Stewart, 1971.

Bocking, D. H., ed. *Pages from the Past: Essays on Saskatchewan History.* Saskatoon: Western Producer Prairie Books, 1979.

_____. *Saskatchewan: A Pictorial History.* Saskatoon: Western Producer Prairie Books, 1979.

Chapman, Evangeline. *Jud Battell's Story of the Early Days of the West.* Moose Jaw: Bowes Publishing, 1953.

Jones, David C. *Empire of Dust: Settling and Abandoning the Prairie Dry Belt.* Edmonton: University of Alberta Press, 1987.

MacEwan, Grant. *The Sodbusters.* Edinburgh: Thomas Nelson & Sons, 1948.

McClung, Nellie R. *Clearing in the West: My Own Story.* Toronto: Thomas Allan, 1935.

Martin, Chester. *Dominion Lands Policy.* Toronto: McClelland & Stewart, 1973.

Minifie, James M. *Homesteader: A Prairie Boyhood Recalled.* Toronto: Macmillan of Canada, 1972.

Morton, Arthur S. *History of Prairie Settlement.* Toronto: Macmillan of Canada, 1938.

Palmer, Howard, ed. *The Settlement of the West.* Calgary: University of Calgary, 1977.

Rasmussen, Linda, et al. *A Harvest Yet to Reap: A History of Prairie Women.* Toronto: Women's Press, 1976.

Robertson, Heather. *Salt of the Earth.* Toronto: Lorimer, 1974.

Stead, Robert, J. C. *Grain.* New York: George H. Doran Co., 1926.

_____. *The Homesteaders: A Novel of the Canadian West.* Toronto: Musson Book Co., 1916.

Stringer, Arthur. *The Prairie Wife.* New York: A. L. Burt Co., 1915.

Waite, Peter B. *Canada, 1874-1896: Arduous Destiny.* Toronto: McClelland & Stewart, 1971.

ASPDIN
Archival Sources
National Archives of Canada
Thomas Aspdin service file. Record group 18, vol. 3319, file 60.
Hyttenrough Mills file MG29 E10.
Saskatchewan Archives Board
Thomas Aspdin homestead file

Beveridge, John. "Origin and Early Development of Moose Jaw as a Service Centre." History paper, University of Saskatchewan, n.d.

"Correspondence of John O'kute-sica," Wood Mountain files R-190.2 and R-834, 1954, 1957.

"Reports of Superintendents and Agents," Department of Indian Affairs annual reports, 1900-1907.

Regina Indian Industrial School, file R-834-35d.

Sitting Bull and the Sioux Indians, file R-151, (three folders).

Unpublished Manuscripts

McLean, Donald. "The Canadian Policy: Causes and Effects of the 1885 Resistance." Paper presented to the Western Association of Sociology and Anthropology at the Gabriel Dumont Institute, Regina, 1984.

Pinno, Erhard. "Temperance and Prohibition in Saskatchewan." M.A. thesis, University of Saskatchewan, 1971.

Published Sources

Assiniboia, Saskatchewan Golden Jubilee Committee. *Golden Memories*. Assiniboia: n.p., 1956.

Atkin, Ronald. *Maintain the Right: The Early History of the North West Mounted Police, 1873-1900*. New York: John Day Co., 1973.

Brown, Lorne and Caroline. *An Unauthorized History of the RCMP*. Toronto: James Lewis & Samuel, 1973.

Hamilton, Zachary M. and Marie A. *These Are the Prairies*. Regina: School Aids and Text Book Publishing Co. [1954].

Haultain, T. Arnold. *A History of Riel's Second Rebellion*. Toronto: Grip Printing and Publishing Co., 1885.

Historical Sketches of the Parishes of the Diocese of Gravelbourg, Sask., on the Occasion of its Silver Jubilee. n.p., 1956.

Kennedy, Dan. *Recollections of an Assiniboine Chief*. Toronto: McClelland & Stewart, 1972.

Longstreth, T. Morris. *The Scarlet Force: The Making of the Mounted Police*. Toronto: Macmillan of Canada, 1974.

MacBeth, R. G. *Policing the Plains: Being the Real-life Record of the Famous Royal North-West Mounted Police*. Toronto: Musson Book Co., 1931.

MacEwan, Grant. *Sitting Bull: The Years in Canada.* Edmonton: Hurtig Publishers, 1973.

Miller, J. R. *Skyscrapers Hide the Heavens: A History of Indian-White Relations in Canada.* Toronto: University of Toronto Press, 1989.

Rondeau, Clovis. *La montagne de bois: The History of Willow Bunch, Sask.*, vol. II. Translated by Sister Gabrielle-Madeleine. Willow Bunch: n.p., 1970.

Spence, Ruth Elizabeth. *Prohibition in Canada.* Toronto: Dominion Alliance, 1919.

Vestal, Stanley. *Sitting Bull: Champion of the Sioux.* Norman and London: University of Oklahoma Press, 1956.

GRAYSON
Archival Sources

Gabriel Dumont Institute of Native Studies and Applied Research, Regina.
Detailed records of Métis land-scrip transactions.

Moose Jaw Public Library Archives
Tannahill, Cecil "Hitchcock & McCulloch: Moose Jaw," pamphlet, n.p., n.d.

Saskatchewan Archives Board
Homestead papers of Albert Grayson, Charles James Grayson, John Hawke Grayson, William Grayson, and Andrew Hardie.
Bates vs. Grayson, Department of the Attorney General, Regina Judicial Centre Court Records, 1st series, file 234 R-304A.

Surrogate Court, Judicial District of Moose Jaw
Last wills and testaments of John Hawke Grayson and William Grayson.

Newspapers, Periodicals
Sprague, D. N. "The Manitoba Land Question, 1870-1882." *Revue d'études canadiennes* vol. 15, no. 3 (Autumn, 1980).

Unpublished Manuscripts
Andrews, Garry. "Commercial Elite in the Development of Moose Jaw, 1882-1914" M.A. thesis, University of Regina, 1977.

Green, George. "A Brief Review of the Experiences of George Malcolm (Mac) Annable." Moose Jaw Public Library Archives, c. 1954.

Heinemann, Larry. "A Research Report: An investigation into the origins and development of the Métis nation, the rights of the Métis as an aboriginal people, and their relationship and dealing with the Canadian government." The Association of Métis and Non-Status Indians of Saskatchewan. Regina, 1984.

"Speculation in Half-Breed Land and Scrip: A Discussion Paper." The Association of Métis and Non-Status Indians of Saskatchewan. Regina, 1979.

Published Sources

Black, Norman Fergus. *A History of Saskatchewan and the Old North West.* Regina: North West Historical Co., 1913.

Barron, Laurie and Waldram, James B., eds. *1885 and After: Native Society in Transition.* Regina: University of Regina, Canadian Plains Research Centre, 1986.

Campbell, Maria. *Halfbreed.* Toronto: McClelland & Stewart, 1973.

Daniels, Harry W. *The Forgotten People: Métis and Non-Status Indian Land Claims.* Ottawa: Native Council of Canada, 1979.

Howard, Joseph Kinsey. *Strange Empire: Louis Riel and the Métis People.* Toronto: James Lewis & Samuel, 1974.

Lowe, Peter. "All Western Dollars," in Clifford Wilson, ed. Papers Read Before the Historical and Scientific Society of Manitoba. Winnipeg: Advocate Printers, 1946.

McLean Don. *Home from the Hill: A History of the Métis in Western Canada.* Regina: Gabriel Dumont Institute, 1987.

Robertson, Heather. *Grass Roots.* Toronto: James Lewis & Samuel, 1973.

Sprague, D. N. *Canada and the Métis, 1869-1885.* Kitchener-Waterloo: Wilfred Laurier University Press, 1988.

Wiebe, Rudy and Beal, Bob. *War in the West: Voices of the 1885 Rebellion.* Toronto: McClelland & Stewart, 1985.

Woodcock, George. *Gabriel Dumont: The Métis Chief and His Lost World.* Edmonton: Hurtig Publishers, 1975.

SMITH
Archival Sources
Saskatchewan Archives Board
"Boharm – An Outpost of Empire, 1882-1990," pamphlet, n.p., n.d.
Homestead papers of Andy Dalgarno, Albert May #569325, Benjamin Smith #169478, and Harry Smith #858940.
Loyal Order of the Orange, pamphlet file.
Moose Jaw Agricultural Society returns, 1887-1934, Department of Agriculture pamphlet file.
Patrons of Industry pamphlet file.
Pioneer School District.
Newspapers, Periodicals
Moose Jaw Times, 1886-1911
Winnipeg Free Press Evening News Bulletin, 1902
Unpublished Manuscripts
Patterson, Robert C. "Moose Jaw in the Territorial Period until 1903. Growth of Business and Industry." History paper, University of Regina, 1968.
Published Sources
Caron History Book Committee. *From Buffalo Trails to Blacktop.* Caron, Sask: Caron History Book Committee, 1982.
French, Goldwin. *Parsons and Politics.* Toronto: Ryerson Press, 1962.
Grove, Frederick Philip. *Fruits of the Earth.* Toronto: J. M. Dent & Sons, 1933.
Herbert, Moorehouse. *Deep Furrows.* Toronto: George J. McLeod, 1918.
Houston, C., and Smyth, W. J. *The Orange Order in Nineteenth-Century Ontario: A Study in Institutional Cultural Transfer.* Toronto: Department of Geography, University of Toronto, 1977.
MacEwan, Grant. *Power for Prairie Plows.* Saskatoon: Western Producer Prairie Books, 1971.
Swainson, Donald, ed. *Historical Essays on the Prairie Provinces.* Toronto: McClelland & Stewart, 1970.

FOOTE/SLEMMON
Archival Sources
Saskatchewan Archives Board
   Homestead papers of Alex Dalgetty, Robert Foote, James Slemmon, John Slemmon.
   Pasqua School Board
Newspapers, Periodicals
Moose Jaw Times, 1900-1926
Unpublished Sources
Letter to Jean Schuster, née Foote.
Published Sources
Dempsey, Hugh A., ed. *The CPR West: The Iron Road and the Making of a Nation*. Vancouver: Douglas & McIntyre, 1984.
MacGregor, James C. *A History of Alberta*. Edmonton: Hurtig Publishers, 1972.
Sharp, Paul E. *The Agrarian Revolt in Western Canada: A Survey Showing American Parallels*. Minneapolis: University of Minnesota Press, 1948.
Wilson, Charles F. *Century of Canadian Grain*. Saskatoon: Western Producer Prairie Books, 1978.

GREEN
Archival Sources
Saskatchewan Archives Board
   Canadian Northern Railway Company and John Robert Green, Supreme Court of Saskatchewan, 1913, file R-304A.
   Homestead records for F. W. Green, Harry Green, John R. Green, and Robert Green.
   Moose Jaw City Council minutes, 1911-1913.
   Tax assessment records for the city of Moose Jaw, 1906, 1916, and 1921.
Moose Jaw Land Titles Office
   Land transfers and certificate of titles, 1900-1938.
Surrogate Court, Judicial District of Moose Jaw
   Last wills and testaments of John R. Green and Harry Green.
Newspapers, Periodicals
Murray, Jean E. "The Contest for the University of Saskatchewan." *Saskatchewan History*, vol. 12, (1959): 1-22.

_____. "The Provincial Capital Controversy in Saskatchewan." *Saskatchewan History*, vol. 5, (1952): 81-105.

Reid, A. N. "Functions of Urban Municipalities in the North-West Territories." *Saskatchewan History*, vol. 10, (1957): 81-96.

Unpublished Manuscripts

Andrews, Garry. "The National Policy and the Settlement of Moose Jaw, Saskatchewan, 1882-1915." History paper, University of Regina, 1977.

_____. "The Role of the Commercial Elite in the Development of Moose Jaw, 1882-1914." Unpublished thesis, University of Regina, 1977.

Richan, Donald Stuart. "Boosterism and Urban Rivalry in Regina and Moose Jaw, 1902-1913." Unpublished thesis, University of Regina, 1981.

Published Sources

Brown, Robert Craig, and Cook, Ramsay. *Canada, 1896-1921: A Nation Transformed*. Toronto: McClelland & Stewart, 1974.

MacEwan, Grant. *Frederick Haultain: Frontier Statesman of the Canadian Northwest*. Saskatoon: Western Producer Prairie Books, 1985.

WHITE

Archival Sources

National Archives of Canada

"Dominion Lands Act," Department of the Interior.

"The Wellington White–John R. Green school land transaction," RG 15, Volume Liber 806, folio 147, file C-6582.

Saskatchewan Archives Board

Homestead records of Wellington White.

Tax assessment records, City of Moose Jaw, 1921.

Moose Jaw Land Titles Office

Land transfers and certificates of title.

Surrogate Court, Judicial District of Moose Jaw

Last will and testament of Wellington White, Oct. 27, 1931; list of assets, 1934; solicitor's bill of costs, 1936.

Published Sources

Abrams, Gary. *Prince Albert: The First Century, 1866-1966*. Prince Albert: Modern Press, 1966.

Anderson, Frank W. *Almighty Voice*. Calgary: Frontier Publishing, 1971.

Beck, Warren A., and Williams, David A. *California: A History of the Golden State*. Garden City, N.Y.: Doubleday, 1972.

Berton, Pierre. *The Great Depression, 1929-39*. Toronto: McClelland & Stewart, 1990.

Diefenbaker, John. *One Canada: Memoirs of the Right Hon. John G. Diefenbaker*, vol. I. Toronto: Macmillan of Canada, 1975.

Francis, D. and Ganzevoort, H. *The Dirty Thirties in Prairie Canada*. Vancouver: Tantalus Research Ltd., 1980.

Gray, James H. *Booze: The Impact of Whisky on the Prairie West*. Toronto: Macmillan of Canada, 1972.

_____. *Men Against the Desert*. Saskatoon: Western Producer Prairie Books, 1967.

_____. *Red Lights on the Prairies*. Toronto: Macmillan of Canada, 1971.

_____. *The Roar of the Twenties*. Toronto: Macmillan of Canada, 1975.

Shackleton, Doris French. *Tommy Douglas: A Biography*. Toronto: McClelland & Stewart, 1975.

Thompson, John Herd. *The Harvests of War: The Prairie West, 1914-1918*. Toronto: McClelland & Stewart, 1978.

Thompson, John Herd, with Seager, Allen. *Canada, 1922-1939: Decades of Discord*. Toronto: McClelland & Stewart, 1985.

Watrous and District History Committee. *Prairie Reflections: Watrous, Venn, Manitou Beach, Renown, Amazon and Districts*. Watrous, Sask: Watrous, and District History Committee, 1984.

EBERLE
Archival Sources
Saskatchewan Archives Board
Homestead files of Joseph Bishoff, Frank Eberle, Johannes Eberle, Joseph Eberle, Meurat Eberle, Nicedamus Eberle, Thomas Eberle.
Rastadt School District 453.
Surrogate Court for Saskatchewan, Judicial Centre of Regina

Last wills and testaments of Frank P. Eberle and Katherine Eberle.

Court of Queen's Bench, Judicial Centre of Regina
Affadavits of RCMP Sergeant Kenneth Burns et al. Q.B. 211.

Queen vs. Kenneth Gerald Sutherland. Transcript of proceedings, November 30, 1987.

Queen vs. Donald James Sutherland. Transcript of proceedings, December 30, 1987.

Public Trustee for Saskatchewan and Carol Anne Ostrander, Donald Sutherland, Sean Ostrander, and Guaranty Trust Company of Canada.

Saskatchewan Provincial Court
Queen vs. Aaron Albert Racette. Preliminary inquiry proceedings, November 20, 1987.

Unpublished Manuscripts
Becker, Anthony. "The German Russians." Speech to the Saskatoon Rotary Club, July 24, 1978.

Pamphlets
Becker, Anthony. "Life and Customs on the Homesteads of the Germans from Russia in the colonies of Rastadt, Katharinental, Speyer and St. Joseph, Balgonie and Kronau, Saskatchewan." University of Saskatchewan, Adam Shortt Library of Canadiana, Becker Collection.

Metzger, Father Henry. "Historical Sketch of St. Peter's Parish and the Founding of the Colonies of Rastadt, Katharinental and Speyer." Translated by A. Becker and Sister Bernadine Kletzel. *Saskatchewan Genealogical Bulletin*, vol. 5, no. 4 (Fall 1974).

Mohr, Mrs. Albert. "The History of St. Peter's Parish, Kronau, Saskatchewan." Pictorial Directory (1971).

Wild, Sister Bernadette. *Golden Jubilee, Sacred Heart Parish, Regina, Saskatchewan, Canada, 1927-1977* (1976).

Zimmermann, Father Andrew. *Fiftieth Jubilee of the Roman Catholic Parish of St. Joseph* (June 1936).

Periodicals
Becker, Anthony. "The Germans from Russia in Saskatchewan and Alberta." *German-Canadian Yearbook* (November 1976).

_____. "St. Joseph's Colony, Balgonie." *Saskatchewan History*, vol. 20 (1967): 1-18.

Kloberdanz, Timothy J. "The Volga German in Old Russia and in Western North America." *Anthropological Quarterly* (October 1975).

Van Gogh, Lucy. "Father Metzger: Painter of Canadian Indians." *Saturday Night* (December 1941).

Published Sources

Aberle, George P. *From the Steppes to the Prairies.* Bismarck, N.D.: Bismarck Tribune Co., 1973.

Combining Communities: Lake Valley Rowletta. Brownlee, Sask.: Lake Valley Rowletta History Book Society, 1986.

Brennan, J. William. *Regina, An Illustrated History.* Toronto: Lorimer, 1989.

Eberle, Irene, Florence Eberle, and Clara Klein. *The Eberle Family History.* n.p., n.d.

Giesinger, Adam. *From Catherine to Khrushchev: The Story of Russia's Germans.* Winnipeg: Adam Giesinger, 1974.

Keller, Rev. P. Conrad. *The German Colonies in South Russia, 1804-1904*, vol. II. Translated by A. Becker. Odessa. n.p., 1905.

Pitsula, James. *Let the Family Flourish: A History of the Family Service Bureau of Regina, 1913-1982.* Regina: Family Service Bureau of Regina, 1982.

Rath, George. *The Black Sea Germans in the Dakotas.* Freeman, S.D.: Pine Hill Press, 1977.

Stumpp, Karl. *The Emigration from Germany to Russia in the Years 1763-1862.* Lincoln: American Historical Society of Germans from Russia, 1978.

_____. *The German Russians: Two Centuries of Pioneering.* New York: Atlantic-Forum, 1966.

Index